Deadball Trailblazers

Single-Season Records of the Modern Era

RONALD T. WALDO

Mechanicsburg, PA USA

Published by Sunbury Press, Inc.
Mechanicsburg, Pennsylvania

www.sunburypress.com

Copyright © 2022 by Ronald T. Waldo.
Cover Copyright © 2022 by Sunbury Press, Inc.

Sunbury Press supports copyright. Copyright fuels creativity, encourages diverse voices, promotes free speech, and creates a vibrant culture. Thank you for buying an authorized edition of this book and for complying with copyright laws by not reproducing, scanning, or distributing any part of it in any form without permission. You are supporting writers and allowing Sunbury Press to continue to publish books for every reader. For information contact Sunbury Press, Inc., Subsidiary Rights Dept., PO Box 548, Boiling Springs, PA 17007 USA or legal@sunburypress.com.

For information about special discounts for bulk purchases, please contact Sunbury Press Orders Dept. at (855) 338-8359 or orders@sunburypress.com.

To request one of our authors for speaking engagements or book signings, please contact Sunbury Press Publicity Dept. at publicity@sunburypress.com.

FIRST SUNBURY PRESS EDITION: July 2022

Set in Adobe Garamond | Interior design by Crystal Devine | Cover by Lawrence Knorr | Edited by Lawrence Knorr.

Publisher's Cataloging-in-Publication Data
Names: Waldo, Ronald T., author.
Title: Deadball trailblazers : single-season records of the Modern Era / Ronald T. Waldo.
Description: First trade paperback edition. | Mechanicsburg, PA : Sunbury Press, 2022.
Summary : Numerous records established during baseball's Deadball Era (1900-1919) still stand today. Record-setting seasons of achievement (like Jack Chesbro's 41 wins) and futility (like John Gochnaur's 98 errors) are brought to life in this book. *Deadball Trailblaers* tells the story of 12 single-season record setters.
Identifiers: ISBN 978-1-62006-899-1 (softcover).
Subjects: SPORTS & RECREATION / Baseball / General | SPORTS & RECREATION / Baseball / History | SPORTS & RECREATION / Baseball / Statistics.

Product of the United States of America
0 1 1 2 3 5 8 13 21 34 55

Continue the Enlightenment!

I dedicate this book to the loving memory of my dear mother, Nancy W. Waldo, who sadly passed away on February 12, 2021. I thank my mother for her gentle guidance, helping me become who I am today. Her kindness and thoughtfulness, along with a loving and caring approach each day grounded in a strong faith, made everyone she touched throughout her life a better person. We all miss her deeply. I love you, Mum.

Contents

Preface vii
Introduction ix

1 Napoleon Lajoie – 1901
    Establishing Baseball's Gold Standard in an Ascending League . . . 1

2 John Gochnaur – 1903
    Dispelling the Good Glove, No Hit Myth 20

3 Jack Chesbro – 1904
    Securing Forty-One and the Game That Got Away 38

4 Rube Waddell – 1904
    Fireballing and Freewheeling His Way to Mound Glory 56

5 Vic Willis – 1905
    Staff Ace Rolls High Twenties in the Loss Column 75

6 Frank Schulte – 1911
    Achieving a New Standard Beyond Those Diamond Barriers 94

7 John Owen "Chief" Wilson – 1912
    Flying Under the Radar Into Baseball's Record Books 112

8 Rube Marquard – 1912
    The Nerve-Wracking Journey to Fame and Glory 131

9 Tris Speaker – 1912
    The Model of Consistency and a Two-Bagger Machine 152

10 Hubert "Dutch" Leonard – 1914
   Master of Precision and a World Beater on the Bump 171

11 Ty Cobb – 1915
   Baseball's Top Player Sets the Standard for Swiping Bases 190

12 Jack Nabors – 1916
   A Season of Futility, Pitching for a Wretched Team 211

13 Deadball Era Pacesetters Writing Baseball History........... 230

   Notes 235
   Bibliography 287
   Index 295
   About the Author 305

Preface

A mission statement regarding a book about baseball's first modern-era, single-season record holders from the Deadball Era seems pretty clear-cut and straightforward. Achievements from some of the greatest players in the game's history, establishing marks that set the standard for others to chase, many of which have endured the test of time, are chronicled to their fullest related to a particular record-breaking season. Numbers and statistics play a huge role in shaping the narrative surrounding single-season marks that brought about glory and, at times, shame for those whose accomplishments garnered them a place in baseball's record books during this particular period of baseball history.

While it certainly may be true that figures don't lie, the stories behind how these numbers came about add some depth to such critical moments in baseball history that continue to live on today. For over a century, numerous variables and factors have impacted diamond performers who chased the windmills of success or were doomed to fall victim to the enigma of failure and futility. This work presents the personalities, facts, statistics, and incidents which shaped and molded these significant record-breaking events. Over time, some of these numbers changed due to inconsistencies and mistakes. Nonetheless, these legacies as record achievers continue to endure the test of time.

I fully utilized *Sporting Life* and Retrosheet for box scores from baseball games related to this project regarding some of these numbers. Regarding statistical indicators, I gleaned information from various sources, including old issues of *Sporting Life* and the *Sporting News*. I also utilized research sites that act as the lifeblood for SABR members and authors, who enjoy immersing themselves in raw data connected to all eras of baseball history.

I researched intensively using articles from old newspapers and other periodicals, while books with connections to various subjects recorded in my work supplied other nuggets of critical information. Each chapter in the book contains extensive footnotes, citing the array of material that acts as the bulwark for telling my story.

Since both glory and heartache exist in baseball, I also selected three unfortunate players who established disastrous single-season marks, which still stand today. Perspective is possible to achieve when examining the adverse circumstances and positive moments in baseball history. This book also contains the stories related to three players who established their single-season records during the Deadball Era's exciting and magical 1912 season. The superlative successes of stalwart performers from that time are chronicled, with a couple of lesser-knowns sprinkled in for good measure, on the adverse side of the historical spectrum.

I decided to chronicle single-season record-breaking achievements related to the modern era rather than tackling this theme utilizing the game's comprehensive history since more clarity arose for baseball at the beginning of the twentieth century. Condensing this down within the Deadball Era seemed logical, given the period's enormous impact on baseball's growth and its continued ascension as America's pastime. As a historian, I have utmost respect and appreciation for those players who performed before the modern era, that were trendsetters when it came to having records etched in stone next to their names on the early tablets of baseball history. These players receive mention at the end of each chapter, alongside their modern-era, pacesetting counterparts.

Of course, a strong admiration for baseball history transcends beyond raw numbers, especially when more than a century has elapsed since these performers cavorted about the diamond. For both writer and reader, a player's personality and temperament are important factors, in conjunction with exciting events and unique characteristics. All these dynamics shape the whole story about a particular iconic season for an individual within the arena of setting records. Today, challenging past monumental achievements continues to be a goal for those who currently play the game, helping formulate opinions for fans in the current baseball environment, just as was the case for their passionate rooting predecessors.

Introduction

Smooth, sharp, and clean lines of delineation go a long way toward bringing a topic or entity into focus. Baseball and its storied history are no exception. When the twentieth century dawned, ushering in a new age of prosperity for the United States, it seemed like a natural progression for baseball to throw down its marker, defining the advent of a new era in its relatively short life. Some people quibble over whether this epoch saw its origin in 1900 or 1901. Nonetheless, the "modern era" was born for a game that had gained colossal traction and support in the 1880s and 1890s. As this age evolved, different eras became defined by a point in time, or baseball's evolving style of play, whether it was the lively years of the Roaring Twenties or the more optimistic period following World War II. With the advent of the modern era, the game's Deadball Era saw its birth, encompassing those early years from 1900 through 1919.

A feeling of constancy permeated as baseball's modern era breathed and grew. Uniformity surrounding baseball rules became the standard, especially after the National League and newborn American League reached a peace accord before the 1903 campaign. Both agreed to coexist on equal footing in the sporting world. Where rule innovation and tweaking had occurred before this time, the traditional tenets we know today saw their implementation at the early junctures of the Deadball Era. Stability for baseball franchises was also the norm after various stages of contraction and relocation. From 1903 until the Boston Braves moved to Milwaukee following the 1952 season, things remained status quo regarding 16 teams, who continued plying their baseball trade in 10 different cities.

The Deadball Era was blessed to have some of the greatest players who ever graced the diamond in baseball history perform their magic. Within the pages of this book, I examine the single-season, record-breaking accomplishments of twelve different individuals from that epoch. Nine of these records are positive achievements, while three offer a negative connotation as unfortunate marks of ineptitude or disappointment. Beyond the numbers, games, and box scores, each chapter contains at least one supplementary or subsidiary story, which supplies some added context to that particular player and season. Background information related to how each chronicled subject received their start playing the game offers another piece of the puzzle.

Although an author's opinion should never enter the picture when creating a historical baseball perspective, this doesn't mean it can't influence the writer's vision. Most of the 12 subjects for this project are incontrovertible, except two, which I chose after much thought and deliberation. The selection of Frank Schulte, establishing a single-season, modern-era record for smacking home runs when he blasted 21 in 1911, was made over Clifford "Gavvy" Cravath of the Philadelphia Phillies. Cravath did hit 24 dingers four years later in 1915. I based this decision on the Chicago Cubs' outfielder being the first player from that period to surpass the 20-homer plateau in a calendar year. Unfortunately, for New York Yankees fans, George Herman "Babe" Ruth's 29 four-baggers as a member of the Boston Red Sox in 1919 didn't enter the calculus since he was another baseball era's most influential figure.

I also decided that Tyrus Raymond "Ty" Cobb of the Detroit Tigers, recording 96 stolen bases in 1915, merited inclusion over the Washington Senators' Jesse Clyde Milan, swiping 88 bags in 1912, since the Georgia Peach's mark stood for 47 years. For six seasons before 1915, the modern-era record for stolen bases in a single season had changed hands on three occasions between Cobb, Milan, and Edward "Eddie" Collins of the Philadelphia Athletics. John "Buck" Freeman (25 home runs) and Edward "Ed" Delahanty (55 doubles) just missed the cut due to achieving their feats one year too soon, in 1899, before the modern era started.

Baseball history has been an ever-changing, constantly evolving organism that continues to progress over time. In December 2020, the Negro Leagues and their players were deservedly given major league status as a baseball organization. This announcement meant exciting additions to the game's statistical dynamic would be forthcoming. The continued longevity of two modern-era records discussed in my book was retroactively updated when Baseball-Reference released the first treasure trove of statistics in June 2021.

While the figures surrounding these marks are relatively cut and dry, the ability to debate which players are worthy of gaining consideration in a discussion is part of the beauty connected to rehashing the grand events and moments of baseball's past. Any journey regarding a life's endeavor requires dedication, commitment, and a first step. That quest is sometimes littered with obstructions, making the road rocky and challenging to navigate. In the end, whether establishing positive or negative marks as the game's standard-bearers, the path traveled by a group of Deadball Era players during such a voyage cemented their place in the record books and the annals of baseball history.

CHAPTER 1

Napoleon Lajoie – 1901

Establishing Baseball's Gold Standard in an Ascending League

Throughout its glorious history, baseball has been a multifaceted entity, combining speed, strength, guts, and cunning. Fans have always held a special place in their hearts for players whose ability surpassed all others, producing special magic with a bat in hand. Before the home run became a key component, greatness in hitting was measured by those who consistently reached base by safely putting the ball in play for hits, sometimes referred to as "bingles" throughout baseball's Deadball Era. Hitting during this period was defined by stalwarts such as Tyrus "Ty" Cobb and John "Honus" Wagner. A third individual also established the measuring stick for batting average in the modern era, at the beginning of the twentieth century, as the perfect nexus existed for this rising star and a new major league. That third man was Napoleon Lajoie.

Napoleon Lajoie was a native of Woonsocket, Rhode Island, and of French descent. The youngest of eight children from a family that lived in Quebec, Canada, before settling in the United States, he was born on September 5, 1874. Four years after his father Jean-Baptiste passed away in 1881, Napoleon quit school and started working in a local textile mill. Referred to as "Larry" or "Nap" throughout his illustrious career, Lajoie became interested in baseball as a youngster. Despite his mother, Celina Guertin Lajoie, objecting to her son's involvement in such a wasteful game, he eventually played semi-professional ball for the hometown team.[1]

Although Napoleon enjoyed the game, it didn't spur him to consider a career in the sport until an unfortunate incident related to his job as a handsome cab driver. One wintry night in Woonsocket, an intoxicated gentleman hailed Lajoie's cab. The man jumped the horse-drawn carriage at some point and stiffed him on the fare. This individual also left behind the wrapped package he had been clutching, a large fish whose odor grew more potent with each passing minute. At this point, Napoleon realized he was ripe for a significant change in his life.[2]

Lajoie's newfound dedication to baseball paid immediate dividends. In February 1896, a *Sporting Life* article announced that Napoleon Lajoie had been signed by manager Charley Marston, on the recommendation of Fred Woodcock, to play first base for his Fall River Indians in the New England League.[3] Lajoie's time with Fall River was brief. He batted .429 in 80 games before jumping to the major league level. On August 8, 1896, the Philadelphia Phillies purchased Napoleon and teammate Philip "Phil" Geier for $1,500. Lajoie didn't exactly make a resounding entrance into the National League. Napoleon's play after joining Philadelphia deemed him a colossal disappointment, in the eyes of sportswriter Francis C. Richter, compared to underachievers on the squad such as William "Billy" Hulen and Duff Cooley.

"The biggest disappointment of all is Lajoie," writes Richter in his article for *Sporting Life*. "He is big and heavy and totally lacking in action, both in fielding and batting. His first base play is accurate enough but machine-like in action, and crude in execution, due, probably, to lack of experience in the position. The latter defect may be remedied by practice, but the inertness is doubtless natural and therefore ineradicable. In batting, however, Lajoie has proved the biggest disappointment. He came here with a great reputation as a slugger and an average of over .400 in the New England League. To date, he has something like .100 in the National League. This great shrinkage has been charitably attributed to nervousness, but in my judgment, it is due to fault of style. He has as little action at the bat as in the field; doesn't swing properly at the ball, and seems to be unable to gauge a drop or slow ball."[4]

Luckily for Lajoie and the Phillies' organization, Richter's judgment was askew, as Napoleon eventually struck his stride and started hitting. Lajoie batted .326 while appearing in 39 contests for Philadelphia. During his first entire campaign in 1897, Napoleon played 127 games, hitting .361 for the Phillies. While Lajoie seemed to be adjusting to life as a major leaguer, a problem arose because of his friendly and good-natured personality. Like many youngsters before him, Napoleon fell into the trap of enjoying the nightlife a little too vigorously, with those lapses into the world of intoxication sometimes affecting his performance. Things reached a critical juncture during a home game against the Pittsburgh Pirates on August 27.

Lajoie's dreadful first-inning performance directly resulted from showing up at the ballpark in an intoxicated condition.[5] Napoleon committed an error in the first frame, leading to Pittsburgh scoring two runs, before manager George Stallings, who had forced his first baseman to play despite being drunk, banished him to the clubhouse.[6] Lajoie was suspended indefinitely without pay. This action taken by Phillies management acted as an epiphany for Napoleon, who was very ashamed and apologetic for his actions. Team management lifted Lajoie's suspension on August 31, following his solemn promise to behave accordingly.

Francis C. Richter offered a bit of advice in his *Sporting Life* prose. Richter claimed that to be "one of the guys" on Philadelphia's squad, along with his good nature and lacking experience, Napoleon was susceptible to succumbing to negative influences espoused by other team members. The writer hoped Lajoie would quickly learn that being a "just fellow," rather than a "good fellow," would serve him well, along with ownership, and the fans, allowing his road in this profession to be a long and prosperous one.[7] Maturity, consistency, and a position change to second base worked wonders for Napoleon in 1898, as he batted .324 while playing 147 games.

Despite suffering an injury, Lajoie's rise to stardom continued one year later as he appeared in 77 contests and swung the willow at a .378 clip. Napoleon was again sidelined in 1900, breaking his thumb in a locker-room altercation with teammate Elmer Flick on May 31 and not returning to the lineup until July.[8] Lajoie ended up batting .337 for the Phillies while also hitting safely in 22 straight games at one point in the season.[9] When Napoleon engaged in his fisticuff folly, Philadelphia stood atop the standings. The Phillies ended the season nestled in third place, with a 75-63 record. That position matched where Philadelphia finished in 1899, their best marks since Lajoie had joined the team in 1896.

Throughout Napoleon Lajoie's tenure with the Phillies, Colonel John I. Rogers and Alfred "Al" Reach owned the team. Many players on the squad didn't appreciate Colonel Rogers's tightfisted policies throughout the 1890s. Following the 1893 campaign, star outfielder Samuel "Sam" Thompson had threatened to never play for Philadelphia again because of ownership's nickel and dime approach regarding travel, hotel accommodations, and meals while the team played on the road.[10] Since the maximum salary permitted for National League contracts was $2,400, this left little room for players when negotiating, giving maximum leverage to ownership.[11]

For the disgruntled baseball proletariat, who had grown tired of being beaten down by the National League ownership hierarchy, a new option emerged following the 1900 season. That year, the American League, a minor league institution cultivated and overseen by Byron Bancroft "Ban" Johnson, had appeared on the scene. Heading into 1901, Johnson intended to raise his organization to major league status and confront the entrenched National League as an equal competitor, the first to do so since the American Association ceased as an organization after 1891. This new major league planned on challenging the validity of baseball's reserve clause as they courted players from National League teams with promises of big salaries.

This fresh choice loomed as a golden opportunity for players, disheartened over not being fairly compensated for their services. Disgusted with his situation in Philadelphia, Napoleon Lajoie fell into that category of disenchanted individuals. Before the 1900 season, Lajoie had demanded a salary of $3,000. Manager William "Bill" Shettsline countered by claiming he could only move up from the standard $2,400 to $2,600, while vowing this would make Lajoie and teammate Edward "Ed" Delahanty the highest-paid members of the Phillies at this equal salary. When Napoleon later discovered Delahanty was earning $3,000 in 1900, he realized that Philadelphia management had bargained in bad faith.[12] Such low-handed tactics indeed established the perfect atmosphere for exploring new possibilities.

Terms such as "war" and "fight" bubbled to the surface shortly after Johnson announced his league planned on challenging the big dog on the block. When the American League was a minor league organization in 1900, former National League catcher Connie Mack managed the Milwaukee Brewers. As 1900 concluded, Mack weighed in on the new association's prospects for success, confronting and battling their established nemesis.

"It is almost impossible to tell just yet what the outcome of the existing conditions will be," said Mack. "The American League is in just as good and, in fact, better position to put up a fight than is the National League. The National League is heavily in debt, as they must owe in the neighborhood of $200,000, and they don't care to carry on a war and add more to their burdens, at least that is the general belief.

"The American League will protect its rights in every way possible, but as to the signing of players from the National League, that is a question that is yet to be settled. The American League will make no move to bring about an understanding relative to this matter, for they have been treated too shabbily by the National League, so if there are any overtures relative to an understanding, it must come from the National League.

"It is possible, of course, that if the National League continued in the attitude it has assumed, that the American League may wade in and sign players right and left, which, of course, it has a perfect right to do, but Mr. Johnson has not as yet decided upon this point. Of course, we are not looking for war, but I can tell you one thing, and that is if there is any argument, you will find Mr. Johnson on the front seat."[13]

Since Connie Mack so eloquently represented the American League, it wasn't surprising that Ban Johnson selected him to manage Philadelphia's entry into that organization, which would be called the Athletics. Shortly after people across the United States celebrated New Year's, Napoleon Lajoie announced he no longer desired to play for the Philadelphia Phillies and indicated he might sign with the new league's Baltimore Orioles, who would be managed by John McGraw.[14]

Phillies president and lawyer Colonel John I. Rogers responded in kind to any player, throwing a covetous glance toward the endless riches offered by the American League. Rogers declared that those individuals who had signed three-year contracts still belonged to their teams for two more seasons. Rogers retained other attorneys to scour contracts of National League performers. They all agreed that blocking players from joining another baseball club was justified for those who intended to jump an agreement.[15] The fact that Rogers believed he had the law on his side didn't deter players from searching for a better baseball life financially. In early February, a person described as a reliable source stated that Napoleon Lajoie had signed to play for the Philadelphia Athletics.

This individual claimed Lajoie had inked a contract two weeks earlier. Still, the announcement was delayed at the Players' Protective Association's urging upon Ban Johnson and American League managers to refrain from propagating offers to players until the National League held their spring meeting. Newspaper reports claimed that the American League planned a massive raid on the Philadelphia Phillies, with Elmer Flick, Francis "Red" Donahue, Edward "Ed" McFarland, Montford "Monte" Cross, Wiley Piatt, and James "Jimmy" Slagle being targeted.[16] Lajoie immediately denied he had attached his signature to any official contract for 1901. The belief existed that the American League didn't want to be hasty in revealing which players they had captured since doing so violated the Protective Association agreement mandating that no individual sign a contract without the consent of that organization's attorney. Johnson and his surrogates also had a second motive. They wanted to keep National League counterparts in doubt regarding the identities of jumping players up to as close to the season opener as possible.[17]

Amid all this speculation about which league players intended to pledge their allegiance, a *Chicago Chronicle* article suggested it would be prudent for the American League to show maximum independence, compared to the National League, by refusing to adopt all the Senior Circuits' rules. This writer surmised that mimicking the league they were fighting, in this respect, would give their adversary legitimacy as both the father and uncle of baseball.[18] One way related to the rulebook where the two leagues ended up differing in 1901 was that the National League adopted the foul strike rule (the first two fouls off a hitter's bat counted as strikes). Things remained status quo for constantly fouling off pitches without penalty in the American League, which continued being a considerable advantage for batters.

Rumor and conjecture finally became fact on March 20 regarding a long-awaited announcement. Napoleon Lajoie had indeed signed a contract to play for the Philadelphia Athletics in 1901.[19] Besides being the second baseman for Philadelphia's new American League entry, Connie Mack selected Lajoie as team captain. Reports claimed that Phillies pitcher Charles "Chick" Fraser and Boston Beaneaters hurler Victor "Vic" Willis would be joining the Athletics.[20] In the end, Willis ended up remaining with Boston. Ironically, Athletics magnate Benjamin "Ben" Shibe was friends, and partners, in various business ventures with part-owner Al Reach of the Phillies.[21] Shibe's field leader, Connie Mack, found the terrain surprisingly smooth while courting National League players for his team.

"I find it much easier to do business with the National League players than I expected," claimed Mack. "Most of them are disgusted with the methods employed by the National League and will welcome a change. The players are surprised, too, that the American League is willing to give up much better salaries than the National."[22]

Phillies president John I. Rogers wasted no time taking action against those players from his team who had breached legitimate contracts. Rogers filed suit in the Pennsylvania Common Pleas Court in Philadelphia at the end of March against Napoleon Lajoie, Chick Fraser, and pitcher William "Bill" Bernhard. The latter had also jumped from the Phillies to the Athletics.[23] The Phillies' organization hired lawyer John G. Johnson as counsel, hoping to compel the court to prevent these three players from joining the Athletics.[24] Rogers offered insight into the suits while talking to the press.

"We gave Lajoie $2,400 per year," stated Rogers, "and the other people promise $4,000–$3,000 salary and $1,000 for captaining the team. We were offered $15,000 for Lajoie. Now, suppose we had bought Kelly [Joe Kelley] for $10,000, and some of those fancy-priced people, and they had jumped, where would we be? If we had done what the American League did in arranging its schedule so as to make conflicting dates, the press of the country would have torn us to pieces. Mack's team conflicts with us 22 games in this city. A schedule could have been arranged whereby they would not have duplicated us more than three or four games."[25]

Colonel Rogers realized that Napoleon Lajoie would be a strong drawing card, as the rebel Philadelphia team went head-to-head against the Phillies for fan support 22 times. Athletics pilot Connie Mack welcomed Rogers's lawsuit and hoped a resolution to the matter would happen quickly. He felt a challenge and adjudication in court were essential to the concept of National League contracts, where servitude for life existed for a player. At the same time, the only requirement for ownership was to give ten days' notice to inform an individual that the team no longer required his services.[26] Ernest J. Lanigan of the *Sporting News* wrote that players had no choice but to accept termination after being handed their releases or risk expulsion.[27] In testing the validity of the option clause in player contracts, Rogers hoped to gain an injunction that prevented Lajoie, Fraser, and Bernhard from playing for any team other than the Phillies.[28] Before the court heard the case, both sides engaged in legal wranglings involving demurrers and amendments.[29]

Proceedings surrounding this suit in equity against these three players and officers of the American League started on Saturday, April 20, in Pennsylvania Common Pleas Court No. 5, with judges Robert Ralston, Jonathan Willis Martin, and Maxwell Stevenson presiding. John G. Johnson handled matters for Rogers and the Phillies. At the same time, attorney Richard C. Dale represented the other side, including co-defendants Connie Mack, Ben Shibe, and American League agent and newspaperman Frank L. Hough. Napoleon Lajoie was called to the stand and grilled by Johnson. In his testimony, Lajoie revealed he had been paid $1,800 (1897), $2,000 (1898), $2,100 (1899), and $2,600 (1900) by Phillies management. That last figure proved the team had violated the National League's salary limit of $2,400 in 1900. Napoleon also stated he was offered $3,200 by manager Bill Shettsline to play for the Phillies in 1901 but had opted to ink his signature to an American League document for $4,000 on February 14.

Lajoie acquitted himself quite nicely on the stand. When Shettsline testified, he appeared to be a better witness for the defense than the plaintiffs.[30] While testifying, Napoleon also said he was unaware of being signed with the Phillies for 1901 until the plaintiffs informed him of this fact while admitting he had indeed agreed to terms on April 18, 1900, to play for what he believed was that one year.[31] Colonel Rogers then testified before others could present oral arguments in front of the court.[32] Rogers, who seemed to enjoy bloviating incessantly, hadn't concluded his statements when the court was adjourned, with the proceedings scheduled to commence on April 27. Since no temporary injunction was requested or granted, Napoleon Lajoie, Chick Fraser, and Bill Bernhard were permitted to play, as the American League slate started on April 24.[33] Reports from April 22 uncovered that Napoleon didn't sign a contract until Connie Mack had placed the salary in escrow.[34]

Following two postponements because of rain, the Philadelphia Athletics played their first game of the season at the Columbia Park home grounds on April 26 against the Washington Senators.[35] Adverse weather for the past three days had soaked the ballpark's infield grass and outfield gravel. Over 15,000 patrons were in attendance as Washington defeated Philadelphia, 5-1. Rows of people standing in roped-off areas of the field reached six and seven deep as enthusiastic fans embraced the new team. Lajoie was presented with a giant floral horseshoe, while Fraser received a basket of posies. The day was rough for Connie Mack's men, who connected for only seven hits and committed seven errors. Napoleon scored the Athletics' one run in the seventh inning and did excellent work with the stick, going 3-for-4 and smacking a double.[36]

The crowd shrunk to 10,000 one day later, as the Senators prevailed again over the Athletics, 11-5. Lajoie continued his scintillating start, going 3-for-3 at the plate and scoring two runs.[37] Philadelphia finally put their first victory on the board on April 29, beating the Boston Americans, 8-5. Showing that he was the new league's marquis player, Napoleon was perfect at the plate for the second consecutive game, going 4-for-4, blasting two triples, and scoring two runs.[38] During the first week of their inaugural season, the Athletics posted a 2-4 record, while Lajoie was an amazing 17-for-25 at the plate. In the game against Boston on May 2, Philadelphia ended up on the losing end, 23-12. Local amateur Ivan "Pete" Loos started the game, allowing three runs, before he was lifted with the bases loaded in the second inning, giving way to Bill Bernhard.[39]

While Napoleon Lajoie was off to a blistering start at the plate, many of Philadelphia's pitchers struggled. Efforts to solidify the staff had been thwarted before the season when Connie Mack conducted his recruitment drive. Mack believed he had secured former Bucknell University hurler Christopher "Christy" Mathewson, who debuted with the New York Giants in 1900. Mathewson had signed a contract to play for the Athletics on January 19, asked for and received $50 in advance money on the eve of the season, and then reneged on the deal, opting to resign with New York. Christy mailed a $50 check to Mack, who sent it back to the pitcher unsigned on the advice of his lawyers.[40] In 1901, Mathewson ended up going 20-17 for the Giants, supported by a 2.41 ERA.

As the season progressed, devoted patrons awaited three judges' decisions related to the suit brought forward by Colonel John I. Rogers since the court had now heard all testimony and arguments. Some believed that if the judges issued an order for Lajoie, Bernhard, and Fraser to rejoin the Philadelphia Phillies, it could prove a death knell for the Philadelphia Athletics.[41] As a precautionary measure, the Detroit Tigers loaned second baseman Robert "Harry" Lochhead to the Athletics on April 28.[42] The battle between the two Quaker City teams was so intense that the *Philadelphia North American* even commented on concessions while discussing the rivalry between Mack and Rogers. The newspaper remarked that the ham sandwiches at Columbia Park were clean and tidy and didn't appear to be sliced with a safety razor while being available for each home game, whereas Rogers only offered this bill of fare on Mondays.[43]

Napoleon Lajoie's hitting cooled off slightly over the next five games, as Philadelphia reached the 11-game mark with a 4-7 record. According to the *St. Louis Republic*, through those 11 contests, Lajoie was 27-for-45 at the plate for a scintillating .600 batting average. He had also scored 17 runs.[44] Napoleon hit safely in all 11 of those games. Lajoie never received an opportunity to make it 12 straight when Philadelphia opposed Boston on May 9 at Huntington Avenue Baseball Grounds. Umpire John "Jack" Haskell ejected Napoleon from the game in the first inning before he received a chance to participate for kicking over a decision related to Phil Geier, Philadelphia's second batter. Changes to the Athletics squad resulted in a weakened unit, leading to substandard play and a 9-3 defeat.[45]

Philadelphia struggled, finding themselves in seventh place on May 17, with a 5-13 record. Lajoie's fine work remained front and center, despite the Athletics' inability to secure victories. On May 11, in a 7-6 win over the Baltimore Orioles, Napoleon went 2-for-5, smacked a double and a triple, and scored two runs.[46] Against the Orioles on May 14, a game Philadelphia lost, 11-5, Lajoie was 2-for-3 at the plate, banged out a triple and a home run, and scored three runs.[47] Another loss on May 17, an 8-7 defeat at the hands of the

Washington Senators, wasn't the big news story related to Philadelphia baseball. Common Pleas Court No. 5 rendered its decision, siding with the defendants and allowing Napoleon Lajoie, Chick Fraser, and Bill Bernhard to continue playing in the American League.[48]

The court's three judges determined that the one-sided contracts put forth by the Philadelphia Phillies, with the reserve clause included, lacked mutuality.[49] This meant the judges also dismissed Colonel John I. Roger's injunction proceedings brought forth before them. In his arguments before the court, defense counsel Richard C. Dale affirmed these contracts were illegal because they deprived the players of their constitutional right to receive the best possible return for their skills and services, making the documents inequitable.[50] This decision firmly established baseball players' rights. Judge Robert Ralston delivered the court's opinion on this case.

"From the testimony, it appears that the defendant is an experienced ballplayer in any position; that he has a great reputation as a second baseman; that his place would be hard to fill with as good a player; that his withdrawal from the team would weaken it, as would the withdrawal of any good player, and would probably make a difference in the size of the audiences attending the game," wrote Judge Ralston. "But something more than this is required to bring the case within the law."

According to these judges, something more was that the "defendant's services must be unique, extraordinary, and of such a character as to render it impossible to replace him, so that his breach of contract would result in irreparable loss to the plaintiff."[51] In this respect, the court felt the plaintiff had failed to meet its burden. In the eyes of these three judges, the ten-day clause and the total "want of mutuality" was the critical point that helped the players win their case. This verdict left Colonel Rogers and the Philadelphia Phillies with the option to file a suit for damages due to the loss of these three players.[52] When asked by a *Philadelphia Record* reporter shortly before the court rendered this decision what further action he might take, Rogers responded by claiming he would file suit in court against those responsible for tampering with his players.

"Who are these people who come along and steal our players after we have paid fancy prices to secure their releases from other clubs?" Rogers asked the reporter. "And yet these are the people that are being lauded to the skies by the newspapers of this city. When the Philadelphia club showed itself weak in any respect, these same papers called out for us to 'loosen up' and such like expressions, urging us to purchase the release of some particular star."[53]

Shortly after Napoleon Lajoie received his freedom to remain with the Philadelphia Athletics, statistics showed the star second baseman carried a .514 average through his first 18 games, with ten doubles, four triples, and two home runs.[54] This positive court resolution seemed to unburden the Athletics, as they finished May by going 8-4. In a game against Washington on May 18, Lajoie and David "Dave" Fultz switched positions, with Napoleon playing shortstop.[55] When Philadelphia opposed the Milwaukee Brewers on May 26, Napoleon lost two home runs due to a two-base ground rule at Lloyd Street Grounds.[56] After the month ended, Lajoie offered an opinion on his work at the plate.

"I consider .300 a good batting average," said Lajoie, "and anyone who can hit near the .350 mark has reason to be more than pleased with himself. My present average, around the .500 mark, is bound to fall off, as I hit but .346 [later adjusted to .337] last season and ranked below Wagner [Honus Wagner], Flick [Elmer Flick], Keeler [Willie Keeler], and Burkett [Jesse Burkett], but, of course, I try all the time and will keep it up as long as possible."[57]

Although Lajoie was hammering the baseball, expecting him to keep up his current hitting pace was unrealistic. After starting the month of June by going 9-for-20 in five games, he went 11-for-43 in his subsequent 11 appearances. The Athletics played poor baseball throughout June, going 8-15. A few bright spots for the squad were back-to-back shutouts against Milwaukee of 6-0 on June 13 and 7-0 the next day. Rookie southpaw Edward "Eddie" Plank did yeoman's work on June 13, while Chick Fraser allowed five hits on June 14, with only one Milwaukee runner reaching third, who was stranded there on a magnificent stop and throw by Napoleon at second base.[58] Plank had done excellent work on the bump for Connie Mack since debuting for Philadelphia on May 13. A writer for the *Philadelphia Telegraph* considered Eddie a true wonder, who "has a beautiful curve that sizzles and twists and batsmen are not sure whether it is going to rake them in the slats, pick off their collar button, or explode at the base."[59]

Following an early June series against Philadelphia at Columbia Park, Detroit Tigers president James D. Burns proffered a novel strategy for stifling Napoleon Lajoie at the plate. Burns opined that only two strikes should be permitted to Lajoie when he batted, while the pitcher had eight balls to work with, rather than the standard four allowed in the rulebook when throwing the pill over the plate.[60] Of course, not everyone bestowed accolades upon the big Frenchman. Boston baseball writer Timothy "Tim" Murnane criticized both Lajoie and Americans' third baseman and manager James "Jimmy" Collins for their tepid leadership skills.⁶¹ When it came to batting aptitude, Napoleon was in a class by himself, finishing off June by going 8-for-15 in the month's final three games.

As the baseball season swung into July, Connie Mack appealed to Ban Johnson for help strengthening his team. Mack mainly wanted permission to invade the Western Association, while Johnson had been leery of provoking minor league organizations.⁶² When Philadelphia defeated the Washington Senators, 9-7, on July 3, the team snapped an 11-game winless streak, as Lajoie went 3-for-4 at the plate.⁶³ This victory left the Athletics with a 22-33 record, good for sixth place in the American League standings. While the season had been a disaster from the viewpoint of wins and losses, Philadelphia started rolling after ending this slide, going 8-5 in their next 13 games, and posting a 13-10 record for July.

As the season proceeded through the summer, people hailed Napoleon Lajoie as the best all-around player in the country.⁶⁴ Statistical information released up to and including July 11 showed that eight American League players were hitting .350 or better. Lajoie stood as king of the hill above all others, leading the league with a .404 average. In 61 games, he had also recorded 25 doubles, eight triples, and four home runs.⁶⁵ Napoleon sizzled in July, only taking the collar at the plate four times while crafting together multiple-hit games on 15 occasions. In a contest against Washington on July 2, Senators hurler Case "Casey" Patten took the novel approach of challenging Lajoie to hit the ball rather than working around him. Napoleon responded by blasting two singles, a double, and a triple.⁶⁶

During a game against the first-place Chicago White Sox on July 23, a 10-6 defeat, Lajoie had to retire from the contest due to an injury after going 3-for-4 and scoring two runs.⁶⁷ Napoleon was back on the field at Bennett Park the following day, smacking two doubles and scoring two runs as Philadelphia beat the Detroit Tigers, 12-5.⁶⁸ Lajoie's scintillating hitting rolled along as the season moved into August. Napoleon drilled two doubles and scored three runs in the Athletics' 8-6 victory over Boston on August 1 at Columbia Park.⁶⁹ When August began, Philadelphia was in fifth place, with a 34-42 record. Thanks to a blistering 22-10 run that month, the Athletics pushed their record to 56-52, leaving them in fifth place but much closer to the teams holding down the third and fourth spots.

In the first game of a doubleheader against Washington on August 7, a 4-1 victory, Philadelphia secured the contest in the sixth inning when Lajoie stroked a double, and Ralph "Socks" Seybold blasted a home run.⁷⁰ On August 8, in a doubleheader sweep of the Senators where Philadelphia accounted for 25 runs, Napoleon went 6-for-10 in the two games.[71] The Athletics achieved another doubleheader sweep over Washington on August 9, as Lajoie went 6-for-9 on the day, smacking two home runs in the second contest.[72]

Philadelphia gained a twin-bill split with the Senators on August 10, losing the first game, 9-4, while winning the second, 13-0. Hurler George "Win" Mercer was the first-game hero for Washington. When it came to the business of playing baseball, Mercer philosophically approached such admiration in the following way: "You're a hero today and a dub tomorrow." While Win was solid for the Senators, Lajoie did crush two home runs over American League Park's fence. Umpire Thomas "Tommy" Connolly also tossed Napoleon in the seventh frame of game one for arguing numerous decisions.[73]

Statistics released on August 12 showed that Napoleon Lajoie was the American League's undisputed hitting king. Through 81 games (there was a considerable lag time regarding the numbers since Philadelphia had played 89 contests up to this point), Lajoie's average stood at .416, up five points from the previous week's mark of .411. Napoleon had also scored 99 runs and stolen 24 bases. Highlighting his importance as a run producer, Lajoie hadn't executed a sacrifice hit in 1901.[74] Following Napoleon's excellent work in three consecutive doubleheaders against Washington from August 8 through August 10, going 18-for-28 in those six games, he slumped a bit at the plate throughout the remainder of the month. Lajoie's record-breaking season was also interrupted by an injury, causing him to miss five games starting August 26 until returning on September 1.[75]

While briefly sidelined, Lajoie received criticism in a Philadelphia newspaper. This writer believed Napoleon could add 50 points to his batting average if he were more patient and selective at the plate instead of being a free-swinger.[76] Although most discussions about Lajoie surrounded his hitting, Athletics manager Connie Mack declared his second baseman was the total player package, possessing a solid work ethic.

"A mistake commonly made by people who follow the game of baseball is that when Lajoie makes an error he is loafing on the ball," said Mack. "I have heard the fans in the grandstand many times pass remarks when he fumbled a ball to the effect that if he had hustled after the ball, he'd have had it. Any such criticism of Lajoie is unjust. He is a player in one respect like Bill Dahlen of the Brooklyn club—he plays ball so naturally and so quickly that it looks as though he was not making any effort to make the plays that are pulled off in a game.

"Lajoie is, without doubt, the greatest second baseman in the business. His reach is long, and he is as fast as lightning, and to throw to at second he is ideal. Any catcher who has worked with him will tell you that he is the easiest man playing ball to throw to. He is sure of everything–high, low, or wide of the bag, it's all the same to him, and his arm is as good as any of them. Combine all these accomplishments with his batting powers, and there isn't a ballplayer in the business that compares with him. If people realized how hard he works in a game, they'd never charge him with shirking."[77]

Upon returning to the lineup on September 1, Mr. Versatility went 1-for-4 against Milwaukee.[78] Napoleon Lajoie's performance at the plate during the season's final month was a mixed bag. Appearing in 28 games, Lajoie took the collar six times, while he recorded multiple hits on 12 occasions, many of which occurred in the second half of September. Posted batting averages in the middle of the month showed Napoleon was still on top, hitting .409.[79] All American League games on September 19 were canceled out of respect for the funeral and burial of President William McKinley in Canton, Ohio.[80] President McKinley had passed away five days earlier from complications after being shot in Buffalo, New York, by assassin Leon Czolgosz, on September 6.[81]

During the season's final two weeks, Lajoie moved to shortstop for Philadelphia. On September 24, in a 5-4 victory against Milwaukee, Napoleon accepted 16 chances in the field, accounting for ten putouts and six assists, while also going 4-for-5 at the plate, with a double and a home run.[82] In that final month, Lajoie and his teammates kept up their torrid pace, posting an 18-10 record in September. When the bell sounded, ending the American League's inaugural major league campaign, Philadelphia came home fourth, with a 74-62 record.

The first, fresh, unofficial batch of final American League statistics on September 30, courtesy of the *St. Louis Republic,* showed that Napoleon Lajoie won the batting title with a .413 average. Lajoie's percentage was 61 points higher than runner-up John "Buck" Freeman of the Boston Americans. According to this initial information, Napoleon was also the leader in runs (146) and hits (227).[83] This mark was corroborated by the *Sporting News.* They also pointed out that 36 men in the American League batted over .300 in 1901.[84] In the middle of October, some publications alleged that Lajoie had batted .440.[85] When the final league statistics were released from Chicago by president Ban Johnson on October 29, Napoleon's official numbers were 145 runs scored, 220 hits, 27 stolen bases, and a batting average of .422.[86]

In his first season playing for the Philadelphia Athletics, Lajoie had established credentials that elevated him to a status as the American League's marquis player. Overall, the first season for this organization as a major league baseball power was a successful one beyond expectations. However, some had been skeptical about their original expansion into Baltimore, Boston, Philadelphia, and Washington. Ultimately, this baseball association challenged the National League on its turf in the East and prevailed.[87] After the season ended, Lajoie was tasked with helping assemble a touring team of All-American players to travel the country when John McGraw backed out due to injuries, starting down South before finishing in California.[88]

When the tourists played a game in Memphis, Tennessee, on October 20, Napoleon struck the baseball squarely with such extreme force that he damaged the sphere. After contact, it appeared two baseballs were in play. The fielders became briefly confused before realizing Lajoie had split the baseball in two, as one half of it landed fair while the other section fell in foul territory. The umpire ruled the smash a foul ball.[89] Napoleon was the big drawing card in New Orleans, Louisiana, when this squad defeated a local team on October 27, 18-8.[90] A double Lajoie smoked over third base, which landed 100 yards from the fence, was given proper plaudits in the *New Orleans Picayune*. The newspaper wrote that it "reached it on first bounce, so great was its impetus, striking with impact like a cannonball."[91] While the team traveled through Texas, Napoleon offered his theories related to hitting.

"The successful batsman is not afraid of being hit by the ball but sets up squarely to the plate and meets it with a chop or a swing," said Lajoie. "When you see a player back away from the plate, you may rest assured that he will not last long in either of the big leagues unless he corrects the fault, and even that is difficult, for batting is hardly a matter of education. Good batters have been developed, but all the greatest men in the country are what are called natural hitters.

"I have been remarkably successful, although, of course, I hit above my normal average this season and will drop off sooner or later, but I could hit well when I first began to play professional ball with Fall River in 1896. It was this quality, I think, which secured me a place with Philadelphia the same year, and there I have played ever since, joining issue with the American League this year."[92]

Napoleon Lajoie's continued success with the Athletics seemed to be a foregone conclusion. On December 4, Connie Mack announced he had signed 17 players for the 1902 campaign, including Lajoie. One such individual was Elmer Flick, Napoleon's former teammate, who jumped after playing for the Philadelphia Phillies in 1901.[93] Lajoie and ten other players, $700 richer in their pockets due to a successful barnstorming series, returned to Chicago from the West Coast in late January. Lajoie, at this time, believed he would be suiting up again for the Athletics.[94] The train ride to California hadn't been very pleasurable for Lajoie, despite the beautiful scenery, as he lost his appetite in one instance while sitting at a dining car table, peering out the window and viewing a 3,000-foot deep precipice. While discussing his travel travails, Napoleon also commented on Phillies president Colonel John I. Rogers challenging him to grab a second bite at the legal apple.[95]

Not one to ignore doing due diligence while exhausting all legal avenues, Colonel Rogers had appealed the original decision of Common Pleas Court No. 5 in Philadelphia to the Pennsylvania Supreme Court.[96] As the baseball world awaited a verdict on this appeal, and American League officials held their collective breath, the National League started a new line of attack, hoping to recoup some of the jumping players. A report claimed that during a meeting at New York's Fifth Avenue Hotel, league magnates pledged to utilize a $100,000 fund established to plunder American League teams of players. Brooklyn Superbas skipper Edward "Ned" Hanlon claimed no such fund existed. Contrary to that assertion, New York Giants manager Horace Fogel supposedly possessed $15,000 cash solely for enticing Lajoie to join his team.[97]

Napoleon did spurn a contract offer from the Giants, calling for him to receive $10,000 a year for three years.[98] In another report, the proposal was the same amount of years, at a rate of $7,000 each season. Lajoie was pestered in Philadelphia for five long hours by an agent acting on behalf of the Giants, starting at 10 p.m. on the evening of April 3. When urged to jump his contract with the Athletics, Lajoie simply laughed at this individual.[99] Napoleon explained how such overtures were futile. "I have received nothing but the best treatment possible from President Shibe and Manager Mack," said Lajoie. "I am under contract to the Philadelphia American League club for two years longer. I have no intention of repudiating that contract, and all the offers of the National League will not induce me to desert the American League. I am satisfied with the treatment I have received from Manager Mack and intend to show my appreciation of it by remaining loyal to him."[100]

When it came to mirthful chuckling, Colonel John I. Rogers had the last laugh. On April 21, 1902, the Pennsylvania Supreme Court overturned the earlier decision of Common Pleas Court No. 5, ruling in favor of the Philadelphia Phillies in their case against Napoleon Lajoie while also upholding the validity of baseball's reserve clause in player contracts. Despite being withdrawn from the suit by agreement of counsel, teammates Bill Bernhard and Chick Fraser were still affected by this decision.[101] On April 23, the judges of Common Pleas Court No. 5 granted Colonel Rogers the new injunction he had filed, preventing Lajoie from playing for the Philadelphia Athletics.[102] That same day, Napoleon appeared in Philadelphia's opening game.

During the bottom of the eighth inning in this contest against the Baltimore Orioles at Oriole Park, Connie Mack received a telegram from Philadelphia informing him of an initial five-day temporary injunction. Mack immediately removed Lajoie from the game.[103] The court made that preliminary injunction permanent on April 28, as this mandate's umbrella also included Bernhard and Fraser.[104] On May 6, the lower judiciary body denied any appeals by the three players to the state's Supreme Court.[105] Fraser returned to the Phillies, while Lajoie and Bernhard chose a different path. Since this court decision was only binding in Pennsylvania, Ban Johnson and other American League officials decided their best course of action was to transfer the organization's preeminent player to a different team.

A rumor surfaced following this last-ditch effort hoping to gain relief from the courts, indicating Johnson may broker a deal, shipping Lajoie to the Detroit Tigers.[106] On May 30, the *Cleveland Leader* wrote that both Napoleon Lajoie and Bill Bernhard would play for the Cleveland Broncos for the season's duration.[107] Reports alleged that Lajoie's salary for 1902 was $7,000.[108] Napoleon debuted for the Broncos at League Park on June 4, as Cleveland defeated Boston, 4-3.[109] Cleveland's new player did solid work, hitting .379 while appearing in 86 games. Such an achievement occurred amid trepidation over potential arrest concerns due to Ohio bordering Pennsylvania, where Lajoie couldn't travel since he had defied a court order. When the two leagues reached a peace accord before the 1903 campaign, Lajoie continued his brilliant career with Cleveland until returning to the Athletics in 1915. Napoleon also received the ultimate honor when Cleveland started being called the Naps in 1903.

Napoleon Lajoie never did top the .400 mark again in his illustrious career. Over time, further research and statistical adjustment brought Lajoie's average for 1901 up to .426, with him later being ordained a triple-crown batter by also leading the American League in home runs (14) and RBIs (125). This recalculation regarding his batting average was due to the addition of 12 hits in 23 at-bats compared to the final statistics released by Ban Johnson's office in October 1901. Before baseball's modern era, three men had topped Napoleon's average. Hugh Duffy's .440 for the Boston Beaneaters in 1894 was the highest.

Pre-1900, a player shattered the .400 mark 15 times, while before the unearthing of new information in 2021, the belief was that this happened on 12 occasions after Lajoie established his modern-era batting achievement. The Detroit Tigers' Ty Cobb hit over .400 thrice, with .419 in 1911 being the highest of his career. For almost a century, Rogers Hornsby of the St. Louis Cardinals seemed closest to outdoing Napoleon when he batted .424 in 1924. This supposition ended up not being true.

A new statistical analysis done by Baseball-Reference related to the Major Negro Leagues blows that premise out of the water. In 1921, Oscar Charleston of the Negro National League's St. Louis Giants topped Lajoie by batting .433. From 1920 through 1948, a qualifying batter from the Major Negro Leagues eclipsed the .400 plateau on 22 occasions. Various individuals surpassed Charleston's 1921 mark. Juan "Tetelo" Vargas of the New York Cubans from the Negro National League II now holds the record, batting .471 in 1943. He barely bested Josh Gibson of that organization's Homestead Grays, who hit .466 that same year.

While it's true that Napoleon Lajoie feasted on diluted American League pitching in 1901, that organization did possess accomplished twirlers like Clark Griffith, James "Nixey" Callahan, Roy Patterson, Denton "Cy" Young, Edward "Ed" Siever, Joseph "Joe" McGinnity, Casey Patten, and Alonzo "Earl" Moore. Of course, the big story behind this record, which stood for 120 years, is about more than base hits and points on a batting average. It is foremost a tale of elite batsman Napoleon Lajoie, the man most responsible for elevating and breathing life into an infant league in 1901.

On April 21, 1902, the Pennsylvania Supreme Court ruled in favor of the Philadelphia Phillies regarding who legally held the rights to Napoleon Lajoie, overturning a previous decision in Common Pleas Court No. 5. Responding to this judgment, American League president Ban Johnson transferred the league's marquis player from the Philadelphia Athletics to the Cleveland Broncos to circumvent the illegality of Lajoie playing for that Pennsylvania team. (Courtesy of the Library of Congress.)

CHAPTER 2

John Gochnaur – 1903

Dispelling the Good Glove, No Hit Myth

Part of baseball's unique beauty is that it's a rare sport where a team maintains control of the ball while playing defense. In football, basketball, and hockey, the offense initiates the attack while possessing the ball or puck. Baseball is drastically different since the players in the field, especially the pitcher, dictate terms and determine how events unfold once a batter steps up to the plate. Given this massive responsibility for those playing the field, hoping to set the tone for a baseball game, placing a high premium on solid glove men and iron-clad defense is essential. The defensive structure was even more critical during baseball's Deadball Era. At this time, teams utilized stealing bases and the hit-and-run play to push precious runs across home plate.

Stretching that defense to its limits was critical to gaining the upper hand. Astute players pushed the envelope when running, forcing defenders out of their comfort zone while attempting to thwart these efforts. As a result, this strategy sometimes led to more errors. Another thing that helped spike high error totals in the Deadball Era was the unrefined fields of major league ballparks. These conditions remained prevalent before constructing new baseball plants in numerous cities. Hard, rocky infields victimized even stellar fielders. In the small-ball era, sacrificing a spot in the lineup with a strong gloveman that was a weak hitter acted as a prudent approach. A problem only arose when that individual couldn't handle either task. When it came to futility at the plate and in the field, Cleveland shortstop John Gochnaur set the standard in both areas during his brief major league career.

John Peter Gochnaur was born on September 12, 1875, in Altoona, Pennsylvania. As a young lad, Gochnaur had gained inspiration watching George "Germany" Smith play shortstop for the Union Association's Altoona Mountain City in 1884 before joining the National League's Cleveland Blues later that year. John started out honing his skills by playing cricket.[1] Gochnaur received his early baseball schooling as a teenager, performing as an infielder for the local Jennings club. John eventually became a star player for the Crickets, a team sponsored by Altoona baseball mogul Charles F. Carpenter.[2] In 1896, Gochnaur started a long sojourn through the minors with the Virginia League's Roanoke Magicians. He was also a member of that organization's Portsmouth Browns and the Cumberland Valley League's Hagerstown Lions.[3]

Gochnaur found some baseball stability in 1897 when he joined the New England League's Brockton Shoemakers.[4] John remained with Brockton for more than a year and then hooked up with the New York State League's Rome Romans in 1898. In 1899, Gochnaur appeared in 60 games with the Atlantic League's Paterson Giants. He continued his nomadic career playing for that association's Scranton Miners and the New England League's Pawtucket Colts that summer.[5] Bad luck certainly plagued John since Scranton disbanded in July and Pawtucket ceased operations in August. Gochnaur finally caught a good break when he became a member of manager William "Bill" Armour's Dayton Veterans aggregation of the Interstate League in 1900. Throughout his minor league travels, Gochnaur had become known as a dependable fielder with a powerful arm.[6]

John found his niche playing for Armour. Previously branded as someone who didn't possess much hitting talent, Gochnaur batted .278 for the Veterans in 1900 and .261 in 1901, when the team became known as the Old Soldiers, playing in the Western Association. On April 28, 1901, in a game against the Columbus Senators, Gochnaur was severely spiked in the seventh inning, forcing him to leave the contest.[7] John didn't miss a beat despite the injury, appearing in 139 games for Dayton. Gochnaur's performance caught the attention of Brooklyn Superbas management, who brought him in for a late-season tryout. John made his major league debut on September 29 against the Chicago Orphans and exhibited strong potential, going 4-for-11 at the plate in the team's final three games.

Brooklyn's fans immediately fell in love with Gochnaur's crack infield work during that short time. Local fans hailed John as one of the young ballplayers, signed by the Superbas for 1902, who possessed a solid chance at becoming a fixture on the squad.[8] Shortly after the season ended, John declared he fully anticipated earning a permanent position on Brooklyn's roster next year. When asked about the intentions of hurler and friend Clarence Eugene "Gene" Wright, who the Superbas had also purchased from Dayton, Gochnaur stated the pitcher confided in him that he would remain with Brooklyn. John's comment contradicted reports that Wright intended to jump to the American League to play for the Cleveland Broncos, with Bill Armour running the ship in 1902.[9]

For the next few months, both John Gochnaur's and Gene Wright's objectives for the coming season were fleshed out in yoyo fashion by the press. In early February, a report claimed Armour had exhausted all hope he could secure Gochnaur and Wright for the Broncos.[10] Interestingly, commentaries indicating Cleveland president John Kilfoyle was in agreement with his manager were unfounded. Finally, on March 7, an announcement came that both players had signed contracts to play for the Broncos and were ready to attend spring training with the squad. A backstory helped explain this decision by Gochnaur and Wright.

When Brooklyn president Charles Ebbets came west the previous season, he approached the two men, informing them he had bought their releases from Dayton. Both players finished the season in Brooklyn uniforms, as the National League campaign ran one week longer than their American League rivals. John and Gene eventually found that Ebbets initially had made a ridiculous, low-ball offer to purchase them, which Bill Armour rejected. Upon discovering this crucial information, Gochnaur and Wright renounced their Brooklyn contracts, pledged allegiance to their former Dayton skipper, and signed with Cleveland.[11] Kilfoyle was confident both players would honor their agreement with the Broncos, despite overtures from Brooklyn.[12]

In his article for *Sporting Life*, writer John B. Foster used this case to criticize the practice employed by both leagues of procuring players bound to legal contracts during this period of all-out war. Foster also condemned pitcher George Mullin, who had jumped his Brooklyn contract before playing for the team, to join the American League's Detroit Tigers. The writer reasoned that while young players such as these felt they could flaunt their obligations and do whatever they pleased, the losses of Gochnaur and Wright would inflict minimal damage to the Superbas' hopes in 1902.

"On the whole," writes Foster, "if they desert, I doubt if the Brooklyn club will lose very much in the long run. There will be a reaction in the case of contract jumpers one of these days that will leave them high and dry, where they will no longer be troubled by the manager who seeks to get them to play.

Gochnaur, Wright, and Mullin need not lay the flattering unction to their souls that they begin their baseball career with flowers and brave speeches when they show a determination to forget what they have promised faithfully to do.

"No doubt exists that both Gochnaur and Wright fully meant to play with Brooklyn when they were with the team last fall. I don't think much of the influence that allured them elsewhere. It is a distinct disgrace to the game of which both leagues have been guilty, and baseball cannot hope to prosper by such methods."[13]

As the Broncos trained in New Orleans, Louisiana, before the 1902 campaign, an interesting story out of Buffalo reached manager Bill Armour. The National Association of Professional Baseball Leagues was ostracizing him in response to fleecing Gochnaur and Wright from Dayton and grabbing Frank Bonner and Harry Bemis from the Eastern League's Toronto Royals to enrich Cleveland's coffers. This story also accused Armour of ingratitude toward the Dayton squad, for which he had a small ownership interest. Cleveland's manager exhibited no concern over the ridiculous accusation. Bill was also in the process of looking for a buyer to purchase his stake in Dayton's team.[14]

One of Armour's first tasks, when spring training started, was to teach his players sign language due to hurler Luther "Dummy" Taylor's addition to the team. After going 18-27 for the New York Giants in 1901, Taylor, a deaf-mute, had jumped to the Broncos in 1902. Each player on the squad was handed instructions with orders to learn the sign manual quickly. Gene Wright, John Gochnaur, and pitcher Adrian "Addie" Joss secured the services of a private tutor, New Orleans ballplayer John "Jack" Law, to become proficient and adept at signing so that they could communicate with Taylor. Before becoming a baseball player, a deaf and mute asylum previously employed Law.[15]

This effort by his comrades ended up going for naught. Taylor became unhappy in Cleveland, perceiving some teammates weren't diligent in conquering sign language. In May, he returned to the Giants with assistance from former teammate and catcher Frank Bowerman. After the season ended, outfielder Charles "Charlie" Hemphill, who had been Dummy's roommate and remained with Cleveland until drawing his release in June, and signing with the St. Louis Browns, explained how Bowerman recaptured the twirler. "'Dummy' Taylor and I were roommates when we were with Cleveland, and I made fine progress in learning the sign language under his tuition," said Hemphill. "Then he 'jumped' us, and I gave up finger talking. It was just after we opened up our first series in Cleveland [starting on May 6]. Taylor had taken a liking to me, and we were much together. The night that Bowerman struck town, I missed

Taylor. I was going to the theater and, walking down the street; I met Taylor and Bowerman. The latter I did not know from Adam, or I would have tumbled in a minute to the object of his Cleveland visit.

"I invited the pair to go to the theater with me, but Taylor declined. I noticed the change in his manner. He seemed to want to 'shake' me as soon as possible and didn't invite me to stay with him. You can bet that Bowerman kept his mouth closed, and finally, they broke away from me, and I went to the theater alone. I returned home to find the bird had flown.

"I went up to our room in the hotel and found the door locked. I thought, 'here is a ruminy go; me with no key and a deaf and dumb man to wake up before I could get in the room to go to bed.' I went back downstairs and there found the key in the box. When I opened the door and struck a light, the first thing I noticed was the 'Dummy's' two uniforms spread out on the bed. A closer search revealed that he had taken his other belongings away with him. I picked up the uniforms and shook out a note which read: 'Goodbye, Charlie—I am back with New York.' Then I knew that he had 'jumped' back, and the man who was with him that night, I found out the next morning, was Frank Bowerman. I did not see the 'Dummy' from that day until I met him at the Southern Hotel in St. Louis. He was with the Giants, and I was a member of the Browns."[16]

Things being in flux were the norm, as the American and National leagues' head-to-head battle over coercing players to join their side continued throughout 1902. On May 30, second baseman Napoleon Lajoie and pitcher Bill Bernhard moved from the Philadelphia Athletics and signed with Cleveland. This maneuver, orchestrated with assistance from league president Ban Johnson, was done in response to an injunction by Pennsylvania courts after a year-long battle. The ruling claimed that Lajoie and Bernhard legally belonged to the Philadelphia Phillies under the reserve clause, the team both men were members of before jumping to the Athletics in 1901.

Cleveland finished the 1902 American League campaign in fifth place, sporting a 69-67 record. John Gochnaur appeared in 127 games at shortstop, batted .185, committed 48 errors, and posted a .933 fielding percentage. In July, the *Brooklyn Daily Eagle* took a backhanded swipe at Gochnaur. While praising his performance in a game against the Washington Senators on July 25, which Cleveland won, 6-3, the newspaper was glowing when referring to John's 11 assists and four putouts in the field, despite committing an error. In a negative context, the publication suggested Gochnaur had jumped to the Broncos because he believed the National League was too fast for him.[17]

Gochnaur remained in shape during the off-season by working for the railroad in his hometown of Altoona. Management expected every team member to be in peak condition when spring training commenced, excluding star second baseman Nap Lajoie, who was recovering from an illness. The anticipation was that Lajoie initially would be limited to a light workload by Bill Armour when players reported to New Orleans in preparation for the 1903 season. Armour also gave pitcher Bill Bernhard permission to skip the trip South and join his teammates the first week of April. Bernhard planned on getting into condition by working out with Los Angeles' minor league aggregation.[18]

On February 1, Cleveland sportswriter Henry P. Edwards responded to baseball pundits working for the *Detroit Journal*, who felt Cleveland wasn't a legitimate pennant contender since they hadn't strengthened the squad after the 1902 season. Edwards didn't see the validity in dismissing Cleveland regarding the flag hunt due to the lack of moves over the winter. In explaining the positive aspects of each player on the roster, the writer gave John Gochnaur a complimentary endorsement.

"And, to tell the truth," writes Edwards, "there are few better fielding shortstops than Johnny Gochnaur; in the opinion of many baseball critics, his speed in the field making up for his shortcomings at the bat, a weakness that seems to be greatly the result of hard luck, as no man on the team hits the ball harder than the little Dutchman."

Edwards claimed a lousy start the previous season before stars like Lajoie entered the scene, preventing Cleveland from joining the pennant conversation.[19] In honoring the American League's best player, a vote by the fans led to a change in the team name from Broncos to Naps, out of deference to Lajoie (they were still referred to as the Blues on occasion). When it came to nicknames, Gochnaur was known as "Dutch," "Goch," and "Johnny" to his teammates. Changes were also coming to the American League in 1903 due to the peace agreement reached with the National League, ending contract jumping and the war between these two entities, which were now equal, co-existing organizations.

As a result of this agreement, the American League adopted the foul-strike rule that had been in vogue for their National League counterpart since 1901. Bill Armour generally believed the new rule of the first two pitches fouled off by a batter counting as strikes would benefit the Naps because his stable of pitchers was speedy and swift.[20] This acceptance wasn't full throttle since he didn't favor the rule.

"It is better," said Armour, "to have a bad rule than to tangle up the public. By having one set of rules in all professional games, a spectator is always at ease.

He always knows what a play is. But when the different leagues have different rules, he must acquaint himself with the peculiar features of the rules of each whenever he goes to a game. Personally, I have never favored the foul-strike rule, but I may be prejudiced against it. Perhaps, the better way will be to give it a fair trial before we condemn it."

Bill Armour also showed little concern over changing the height of the pitcher's mound to a league-wide standard of 15 inches.

"Last season," declared Bill, "we started with a mound that was about 21 inches high, and before the year ended, we had lowered it to about six inches. Fifteen inches is plenty high enough. And so far as that is concerned, I don't know that we shall have a mound at all. Cleveland's pitchers are such big fellows that they look like mountains to opposing batters without having a pedestal under them."[21]

When the time arrived to play spring exhibition games, one of Cleveland's little fellows stood above all others. John Gochnaur, who showed up at spring training in excellent condition, carried away top honors in the Naps' first spring battle on March 23, a 7-3 victory over the Southern Association's New Orleans Pelicans. Gochnaur smacked three hits and distinguished himself in the field, accepting all six chances at shortstop cleanly, four of which were tough plays.[22] Unfortunately, John's performance slipped a bit. He batted .209 in seven games against New Orleans before Cleveland broke camp, started north, and finished the pre-season campaign with exhibition contests against the Birmingham Barons, Louisville Colonels, and Nashville Volunteers. As an added treat, Naps' management decided to take the entire team to Cincinnati for the Reds' April 16 opening game against the Pittsburgh Pirates.[23]

Cleveland started their season on April 22, losing to the Detroit Tigers, 4-2, at Bennett Park. Detroit's crowd, the largest to ever witness a game in that city, went home happy, thanks to a Tigers rally in the eighth inning that broke a 2-2 tie.[24] Detroit slaughtered the Naps on April 23, 11-1, as John Gochnaur and third baseman William "Bill" Bradley each committed an error.[25] The Tigers made it a clean sweep on April 25, shutting out Cleveland, 2-0. Gochnaur went 2-for-3 at the plate and made an error, while Naps hurler Earl Moore allowed only one earned run.[26] Following this series, manager Bill Armour offered impressions regarding the state of his team.

"We have the best team in the league," said Armour, "and we have to show the public that we have. Our Southern trip was a frost as far as securing practice was concerned, and now we will have to make up for lost time upon the home grounds. We really did not have a warm sunshiny day after we left New Orleans, and as a result, the men are not thawed out. Rain kept us from playing at Louisville, and at Indianapolis and Columbus, we were playing when we should have been hugging the stove. At Detroit, it was worse yet, the cold there being intense. In fact, it was so cold that the large attendance there was a huge surprise to me."[27]

Nearly 20,000 raucous members of that public were in attendance at League Park for the Naps' home opener on April 28. Cleveland prevailed over the St. Louis Browns, 6-3. During this contest, recently erected temporary bleachers in right field collapsed, injuring some people with severe bumps and bruises. The Naps secured the game by bunching their hits off Browns hurler John "Jack" Powell.[28] The ballpark was so jammed that people took up residence on the roofs and fences while thousands of fans sat or stood on the grounds, forcing special ground rules to be adopted. Although Gochnaur went 2-for-2 at the plate and drew two walks, his wild throw, after fielding Roderick "Bobby" Wallace's ground ball in the seventh inning, allowed Charlie Hemphill and Emmet Heidrick to score.[29] The Naps pushed their record to 2-3 on the young season by beating St. Louis, 4-1, on April 29.

Cleveland started May by losing four consecutive games. On May 1, the Naps succumbed to St. Louis, 9-8, as errors by Gochnaur and John "Jack" Thoney in the eighth inning contributed to the Browns scoring four runs and tying the game.[30] John also made a miscue on May 2, as Cleveland lost to the Chicago White Sox at South Side Park, 16-6.[31] Although Gochnaur's fielding had been unsteady, as the last place Naps' record stood at 2-7 on May 4, he was the season's surprise with the willow thus far. John was smacking the ball for an average of around .400.[32] Armour and his troops righted the ship, going 15-8 throughout the rest of May and moving up to fifth place by month's end. Despite Cleveland's turnaround, Gochnaur's leaky defense continued, as he made 17 errors over those 23 games, giving him 20 for the entire month.

Although John committed two fielding gaffes against Detroit on May 7, he was the hero. Tigers outfielder Samuel "Sam" Crawford misplayed Gochnaur's long fly in the eighth inning, allowing two critical runs to score, as the Naps prevailed, 6-5. Umpire Francis "Silk" O'Loughlin also expelled Bill Bradley from this game due to arguing over one of his decisions.[33] Two days later, as Detroit mauled Cleveland, 13-1, Gochnaur committed an error as part of the team's patchwork infield since Bradley received a suspension, and Nap Lajoie was sick.[34] On May 12 against the Boston Americans, John was flawless in the field. Unfortunately, five errors aided Boston in scoring six unearned runs and beating the Naps, 10-5. Umpire Tommy Connolly also ordered Nap Lajoie from the field for disputing one of his calls.[35]

John Gochnaur helped the Americans' cause on May 14, as Boston defeated Cleveland, 10-4. With two outs in the fifth inning, errors by Gochnaur and first baseman Charles "Charlie" Hickman allowed the parade to continue as Boston piled up five runs. Naps pitcher Earl Moore fanned eight batters in the first four frames before his defense abandoned him.[36] John received accolades for brilliant fielding in a game against the New York Highlanders on May 17.

Cleveland won the contest at Neil Park in Columbus, Ohio, 9-2, as Armour's boys pounded hurler Clark Griffith in the first two innings.[37] Amazingly, Bill Bernhard handled the Washington Senators, 5-2, on May 21, despite Gochnaur's four errors. Bill would have experienced a much more leisurely afternoon if not for John's miscues. Gochnaur did participate in one of his team's three fast double plays at critical junctures of the game.[38] Each time John booted a play, Bernhard's resolve on the mound grew stronger.[39]

In Cleveland's 2-1 win over the Philadelphia Athletics on May 25, Earl Moore lost his shutout bid in the ninth inning when Gochnaur's wild throw allowed Oliver "Ollie" Pickering to cross home plate.[40] On June 1, the *Washington Times* claimed that while he was fielding at about a .840 clip, John was batting far better than in 1902.[41] Naps fans reasoned Gochnaur was having a tough time with those grounders, while they alleged double-play partner Napoleon Lajoie lacked ginger and snap.[42] Cleveland closed out May by winning three consecutive games against Chicago. This victory tonic came at the right time since disgruntled rooters were starting to knock the team's inconsistent play. Writer Henry P. Edwards claimed part of the problem was that high expectations had been placed on the team by local scribes before the season started. Edwards surmised that pennants were won on the diamond and not on paper.[43]

John Gochnaur slightly stemmed the tide by butchering plays over the next month, committing 12 errors in June. In a game against New York at American League Park on June 5, John was responsible for two miscues as the Highlanders defeated Cleveland, 8-7. Wild throws by Gochnaur and catcher Harry Bemis in the ninth inning allowed New York to secure victory. Highlanders pitcher Jesse Tannehill was banished from the game for kicking over a decision by umpire Silk O'Loughlin.[44] Following an 8-4 win over New York on June 6, Cleveland swept a three-game series against Washington. Many Naps seemed to be wielding deadly cudgels, as Napoleon Lajoie, Bill Bradley, Harry Bay, Elmer Flick, and Charlie Hickman impressed at the plate. On the downside, Gochnaur and John "Jack" McCarthy were experiencing devastating hitting funks.[45]

John made fielding gaffes in five straight games against Washington and Philadelphia from June 9 through June 13. The Naps posted a 3-2 record in those contests, while Gochnaur went 3-16 at the plate. Cleveland's 3-2 victory over the Athletics on June 11 was a homecoming for three players. A peace agreement and lifted injunctions permitted Nap Lajoie, Bill Bernhard, and Elmer Flick to play baseball in Pennsylvania without worrying about being arrested for taking the field in a professional game within the state's boundaries.[46] On June 12, Cleveland's Addie Joss and Philadelphia's George Edward "Rube" Waddell both pitched brilliantly, as the Athletics were victorious in 14 innings, 2-1.[47] One day later, 24,277 patrons packed Columbia Park, braving cool weather and the threat of rain, to watch Philadelphia demolish the Naps, 12-1.[48]

Gochnaur continued fumbling about in the field, committing one error each in consecutive losses against Boston on June 19, 20, and 21. After taking two out of three from the Americans on the road and winning the first game against them at League Park, 5-4, on June 18, Cleveland was defeated by scores of 5-3, 5-4 (in ten innings), and 12-7 in those three contests that John made fielding mistakes. After committing so many blunders, manager Bill Armour decided a change was prudent, briefly benching Gochnaur and installing William "Billy" Clingman at shortstop. Dutch's performance certainly had been erratic up to this point. John blamed his substandard play on poor health.[49]

As John watched from the bench on June 24, Cleveland split a doubleheader with New York. In the first game, a 6-3 Highlanders victory, the Naps committed five errors, including one by Clingman.[50] During Goch's short hiatus, Billy generally played fine ball in the field, but his batting was highly anemic. This reality prompted Armour to reinstall Gochnaur at shortstop in the game against Philadelphia on June 29. Although the Athletics defeated the Naps, 4-2, a rejuvenated Gochnaur was a demon in the field, gobbling up everything the opposing team hit his way. John also drove in one of Cleveland's runs with a double.[51] One day later versus Philadelphia, John scored the winning run in the ninth inning after Harry Bay singled, giving the Naps a 4-3 victory.[52]

Cleveland stood in third place with a 31-26 record, 5 ½ games behind league-leading Boston as the campaign entered July. While accessing the American League race, veteran Boston writer Jacob C. "Jake" Morse claimed the Naps looked solid and impressed fans so much they believed a flag was a strong possibility. Morse offered positive impressions regarding the play of various infielders in games against the Americans.

"Charley Hickman put up great ball at first," writes Morse. "Bradley played by all odds the best third seen in this city this year and is assuredly the best all-round man in the position today, without the possibility of doubt in the matter.

"Johnny Gochnuar (how they do stumble on this name) made many a fine play at short, and the first base work of Charley Hickman was a revelation to the 'fans.'

"'Hick' made many a good play, and the 'fans' rejoiced in his ability to make good, for he is deservedly one of the most popular players there is in the business today."[53]

Morse failed to grasp one key point concerning Gochnaur. Cleveland's shortstop was equally capable of making outstanding plays and losing focus on more pedestrian chances. July was none too kind to Goch's fielding percentage, as John committed 18 errors that month. The official scorer charged John with two miscues in six different July games. After not making an error in the morning affair of a July 4 doubleheader against Washington, Gochnaur didn't get a chance to press his luck in the afternoon contest on a strange day. The Senators won the first game, 10-3, as Nap Lajoie was banished from the proceedings as the first inning ended. Lajoie failed to heed the instructions of umpire Robert "Bob" Caruthers before a police officer escorted Nap from the premises. After being overcome by the heat in the fourth inning, Caruthers then relinquished his duties, with the task falling to Washington denizen Harry Mace. Rain caused the afternoon contest to be postponed.[54]

On July 10, Addie Joss defeated Philadelphia at Columbia Park, 4-1, although Goch committed two errors. Players from both squads wore bows made of crepe, honoring former Philadelphia Phillies great Ed Delahanty. The remarkable player had died days earlier when he fell from a railroad bridge near Niagara Falls after being ordered off a train for initiating a disturbance.[55] An electrical storm caused a one-hour delay in the game against the Athletics on July 11. The contest was played in muddy conditions, as the Naps sent Rube Waddell to the showers in the fifth inning, claiming a 10-3 victory. Indeed, such conditions weren't conducive to staunch fielding, as Gochnaur made two errors.[56]

More weirdness, and another duo of miscues by John, highlighted Cleveland's 11-4 loss against Boston at Huntington Avenue Baseball Grounds on July 16. Four of the Americans' runs resulted from umpire Tommy Connolly inexplicably calling time in the first fame, as the Naps recorded the third out. Connolly did so because he turned to the bench, demanding new baseballs. Umpires shortened the game to eight innings so Cleveland could catch a train to New York.[57] Gochnaur was flawless in the field in the first two contests of the series with the Highlanders until he flubbed two plays in the second game of a doubleheader on July 20. In that contest, the Naps' two runs scored off Jack Chesbro, after replacing Wilbert "Barney" Wolfe, who retired because of an injury, were the game's only tallies.[58]

Johnny committed two errors against St. Louis at League Park on July 25, as hurler Alexander "Alex" Pearson, formerly of the St. Louis Cardinals and recently secured from Homestead, Pennsylvania, debuted for Cleveland.[59] Pearson did marvelous work, restricting the Browns to six hits and one earned run as Cleveland won the game, 7-4. Although Nap Lajoie committed a throwing error after making a sensational play, allowing two runners to score in the sixth frame, he was the hitting star, smacking a two-run double in the first and blasting a home run over the left-field fence in the third. St. Louis registered their other unearned run in that inning when Gochnaur fumbled William "Bill" Friel's grounder, killing a potential double play. Following a force out and a walk, Friel scored when Mike Kahoe flew out to center field.[60]

In the game against Chicago on July 30, John's old buddy Gene Wright was horrendous on the mound for the Naps. The White Sox claimed a 10-0 victory, as Wright passed eight men and allowed four hits. Two stolen bases, two sacrifice bunts, and two errors aided Chicago's ability to put runs on the scoreboard. One of those miscues came courtesy of Gochnaur.[61] Two days later, on August 1, Gene was shipped to St. Louis for fellow pitcher Red Donahue. After the Naps finalized the deal, Wright expressed his displeasure and refused to report to the Browns. Gene only consented to the move after a long talk with manager Bill Armour, president John Kilfoyle, and owner Charles Somers.[62]

As the season swung into a new month, Cleveland remained in third place, with a record of 45-39. The Naps trailed first-place Boston by 8 ½ games. Thus far in 1903, Dutch had already surpassed his total from the previous year by being charged with 53 errors. Gochnaur did some of his worst work in August, committing 21 miscues when it came to booting, fumbling, and making wild throws. John was particularly wretched at the beginning of the month, making one error in each game, as Cleveland lost to Chicago, 5-0, on August 1, and 2-0, the following day. Gochnaur then committed an error on August 4, when Detroit defeated the Naps, 5-2. One day later, John was at it again, although the Naps prevailed over the Tigers, 8-2. Detroit was gifted the game in a 5-3 loss on August 7 thanks to five Naps errors. John did his part, being responsible for two of those fielding gaffes.[63]

On August 8, Cleveland lost their third straight game against the Tigers due to a forfeit. With the contest tied 5-5 in the eleventh inning, Detroit catcher

Frederick "Fritz" Buelow tossed an old, worn, soiled baseball into play. The Naps' players protested, but umpire Tommy Connolly rejected their complaints. Deciding to take care of matters, Napoleon Lajoie grabbed the ball and threw it over the grandstand. In response to this action, Connelly promptly awarded the game to the Tigers through forfeit, 9-0. Although an angry mob of League Park fans surrounded the umpire, they didn't subject him to any violent acts before he exited the field. John Gochnaur also committed two errors in the game.[64]

After starting the month 2-6, Cleveland reeled off an eight-game winning streak from August 10 through August 17. Gochnaur didn't get cheated in the error department during his team's surge. The shortstop committed single gaffes against Chicago on August 12, New York on August 13 (in game two of a doubleheader) and August 15, and Boston on August 17. The winning run ended on August 18, when Boston crushed the Naps, 10-2. Undaunted by this minor setback, Cleveland began another streak the following day, reaching five games. John had a hand in starting things positively for the Naps as they defeated the Senators, 2-0, on August 19. Gochnaur scored a crucial insurance run in the eighth inning when he reached on a single, moved to second on a sacrifice bunt by Earl Moore, and scored on Elmer Flick's base hit.[65]

Sloppy play returned to John's game, as he committed two errors in an 11-3 victory over Philadelphia on August 22 and made a single fielding mistake on August 24, when Cleveland defeated the Athletics, 3-0. Muddy conditions contributed to more struggles for Gochnaur on August 25, as Philadelphia beat the Naps, 9-3.[66] Dutch had numerous opportunities to retire the side in the sixth inning without allowing a single runner to cross the plate.[67] The Athletics scored six runs, as John's defensive line score included three errors.[68] In the game against the Browns at Sportsman's Park on August 29, a 4-0 loss, Gochnaur committed two fielding gaffes. Cleveland and St. Louis were supposed to play a doubleheader that afternoon. All parties agreed upon changes since a train wreck had delayed the arrival of both teams.[69] John finished his rough month with one final error in game one of a doubleheader on August 30, as the Naps defeated the Browns, 7-4.

A strong showing in August elevated Cleveland to second place as the season entered its final month. The Naps' record stood at 63-50, leaving them 9 ½ games behind pacesetting Boston. John Gochnaur's error total in 1903 now stood at 74. Regarding a possible upgrade at shortstop, correspondent Henry P. Edwards believed third baseman Terrance "Terry" Turner's acquisition two weeks earlier from the American Association's Columbus Senators was done with 1904 in mind.[70] Gochnaur certainly didn't do anything in the field to circumvent an inevitable change, as the shortstop added 19 errors to his total in September.

On September 2, John committed two errors, while the Tigers defeated Cleveland, 4-2. An article in the *Detroit Free Press* characterized Gochnaur's work as minor-league. Frustration also led to abject stupidity by John. In the fourth inning, Gochnaur failed to tag Detroit's Lewis "Sport" McAllister on an attempted steal of second base. As umpire Silk O'Loughlin turned away after calling McAllister safe, John petulantly tossed the baseball toward the arbitrator. The ball rolled to the grandstand, allowing Sport to reach third. He then came home when Gochnaur failed to handle Herman Long's ground ball hit to short. Sam Crawford scored the Tigers' final tally in the eighth when John overran Charles "Charlie" Carr's infield chopper.[71]

Two-error games were standard for Dutch in September, as he turned the trick five times. On September 6, Cleveland only managed to collect one hit against Chicago hurler Guy "Doc" White, a double by Bill Bradley in the ninth inning. Naps pitcher Martin Glendon also neutralized the White Sox at the plate. With the game entering extra innings, two miscues by Gochnaur in the tenth aided Chicago in scoring the contest's only run.[72] Cleveland finished off the 1903 slate with a crippled pitching staff. Bill Bernhard had been out of commission with a broken hand. Addie Joss was in the hospital suffering from a fever, brought about related to the recent railway accident at Napoleon, Ohio, and Earl Moore was sidelined due to a muscle injury resulting from two batted baseballs hitting his pitching arm.[73]

After his extra-inning butchery against Chicago, Gochnaur committed errors in three out of four games. John was responsible for one fielding mistake in a 7-0 victory over the White Sox in the back end of a doubleheader on September 7. He then blundered twice in game one of a twin bill on September 9, when St. Louis beat Cleveland, 6-0. Although the Naps rebounded against the Browns in the nightcap, 2-1, Goch committed another error. John made the most of the opportunity to screw up in two games against Detroit on September 12, as he made one fielding miscue in each end of a doubleheader. On September 17, Boston clinched the American League pennant by defeating the Naps, 14-3, as umpires called the game after eight innings because of darkness. Gochnaur commemorated the moment by making two errors.[74]

In the game against Washington on September 23, Nap Lajoie's two home runs helped Cleveland overcome a considerable deficit.[75] Everything was erased in the blink of an eye as Gochnaur fumbled William "Barry" McCormick's ground ball and threw wide to first.

Harry Bemis, guarding the initial sack, believed McCormick had missed the bag. Rather than tag out Barry, Bemis argued over umpire Tommy Connolly's "safe call" as two runners crossed home plate with the deciding markers in the Senators' 7-5 victory.[76] John made sure he left his negative imprint in a defensive sense on Cleveland's final two games. He committed one error in each of those contests, the first a 4-3 loss against Philadelphia in ten frames on September 28 and a ten-inning, 7-5 victory over the Athletics on September 29.

The Naps finished the 1903 campaign with a 77-63 record; good for third place, 15 games behind pennant-winning Boston. Unofficial statistics at year's end credited John Gochnaur with 93 errors at shortstop. Based on this information, Cleveland posted a 36-33 record in the 69 games he committed a fielding blunder. In those 69 contests, Goch went 42-for-228 at the plate, suitable for a .184 batting average. An eventual statistical revision was unkind to John, as adjustments ultimately added five more errors to the record books, for a final total of 98, giving him an American League worst .869 fielding percentage. Statisticians took away mistakes in games from June 9, June 11, July 16, and September 18. Unfortunately, they added gaffes to contests played on May 3, May 27, May 31, June 2, June 18, August 2, August 11, and September 17 (two errors). For the second straight year, official statistics showed that Gochnaur batted .185.

After the campaign ended, the Naps opposed the Cincinnati Reds in a postseason series. Napoleon Lajoie did fine work against the Reds at shortstop after an ankle injury sidelined Dutch.[77] Fans and baseball writers surmised Gochnaur would remain on the roster until Cleveland management could fully access Terry Turner's ability. John had been horrendous at the plate, and his perceived 93 errors at that time were extremely high for a player in any league.[78] Of course, Gochnaur wasn't the only offender, as Bill Bradley's 37 errors tied for the lead among all American League third baseman, and Charlie Hickman topped the circuit with 40 miscues at first base. In the series against Cincinnati, Cleveland convincingly exhibited their superiority in all facets of the game.[79]

Committing 98 errors and hitting .185 was an excellent recipe for ensuring discontinued major league employment. It turned out that Bill Armour benched Gochnaur during the Cincinnati series.[80] In November, word leaked out that John could draw his release from the Naps, giving him the freedom to play wherever he pleased. Armour, John Kilfoyle, and Charles Somers all agreed the shortstop's play was lacking and subpar.[81] A possible explanation behind his wretched performance rose to the surface as the year ended. Reports claimed that John had failed to take care of himself and keep in condition, terminology from that era indicating his downfall was due to drinking and partying with too many so-called friends, who led him down the wrong path.[82] When pressed, Armour defended his decision to stick with Gochnaur in 1903.

"I have been blamed for keeping 'Dutch' all year," stated Armour. "Now, I would like to know where they would have got a man to take his place. The good shortstops are not hanging on bushes waiting to be picked off like berries. Shortstops of major league caliber are a very scarce article. For instance, look at our own experience. We had a chance to get Billy Clingman, touted by many as being one of the best fielding shortstops in the business, although a weak hitter. Well, we took 'Dutch' out for a week and sent Clingman to his place and then discovered that rotten as 'Dutch' was he was better than Clingman. We then looked all over, but we could not find any man that we wanted that we could get right away. Consequently, we left 'Dutch' in for the remainder of the season. I still think that Gochnaur is a great shortstop, and I know he has it in him to show the public a few things."[83]

It was apparent Dutch wouldn't be showing the Cleveland public a few things in 1904. Although Gochnaur had sent Armour numerous letters expressing a desire to remain with the Naps, rumors indicated a berth with the Pacific Coast League's San Francisco Seals or being waived to Washington was the most likely scenario. In one correspondence, John claimed he took the temperance pledge for one year and offered a mea culpa for his behavior in 1903. "I don't blame the people for being disgusted with me," writes Gochnaur, "for I certainly made a fool of myself."[84]

On February 13, manager Charles F. Carpenter of the Tri-State League's Altoona Mountaineers announced Gochnaur was returning home to play for his squad.[85] John remained with Altoona until joining San Francisco later that summer.[86] When Cleveland's 1904 season ended, Bill Armour stated he hoped Dutch would succeed wherever he played. He then related a tale about wishing the shortstop good luck after the 1903 campaign had concluded. Armour found John, who had just received his final lump sum salary payment of $700, in a Cleveland saloon. Gochnaur was just about to plunk down 35 twenty-dollar bills to buy the establishment when Bill walked in, stopped the transaction, and assisted Dutch in boarding a train for Altoona.[87]

A humorous tale saw its birth during John Gochnaur's time playing for San Francisco. On one occasion, when the Seals opposed the Seattle Siwashes, an enterprising California sport offered a bottle of champagne to the player who connected for a home run. During Saturday's contest, he bet $50 on a San Francisco victory. The score was tied heading into the seventh inning. A Seals player occupied third base with two out. The next batter, a heavy hitter, was issued an intentional walk. Gochnaur, with his anemic average, prepared to bat. As John stepped up to the plate, the gambling sport shouted: "A case of bubbles, 'Dutch,' if you make a hit!" Many in the crowd laughed over such a preposterous suggestion.

Seattle's hurler quickly slipped two strikes past Gochnaur. As the pitcher whipped in the third offering, Dutch closed both eyes and swung with all his might. The bat connected against the ball with a loud crack, sending the sphere past the Siwashes' center fielder. By the time Seattle's outfielder pulled the baseball out of the long grass near the fence, three Seals players had crossed home plate, and Gochnaur was sitting in the stands, negotiating with the sport over the most suitable place to receive his case of the bubbly.[88]

After retiring as a player, John Gochnaur remained in the game as a minor league umpire, starting in Charles F. Carpenter's Tri-State League.[89] When it came to establishing the modern-era record for most errors committed by a player in a single season, those five added gaffes pushed Gochnaur over the finish line. Baltimore Orioles shortstop William "Bill" Keister had committed 97 errors in 1901. Philadelphia Phillies shortstop Rudolph "Rudy" Hulswitt made 81 errors in 1903, while Cornelius "Neal" Ball of the New York Highlanders came closest to eclipsing John's record, with 81 miscues in 1908. Before the modern era, when cruder equipment and inferior field conditions existed, 122 errors were the standard, established by Herman Long of the American Association's Kansas City Cowboys in 1889 and William "Billy" Shindle of the Players' League's Philadelphia Quakers in 1890.

In 1905, former Naps teammate Harry Bemis stated that Gochnaur was always a fierce competitor who became angry and grumpy after losing a game.[90] That same year, pitcher Earl Moore proclaimed Dutch had made the most remarkable play by a shortstop he had ever witnessed.

"In the tenth, the home team had a man on third and two out," said Moore, "when a ball was hit straight at my feet. As I reached for it, the ball struck a stone and bounded over my head. I could almost see 'Washington 4, Cleveland 3,' on the blackboard when I looked around, and there was 'Dutch' picking the ball off my left heel and humming it over to Hick [Charlie Hickman] like a rifle shot. It beat the runner by a step, and we won the game, but how 'Dutch' ever got to that ball in time to make the play is a wonder to me to this day."[91]

Quite the statement regarding record-setter John Gochnaur, who was known to struggle making basic plays, but could sometimes turn tough chances into smooth outs.

Statistical revision proved unkind to blundering Cleveland Naps shortstop John Gochnaur in 1903. After initial statistics showed Gochnaur committing 93 errors that year, adjustments added five more miscues to the record books, bringing the final tally to 98. For the second straight year, John batted .185 for Cleveland. Before the 1903 campaign, Gochnaur had a reputation for being a solid fielder. (Photo in the Public Domain.)

CHAPTER 3

Jack Chesbro — 1904

Securing Forty-One and the Game That Got Away

Teamwork, constantly giving maximum effort on the diamond, and entertaining the fans are vital components that have allowed baseball to grow and thrive throughout its storied history. While dissecting statistics and feverishly rooting for a favorite player or team adds to the love affair for this game, in the end, one basic premise remains vital when it comes to achieving success and rejecting disappointment. The goal and desire of each player and manager have always been to win games during that season-long struggle, hoping to contend for pennants and achieve baseball glory. The individual tasked with being the critical organism toward this goal is the player credited with a "W" when his team is victorious, called the pitcher, hurler, twirler, or moundsman throughout baseball history.

Concerning establishing the modern-era, single-season standard for victories by a pitcher, during baseball's Deadball Era, one man executed a campaign for the ages. He accomplished this playing on a squad that, while only competing in its second season for the American League, eventually became the most famous franchise in baseball history. In 1904, while pitching for the New York Highlanders, John Dwight "Jack" Chesbro established a record that stands above all others regarding mound excellence, leading his squad to victory and piling up wins.

Chesbro was born on June 5, 1874, in the farming community of North Adams, Massachusetts.[1] When Jack was born, the family still used the original spelling of Chesebrough (pronounced Cheese-bro). In his formative baseball years, Chesbro played for various amateur baseball teams in western

Massachusetts.² One of those squads that Jack pitched for in 1894 was an insane asylum in Middletown, New York, where he worked as an attendant. It's believed Chesbro might have received his nickname of "Happy Jack" from a patient at this institution. At the same time, another story claimed he was given the moniker because of his pleasant and cordial temperament when working on the mound. As a youngster, Jack was merely known as "Chad" to his North Adams friends, which was his father's first name.³

Chesbro received his first big chance professionally in 1895, signing a contract to play for the New York State League's Albany Senators. Jack joined the league's Johnstown Buckskins when that franchise folded, remaining with them through July, before inking his signature to a contract to play for the Eastern League's Springfield Maroons. In 1896, Chesbro hooked up with the Virginia League's Roanoke Magicians. Unable to weave any magic in Roanoke, going 8-11 before this team disbanded, Jack cast his fortunes for the remainder of the year with a squad in Cooperstown, New York, called the Athletics. While playing here, the shortened version of his last name became standard, pared down to fit into the local newspaper's box scores. In 1897, Chesbro's long baseball odyssey brought him to Richmond, Virginia, to pitch for the Atlantic League's Giants. After going 16-18 that season, Jack posted a 23-15 record in 1898, when Richmond became known by their Virginia State League nickname of the Bluebirds.

Jack Chesbro's work on the bump in 1899 attracted attention from major league teams. Sporting a stellar 17-4 record in July, the Pittsburgh Pirates purchased Chesbro for $1,500.⁴ Richmond had acted as an excellent feeder team for Pittsburgh. Chesbro joined Pirates hurlers Jesse Tannehill, Samuel "Sam" Leever, and Thomas "Tully" Sparks, who had also pitched for Richmond.⁵ Jack debuted against the New York Giants on July 12 and made his first three starts on the road during Pittsburgh's swing through the East. Chesbro finally pitched in front of Exposition Park's home patrons on July 21 against the Philadelphia Phillies.

Jack defeated the Phillies, 6-3. One Pittsburgh sportswriter described Chesbro as unflappable, calm, and deliberate at all stages of this commanding performance. The writer also stated that Chesbro possessed exceptional control and didn't become flustered in the third inning when Philadelphia cracked out three consecutive safeties. Jack also smacked two hits against the Phillies and had allowed 14 runs in his first four games.⁶ When posing for a picture shortly after joining the Pirates, people mentioned that Chesbro had beautiful bangs, making him quite the photogenic, handsome subject.⁷ Jack's solid pitching at the outset for Pittsburgh became a distant memory, as he ended up going 6-9 in 1899, with a 4.11 ERA, while appearing in 19 games.

Despite Chesbro's rough rookie campaign, Boston sportswriter Jake Morse deeply admired the hurler's ability and potential. Pittsburgh management didn't share that opinion, having sent Jack back home before the season ended. They didn't believe him to be a high-class twirler, lacking key intangibles, although he had performed well occasionally.[8] Because of this assessment, it came as no surprise that Pittsburgh packaged Chesbro in a deal considered at the time to be the most significant transaction in baseball history. On December 8, 1899, the Pirates shipped Jack to the Louisville Colonels with three other players and cash for a bevy of talented baseball flesh, including Fred Clarke, Honus Wagner, Claude Ritchey, Rube Waddell, Charles "Deacon" Phillippe, and Thomas "Tommy" Leach. This transfer of stars was in conjunction with Louisville magnate Barney Dreyfuss becoming part-owner of the Pirates. Eventually, the Colonels were part of the National League contraction, from twelve teams to eight.[9]

Jack Chesbro was officially reassigned to the Pirates when the league eliminated Louisville, Baltimore, Cleveland, and Washington. Under the careful and brilliant guidance of Pittsburgh manager Fred Clarke, who replaced Patrick "Patsy" Donovan upon joining the club, Chesbro showed signs of realizing his potential in 1900, going 15-13 with an ERA of 3.67. Jack's development reached another level for the pennant-winning Pirates in 1901, as he posted a 21-10 record, bolstered by a 2.38 ERA. Exhibiting such dominance on the mound was only the beginning for the Smoky City twirler. In 1902, Chesbro assumed the mantle as the National League's top pitcher, blazing away on the bump to the tune of 28-6, with a 2.17 ERA. Pittsburgh cruised to their second consecutive flag in 1902, finishing at 103-36, 27 ½ games ahead of the second-place Brooklyn Superbas.

Up to this point, Pirates owner Barney Dreyfuss had been very fortunate to prevent players from jumping to the American League. Dreyfuss's generosity regarding player contracts and foresight in assessing the baseball landscape allowed Pittsburgh to continue at almost full strength. Third baseman James "Jimmy" Williams was the only defector before the 1901 campaign. Things changed on September 20, 1902, when American League president Ban Johnson and vice-president Charles Somers made a trip to Pittsburgh, hoping to entice Pirates players with the promise of better salaries if they joined their organization.[10] Jack Chesbro and fellow hurler Jesse Tannehill were two of the players courted by Johnson. The American League president hoped to pull off a vital coup, crippling the National League's best team, while also attempting to stock a new entry for his league in New York for 1903.

Weeks after Johnson and Somers made their pitch, Dreyfuss connected with Chesbro and Tannehill at the team hotel while Pittsburgh played the Giants in New York. On the morning of September 9, Pittsburgh's owner asked what it would take regarding salary to keep them in the fold. Their demands shocked and stunned Dreyfuss.

"I want a two years' contract calling for $17,000," said Chesbro.

"I'll sign for the same figure," chimed in Tannehill.

Dreyfuss emitted a long, low whistle before responding softly: "Is that all?"

"Yes, that's all," said Chesbro, who acted as spokesman for the pair, "and we'll get it, or we'll jump to the American League."

Dreyfuss excused himself and walked into the hotel bar to contemplate this ridiculous request. The magnate took some time thinking things over before rejoining Chesbro and Tannehill to issue his decision.

"Boys," he said, "the Pittsburgh club is not owned by Andrew Carnegie, nor are we in business solely for your benefit. I'll give each of you $11,000 for two years, and if this isn't satisfactory, you may jump to the Johnson crowd if you see fit. Will you except."

The two players declined Dreyfuss's generous proposal, which happened to be $1,000 more than the American League offered.[11] When the season ended, Jesse Tannehill was cast adrift and told to empty his locker at Exposition Park.[12] Jack Chesbro was still mulling over his options when Pirates teammates helped the stalwart hurler make a final decision. After claiming the National League pennant, Pittsburgh's players agreed to play a short series against a team of American League all-stars. When Chesbro refused to pitch in one of the games on October 8, although he agreed to do so, his teammates held a meeting that evening. They decided not to include him concerning any extra money realized from this series. They maintained Jack was a quitter before informing him that he wouldn't receive any financial benefits from these games.

Chesbro refused to pitch because American League rules were being used (including the no foul-strike rule, which was disadvantageous for pitchers). His teammates threatened to cut Jack out of any monetary proceeds if he didn't play. The pitcher responded by laughing. Chesbro later sent word to Exposition Park that he couldn't suit up due to being sick.[13] Of course, this was an excuse since Jack looked in the best of health before and after the game.[14] This dereliction of duty led Pittsburgh's players to take action while also categorizing Chesbro as a deserter.

Angered over this decision, Jack appealed to Barney Dreyfuss, who responded that he couldn't offer an opinion on the situation while supporting the stance taken by the players, whom he had given complete control over all proceeds from this series against the American League all-stars. On October 9, Chesbro informed the Pittsburgh club that evening he quit the team to join the rival organization (where the foul strike rule would take effect next year). Jack then left for Chicago to hook up with a squad of National League all-stars headed for the Pacific Coast. Dreyfuss showed little concern over his star pitcher's defection.

"Chesbro is gone, and I am glad of it," said Dreyfuss. "He showed himself a quitter when he had a chance to help the boys out. He refused to go in under American League rules. I wish the American all kinds of luck with him, but no more of him in Pittsburgh."[15]

Jack Chesbro joined ex-Pirates Jesse Tannehill, John "Jack" O'Connor, William "Wid" Conroy, and Alfonzo "Lefty" Davis on the New York Highlanders in 1903, under the guidance of manager and hurler Clark Griffith. Chesbro pitched the first game in franchise history on April 22, 1903, losing 3-1 to Albert "Al" Orth and the Washington Senators at American League Park. Jack didn't entirely build upon his sensational season in 1902, as the Highlanders came home fourth in the American League, sporting a 72-62 record. Chesbro went 21-15, with a 2.77 ERA. Fellow contract jumper Jesse Tannehill, who had gone 20-6, supported by a 1.95 ERA with Pittsburgh in 1902, could only post an even 15-15 record for New York in 1903.

After his first American League season ended, Tannehill offered thoughts on how American League Park's home grounds were brutal for hurlers. "No pitcher can last long on the New York American grounds," said Tannehill. "The grounds are on a high bluff overlooking the river, and the cold wind blows over the diamond morning, noon and night. A man would have to have a cast-iron arm, to pitch winning ball under these circumstances."

While making excuses for his mediocre showing, the Kentucky native also claimed he would rather play in Cincinnati than anywhere else in the country.[16] Tannehill received his wish to gain freedom from American League Park when New York traded him on December 20, 1903, to the Boston Americans for pitcher Thomas "Tom" Hughes. A person who could be pretty obstinate at times and a less than perfect teammate while playing for Pittsburgh, Jesse exhibited no inhibitions after learning about the deal.

"Well, I see I was traded a few miles away," said Tannehill. "Now, there are some places to which I have no objection to going, and there are others

I wouldn't travel to reach for a bucket of coin. If I'm to be swapped around like old junk, they've got to give me my share of the junk. I've got a two-year contract with New York, and would like to remain there. One thing is certain, Clark Griffith can't send me to Detroit. I'll not go. I've got too nice a proposition from the Pacific Coast people to be worried about the future. Before anything is done they've got to talk to Jess."[17]

Junk aside and the desire of this pioneer to dictate his terms from a financial standpoint, more than 70 years before baseball free agency was born, Jesse Tannehill pitched for Boston in 1904. Back in New York, an announcement in December stated that Jack Chesbro and teammate William "Willie" Keeler had been selected to coach Harvard University's varsity baseball team for a few days in the spring.[18] This was the second consecutive year that Chesbro mentored the Cambridge boys. Jack spent his off-season at his home in Conway, Massachusetts. Chesbro had bought a farm there a few years after marrying Conway native Mabel Shuttleworth in 1896.

Jack donned his overalls over the winter to build a new barn on his property. Chesbro was considered an icon to the boys in the farming town. These youngsters were thrilled with the hurler, who bought baseballs and bats for the lads and sometimes umpired their games. While these boys were residents of Massachusetts, they passionately rooted for the New York Highlanders.[19] Jack had purchased the former residence of Parson John Emerson, the first Congregational minister who settled in Conway, and built the home around 1771.[20] This acquisition, along with procuring additional property, brought Chesbro's land holdings in Conway to ten or 12 acres, where he raised hay.[21]

Such adulation from Conway's youngsters was something Jack didn't consistently achieve in his first season with New York. During a game on June 4, 1903, against the Cleveland Naps at American League Park, Chesbro exhibited a sour temperament, sulking throughout most of the contest and making comments to arbitrator Silk O'Loughlin. After Jack had interrupted the game a sixth time, O'Loughlin confronted New York's hurler.

"Come, Jack, enough of this," said O'Loughlin. "Descend from your elevated palfrey and allow hostilities to be resumed."

"Wonder what he meant by that," remarked Chesbro as he walked moodily back to the Highlanders' bench.

"He meant fer yer to git down off yer high horse and play de game," yelled a small boy sitting close by.[22]

The sometimes moody Jack Chesbro left his domicile to begin working with Harvard's pitchers before spring training started for the Highlanders. Jack planned on remaining in Cambridge, Massachusetts, until March 23, hoping to join his teammates for spring training in Atlanta, Georgia, three days later.[23] During his time coaching Harvard, Chesbro was asked by writer Jake Morse about the trade involving his friend and former teammate Jesse Tannehill and Tom Hughes. Jack offered a brief comment while rating both as first-class hurlers. "Tannehill has no superior as a pitcher," said Chesbro, "and as for Hughes, I always rated him as a king."[24]

Besides coaching Harvard's pitching staff, Chesbro followed his strict workout regimen to get in shape for the upcoming season. Jack spent time trying to hone a "slow ball" or "slow curve" that had been perfected years ago by the great Charles "Old Hoss" Radbourn.[25] Chesbro also tinkered with another pitch that utilized saliva from the mouth, applied to fingers on the pitching hand. This offering became known as the "spitter" or "spitball." Jack first saw Elmer Stricklett use it while pitching in a game at Columbus, Ohio. Many people credited Stricklett as being the wet delivery's innovator. However, Elmer learned the pitch from former teammate Frank Corridon.[26] Pitcher William "Bill" Hart claimed Baltimore Orioles catcher Frank Bowerman showed him how to throw the pitch when he played for the St. Louis Browns in 1896.[27] Some baseball experts believed old-time hurler and former American Association standout Robert "Bobby" Mathews had utilized an offering similar to the spitter that Chesbro hoped to conquer.[28]

When Jack joined the Highlanders, he was in excellent condition, dropping 20 pounds from the previous season. Chesbro put on a uniform and got some work on the mound, helping shut out the Southern Association's Atlanta Crackers. Jack also heaped praise upon a Harvard hurler he had coached named Walter Clarkson, who eventually signed with New York in the summer.[29] Shortly before the season opener, sportswriter William M. Rankin, who covered both New York teams for the *Sporting News*, criticized an opinion offered by colleague and Pittsburgh scribe Ralph S. Davis. Davis suggested that Ban Johnson had decreed the Highlanders must be crowned American League pennant winners in 1904. Rankin considered the claim ludicrous, offering that the other seven clubs wouldn't be receptive to tanking the season while avowing those days of crooked baseball received a burial many years ago.[30]

Despite morning snow and arctic weather, pageantry was the theme as the Highlanders opened the 1904 season on April 14 at American League Park.[31] Their opponent was the Boston Americans, who had won the pennant, and the first modern World Series over the Pittsburgh Pirates in 1903. A raucous, excited crowd descended upon the ballpark via elevated trains, automobiles, streetcars, and foot.[32] The 69th Regiment Band entertained the masses before the first pitch, while a wide range of people from New York's political spectrum was in attendance. Former judge William Olcott, with law partner Abe Gruber at his side, threw out the first pitch to umpire Frank Dwyer.[33] Clark Griffith selected Jack Chesbro to pitch for New York, while Denton "Cy" Young received the assignment to take the bump for Boston. Ballpark improvements were evident to those who turned out, especially the raising and extending of right-field territory so that fans from any vantage point could now see Willie Keeler patrol his position.

New York's *Evening World* reported that 20,000 fans attended the opening game.[34] *Sporting Life* put the number at 15,840, as the Highlanders were victorious over Boston, 8-2. Chesbro was touched for two runs on inside-the-park home runs by Buck Freeman and Alfred "Freddy" Parent. Jack also thrived at the plate, going 2-for-3 while legging out a four-bagger of his own.[35] The fact that none of these home runs left the yard could be attributed to changes at the ballpark. Highlanders team president Joseph Gordon tasked a large group of workers with transforming the grounds into sparkling, first-class condition throughout the previous winter. Besides eliminating the ravine in right field, the fence in that part of the ballpark now stood 420 feet from home plate.[36]

Chesbro saw his record drop to 1-1 against the Philadelphia Athletics on April 18. Jack lost the game, 5-1, going the distance while strafed for 12 hits by the Athletics.[37] Chesbro rebounded nicely on the road against the Washington Senators on April 22. He tossed a one-hit shutout as New York prevailed, 2-0.[38] Jack split his subsequent two decisions, losing to Philadelphia at Columbia Park, 6-2, on April 30, and beating Washington again on May 4, securing a 6-3 victory at American League Park. Chesbro's brilliance continued against Boston on May 7, as New York gained a 6-3 decision at Huntington Avenue Baseball Grounds.

As Chesbro and New York prepared to play a home game against the Cleveland Naps on May 12, Happy Jack sported a 4-2 record in six starts, having completed each game. Jack went the distance but struggled, as he was battered from the outset, allowing seven runs on 13 hits and losing to the Naps, 7-0. Highlanders shortstop Norman "Kid" Elberfeld was forced to leave the game in the eighth inning after Cleveland's Nap Lajoie spiked him at second base.[39] Chesbro took the ball again two days later and reversed fortunes, tossing a complete game and beating the Naps, 10-1, on May 14. Cleveland's third baseman, Bill Bradley, had to retire from the contest in the third frame when one of Jack's inside shoots struck his hand.[40] Chesbro pushed his record to 6-3 for the young season when he defeated the Detroit Tigers, 5-1, on May 17.

When New York finished the series against Detroit by losing 6-1 on May 18, their record stood at 14-10, placing them third in the American League race. In his *Sporting News* article, William M. Rankin claimed the Highlanders weren't playing consistent baseball. While Rankin felt they performed brilliantly at times, the height of mediocrity resembled Class C level baseball on many occasions. He praised the team for their work in the series against Boston and Cleveland but doled out harsh criticism for their performance against seventh-place Detroit. Rankin believed one of the main problems, which many expected to be a strength when the season opened, was New York's pitching.[41]

Jack Chesbro certainly couldn't be included among those who had disappointed on the mound for the Highlanders. On May 20, against Chicago at American League Park, Chesbro pitched the entire 12 innings, defeating the White Sox, 3-2. New York secured victory in the twelfth when John Ganzel doubled and scored on Jack Thoney's single.[42] Jack was invincible against St. Louis on May 24, scattering three hits and prevailing, 3-0, over the Browns.[43] On May 28, Chesbro locked horns in a classic pitcher's duel against Philadelphia's Eddie Plank at Columbia Park. Jack limited the Athletics to four safeties, while the Highlanders scored the game's only tally in the eighth inning when Willie Keeler singled, moved to second on Wid Conroy's sacrifice bunt, and scored when John Anderson blasted a double. Jack struck out Freeman Osee Schrecongost and Monte Cross to end the game with two on and one out for Philadelphia in the ninth frame.[44]

Chesbro secured his tenth victory of the season on June 1, when he defeated Detroit, 5-3, at Bennett Park. As a pinch hitter against the Tigers on June 3, Jack's single drove home Thoney. It tied the game 3-3 in the ninth frame before New York lost in extra innings.[45] Chesbro delivered more punishment against the Tigers on June 4, tossing a complete game and securing a 5-1 victory. The contest was tight until Jack drove home two runs with a seventh-inning double, and his teammates assaulted Detroit hurler George Mullin in the ninth.[46] Although Chesbro's record was 11-3 after his win over Detroit, New York was 22-16, leaving them in third place. Jack's solid run looked to be in jeopardy when Clark Griffith handed him the ball to pitch against the Cleveland Naps at League Park on June 9. Solely throwing only fastballs and curves in the first inning, Cleveland victimized New York's star pitcher for two runs.

Upon returning to the bench after retiring the side, Chesbro confided to Griffith that he lacked strong stuff that afternoon. Jack then asked for and received permission from his manager to exclusively throw spitballs for the remainder of the game.[47] This tactical change on Chesbro's part was pure genius, as he baffled the Naps from that point forward, allowing only one hit. The Highlanders finally solved Cleveland hurler Earl Moore in the ninth, scoring three runs, which allowed them to walk away with a 3-2 victory.[48] With Jack's new deceptive pitch acting as the bulwark of his arsenal, the spitball twirler forged onward, defeating Chicago, 6-3, at South Side Park on June 11. Throughout New York's western swing, baseball enthusiasts showered Chesbro with accolades.

In the game against Chicago, Jack allowed five hits. Following Chesbro's earlier virtuoso performance opposing the Athletics' Eddie Plank, Philadelphia manager Connie Mack had remarked that it was the best-pitched game he witnessed that year.[49] Not everyone jumped aboard the Happy Jack bandwagon. Amid discussion about Pittsburgh needing pitching assistance for a squad that would fail to win the National League pennant for the first time in three years, owner Barney Dreyfuss was dismissive when a writer suggested rumors pointed toward Jack Chesbro.

"The man that says I am dickering for Chesbro is a pipe-hitter for sure," said President Dreyfuss. "I don't care how well Chesbro may be pitching. He could not get back with the Pittsburgh Club if he offered to work for nothing."[50]

If Dreyfuss were truly dickering for Chesbro's services, it's doubtful Highlanders ownership would be willing to listen. When Jack and his former Pirates teammates crossed paths while the two teams played in St. Louis, some remarked he had never looked in better physical condition. Manager Fred Clarke echoed that sentiment when asked about the subject at the team's lodging at the Southern Hotel, on the evening of June 19, following Pittsburgh's doubleheader that afternoon against the St. Louis Cardinals.

"He's lighter by fully fifteen pounds than when he was with me," said Clarke. "Chesbro was always a good pitcher. Occasionally in the spring he would report way overweight, and he wouldn't be any good until he chased all the superfluous flesh off his frame. I never saw him looking as well as he does right now, so it is not to be wondered at that he is twirling such wonderful ball."[51]

Superlatives aside, Jack Chesbro continued rolling along, winning his tenth consecutive game on June 16, beating the St. Louis Browns at Sportsman's Park, 10-3. Chesbro was nearly unhittable against Washington on June 21, scattering four hits, three being scratch safeties, while claiming his eleventh straight victory, 3-0.[52] As Jack prepared to battle Boston at Huntington Avenue Baseball Grounds on June 25, New York's record was 32-21, good for second place in the standings, 2 ½ games behind the first-place Americans. Chesbro went the route, defeating the league leaders, 5-3. Jack's twelfth consecutive win also matched the mark of New York Giants hurler Joe McGinnity in 1904.[53]

The Highlanders were one of the American League's hottest teams when they returned home after a long road trip to oppose Washington on July 1. While away for an entire month, New York went 15-7. When they had started the western swing after a doubleheader at American League Park on May 30, the Highlanders occupied fourth place. Before the game on July 1, the team stood second behind Boston. Such a record was remarkable, given that injuries had sidelined Kid Elberfeld and Dave Fultz before New York began their travels, along with Willie Keeler and Wid Conroy, both of whom became incapacitated in St. Louis.[54] Some assistance had come in the form of a deal with Boston on June 17 that sent rookie infielder Robert "Bob" Unglaub to the Americans for veteran outfielder Patrick "Patsy" Dougherty. When individuals discussed the player procurement subject, Clark Griffith became annoyed over constant ramblings about Ban Johnson becoming involved.

"I think so little of Mr. Johnson's judgment," said Clark, "that I wouldn't take a player he recommended. I am wholly responsible for the good, and bad players picked up by the New York club."[55]

The Highlanders' star player that Johnson was responsible for bringing into the fold before the 1903 season showed that 13 wasn't an unlucky number. Jack Chesbro chalked up another victory on July 1, beating Washington, 8-3. A trip to Philadelphia for a holiday doubleheader on July 4 saw Chesbro take the mound for the day's morning contest. Jack recorded his fourteenth straight victory, tossing a complete game and allowing seven hits, as New York defeated the Athletics, 9-3.[56] The win pushed Chesbro's record to 18-3 in 1904. One day later, on July 5, big news coming out of New York focused on Giants owner John T. Brush rather than Jack's achievement. Brush directly violated an agreement reached before the season between the National and American leagues to participate in a series for the world's championship as had been done in 1903. He asserted the Giants wouldn't play their counterparts from the city under any circumstances if the two teams won their respective pennants. The basis for John's stubborn stance was his strong disdain for Ban Johnson's organization.[57]

Against Boston on July 7, Jack proved he didn't possess superhuman powers. Chesbro saw his winning streak end, losing 4-1. The Highlanders' batters couldn't solve Americans hurler Norwood Gibson, Boston played better inside baseball, and Albert "Kip" Selbach drove in three runs.[58] When Jack took the mound two days later, on July 9, Boston won their third consecutive game of this series at American League Park. Cy Young bested Chesbro in a tight matchup, 2-1. Jack didn't see action again until relieving Clark Griffith against Cleveland on July 13, a game the Naps won, 16-3. Chesbro allowed six runs, with two being earned, in three innings of relief work.⁵⁹ Although he had lost two games in a row against Boston and was ineffective versus the Naps, Highlanders fans still marveled over the fact that Happy Jack beat every team in the American League during his winning streak while going the distance in each of those 14 triumphs.⁶⁰

Life was a breeze for Chesbro, and the Highlanders, on July 14, as New York crushed Cleveland, 21-3. Jack secured his twentieth victory of the season two days later, relieving Walter Clarkson in the eighth frame, as New York won a ten-inning affair over Detroit, 9-8. Chesbro ended the game in the bottom of the tenth when he made it over to third after walking and then dashed for home plate, winning the festivities with a daring steal.⁶¹ Jack added another notch on his belt, besting the Tigers, 2-1, on July 19, in a game that lasted 11 innings. To improve New York's pitching staff, the Highlanders shipped hurlers Barney Wolfe and Tom Hughes to the Washington Senators for veteran pitcher Al Orth. Besides being expected to add crucial stability on the mound, Orth's ability to play the outfield, and usefulness as a hitter, made him a very valuable commodity.⁶²

Chesbro gained a split in his final two decisions of the month, losing to Chicago, 5-4, on July 23, and defeating St. Louis, 3-2, in ten innings during a July 30 doubleheader opener. As the American League's scintillating race moved into August, only 5 ½ games separated first-place Boston from fifth-place Philadelphia. New York was in the second spot, one game back, with a record of 50-33. Jack remained red-hot as the season progressed into a new month, beating Detroit, 5-2, on August 3, and then nipping Cleveland three days later, 4-3, in a tight battle against Addie Joss. In the game against the Tigers, Chesbro fanned 13 batters and didn't allow a walk. When facing the Naps on August 6, Nap Lajoie and Elmer Flick whiffed on six pitches in the first inning. In the second, after Bill Bradley reached first on a free pass, Jack struck out Charlie Hickman, William "Billy" Lush, and Terry Turner on ten offerings.⁶³

Jack lost a tough one against Chicago at South Side Park on August 10. Although Chesbro only allowed three hits before exiting in the seventh inning, the White Sox touched him up for five runs. Two walks opened the floodgates to three tallies in the first, while Highlanders' errors aided the White Sox's cause with two more runs in the third.⁶⁴ On August 13, Jack registered a no-decision, as umpires canceled the game versus Chicago after five innings, with the score tied, 3-3. A horrendous rainstorm fell throughout the entire contest. As "National Union Day" was celebrated, a big crowd was in attendance, with a band concert and lacrosse match preceding the baseball tilt.⁶⁵ Chesbro was brilliant against St. Louis on August 15, allowing five hits, striking out seven batters, and gaining a 3-1 victory.⁶⁶ After claiming the first three games of this series against the Browns, New York was listless during the final contest on August 17, losing 3-1. St. Louis's "World's Fair" was the culprit, as too much revelry and high living led to adverse consequences.⁶⁷

When the Highlanders returned home on August 19, Jack efficiently handled Chicago, 6-1. Four days later, Chesbro smothered the White Sox again, 1-0, while allowing only four hits and walking no batters. Willie Keeler scored the game's only run when he reached third on Chicago hurler Doc White's wild throw and came home on John Anderson's single.⁶⁸ The victory allowed New York to remain atop the American League standings, ½ game ahead of Boston. Jack secured a victory in relief over St. Louis on August 26, with the Highlanders winning in 11 innings, 3-2, as hits by John Ganzel and Wid Conroy brought home the bacon.⁶⁹ Jack finished the month by splitting two decisions, losing to St. Louis in the second game of a doubleheader on August 27, 4-3, before defeating Cleveland, 3-1, on August 31.

The pennant race became a two-team battle between New York and Boston heading into September's stretch drive. On September 3, the Highlanders leapfrogged their nemesis as Jack Chesbro claimed his thirtieth victory of the season, defeating Detroit, 2-1. Tigers' errors facilitated both New York runs.⁷⁰ Jack stood tall on September 5 against Philadelphia, besting the Athletics in the first game of a Labor Day doubleheader, 2-1. Chesbro was victorious in a marquee matchup against eccentric southpaw hurler Rube Waddell and the Athletics in game one of a twin bill on September 8. Jack and his Highlanders came out on top, 3-2, when Waddell's wild throw led to a New York tally in the first inning, while his inability to field two bunts proved fatal in the third as John Anderson's single then plated two runs.⁷¹

On September 9, hoping to strengthen New York's pitching staff, Clark Griffith claimed veteran twirler Virgil "Ned" Garvin off waivers from the Brooklyn Superbas. Garvin had been cut loose by Brooklyn for dissipation and insubordination.⁷² According to reporting in the *Pittsburgh Press* on August 28, while Superbas manager Ned Hanlon was on a scouting trip and the team had traveled to St. Louis for a series a little over a week earlier, Garvin and four teammates became drunk and unruly on the train. Ned, who was highly intoxicated, punched team secretary George Watson. The five men hurled beer bottles throughout the team's car, with some even breaking windows. This behavior continued when the team reached St. Louis, and these individuals soaked in the city's World's Fair atmosphere. Given the choice of either unconditional release or suspension by Hanlon, Garvin opted for the former.[73] Watson later denied that any member of Brooklyn's squad had assaulted him.[74]

Back on the diamond, Jack Chesbro pushed his record to 33-8 on September 12, beating Washington, 4-2, and fanning six batters.[75] As New York prepared to open a big series against Boston at Huntington Avenue Grounds on September 14, the Highlanders trailed the Americans by ½ game in the race. The schedule called for six games over three days. Nothing was solved, with only four official contests reaching their conclusion, as the two contenders played doubleheaders on September 14, 15, and 16. Boston and New York split four games, while umpires called the other two at the backend of twin bills on September 14 and 15 with the score tied, 1-1 (the first one ended after five innings). In front of 23,000 people for the series' initial battle on September 14, 10,000 of those standing in roped-off areas on the field, Chesbro bested William "Bill" Dinneen and the Americans, 3-1.[76] Jack gained a second victory in the first game of a doubleheader two days later, as he defeated Dinneen once again, 6-4.

Chesbro's mother, Martha, had watched him pitch for the first time on September 12 in New York.[77] She also accompanied her son on the trip to Boston.[78] Jack exhibited his versatility when working on the mound at Washington on September 20. Arriving late from his Massachusetts home during the first game of a doubleheader, Chesbro entered the fray in the tenth inning, pitched two shutout frames, and gained a 3-2 victory when Willie Keeler scored the winning run. Jack started the nightcap, beating Washington, 5-1, as umpires called the game because of darkness after six innings.[79] In the first game of a doubleheader at League Park on September 26, Cleveland handed Jack his ninth loss of the campaign. George Stovall's bases-loaded triple in the eighth inning proved the difference, as the Naps claimed a 4-3 victory.[80]

Chesbro split his following two decisions, beating Detroit in eleven innings, 4-1, on September 27, and losing to Chicago three days later at South Side Park, 4-0. The game against the Tigers at Bennett Park was a rowdy affair. The crowd's discontent over umpire Silk O'Loughlin's work almost precipitated a riot. O'Loughlin ejected Detroit's George Mullin in the eleventh inning after the pitcher threw his glove at him.[81] Jack's heavy workload in the season's closing weeks, which was logical given his status as New York's staff ace, continued as September ushered in October. Following his loss against the White Sox on September 30, Chesbro was handed the ball again on October 1, defeating Chicago, 7-2. Jack was magnificent against St. Louis at Sportsman's Park on October 4, securing his fortieth victory. He tossed a seven-hit shutout and beat the Browns, 6-0.[82] New York claimed their ninetieth victory of the campaign on October 5, when Jack Powell defeated St. Louis, 8-1.

Appropriately, the American League's two best teams went head-to-head during the season's final days. As the Highlanders prepared to play Boston on October 7, the Americans held down first place, with a record of 92-57, while New York was ½ game back, at 90-56. Timely hitting by Patsy Dougherty, Jimmy Williams, and John Anderson nudged New York into first place as they defeated Boston, 3-2. Jack Chesbro went the distance for the Highlanders, allowing only five hits, as he picked up victory number 41 in 1904.[83] Around 12,000 fans passed through American League Park's turnstiles to witness this crucial battle. When the contest ended, admiring patrons hoisted manager Clark Griffith on their shoulders and carried him off the field.[84] For Highlanders fans exhibiting legitimate concern that Chesbro was being used too frequently by Griffith, those fears were slightly allayed by the hurler, who told his manager he would pitch every game, if necessary, during the season's final week.[85]

When things shifted to Boston for a doubleheader on October 8, the Americans regained first place, sweeping New York in front of 28,040 passionate fans, 13-2 and 1-0 in the nightcap, that umpires called after seven innings on account of darkness.[86] Jack Chesbro was highly ineffective in the first contest. Manager Clark Griffith sent the star hurler to the clubhouse after five earned runs and six hits were allowed in four innings of work.[87] The entire season for these two teams came down to a doubleheader on the schedule's final day of October 10, at American League Park. New York needed to sweep the twin bill to clinch the American League pennant. Twenty-eight thousand five hundred eighty-four enthusiastic spectators, the largest crowd ever to witness a baseball contest at that venue, attended this monumental clash.[88] Ropes were stretched in front of the bleachers to hold the mass of humanity jammed into that area. The stands were also congested, while a large congregation stood along the right-field fence. One grandstand fan found a ladder, using it to climb to a beautiful vantage point on the roof.

Jack Chesbro was given the assignment in game one against Boston's Bill Dinneen. New York's players received a rousing ovation as they took the field. When Jack stepped up to the plate to bat in the third frame with one out, a group of friends from North Adams delayed the contest and presented him with a fur-lined overcoat. Jack responded by blasting a triple but was stranded at third base. The Highlanders finally drew first blood with two out in the fifth inning. Catcher John "Red" Kleinow started the parade by smacking a single to right. Chesbro then reached first when Dinneen knocked down but couldn't handle his blistering liner to the box. Kleinow scored the game's first tally on Patsy Dougherty's single to right field. The Highlanders added a second run when Willie Keeler and Kid Elberfeld drew consecutive walks.

Boston rallied with two tallies of their own in the seventh. George "Candy" LaChance got things rolling by reaching first on an infield single to Highlanders' second baseman Jimmy Williams. Albert "Hobe" Ferris followed by drilling a single to right. Americans catcher Louis "Lou" Criger successfully moved the runners to second and third with a sacrifice bunt. Dinneen stepped to the plate and struck a groundball to Williams at second. Believing he had an easy play on LaChance motoring toward the plate, Jimmy fired to Red Kleinow. Regrettably, Williams's throw was low, bounding away from Kleinow as both LaChance and Ferris scored to tie the game, 2-2.

Tension built as the score remained knotted heading into the ninth inning. Criger led off that frame by beating out an infield hit and moved over to second on Dinneen's sacrifice bunt. Boston's catcher sauntered to third when Kip Selbach was retired on a grounder to Highlanders shortstop Kid Elberfeld. Chesbro quickly got ahead in the count against Freddy Parent with two strikes. The confident moundsman, determined to spike this rally, wound up and fired a spitter toward the plate. Unfortunately, the moist offering eluded catcher Red Kleinow, bounded to the backstop, and allowed Criger to score on the wild pitch (his second of the game), giving Boston a 3-2 lead. Visibly disturbed, Chesbro allowed Parent to reach on a single before retiring the Americans.

The bottom of the ninth started with Dinneen fanning John Ganzel. Wid Conroy then drew a walk before Kleinow became the second out when he popped out to Ferris at second. Pinch hitter James "Deacon" McGuire kept New York's season alive by reaching first with a base on balls. Dougherty dashed any flickering pennant hopes, ending the game by striking out. New York won the meaningless nightcap by securing a 1-0, 10-inning victory.[89] Although Boston had clinched the pennant by claiming the earlier contest, 3-2, the devoted crowd's enthusiasm never waned from the first pitch to game two's final play.[90]

Pitcher Jack Chesbro produced a monumental season in 1904, posting a 41-12 record, supported by a 1.82 ERA. Chesbro appeared in 55 contests, started 51, completed 48 games, hurled 454 ⅔ innings, and struck out 239 batters. In the end, a wild pitch preventing him from adding one more victory to the ledger couldn't diminish this phenomenal achievement. Jack never approached those numbers and the lofty heights of 1904 again throughout his major league career, which lasted until 1909. Although Boston won the American League pennant for the second straight season, there was no World

Series. At the beginning of October, New York Giants owner John T. Brush had decreed that his team wouldn't play any postseason championship series, no matter who won the American League bunting.[91]

After the season concluded, sportswriter Francis C. Richter explained in *Sporting Life* that pitchers utilized a spitball by moistening the baseball on one side with saliva before delivery. According to Richter, this caused the air in passage to give erratic courses to the ball. When the pitch was thrown low, it had a tremendous drop, while it wobbled and moved with an upshoot when tossed high. Richter concluded by stating that a hurler didn't always possess control over how the pitch would break.[92] Over the winter, Jack Chesbro sat down for an interview with Boston writer Frederic P. O'Connell. Chesbro explained that it was logical to call a spitball a thumb ball since the sphere left the fingers first and the thumb last when throwing the pitch. Jack also stated he could make the spitter drop anywhere from two inches to a foot and a half and that it placed no stress on his arm.[93]

When some insinuated later arm problems were due to throwing the spitball, Jack declared the ailment resulted from getting a cold in his arm while pitching for New York on a rainy day.[94] In 1912, three years after he retired from baseball, Chesbro corroborated an earlier claim from former teammate Jesse Tannehill. Jack said two years of pitching at Hilltop Park (the name eventually attached to the Highlanders' ballpark) was the limit for hurlers, given the chilly Hudson River breezes and hard infield.[95]

When it comes to his place in baseball history, in totality, related to single-season victories achieved, Jack Chesbro is in a tie for 24th all-time with 41 wins in 1904. Old Hoss Radbourn lays claim to the top slot with 59 victories, pitching for the Providence Grays in 1884. On the other hand, Chesbro's record still glistens above all other pitchers who performed during baseball's modern era. Edward "Ed" Walsh of the Chicago White Sox came closest to beating that mark, securing 40 victories in 1908, while there hasn't been a 30-game winner since Dennis "Denny" McLain of the Detroit Tigers went 31-6 in 1968. Armed with a tricky spitball, Chesbro set the standard for victories in 1904; while in the process, he almost brought his team across the finish line on top, 17 years before Babe Ruth's 1921 Yankees secured the first American League pennant in franchise history.

Jack Chesbro – 1904

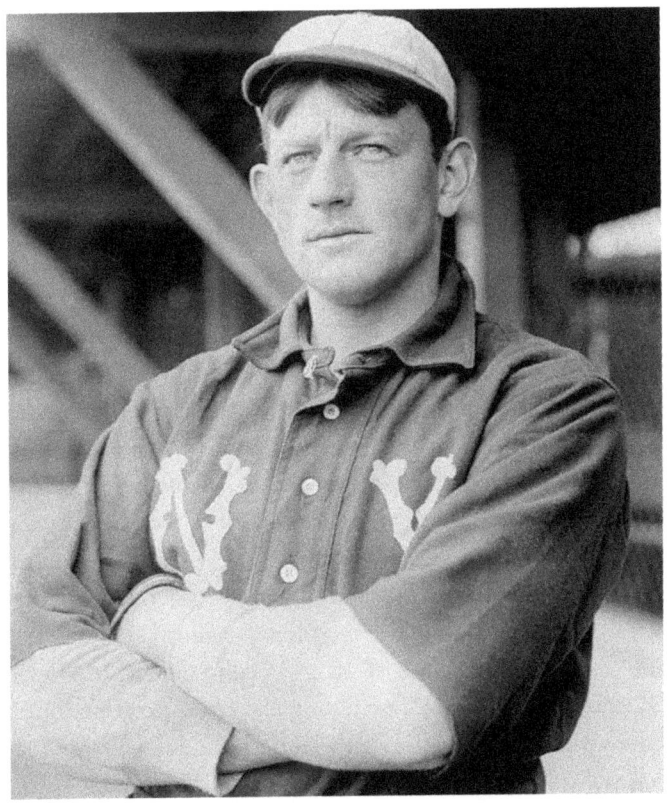

New York Highlanders spitball hurler Jack Chesbro pitched phenomenally in 1904, going 41-12 with a 1.82 ERA. Chesbro's 41 victories established the modern-era, single-season record that still stands today. A ninth-inning wild pitch by Jack in game one of a doubleheader on October 10 at American League Park, allowing the Boston Americans to win the contest and secure the American League pennant over New York, doesn't diminish his great achievement. (Photo in the Public Domain.)

CHAPTER 4

Rube Waddell – 1904

Fireballing and Freewheeling His Way to Mound Glory

Exciting and unique characters dominated the conversation as baseball became more popular, transforming from its early version to the brand of diamond action that entertained fans throughout the Deadball Era. The combination of exquisite, beautiful athletic poetry, courtesy of talented players, along with a rough-and-tumble attitude, allowed some of these distinctive personalities to rise in stature and become deeply loved by adoring rooters beyond the city those individuals called home. One player stood above all others, merging eccentric and oddball traits with a high level of raw diamond talent, allowing him to become one of the period's most fascinating and remarkable performers. Inimitable southpaw pitcher George Edward "Rube" Waddell was that player.

Waddell was a fireballing, firefighting, fun-loving, carefree spirit who possessed bundles of ability and an unmanageable soul that burned freely on its own terms. Rube enjoyed fishing, took his role in helping fireman do their work very seriously, and loved having a good time with alcohol as his companion. Waddell was one of the Deadball Era's greatest hurlers when the mood suited him, laying the groundwork for inclusion among those considered the most dominant pitchers in baseball history.

George Edward Waddell was born on a farm outside Bradford, Pennsylvania, on October 13, 1876. George was a boisterous, energetic youngster. Waddell's sister avowed that her brother broke his crib at the age of two and ran away from home to sleep in a firehouse when he was three. As a seven-year-old, George dove into a stream to snatch a fish that had evaded his hook. While Waddell missed school more often than he attended, the lad spent most of his young days receiving an education, fishing, chasing fire engines, and playing baseball.[1] Rube acquired power in his left arm as a youngster by throwing rocks at birds.[2] Only a select few companions were willing to play catch with Waddell since the southpaw's slants stung their hands. When George was 18, he started hurling for the town team. Unreliability was a concern since he didn't always appear to pitch in a game and couldn't be counted upon to finish a contest.

In 1896, drummer (door-to-door salesman) Wesley Baker saw Rube pitch while stranded in the town of Prospect, peddling goods in Western Pennsylvania. Enamored with Waddell's talent, Baker recommended him to the Franklin baseball club. Rube received his breakthrough opportunity in 1897 when the Louisville Colonels expressed an interest in the blazing southpaw. Upon being extended his first major league contract, Waddell requested $25 a game. When Colonels manager Fred Clarke offered him $500 for the season, a giddy Rube wasted no time signing. After making his major league debut on September 8, Waddell only appeared in one more game and immediately irritated his impatient skipper due to a penchant for drinking. Louisville farmed Rube out to the Western League's Detroit Tigers in 1898. After being plastered with a $50 fine, he jumped that squad, joining a semi-professional team in Chatham, Ontario, and immediately amazed fans with his mound feats.

The following year, Rube joined the Western League's Columbus Buckeyes/Senators, managed by Thomas "Tom" Loftus. The team quickly shifted to Grand Rapids, where Milwaukee Brewers manager Connie Mack saw Waddell pitch for the first time. Rube went 26-8 in 1899 and struck out over 200 batters playing in the two cities. Before a contest between Milwaukee and Grand Rapids, Loftus walked over to Mack and told the Brewers' skipper to keep an eye on his screwball pitcher, whom he would be sending to the mound that day. The Grand Rapids manager also informed Connie that the superstitious Rube, before the third inning started, would leave the field, stroll over to the bleachers, and have a fan cut one-half inch off his undershirt sleeve. Waddell shut out Milwaukee on two hits while fanning 13 Brewers.

In September, Rube reported to Louisville, where he went 7-2 with a 3.08 ERA.[3] Before the Colonels were victims of National League contraction in 1900, Waddell was part of an extensive transaction with the Pittsburgh Pirates on December 8, 1899. Many talented players, including Fred Clarke and Honus Wagner, joined him in the Smoky City, while Louisville magnate Barney Dreyfuss merged with that team's ownership group.[4] Before the start of the 1900 season, Rube made four trips from Plano, Butler County, to Pirates offices, touching up Dreyfuss for $10 each time.[5]

Although he fashioned a league-leading 2.37 ERA pitching for his hometown team in 1900, Waddell's antics exasperated Fred Clarke, who had assumed the managerial reins following the Louisville deal. On Saturday, July 7, Rube received a suspension and fine after Pittsburgh's manager tired of hearing numerous stories about his mound giant drinking the previous night, entertaining groups of people at saloons and taverns.[6] Waddell responded to this punishment by jumping the Pirates and pitching for a squad in nearby Punxsutawney, Pennsylvania.

Locked in a colossal pennant fight with the Chicago White Stockings in the newly designated American League minor organization, Milwaukee manager Connie Mack hoped to search out pitching assistance for his team. Remembering Rube Waddell's performance one year earlier, Connie boarded a train for Pittsburgh and requested permission to sign him. Understanding that Pirates management had failed to control his idiosyncrasies, Dreyfuss gave his blessing to Mack. The Brewers' manager made a mistake when calling up the husky hurler by telephone to persuade him to join Milwaukee. When Connie asked if it genuinely was Rube after the proprietor of a Punxsutawney hotel put him on the phone, Waddell responded: "Who in hell are you?" Remembering that Waddell didn't like being called "Rube," Mack referred to him as "Eddie," and the conversation from that point went smoothly.

Despite being offered good money, Waddell balked at the proposal, claiming the people of Punxsutawney liked him so much that he didn't want to upset them by leaving. Connie eventually swayed Rube to change his mind after besieging the hurler with telegrams and letters for two weeks. Waddell told Mack to come and get him. Shortly after arriving in Punxsutawney, Connie and Rube ate breakfast in the dining room at the hotel where Milwaukee's skipper took up lodging. Waddell consumed four eggs, a stack of pancakes, home-fried potatoes, and coffee.[7] Rube then told Milwaukee's manager he needed to take care of some obligations before departing. Mack ended up paying off each of Waddell's debts at 12 different businesses, including a dry goods store, hardware store, saloon, and pressing establishment. The final stop was the Adams Express Co., where Rube owed eight dollars for a dog, recently shipped to him C.O.D. by a friend. Connie wondered how Rube had procured the canine without paying for the mutt.

Waddell became an instant fan favorite in Milwaukee. When the team made an early August trip to Chicago, they trailed the White Stockings by three games. In the first contest of a doubleheader, Rube went the route, pitching an extra-inning affair that lasted more than three hours and winning it for the Brewers, 3-2, when a teammate tripled home the deciding run in the seventeenth frame. Both teams decided to limit the second game to five innings. Mack searched out Rube, proposing to his star hurler that he could go fishing at Pewaukee Lake in Wisconsin for three days and skip the team's next trip to Kansas City if Waddell pitched the second game. Rube agreed and secured victory for Milwaukee. The following day, headlines in sports pages across the country praised Rube's double triumph. Aware of Waddell's heroics, Barney Dreyfuss requested the southpaw hurler immediately report back to the Pittsburgh Pirates. Connie Mack responded to the telegram by wiring that if Dreyfuss wanted Rube, to come and get him.[8] Mack realized he couldn't rebuff this directive since Waddell legally belonged to Pittsburgh.

Rube rejoined the Pirates and remained with them throughout the remainder of the season. Before leaving Milwaukee, Waddell had exhibited steadfast composure under pressure when participating in one of his favorite activities, other than tossing a baseball. During a severe storm, lightning struck the dairy barn of George Hodgson, causing it to catch fire. When Rube arrived on the scene, he found farmers standing idly by watching the flames. Under Waddell's diligent guidance, the farmers saved forty heads of stock, wagons, buggies, and machinery. The fire severely burned Rube's hand while pulling a wagon to safety.[9] When Pittsburgh's players held their field-day festivities at Exposition Park as the campaign concluded, one of the participating teams was called the "Buckwheats" in Waddell's honor. While goofing around, Rube also wrenched the leg of the swine players had selected for the "Lubricated Hog Chase."[10]

Waddell experienced a full and busy off-season. Rube showed up at Pirates offices weeks after the campaign concluded, touching the team for money following standard protocol. Newspapers announced that Waddell was to participate in a stage melodrama. A butcher was the main character of this production, starting in Butler and traveling by wagon along the Pennsylvania oil circuit.[11] When this show, *The Union Scout*, was staged in Brookville, Pennsylvania, on December 5, theater patrons lauded Rube as a great success and an actor of rare ability. Between acts of the play, Waddell sold 25-cent songbooks, reduced to a dime, even though the playbill contained a photo of himself, the "greatest baseball pitcher in the world."[12]

Rube played for the Butler football team in their game on November 20 against Grove City College. On the game's first drive, Grove City coach George Lowrey disagreed with a penalty call by umpire Joe A. Heinemann, following an aggressive tackle on the initial play after Waddell, gained good yardage on the kickoff. Players from both teams became involved, with Rube wading into the tumult, willing to fight everybody. It took about a dozen men to pull Waddell away from the group of players. Police officers escorted Lowrey off the field and then were required to shift their attention to Rube, who was engaged in a heated argument with Referee Collingwood. After the referee ran away for his life, these officers saved the arbitrator and restored order before Grove City refused to continue the game.[13] Combative on another occasion, while traveling by train on the West Penn Railroad near Leechburg, Pennsylvania, Eddie became involved in a fight. Waddell supposedly challenged the entire train, stating he could lick any man and took off his coat to underscore the pronouncement.[14]

Such a belligerent attitude probably didn't foreshadow a lasting, loving relationship between pitcher Rube Waddell and manager Fred Clarke once the bell rang to start the 1901 season. Waddell's behavior continued infuriating Clarke after the campaign began. Rube's critics declared he was in terrible odor with Pittsburgh's rooters.[15] Waddell's days of playing in his backyard ended when the Pirates' manager finally rid himself of the problem child, selling the hurler to the Chicago Orphans on May 2, 1901. Pitching for Tom Loftus, Rube's former minor league skipper, the big southpaw went 14-14 with a 2.81 ERA. Rube's restless spirit took hold as he joined a team managed by Joseph "Joe" Cantillon, which traveled to the West Coast. Enjoying the adulation he received while in the West, Waddell hooked up with the California League's Los Angeles squad. Although many expected him to return to Chicago, a photographer was hired to create 500 photos that could be handed out on the first ladies' day once Los Angeles' season started.[16]

Leaving his heart in California was undoubtedly difficult when Rube received adoration and worship from the citizens. While visiting a theater one evening in the spring, Waddell reached his center-row seat as the curtain rose. When other theater patrons fixed their gaze upon him, Rube determined he was the main attraction, turning his back to the stage and bowing before being dragged back to his chair.[17] As Waddell experienced a grand time in Los Angeles, back in Butler, Pennsylvania, his wife, the former Florence Dunning, was granted a divorce from her prodigal husband. A family friend confided that Rube wasn't the type of individual to spend an evening with the family by his fireside.[18]

While Waddell enjoyed California life, former manager Connie Mack was looking to add pitchers to his Philadelphia Athletics' American League squad. This organization was battling the established National League for fan support in its second year as a major league. Remembering Rube's ability when pitching for him in 1900, Mack wired the twirler in Los Angeles, asking him to join the Athletics. Waddell responded by requesting $100 and transportation funds.

Connie agreed, but Rube still hadn't appeared in Philadelphia after one week. While the Athletics were in Chicago, a man walked up to Mack and informed him he had seen Waddell board a train in Los Angeles. Before the locomotive departed, a group of men had engaged Rube and talked to him for about ten minutes. Waddell started crying, told the gathering he never wanted to leave since the people had treated him well, and exited the train.

Connie Mack elicited Ban Johnson's assistance, who took him to the Pinkerton Detective Agency. Two detectives dispatched themselves to San Francisco, where Rube's Los Angeles team was playing. Mack received a telegram from the two men one day later, informing him that Waddell was now in their custody. While the Athletics were in St. Louis, Connie journeyed to Kansas City, Missouri, and secured Rube, who had spent the entire train ride walking around in a trance, affording fellow passenger and boxer James "Jim" Corbett consummate admiration and attention.[19]

On June 26, 1902, Rube Waddell debuted for the Philadelphia Athletics, losing to the Baltimore Orioles at Oriole Park, 7-3. Rube, facing these same Orioles days later on July 1, secured a 2-0 victory at Columbia Park. Despite getting a very late start participating in the American League campaign, Waddell was brilliant for Philadelphia in 1902, going 24-7 while posting a 2.05 ERA and fanning 210 opposing batters. The Athletics also claimed the American League pennant with an 83-53 record, finishing five games ahead of the St. Louis Browns. Philadelphia's baseball fans expected big things from Rube and his team in 1903. Although not terrible, Waddell's numbers that year weren't quite as sterling when Philadelphia came home second behind the Boston Americans. With Rube's record standing at 21-16, old problems that had caused Fred Clarke grief brought about a day of reckoning with Connie Mack.

Disgusted over incidents involving revelry and alcohol, Mack confronted Waddell about his unsavory behavior and suspended him. Rube denied engaging in objectionable conduct before mentioning he kept in top shape, spending time at a Turkish bath.

"Was there a threshing machine in the bath?" asked Mack. "You look like you had been through one. And how about that sloe gin?"

Waddell denied drinking anything other than beer while engaging in his recent escapades.

"Oh, I know all about it," continued Philadelphia's manager. "Part of the time, you tended bar in one of the toughest dives in the city. The Bartenders' Union ought to boycott our games because you had no card, and that is one of the reasons why I had to suspend you."

The fact that Rube missed the train for a Sunday exhibition game in Zanesville, Ohio, added to Mack's calculation, punishing the husky southpaw. Waddell initially didn't believe the Athletics manager had suspended him before resigning himself to that fact and vowing to return home to get in shape so Philadelphia could capture the pennant.[20] While Connie initially insinuated that Rube's days of playing with the Athletics might be over and he could be released, Mack softened that stance, saying he would be in the fold for 1904 after the New York Highlanders expressed interest in the suspended hurler.[21]

Rube Waddell briefly rearranged his priorities after being sent home for the season, putting baseball on the back burner, and entering the thespian world. Waddell secured a role in the production *The Stain of Guilt*, written by Walter Mathews of Louisville, Kentucky. Waddell played the role of rescuer for terrified maidens in the story. Critics viewed the traveling acting company as very accomplished. Oscar Dane played the story's detective, while Rachel Acton was the pretty, attractive heroine facing danger. Mattie Lockette's singing and dancing were phenomenal, while George D. Melville did a commendable job in the villain role as a blood-thirsty Italian thug.[22]

Before the show hit Chicago in early October, the *Washington Times* reported that "a sharp advance in the price of vegetables and eggs has already been noted in the commission market," anticipating Rube's stage arrival. The newspaper article suggested that members of the Chicago White Sox might be in attendance, armed with such items. While promoting Waddell, the show's handbill characterized his acting as "the most daring and sensational piece of human deviltry in all the records of crime."[23] Rube's performance was passionately lauded by patrons during two shows in one day at the Park Theatre in Indianapolis, Indiana.[24] His defined role was that of a detective's assistant, thwarting scoundrels by tossing them about or grabbing their guns and biting off the triggers before returning the weapons. In the first act, Waddell appeared onstage wearing a brown baseball suit, with a small tear in one stocking. Rube scoffed when someone suggested the stocking should be darned.

"Never," replied the hero. "Any king might have a torn place in his royal robes, but a darn is evidence of poverty."[25]

Friction first appeared regarding Waddell's eccentricity when the show reached Washington, Indiana. Rube refused to go onstage after the show's manager, Charles W. Daniels, wouldn't allow him to add a musical number highlighting the big hurler's singing skills. Daniels then tossed Waddell's baggage out to the curb. During the first act, Waddell pleaded with the theater manager to intervene, who convinced Daniels to give Rube another chance. The ecstatic pitcher grabbed his trunk, placed it on his shoulder, and made his way through the playhouse, bumping patrons as he bounded down the aisle.[26] When the acting troupe reached Cincinnati in early November, rumors abounded that Reds manager Joseph "Joe" Kelley was vigorously trying to bring Waddell into the fold. Kelley supposedly made a magnificent offer for the southpaw's services. Still, Connie Mack declined, stating no proposal could sway him to part with Rube, who had given Philadelphia's manager necessary guarantees for the 1904 baseball campaign.

"Waddell has told me," said Mack, "that he will be more attentive to his work next year than he was last, and if he does, my team will surely carry off the pennant."[27]

Joe Kelley denied he was making overtures to acquire Rube.[28] While in Cincinnati, Waddell met with Reds owner Garry Herrmann and stated he would call on Kelley when *The Stain of Guilt* played in Baltimore.[29] When the production reached Wheeling, West Virginia, reports claimed on December 6 that Rube had drawn his release from the show after another dispute with its manager. Rumors alleged Waddell had left the acting company to tend bar for old Western Association outfielder Sam Nicholl, who owned a saloon in Wheeling. Rube's second wife, May Wynne Skinner Waddell, also brought suit against her husband. The hotel where his wife was staying seized her clothing for not paying board. May Waddell then took shelter with the Humane Society. She alleged Rube had been paying the bills until recently but never actually gave her any money.[30] While high drama occurred on the stage and in the Waddell household, Connie Mack reiterated that the southpaw pitcher would wear an Athletics uniform in 1904.

"Do you suppose I would leave Rube get away from me and allow him to do great work for some other club, when I know he can do it for the Athletics?" opined Mack. "Not much. I have fixed up my pitching staff so that I can afford to take a chance on 'Rube.'

"He may come around next spring on his good behavior and pitch great ball, in which event the Athletic Club will need his services as much as any other team. 'Rube' is satisfied with the treatment he has received from the club, and I don't think he is trying to get away. Any time he gets tired of playing with the Athletics he can jump out and play with some independent club, and with our present staff of pitchers we will never miss him. But no other club will get the benefit of Waddell's pitching."[31]

Mack had good reason to be confident that Rube Waddell would be a valuable contributor to his team. One of Rube's Athletics teammates wrote to a

Chicago friend that Connie had agreed to pay Waddell $5,000 for the 1904 season, with special provisions in the contract. Waddell was required to pitch 40 games to earn that money. Once Rube met that threshold, the pitcher was free to do what he wanted for the campaign's duration. According to the Cleveland Naps' Harry Bay, Waddell had been paid $25 by Connie when he showed up to pitch in 1903 and nothing when he didn't.[32] The 1904 contract was adjusted to $7,000 a year when Mack and Waddell met in Philadelphia. Rube happily inked his signature to the document.[33]

Waddell's theatrical career was also slowly fading. On December 4, before the show reached Pittsburgh, publicity manager and advance agent Joe Finnigan (or Finnegan), a St. Louis newspaperman, made a trip to Butler County, hoping to convince Rube to rejoin the company. Finnigan gave him six dollars advance money but balked when Rube asked for ten more. The publicist then set about on a fruitless mission to Carnegie, Pennsylvania, to ask Honus Wagner to take the place of Waddell in the production.[34] In the end, as interest declined, Rube abandoned the troupe for good in Philadelphia when the show's manager barred teammate and catcher Osee Schrecongost from visiting him in his dressing room. The two players exited the premises and traveled to the other side of the Delaware River, where Rube put on an apron and worked behind the bar of an establishment in Camden, New Jersey.[35] Rumors abounded that Waddell was tipsy at times due to pouring schooners of beer in this Camden saloon.[36]

In the middle of January, Rube Waddell sent a letter to Peter Agnew, manager of the Tri-State League's Harrisburg Senators, asking if he could pitch for his team next season.[37] On January 26, word out of Pittsburgh indicated manager Howard Risher of the nearby Homestead baseball club planned to offer Rube big money since the hurler had expressed a desire to play for that club through written correspondence.[38] In early February, news from St. Marys, Pennsylvania, chronicled that Waddell was working in his brother John's butcher shop. Rube's skill with butcher knives and hatchets became legendary, mesmerizing denizens with his uncanny talent for working the chopping block.[39] Waddell also performed diligent service as a member of St. Marys' Volunteer Fire Department.[40]

Being a nomadic renaissance man during the off-season was fine for sowing wild oats before the campaign started, but making written overtures to join other teams after agreeing to terms with Philadelphia was a waste of paper. Part of that 1904 Athletics contract called for Waddell to adhere to all club rules or lose large chunks of salary.[41] Once the time came to report for spring training; it was surprising that Rube had any energy left as the season beckoned.

One month before the first slate of regular-season games, Waddell offered his thoughts regarding the upcoming American League race.

"We'll win the pennant in a walk this year," said Waddell. "We are all in fine shape, and I can't see anything but the Athletics. If we don't win, it will not be my fault. I'll pitch my arm off to win for Connie Mack. I know I made a mistake last year, but you can bet I won't make the same one again this season."[42]

When Rube arrived to leave by train for spring training at Spartanburg, South Carolina, the hurler told Connie Mack he felt great. Waddell further vowed that Mack could count on him for the upcoming season, promised no boozing or funny business, and informed his manager to order a new championship flag for the forthcoming year.[43] While one Philadelphia writer felt Rube could stand to lose about a dozen pounds, to this individual, the hurler appeared to be in great shape.[44] When the battle to win a pennant started on April 14, the Athletics' Eddie Plank claimed an eight-inning victory over the Washington Senators at American League Park, 8-3. Amid silly rumors that Waddell would be joining a western minor league team in the summer, the husky southpaw took the bump on April 16.[45] Rube was on top of his game, striking out seven batters, as Philadelphia crushed Washington, 12-2.[46] When the Senators loaded the bases with one out in the fifth inning, Waddell snuffed out the rally by striking out Garland "Jake" Stahl and Barry McCormick.[47]

One day after Rube secured his first victory of the season, Boston Americans veteran hurler Cy Young modestly denied he was the league's most outstanding pitcher. Young bestowed that honor instead upon Waddell as the world's top hurler.[48] Cold weather led to the postponement of Philadelphia's home opener on April 20.[49] Wintry winds gave way to the bright, warm sun one day later, as Waddell opposed the New York Highlanders at Columbia Park. The First Regiment Band entertained the 5,000 spectators present around 2:30 p.m. Rube appeared on the field wearing a red coat with gray facing, batting out fly balls and keeping time with the music. At 3 p.m., both squads lined up in front of the benches. They marched in unison to the outfield to prepare for the flag-raising and the band performing the National anthem. A group of fans then presented Waddell with two bouquets of assorted flowers. At 3:40 p.m., Philadelphia's mayor, John Weaver, threw out a new baseball wrapped in foil to umpire Tommy Connolly.[50]

Rube Waddell was brilliant, striking out 16 Highlanders, as Philadelphia claimed the 12-inning game, 3-2. Rube would've tossed a shutout if not for an error by shortstop Monte Cross and his wild pitch. Athletics' first baseman Harry Davis was the batting star, smacking a homer in the fourth and driving home the winning run with a double in the twelfth.[51] Kid Elberfeld connected for three of New York's four hits.[52] Waddell struck out at least one opponent in ten of the game's innings while turning the trick twice on six occasions.[53] Rube's mastery continued against Boston on April 25. Waddell tossed a six-hit shutout, beating the Americans, 2-0, although he only fanned three batters.[54] As the season entered May, many newspapers crowned Rube as the swiftest pitcher in baseball, with his fastball possessing so much velocity that it was dangerous for the catcher's hand, while curves shot across the dish with a speed that nearly burned up home plate.[55]

Philadelphia's stalwart southpaw was even better when he faced Boston at Huntington Avenue Baseball Grounds on May 2. Waddell allowed one hit and fanned seven, as the Athletics were victorious, 3-0. The Americans' only hit came when the official scorer ruled Patsy Dougherty's bunt a single, although Rube blundered by overrunning the ball, which he should have cleanly fielded.[56] On May 5, Waddell was in the box again, facing Boston ace Cy Young.

Rube suffered his first defeat of the season, 3-0, as Young was perfect for the Americans. Although Waddell had promised before the contest not to allow a hit, Boston hammered him for ten safeties. At the same time, Cy achieved pitching infamy, not permitting an Athletics runner to reach base.[57] In tossing a perfect game, Young fanned eight, while only six Philadelphia batters lifted fly balls to the outfield.[58]

His next time out against Washington on May 7, Rube Waddell secured an 11-4 victory. On May 11, Rube pitched twelve innings against the Chicago White Sox at Columbia Park. Philadelphia claimed the contest, 6-5, when Daniel "Danny" Murphy's single drove home the winning run. Murphy smacked three doubles and two singles on the day, while Waddell did his part, striking out six batters.[59] Rube was highly effective after the first inning against Chicago on May 14, fanning eight White Sox players and scattering five hits, as Philadelphia proved victorious, 2-1. Murphy was the batting hero again, as his two-out double in the fourth knocked in the deciding run.[60] Waddell dropped two straight heartbreakers, losing to the Browns, 2-0, on May 17 and coming up short against Cleveland, 4-3, on May 23. In the game against St. Louis, Rube failed to go the distance for the first time in 1904, lasting eight innings. Waddell combined for ten strikeouts in those two games.

Rube ended this short skid with a masterful performance against the Detroit Tigers at Columbia Park on May 26. Waddell tossed a four-hit shutout, struck out 12 Tigers, and secured a 5-0 victory.[61] The win left Rube with an 8-3 record. Rube's stingy mound work continued against New York on May 30, when he pitched the Memorial Day doubleheader's afternoon contest. Waddell scattered seven hits, fanned eight, and came away with a 1-0 victory. The nightcap's only run occurred when Osee Schrecongost tripled and scored on Monte Cross's single.[62]

Rube's proficiency deserted him against Chicago on June 5, as a White Sox onslaught resulted in a 14-2 win over Philadelphia. Rube only lasted two innings, being roughed up for three runs and six hits.[63] Connie Mack handed Waddell the ball one day later, as the southpaw hurler exacted revenge by beating Chicago, 6-3. Rube made it a twirling trifecta, opposing the White Sox for the third consecutive day on June 7. Chicago's hitters were most effective at critical times, defeating Waddell, 6-1.[64] When Mack's team had arrived in Chicago, Rube boasted he would pitch all four games of this series. After showing signs of fatigue in the third contest, Waddell announced he was going to the bump again on June 8, but Connie selected Eddie Plank to take up the task.[65] Had Rube been pitching at home, help would've been nearby to galvanize the exhausted hurler. During games at Columbia Park, five rooters in the bleacher section opposite first base offered psychological assistance, putting Waddell in the proper frame of mind, shouting out fishing terminology concerning game situations.[66]

As Philadelphia continued its road trip in Cleveland, one of those innocent Rube Waddell stories made its way into print for public consumption. At one time, it seemed Rube had conceived the idea of spending his spring months playing baseball for a college squad. Upon asking a friend what course of study he should consider, this individual recommended shooting and fishing.

"Great," said Waddell, "I could pass that easy."

Waddell diligently sat down and wrote to the dean of a Southern learning institution, explaining that he wanted to attend the school, taking shooting and fishing as his major. Rube later received a harsh response from the dean, who believed the pitcher was poking fun at him.[67]

Waddell experienced loads of fun in his next outing against Cleveland on June 13, defeating the Naps, 9-2, in ten innings. Rube locked horns with Earl Moore in a tight mound duel until Philadelphia exploded for seven tallies in the tenth frame. Waddell also fanned 13 batters.[68] Detroit was victimized by Rube on June 17, with Philadelphia claiming an easy 7-1 victory, as the eccentric southpaw recorded nine strikeouts.[69] On June 22, Waddell was knocked out of the box after two innings, as Boston assaulted him for six runs and eight hits, defeating the Athletics, 7-6.[70]

Rube split his final two decisions of the month, beating Washington, 6-3, on June 25, and losing to Boston, 4-3, on June 30. In the Senators' game,

Waddell showed so much determination and speed when scoring a run that he took three wide turns after crossing home plate to prevent colliding with the grandstand.[71] While facing New York in the afternoon game of a holiday doubleheader on July 4, Rube fanned eight Highlanders but lost his second straight game, 5-2.[72] Eight once again was the magic number in the "K" department on July 9, as Rube bested Washington in the first game of a doubleheader, 3-0. Fourteen thousand three hundred twelve enthusiastic Columbia Park spectators viewed Waddell's mound mastery.[73] Waddell had taken the hill against the Senators on July 7, but a violent thunderstorm ended that day's double proceedings in the first game's second inning.[74]

When Eddie Plank defeated Chicago on July 15, Connie Mack courteously awarded him a suit of clothing. Mack offered this extra-effort perk when one of his hurlers won three consecutive games.[75] Waddell had pushed his record to 15-8 for the season on July 14, trimming Chicago, 2-1, and striking out 11 White Sox batters.[76] Rube lost a tough one, 1-0, against St. Louis on July 19, despite pitching well in the pinches, allowing ten hits, and fanning nine batters.[77] In game one of a doubleheader on July 23, Cleveland defeated Waddell in 11 innings, 3-2.

Rube rebounded by thumping Detroit two times at Columbia Park. He cruised to a 5-0 victory on July 27, scattering three hits and striking out 11 batters.[78] Henry Chadwick, the "Father of Baseball," was in attendance watching Waddell weave his magic.[79] On July 30, Rube fanned seven Tigers and secured a 4-1 victory, losing his shutout bid by allowing three singles in the eighth inning.[80] As the campaign moved into August, Philadelphia found themselves in fifth place with a 46-38 record, 5 ½ games behind the pacesetting Boston Americans.

The Athletics secured a 9-3 victory against St. Louis at Sportsman's Park on August 2, with Waddell on the hill. In the sixth inning, Browns utility infielder Harry Gleason was struck on the head by an inside fastball. Rube's pitch rebounded with such a reverberating crack that some thought the baseball hit Gleason's bat. Harry slumped to the ground. Teammates rushed to his aid, picked Gleason up in their arms, and carried him to the bench. Dr. Max C. Starkloff, St. Louis's former city health commissioner, who was in the grandstand, attended to the player.[81] Dr. Starkloff worked on Gleason for ten minutes as blood ran from his nose and ears. Players commissioned a clubhouse door and used it as a stretcher to carry the injured man off the field.[82] Harry ended up in the Missouri Baptist Sanitarium. Listed in critical condition with a concussion to the brain, doctors expected him to recover.[83] Although Gleason had indicated after spending weeks in the hospital that his baseball career was likely over, he eventually returned to the diamond.[84]

On August 7, Rube Waddell defeated Chicago, 5-2. The blazing southpaw struck out 11 White Sox batters, including a critical fanning of John "Jiggs" Donahue with the bases loaded, in the ninth inning.[85] The White Sox stranded 12 men, with Rube recording nine of his 11 strikeouts when opponents occupied a bag.[86] Through 29 starts, Waddell had fanned 212 batters. In 1903, Rube struck out 301 batters in 39 games (research later adjusted this to 302).[87] Rube recorded his twentieth victory of the season on August 11, beating Cleveland, 2-1, in a 13-inning affair and fanning 14 Naps.[88] Waddell secured his sixth consecutive win on August 15, shutting out Detroit, 2-0. Rube allowed eight hits and struck out seven Tigers batters.[89] That winning streak ended against Cleveland on August 19. Although Waddell fanned 15 batters, the Naps claimed a 2-1 victory in 11 innings. Nap Lajoie scored the winning run, racing around the bases when Monte Cross threw the ball into the right-field bleachers after fielding his grounder.[90]

Achieving victories suddenly became difficult for Waddell, as he failed to secure wins in games against Cleveland on August 23 and Detroit on August 25, although the southpaw struck out 19 total opponents in those contests. Rube became confused over his whereabouts before pitching against Chicago on Monday, August 29. Waddell was in Reading, Pennsylvania, umpiring a baseball game on Saturday. Rube enjoyed this diversion so much that when it came time to catch a train, he mistook the "Queen of the Valley" flyer from Harrisburg to Allentown as the locomotive along the Reading Railroad's Main Line, whose destination was Philadelphia. When Waddell reached the Allentown terminal station, he believed he was in Philadelphia before being told that wasn't the case.

"I must get to Philadelphia today to pitch for the Athletics against Chicago," said Waddell. "Where in [blank] am I?"

Rube immediately was put on the Scranton flyer bound for Philadelphia.[91] Waddell arrived in time and defeated the White Sox, 4-1, fanning 11 batters.[92] When September started, the Athletics found themselves in third place with a 62-45 record, 4 ½ games behind league-leading Boston. Rube mowed down Browns' batters when he faced St. Louis on September 1 but lost 2-0, despite striking out ten. Neither team could break through until St. Louis scored two runs in the ninth inning.[93] Facing New York in the second game of a Labor Day doubleheader on September 5, Waddell retired to the showers in the first inning.[94]

Two losses followed in the first games of twin bills against these Highlanders; on the road on September 6 and at Columbia Park against Jack Chesbro on September 8. Rube combined for 21 strikeouts in the two contests. Waddell was directly responsible for the 3-2 loss on September 8, making a wild throw that allowed a run to score in the first and failing to field two bunts in the third.[95] Rube finally placed a game in the win column one day later, defeating New York, 5-1, in game two of a doubleheader. Against Boston in the opening round of a twin bill on September 12, Waddell was wild and unproductive in the first three innings, being pulled by Connie Mack, as Philadelphia lost, 6-4.[96] Rube also failed to finish game two of a doubleheader versus Washington on September 15, due to suffering an injury. In the second inning, Waddell slipped and fell heavily on his right shoulder, straining it severely.[97] Rube sustained the injury while attempting to tag a runner with his left hand. X-rays were taken on his shoulder the following day, but Mack offered no timetable for Waddell's return.[98]

This incident meant Rube Waddell's invincible persona that year was compromised on a second occasion. Months earlier, Waddell succumbed to temptation for the first time in 1904. In a game against Boston on July 1 at Huntington Avenue Grounds, Americans hurler Jesse Tannehill had beaned Athletics outfielder Daniel "Danny" Hoffman. Dr. Theodore Erb, who tended to Hoffman's injury, later shared a good story about the situation related to Waddell. Rube was so concerned over Danny's condition that night that he ordered a whiskey at a saloon for his teammate. The dazed Hoffman rejected the liquor when it arrived.

"Well, it would be a shame to see that wasted, and as I ordered it and paid for it, I might as well put it away," declared Rube.

Minutes later, when Connie Mack appeared at the bar, Waddell quickly smoothed things over with his manager in a diplomatic fashion.

"Conny, I just absorbed one whiskey to save it!" said Rube.[99]

Rube remained out of the lineup for two weeks. When Waddell suffered his injury, Philadelphia was in third place, six games from the top spot. Two weeks later, as Rube resumed his turn in the rotation, the Athletics held down the fifth spot, ten games behind first-place Boston. Besides his star hurler missing time, Mack was also without catcher Michael "Doc" Powers and first baseman Harry Davis due to injuries.[100] Waddell returned to the mound in a blaze of glory on September 29, tossing a two-hitter in game one of a doubleheader and defeating St. Louis, 1-0.[101] Rube gained a split in his subsequent two decisions, losing the first contest of a twin bill to Detroit, 3-2, on October 1, and securing victory over Washington, 3-2, in game one of a doubleheader on October 7. Waddell didn't allow a walk and fanned 13 Senators.[102]

Philadelphia played their last six games of the 1904 season, courtesy of three doubleheaders in Washington. Before making his final appearance in game two on October 10, Rube Waddell exhibited true heroism, facing a hectic situation. On October 9, a fire ravaged the upper stories of the William F. & B. F. Downey's livery stable, located at 1622 to 1628 L Street Northwest. Within this building were carriages that belonged to senators, diplomats, and wealthy Washington citizens. Damage estimates from the fire approached $100,000. When firefighters arrived, Rube was among them, eager to volunteer as he entered the building with a handkerchief tied across his mouth.[103] Waddell's assistance was exemplary, rushing into the burning structure and rescuing many fine horses that were the property of foreign diplomats.[104]

On October 10, the Athletics claimed the doubleheader's first game, 7-6. Before the second contest, both team captains agreed to shorten the final tilt to five innings.[105] Rube started and lost the abbreviated game, 4-3. When Senators manager Patrick "Patsy" Donovan batted in the fourth inning, Waddell walked toward him, pulled a parcel wrapped in a newspaper out from under his sweater, and handed it to his surprised opponent. Donovan backed away for a moment without speaking before Rube, who had piqued the interest of spectators, broke the silence using a booming voice.

"You cannot refuse," yelled Waddell, "'tis the Stars and Stripes! Pay homage to it, patriot! Keep it in remembrance of the team that won the cellar championship of the year 1904."

Patsy Donovan accepted the gift, shook Rube Waddell's hand, and had someone carry the tattered flag to the Senators' bench. Donovan declared that this memento, given to him by Waddell since Washington finished dead last in the American League race by going 38-113, would be displayed on a wall in his house.[106] At the season's end, Philadelphia sat in fifth place with an 81-70 record, 12 ½ games behind the pennant-winning Boston Americans. Regarding Rube fanning batters in 1904, 343 strikeouts were the official total recorded at that time.[107] This mark stood for decades, with the Washington Senators' Walter Johnson coming closest in 1910 when he whiffed 313 batters.

Baseball enthusiasts believed the modern-era record for strikeouts by a pitcher in a single season fell in 1946, with Robert "Bob" Feller of the Cleveland Indians fanning 348 batters. As Feller assaulted Rube Waddell's record throughout the season, statisticians revisited the big southpaw's numbers from 42 years earlier. Two men had challenged George Moreland's *Little Red Book* figure of

343 strikeouts before Feller purportedly established a new record. Historian and statistician Ernest J. Lanigan, the director of the National Baseball Museum in Cooperstown, New York, and Leonard Gettleson of Long Branch, New Jersey, undertook this analysis. In 1942, while compiling the *Dope Book* for the *Sporting News*, Gettleson had placed Waddell's 1904 total at 352 strikeouts. Lanigan scoured box scores in *Sporting Life* and found the number to be 347.

Earl J. Hilligan, chief of the American League's Service Bureau, continued accepting Rube's figure of 343, claiming it would be unfair to Feller for a change to occur without indisputable evidence to challenge this total. In 1904, the American League hadn't kept official statistics independently, not starting this practice until 1905. Hilligan's stance didn't stop Ford Sawyer, of Dorchester, Massachusetts, who did work regarding baseball records for the *Sporting News*, from digging into research files of Boston newspapers. Sawyer's diligence in 1946 found Waddell had fanned 349 batters in 1904. Sportswriter Allen Lewis of the *Philadelphia Inquirer* scanned box scores from various publications in the Quaker City. Lewis reached a figure of 348 strikeouts. This meticulous research by these two writers found eight discrepancies related to the original numbers when combining their findings.

Since only one source didn't match in disputed games from 1904, for June 17, June 30, September 1, and September 9, the consensus reached pointed to typographical errors being the culprit regarding this publication. Washington correspondent George Zielke checked out the other four incongruities, utilizing the *Sporting News* from the Library of Congress, including lists of victimized batters and play-by-play accounts. In the end, this tireless research placed Rube Waddell's strikeout total at 349, leaving Bob Feller one shy at 348 in 1946.[108] Minor tweakings on a game-by-game basis at a later date still left the figure at 349. That mark is the final total we know today, as Waddell's adjusted numbers in all departments left him with a 25-19 record in 1904, supported by a 1.62 ERA.

After Feller came up short, besting Rube's record, his standard stood until 1965, when Sanford "Sandy" Koufax of the Los Angeles Dodgers toppled the mark by whiffing 382 opposing hitters. Lynn Nolan Ryan established the modern-era record that still stands today, besting Koufax by striking out 383 in 1973 as a member of the California Angels. Waddell still holds the mark when the conversation centers on southpaw hurlers from the American League. With respect to those who came before Rube, Matthew Aloysius Kilroy of the American Association's Baltimore Orioles tops the list. Statistics credited him with fanning 513 batters in 1886 while pitching 583 innings. Had Waddell worked that many stanzas on the bump in 1904, at the beginning of the modern era where such a workload in comparison was even ridiculous, based on his .91 strikeouts per inning pitched, the great southpaw would have fanned 531 batters. Approaching that many innings pitched would have been an interesting case study for Rube since fighting fires and fishing always offered suitable alternatives.

When it came to living life to its fullest and enjoying every minute of a particular moment, George Edward "Rube" Waddell had few equals. Whether Waddell was fighting fires, fishing, hunting, acting, or firing bee bees past helpless American League batters, he squeezed every drop of vivacity and energy from his heart and soul. Of course, this was the case, as long as the attention span was willing while partaking in something he loved. While many were methodical and mechanical, establishing the first records of baseball's modern era, Rube did so with flair and panache, never taking a backseat to anyone regarding baseball endowment and diamond supremacy.

Philadelphia Athletics manager Connie Mack received assurances from pitcher Rube Waddell that he'd behave in 1904. Mack placed a special provision in Waddell's contract requiring him to pitch 40 games in order to earn his salary. Once reaching that threshold, Rube had the freedom to do as he pleased for the remainder of the season. The contract also called for Rube to adhere to all club rules or lose large chunks of salary. (Courtesy of the Library of Congress.)

CHAPTER 5

Vic Willis – 1905

Staff Ace Rolls High Twenties in the Loss Column

Before specialization became a vital facet in how managers handled their pitching staffs, hurlers possessing strong pedigree could expect a heavy workload on the mound, with concerns over pitch counts being a foreign concept. In the case of Jack Chesbro, undisputed ace of the New York Highlanders' twirling unit in 1904, high numbers in both innings pitched and victories resulted from manager Clark Griffith expressing supreme confidence in his mound reliability. Throughout the Deadfall Era, those with extreme talent thrived, winning baseball games, in most cases, no matter the circumstances. Victory totals grew for individuals with pennant contenders unless a manager was lucky enough to be blessed with an arsenal of supreme talented hurlers. Such was the case for Fred Clarke and his 1902 Pittsburgh Pirates when Chesbro, Jesse Tannehill, Deacon Phillippe, Samuel "Sam" Leever, and Edward "Ed" Doheny were at his disposal on a team that won 103 games.

It was sometimes inevitable that teams could reach a fine line between fighting for the flag and floundering in the second division. The obliteration of this line led to games once won with ease now becoming a struggle. A pitcher, achieving the critical benchmark of surpassing 20 victories in a season, quickly saw things reversed in a heartbeat, piling up losses at a much higher rate. Boston Beaneaters hurler Victor Gazaway "Vic" Willis was one such player, exposed to both sides of this coin. He succeeded when times were good, before battling for every inch of diamond territory, after Boston transformed into a perennial second-division citizen, fighting to avoid residing in the basement. When it came to the magical number "20," Willis tasted both sweet success and agonizing defeat.

Vic Willis was born on April 12, 1876, in Cecil County, Maryland. James, a carpenter, moved the family to Newark, Delaware, when Willis was a young boy. As an athlete, Vic thrived playing sandlot and amateur baseball in Newark.[1] Willis was also a collegiate football performer, although he never attended a university. Vic played fullback for the Delaware College team in 1893. Since the college had a small enrollment, it recruited young Newark men for the sole purpose of playing for the school's athletic squads. By age 17, Willis had already grown to six feet, two inches tall. This slender build served him well, pitching in leagues across Newark and Wilmington.

Vic received his first chance as a professional in 1894, earning a modest five dollars each game as a Wilmington YMCA squad member. Willis made the jump to Organized Baseball in 1895, signing to play for the Pennsylvania State League's Harrisburg Senators. Vic showed bright promise as a hurler before the league folded in August. Undaunted by this misfortune, Willis hooked up with the Virginia State League's Lynchburg Hill Climbers. Vic's strong performance with Lynchburg garnered him a promotion to the Eastern League's Syracuse Stars in 1896.[2] Willis was phenomenal for manager George Kuntzsch's Stars, doing exceptional mound work before being sidelined due to illness. In August, Kuntzsch forged onward without the young prodigy, who suffered a severe attack of diphtheria that left him in a weakened condition.[3]

In 1897, Vic Willis bounced back from the previous year's ailment under new manager Albert "Al" Buckenberger, as Syracuse claimed the Eastern League pennant. Utilizing a devastating overhand curveball he perfected upon joining the team, Vic went 21-17 for the Stars and posted a minuscule 1.16 ERA. As the season progressed, Willis became a hot piece of baseball property. The Baltimore Orioles expressed interest in the elongated slab artist but found the $3,000 asking price too rich for their blood. Skipper William "Billy" Murray, of the league's Providence Clamdiggers/Grays squad, recommended Vic to Boston Beaneaters manager Frank Selee, advising him to sign the pitcher.[4]

An earlier agreement posed a big problem for Selee or any other major league team interested in Willis's services. During the 1896 campaign, Syracuse's George Kuntzsch brokered a deal with Pittsburgh Pirates owner William Kerr. Kuntzsch purchased from Pittsburgh the release of third baseman Judson "Jud" Smith, and first baseman Abel Lizotte, for $750. A critical proviso attached to this agreement stated Kerr would be permitted to select any player from Syracuse's squad before the 1898 season concluded. The Pirates would then pay $500 to secure that individual.

Around August 6, 1897, Selee opened negotiations with Stars management, hoping to sign Vic. A sticking point remained regarding the earlier promise that Pittsburgh retained first rights to select any player from Syracuse's roster through the 1898 campaign's conclusion. Realizing Willis could easily be peddled to another team for more than $500, Al Buckenberger, who had managed the Pirates at one time under William Kerr, attempted to gauge the Pittsburgh magnate's interest in his star pitcher.

"Do you want Willis?" Buckenberger wired to Pittsburgh's owner.

"Do not want Willis," responded Kerr.

Earlier dickering had indicated Kerr was initially interested in former major league backstop John "Jack" Ryan.[5] With this obstacle now removed, Frank Selee swooped in, purchasing Vic Willis in September.[6] Selee forked over $1,000, and catcher Frederick "Fred" Lake to bring Willis into the fold.[7] This acquisition was lauded back in Boston. Syracuse catcher Jack Ryan did fantastic work in 1897, assisting Vic's rapid development. Willis gained impeccable control while exhibiting excellent speed. This combination and Vic's tantalizing curveball allowed him to become the league's most effective twirler. Willis's motion was effortless when throwing his ace pitch, the drop ball. Veteran Eastern League players found this pitch more efficient than anything other young hurlers had to offer. That year, Vic pitched four games where he only allowed three hits in each and had averaged seven strikeouts per game since June. Willis also became known as "The Wolf" because of his haggard and hungry appearance.[8]

Willis was joining one of the National League's elite organizations. Boston won the 1897 pennant, finishing two games ahead of the Baltimore Orioles with a record of 93-39. The Beaneaters' loaded roster included star performers such as Jimmy Collins, Hugh Duffy, William "Billy" Hamilton, Herman Long, Robert "Bobby" Lowe, Frederick "Fred" Tenney, Charles "Kid" Nichols, and rookie Charles "Chick" Stahl. Talented but temperamental Martin "Marty" Bergen, considered the best catcher in the league, was also a squad member.

Boston repeated as champions in 1898, posting a 102-47 record in the first season the National League played a lengthened schedule. The Beaneaters topped the second-place Orioles by six games. Vic Willis experienced a sensational rookie campaign for the pennant winners, going 25-13 with a 2.84 ERA. As the season wound down, an article revealed that a story regarding team disharmony had been suppressed for months by agreement, involving the young pitcher and his battery mate. When accounts of the incident became public in

October, Boston's fans found that Willis and Bergen had tangled in a summer confrontation months earlier.

This clash occurred on July 28, while the team was in St. Louis. Trouble had first bubbled to the surface the previous night when the Beaneaters traveled by train from Brooklyn. Tired due to the long trip, Boston's players engaged in horseplay and harmless practical jokes to lift their spirits and break the monotony before retiring to their berths. Initially, Bergen participated in the merriment, and camaraderie was present among all players. Suddenly, Marty became moody and detached, refusing to continue in the tomfoolery. He growled at Willis, but nobody gave this reaction much thought since the catcher slipped into these lapses often, preferring to be aloof.

The following morning in St. Louis, when Vic entered the dining room of Boston's lodging at the Southern Hotel, he was seated at a table by the head-waiter next to Bergen, who had walked in minutes earlier. While sitting down in his chair, the rookie hurler greeted his teammate. Bergen, exhibiting belligerence, didn't follow standard decorum, ordering Willis instead to sit at another table.

"If you don't get away from me," Bergen growled, "I'll smash you, sure."

Willis refused to move, prompting Bergen to slap him across the face. Teammates and hotel employees quickly intervened, preventing further chaos. Seething over being struck, Vic adopted an aggressive demeanor but kept his anger in check with the help of sympathetic friends. Willis moved to another table, sat down, ate breakfast, and then retired to his room, accompanied by two or three teammates. Bergen finished his meal, receiving unflattering comments the entire time from whispering hotel guests. Shocked women who witnessed the altercation immediately exited the dining room.

An accommodating employee alerted a Boston sportswriter to what had happened. This scribe immediately searched out manager Frank Selee, who was vague about the incident, until peppered with pieces of information provided by the hotel employee. Selee shifted gears, agreeing to speak about the matter if the writer promised to quash the story until the season closed.

"It is useless for me to deny," said Selee, "that Bergen and Willis had a difficulty, but I must decline to give you the particulars or inform you whether I will discipline either or both of the men. Print that story, and Boston is out of the race. We are shorthanded now with Hamilton, Tenney, Stahl, and Klobedanz [Frederick "Fred" Klobedanz] in the hospital, and once this affair is ventilated, either Bergen or Willis and maybe both will be useless to us. I have made up my mind, of course, where the blame lies, but unless compelled to, will not take any action. I have talked to the parties and told each plainly that a renewal of hostilities will result in a heavy fine and suspension of the guilty man, even if it costs us the championship."

Selee had talked to both parties shortly after the unfortunate incident occurred. While speaking to Vic Willis, Frank received a pledge from his pitcher that he wouldn't pursue renewing hostilities in this instance. However, that promise didn't extend to future encounters with Bergen.

"I will make a sacrifice of my personal feelings and swallow the insult in the interests of the club," said the pitcher, "but if Bergen makes another break at me, we will settle the question of which is the better man, whatever the effect on the discipline and pennant prospects of the team."

Boston's manager offered Vic assurances there would be no more trouble. Selee then talked to Marty Bergen and issued an ultimatum to his catcher, who pleaded with the justification that he lost control of his temper, believing he had been made a mark by Willis, leading to the incensed outburst. Frank informed Bergen that it was totally up to him to remain with Boston or go elsewhere. One stipulation for continuing with the Beaneaters was that Marty couldn't instigate further trouble with Willis.

"If you say the word," said Selee, "I'll begin negotiations at once to trade you. We must have you or another catcher, and you can depend on going to another club if you are not satisfied to remain with us."

Bergen responded that he wished to remain with Boston but wasn't receptive to allowing team members to impose on him.

"All right," continued Selee. "I see you are not willing to do what I, as manager of the Boston Club, have a right to expect, so I'll do what I consider my duty in the matter."

Bergen played in the Beaneaters' game that afternoon but wasn't behind the dish when Vic Willis pitched against the St. Louis Browns on July 30, after rain postponed the previous day's contest. Selee used the excuse of a riding accident to explain Marty's absence. Believing the catcher had learned his lesson, Selee allowed Bergen to return and play both games of a doubleheader against St. Louis on August 1. In the aftermath of Marty's slapping challenge against Willis, a Beaneaters player, who preferred anonymity, offered insight regarding the team's paranoid, troubled catcher.

"Bergen is the greatest catcher in the business," said Boston's player, "and a harder worker for his team's success never wore a wind pad. He hustles all the time and is a great help to the gang on the field, but he is anything but companionable, and when on the road, he always has one or more fancied grievances.

It's his disposition to be gloomy and morose, and we give him all the latitude we can in order to keep peace with him. That scrap with Willis was an outrage. Bergen made an ass of himself and brought discredit on us all by his inexcusable conduct at the table.

"It would have been bad enough to have had two of the boys scrap in a barroom or an alley, but Bergen selected a small hotel dining room for his break, and it is a surprise to me that we were not all thrown out bag and baggage. Willis acted with rare good sense, and I feel certain that our repeated assurance that we, to a man, condemned Bergen's actions gave him the courage to take the blow and let it go at that. He is not a cur. All of us showed him that we considered him a courageous fellow and were glad to have him for a friend.

"There is no boycott on Bergen, but there is nothing cordial in our relations with him, and so he understands. He has made trouble with a good many of the boys, and we just give him a wide berth. But he's a ballplayer, and once we get into a game, personal feelings are set aside in admiration of the artist, for such he is. Will he be with Boston next year? None of us know, but we think not. He jumped the Kansas City team toward the close of the season that Selee bought him [in 1895]. He's liable to pack up and leave us when in one of his moods."[9]

Although Marty Bergen remained with Boston in 1899, his teammate's foresight regarding potential club jumping was genuinely prophetic. Bergen's behavior became more erratic following the death of his son, Martin, Jr., in April 1899.[10] The catcher's paranoia was so intense that Marty thought fellow players were purposely reminding him of his son's death for their amusement.[11] One night, when the Beaneaters were residing at the Burnet House while playing in Cincinnati, a local writer talked to Bergen, standing next to pitcher Frank Killen, about the team's pennant aspirations. After stating Boston would easily win another flag, his mood suddenly changed before declaring it would be inconsequential to him, whatever the outcome.

"Why not?" asked the writer.

"Because I won't be with this bunch much longer," was Bergen's surly reply. "I am going to quit them. I am tired of traveling with a lot of knockers and backbiters. They are all giving me the worst of it. I'll shake the gang just as soon as we get to Boston."

Marty suddenly became quiet when other players joined the group. Ten minutes later, as the writer talked to manager Frank Selee, Killen pulled Boston's pilot aside and informed him that Bergen, crying like a baby, asked not to be quoted in the newspaper. After the scribe initially promised not to report this discussion, he approached Selee, questioning what troubled the catcher.

"He is insane," said Boston's manager.[12]

Marty abandoned the team numerous times in 1899, although not permitted to do so by Selee, returning to the solace of his "Snowball Farm" in North Brookfield, Massachusetts, where he seemed most content.[13] Amid all the drama perpetuated by Bergen, Boston came home in second place with a 95-57 record, finishing eight games behind the pennant-winning Brooklyn Superbas. Vic Willis rose to star status as a hurler, going 27-8 with a 2.50 ERA. Years later, Vic gave much credit for his immediate success to troubled catcher Marty Bergen for converting him from a wild pitcher into a dominant performer.[14] Willis also secretly married Mary Minniss (Minnis) of Elkton, Maryland, after the season. The couple didn't announce their union until the following March.[15]

Before the 1900 season, a significant tragedy rocked the organization. On the morning of January 19, Marty Bergen's father, Michael, walked through the snow of his nearby farm to his son's residence. Knowing that dairy farmers always rose early, Michael Bergen became concerned upon noticing drawn shades in the house. Since both doors were closed and secure, he entered the premises by prying open a window.[16] Michael Bergen came upon a horrific scene. Marty Bergen had killed his wife and two children with an ax before cutting his own throat with a straight razor so ruthlessly while standing in front of a mirror; it almost severed his head.[17] The demented individual had murdered his 32-year-old wife, Mrs. Harriet Gaines Bergen, first before killing his five-year-old daughter Florence, and son Joe, who was three.[18]

Realizing at some point Marty Bergen's days with Boston would end, although never expected under such tragic circumstances, the Beaneaters forged ahead without the temperamental catcher. After eliminating four squads to an eight-team league in 1900, Boston slipped to fourth place, going 66-72. Vic Willis experienced a horrendous season, posting a 10-17 record with a ghastly 4.19 ERA. One writer blamed honeymooning as the reason for Willis, whom he referred to as "Granddaddy Longlegs," performing miserably in the season's early stages.[19] Although Vic pitched horribly in 1900, the brand new American League came knocking, hoping to lure him away from Boston with the promise of more money.

In January 1901, Philadelphia Athletics manager Connie Mack journeyed to Newark, eager to sign Willis. Mack offered to pay Vic $3,500, a significant increase over the $2,400 National League salary limit he had received in 1900. To seal the deal, Connie proffered Willis $450 in advance money. When Vic signed a receipt for that amount, Mack believed he had reached an agreement. Expecting his new pitcher to report for duty on April 1, Willis notified the

Athletics manager he wouldn't be arriving until April 6. On April 2, Boston team treasurer and part-owner James B. Billings visited Vic in his Newark home and pledged to match Mack's offer. Willis agreed, immediately joining the Beaneaters for spring training at Norfolk, Virginia. Connie was furious upon finding out that Vic had double-crossed him. While Mack took no legal action, Philadelphia's skipper refused to cash the $450 check he received from Vic to remit the advance payment.[20]

Willis bounced back nicely in 1901, posting a 20-17 record, supported by a 2.36 ERA, as Boston came home in fifth place. With Frank Selee leaving to manage the Chicago Cubs, the Beaneaters hired someone familiar to Vic. His former minor league skipper, Al Buckenberger, was brought in to run the team. Vic experienced a monstrous season in 1902, going 27-20 with a 2.20 ERA. Vic also led the National League in games (51), games started (46), complete games (45), innings pitched (410), and strikeouts (225). Boston moved up two spots in the race from the previous season, finishing third with a record of 73-64.

Unfortunately, such a high position and competitive baseball became things of the past. The Beaneaters slid down to the sixth spot in 1903, with a mark of 58-80. Vic crashed and burned as well, going 12-18, supported by a 2.98 ERA. Before this campaign, Willis had dipped his toes into American League waters a second time, agreeing to play for the Detroit Tigers in 1903. Once again, he walked away from that obligation when Boston matched the offer.[21] The bottom fell out in 1904, as Boston sunk into seventh place, finishing 2 ½ games above the cellar-dwelling Philadelphia Phillies. Two years after winning 27 games, Willis's record stood at 18-25. Buckenberger quickly announced that he was jumping ship to manage the Eastern League's Rochester Bronchos.[22] Initial rumors indicated first baseman Fred Tenney would be amenable to overseeing the Beaneaters if asked.[23]

"I would like to manage the Boston National League Club very much," said Tenney. "I feel that I can become a successful manager, and I feel that with our last year's team and with the new men we have secured, I can mold together a first division team."

Tenney further added that many youngsters, who secured major league experience in 1904, would play essential roles in the team's fortunes for 1905. Fred concluded by saying that while Vic Willis's previous season was rather bad, he should exhibit his best form going forward. Tenney considered the outlook for the upcoming campaign to be quite promising.[24] Boston's ownership group was previously known as the Triumvirate when James B. Billings was also a magnate. It now consisted of only Arthur Soden and William Conant, who mulled over this decision, attempting to reach terms with Fred.[25] On February 2, team president Soden announced Tenney had been hired as manager and named team captain, while longtime treasurer William H. "Billy" Rogers was appointed as Boston's business manager.[26]

With the management team now in place, the next step was assessing who would be the critical diamond contributors in 1905. A salary dispute brought about the possibility that Boston wouldn't sign a vital component of the mound corps before the season started. After drawing a $4,500 salary in 1903, Vic Willis saw that figure cut significantly to $2,400 for 1905.[27] Willis remained a holdout when the Beaneaters arrived in Charleston, South Carolina, on March 20, to begin spring training.[28] Rumors abounded that Vic might jump to play baseball for an outlaw league. Although Willis initially felt confident he would be with Boston in 1905, newspaper reports weeks before the season opened claimed that the tall hurler had inked a deal to play for the Tri-State League's Altoona Mountaineers. Altoona, along with the league's York Penn Parks, had been attempting to sign Vic for over a month.[29]

Willis had already received a reduction in pay after the 1903 campaign, from that high-water mark of $4,500 to $3,300. He couldn't understand why ownership was slicing another $900 away from his earnings. Vic took his case to National League president Harry Pulliam, futilely requesting permission to remove the monetary shackles imposed by Boston management and become a free agent. Willis wrote a letter to a Syracuse friend, explaining he would never play for the Beaneaters again.

"I beat New York, Chicago, and Cincinnati, the best teams in the league," writes Willis, "with a tail-end team behind me. I don't understand why I should be cut almost in half in salary. They'll find your Uncle Victor will not stand for it."[30]

Although Willis had pitched horribly in 1904, he still carried elite hurler status. While true, he had lost some speed; players around the league considered him a fox in the box, especially when it came to his unhittable drop pitch.[31] When Boston opened the season against New York on April 14, Willis remained unsigned. Vic's holdout didn't last much longer. Arthur Soden finally acquiesced, agreeing to pay the pitcher his figure of $3,500.[32] One month after Willis agreed to the deal, Boston writer Tim Murnane revealed an essential point about his signing. Frank V. Dunn, who was making overtures to purchase the Beaneaters, had demanded that current ownership reach an agreement with the pitcher. For Mr. Dunn, any potential deal to buy the club hinged on Vic being a positive asset in the ledger book.[33] Willis joined the club on April 21 as they prepared to open a series at Washington Park against the Brooklyn Superbas. Despite having his staff ace in tow, manager Fred Tenney said he planned on using young hurlers against Brooklyn.[34]

The previous day, newspapers revealed sad news about the Beaneaters' organization. Business manager Billy Rogers, who was in poor health, passed away on April 20 from typhoid-malaria fever at his sister's New York City home.[35] In the world of baseball wheeling and dealing, a report claimed that Superbas president Charles Ebbets had made an offer for Vic days earlier when the two teams played in Boston.[36] Tenney had a change of heart regarding his rotation for this series, sending Willis to the mound for the first time to face Brooklyn on April 25. While Vic tossed his drop ball with sublime skill and grace, Superbas batters feasted on his swift offerings, which lacked steam.[37] Brooklyn hammered Willis for 11 hits and won the game, 3-1.[38] Vic dropped his second game of the season against Philadelphia, April 29, on a rain-soaked field, as the Phillies claimed a 6-4 victory. Philadelphia did heavy damage in two innings, scoring all six runs while recording ten hits, five of which were bunts.[39]

As Boston played mediocre baseball through the season's first few weeks, plans to become a baseball executive were moving along for Frank Dunn. The latter had given present ownership a $5,000 deposit toward securing the team. Dunn had grand intentions, believing $20,000 worth of improvements to South End Grounds would make it one of the National League's best baseball plants.[40] Vic Willis lost his third consecutive start of the season against the New York Giants on those home grounds on May 4. Vic was strafed for 12 safeties as the Giants secured an easy 6-1 victory. Hurler George "Hooks" Wiltse dominated the Beaneaters, allowing two hits and striking out ten batters.[41] Willis only lasted four innings on May 8 after switching the venue for these two teams to the Polo Grounds, as Boston lost to the Giants, 9-1.[42] In his first four starts of the season, Vic had allowed 46 hits.

The Beaneaters' organization held a special event when they opposed the Chicago Cubs at South End Grounds on May 11. Boston writer Jake Morse had done diligent work putting together a benefit where Billy Rogers's widow would receive all donations.[43] Boston won the game, 5-0, as the team bequeathed a portion of the gate receipts to Rogers's family. National League president Harry Pulliam and owners Barney Dreyfuss of the Pittsburgh Pirates and Garry Herrmann from the Cincinnati Reds donated $100 to the fund. Former Beaneaters manager Frank Selee also exhibited supreme generosity, as did the entire Cubs organization. Even an individual from Winnipeg, Manitoba, who didn't know Rogers, donated five dollars. The original hope was that this fundraiser would realize $750.[44] Unfortunately, the crowd ended up being sparser than was expected.[45] Horrible spring weather had wreaked havoc on Boston's attendance throughout the campaign.[46]

Vic Willis took the bump against Chicago on May 12. Although he pitched much better, the outcome was the same. Vic battled for 11 innings before losing to the Cubs, 5-4.[47] Hard luck plagued Willis against St. Louis on May 18, as the Cardinals prevailed, 5-2. Two hits, two errors, and a walk allowed the visiting Cardinals to score four runs in the fourth inning. Boston's rally in the ninth averted a shutout.[48] Vic finally secured a victory against St. Louis on May 22, although the performance certainly couldn't be categorized as a pitching gem. Boston bombarded Cardinals' hurler John "Jack" Taylor in the early going before he settled down and was unhittable. Thanks to their early onslaught, the Beaneaters won, 6-4. Willis was credited with the victory, despite wildness and ineffective pitching, leading to his fifth-inning exit in favor of Irvin "Kaiser" Wilhelm.[49]

Vic's winning mojo didn't last long, as he dropped his following two decisions. Willis was beaten by Philadelphia, 6-0, on May 31, and succumbed in the second game of a doubleheader against New York, 8-3, on June 3. Vic pitched his best game of the season versus Chicago on June 9 at West Side Grounds. He only allowed four hits but lost the ten-inning affair, 3-2. The Cubs scored the winning tally when William "Billy" Maloney reached first on an error by Beaneaters shortstop Edward "Ed" Abbaticchio, stole second base, moved to third on Frank Chance's sacrifice bunt, and scored when John "Johnny" Evers lashed a single.[50] Willis lost his fourth consecutive game on June 13 against Pittsburgh at Exposition Park. Vic only lasted four innings, as the Pirates defeated Boston 6-0.[51] After this loss, Willis's record stood at 1-10, while seventh-place Boston was 16-33.

Compounding matters for manager Fred Tenney, aside from his team's offensive play, was that he happened to be wearing many organizational hats due to Billy Rogers's death. Tenney approached ownership in assuming the business manager's duties and volunteered to look after the money when Boston was on the road.[52] One day after losing his tenth game of the season, Vic gained revenge against Pittsburgh on June 14. Willis tossed a complete game as Boston defeated the Pirates, 5-3. The Beaneaters scored three runs in the game before recording a hit, while Pittsburgh didn't fully utilize their ten safeties.[53] This positive vibe was quickly shattered as Cincinnati defeated Vic and his teammates, 5-2, on June 17. Willis rolled along until the seventh, when two walks, two stolen bases, and two singles allowed the Reds to score three runs and take command of the game.[54]

Vic finally had an easy day at the office, defeating St. Louis, 10-2, on June 22. Thanks to no run support, Willis suffered three straight heartbreaking defeats in a row by the identical 2-1 scores. New York bested him on June 27, Philadelphia took care of business in the second game of a doubleheader on June 29, and Brooklyn defeated Vic on July 3. Realizing that the logical path to victory was by thoroughly eradicating an opponent's damage, Willis tossed a three-hit shutout two days later, on July 5. Of course, on a day Vic was unhittable, Boston's bats came to life as the Beaneaters claimed a 7-0 victory over the Superbas.[55] Willis came out on the losing end once again versus the Phillies on July 8. Philadelphia claimed a 4-3, ten-inning victory. After tying the game in the ninth frame, the Phillies scored the winning run in the tenth when John Titus singled, moved to second on a sacrifice bunt, and scored on a wild throw by Beaneaters second baseman William "Bill" Lauterborn. Umpire William "Bill" Klem tossed Boston's Ed Abbaticchio in the fourth inning for arguing over one of his calls.[56]

Willis reversed fortune in game two of a doubleheader against Cincinnati on July 12, defeating the Reds, 3-2. Vic clamped things down on the hill after walking three batters in the opening frame and then committing a balk.[57] On July 15 against St. Louis, Willis was driven from the box after the Cardinals scored six runs in the sixth inning. The bright spots for Boston, who lost 11-8, were home runs by James "Jim" Delahanty and Harry Wolverton.[58] Vic was tagged for a loss against the Cardinals, 7-4, on July 19. Lack of control in the sixth inning and a cavalcade of hits by St. Louis' batters in the seventh sunk the elongated slab artisit.[59]

As Boston's season moved into the heat of summer, local scribe Frederic P. O'Connell wrote in his *Sporting News* article that Vic Willis's performance in 1905 had been a joke. O'Connell added that Vic couldn't even secure victory in one out of every three games. The writer also declared that Willis most likely would've been pitching in an outlaw league if owners Arthur Soden and William Conant had gotten their wish. Soden and Conant initially weren't willing to give Vic one cent more than $2,400 in salary. Frank Dunn had altered this stance when he demanded that Willis be a part of the Boston organization upon purchasing the team in the fall.[60]

Vic was shelled by Pittsburgh on July 26, at South End Grounds, as the Beaneaters suffered an 8-2 defeat. After falling behind 2-0, Boston tied the score in the seventh inning before the Pirates exploded in the eighth, solving Willis and putting six runs on the scoreboard.[61] As the Beaneaters embarked on a long road trip through the league's western cities, the Boston press reported two stories of significance. The first centered on potential owner Frank Dunn's interest in bringing Hugh Duffy aboard as manager in 1906. The second piece of news accentuated the sportsmanship of Boston Americans magnate John I. Taylor for expressing interest in playing a postseason series against their National League counterpart.[62]

On July 30, in the first game of a doubleheader, Vic and Cardinals hurler Charles "Buster" Brown locked horns in a classic pitcher's duel. St. Louis scored the game's only run in the first inning on a wild pitch.[63] When August started, Boston found themselves in last place, with a 29-65 record. Willis pitched well enough to win again on August 4 but suffered defeat against Chicago, 2-1. After two singles and a long fly ball gave the Beaneaters their only run in the seventh inning, the Cubs scored twice in the eighth, thanks to two singles, a double, and an out.[64] This tough loss dropped Vic's record to 6-20.

Willis found the perfect foil for placing two games in the win column. In the first game of a doubleheader on August 7, Pittsburgh was unable to solve Vic, as Boston won the game, 3-0.[65] Willis made it two in a row against the Pirates on August 10, when he cruised to a 7-4 victory. Vic pitched the final game of the road trip against Cincinnati on August 13. The two teams couldn't complete a scheduled doubleheader as heavy rain stopped the second game. Willis lost the first contest, 7-2, as the ugly combination of hits, errors, walks, and a passed ball led to four Reds runs in the fourth inning.[66]

While the Beaneaters finished their baseball sojourn, a baseless rumor made the rounds back in Boston. Talk of the National and American leagues possibly consolidating was being bantered about, propagated by some connected to the Senior Circuit. Such a thought was ludicrous since American League president Ban Johnson would be unwilling and had the strong backing of that organization's eight owners. Americans magnate John I. Taylor certainly wasn't a proponent of such a ridiculous concept. Taylor reasoned this merger would force him to buy out the Boston Beaneaters' interests, while a hefty monetary compensation price tag would be in effect, related to rival owners.[67]

Back at the home ballpark of South End Grounds, Vic Willis tossed a shutout over Cincinnati in game one of a doubleheader on August 18, scattering eight hits, and defeating the Reds, 12-0.[68] Willis exhibited pure brilliance on the mound against St. Louis on August 22, but still lost. Although he only allowed five hits and fanned 11 batters, Vic was defeated, 1-0. Cardinals hurler Jack Taylor tripled home Michael "Mike" Grady, who had reached base on an error by Beaneaters third baseman Frederick "Fred" Raymer, for the game's only tally in the third frame.[69] Willis suffered another defeat on August 24, as Pittsburgh claimed a ten-inning contest in game two of a twin bill, 7-4. A batting surge in the tenth frame allowed the Pirates to plate three runs.[70] Vic finished off the month watching his offerings get smacked all over South End Grounds, as Chicago bolted to a 10-2 victory on August 29.[71]

As the 1905 campaign moved into September, the Beaneaters were a deeply entrenched second-division team, holding the seventh spot in the standings with a 39-83 record. A light rain shower before the game against Brooklyn on September 2 didn't hamper Willis, as he pitched marvelously, beating the last-place Superbas, 1-0. Heading into the ninth inning, Vic had only allowed a scratch single by fellow hurler John "Harry" McIntire. In the final inning, Brooklyn added two more safeties, as McIntire recorded another hit, and John Dobbs followed suit. The contest's single run came in the third inning when Boston's Ed Abbaticchio doubled and scored on Fred Tenney's single.[72]

Willis's diamond spirit was crushed again on September 7, losing a tough battle against Christy Mathewson of the New York Giants, 3-0. The game remained scoreless through six innings in this second tilt of a doubleheader at the Polo Grounds before New York added one run in the seventh inning and two more in the eighth, with Michael "Mike" Donlin's solo homer to left field being the big blow.[73] As Vic's record plummeted to 10-25, the man most responsible for him still pitching in Boston was running into roadblocks, attempting to purchase the Beaneaters. Realizing a new ballpark was essential to being competitive, Frank Dunn hoped to find a better location for his potential team. One possible piece of prime real estate, near Huntington Avenue Baseball Grounds, home of the Boston Americans, was plucked off the market when their owner, John I. Taylor, secured a lease on that land before Dunn was able to inspect the property.[74]

Back on the diamond, Vic Willis pitched the first game of a doubleheader versus New York on September 16. He was knocked out of the box in the second inning as the Giants secured a 7-1 victory.[75] One day later, Taylor stated he had agreed to his Americans facing the Beaneaters in a seven-game postseason series. An announcement also came that Frank Dunn was industriously selling stock options for the reorganized Beaneaters, with a caveat contained in the distributed prospectus stating that he would use South End Grounds as a revenue-generating amusement resort during the winter months.[76] Although rare when working the bump in 1905, enjoyment, amusement, and delight were prevalent for Willis while opposing Brooklyn in game two of a doubleheader on September 18. Vic exhibited total command the entire contest, beating the Superbas, 4-1. Umpires called the game after eight innings because of darkness.[77]

Willis took it on the cuff again on September 24, losing to St. Louis, 5-3. In his next start on September 27, Vic won a wild game over Cincinnati, 14-10. Boston's tall hurler came up short in extra innings on October 3, suffering defeat in the second game of a doubleheader against Pittsburgh at Exposition Park. The Pirates won the contest, 4-3, in the tenth inning, when Claude Ritchey doubled, moved to third base on Henry "Heinie" Peitz's sacrifice bunt, and scored on pitcher Albert "Lefty" Leifield's single.[78] Willis took the mound one final time against Brooklyn on October 6 at Washington Park. Fittingly, in keeping with the 1905 campaign's theme, Vic lost the game, 7-3. Willis was administered his lumps in massive doses, as the Superbas scored two runs on four hits in the second inning, while three more safeties and a muff by outfielder Patrick "Cozy" Dolan led to four more tallies in the sixth.[79]

On the season's last day for Boston, October 7, they split a doubleheader with Brooklyn. The Beaneaters' final position in the league race was seventh place, with a 51-103 record, 54 ½ games behind the pennant-winning New York Giants. Pitcher Vic Willis finished at 12-29 in 1905, supported by a 3.21 ERA. Willis appeared in 41 games, all starts, completed 36, and tied for the league lead by allowing 340 hits. One day after the regular season concluded, the postseason city series between the Beaneaters and Americans began on October 9. Potential new owner Frank Dunn reportedly considered betting $5,000 on the Beaneaters being victorious. Such a proposition seemed rife with folly, even before the series commenced.[80]

While most of the baseball world was enthusiastic over the upcoming World Series between the New York Giants and Philadelphia Athletics, Boston's baseball patrons experienced the treat of a battle between a seventh-place club and an American League squad that had finished fourth. Vic Willis secured victory for his Beaneaters over the Americans on October 9, 5-2. This game ended up being the only victory the National League squad achieved. The Americans won the next six contests in a series, scheduled to go a full seven games, rather than both teams fighting to see who could first be victorious four times. Willis also pitched Game Five on October 13 and lost that contest, 5-2. The squads played all seven matches at Huntington Avenue Baseball Grounds to achieve higher gate receipts.[81]

With the baseball season now completed, attention turned to who would run the show in 1906. Possible changes included both the front office and field leadership. Weeks earlier, while the Beaneaters were in Cincinnati, ready to travel to Chicago, manager Fred Tenney acknowledged that he could be preparing to find a new baseball home. Tenney's decision was based on Frank Dunn not seeming to be interested in improving the team, for which he held a purchase option.

"I feel," said Tenney, "that if A. H. Soden and W. H. Conant really retire from the control of the National League game at the South End that I would like to get out, too."

"Do you mean to quit the game?" queried the sportswriter who was talking to Tenney.

"There isn't enough money floating around to drive me off the ball field," replied Fred. "I love the game too well for that. Still, I think I have done enough for Boston to deserve a little consideration and I'd like to be permitted to choose some new stamping ground. Of course, that idea that the Boston Americans can secure me is absurd. I expect to be back in Redland [Cincinnati] next season, but, whether in Boston uniform time alone will tell."[82]

Tenney ended up returning to manage Boston in 1906. The paperwork surrounding Frank Dunn's deal to purchase the Beaneaters was due to be finalized on November 1.[83] That date passed without completing this transaction. Dunn was left in a lurch when his stock subscription plan, enticing Boston fans and business owners to partner with him, was a colossal failure.[84] The prospective owner ended up pulling out of the deal. According to Dunn's lawyer, the primary reason was a discrepancy in negotiations over the price for title to Boston's baseball grounds.

Another minor problem that arose when parties started dickering last spring was over players. Of the 18 individuals under contract at that time, Dunn demanded 14 be delivered when he took control of the organization. Of those 14, current ownership could release five throughout the year, only with Frank's blessing.

Along with Vic Willis, included on the list were fellow hurlers Kaiser Wilhelm and Irving "Irv" Young and outfielder Wirt "Rip" Cannell. If Arthur Soden and William Conant wanted to release these individuals during the season, and Frank Dunn wasn't in agreement, he would be responsible for paying the remainder of their salaries. When Frank received a letter in July requesting permission to release Young, Wilhelm, and Cannell, he refused. At season's end, Soden and Conant forwarded to Dunn a bill for the three players' salaries over the past three months, totaling $2,700. Given that Young was Boston's most effective pitcher in 1905, going 20-21, Frank believed Soden and Conant were disingenuous, neglecting their financial responsibilities.[85] Unable to enter the realm of major league baseball ownership, Mr. Dunn was sighted in early

November, assessing some theater ventures in Philadelphia that had attracted his interest.[86]

Boston not shifting to new ownership supplied some positive karma for Vic Willis. Heading into the December league meetings, the Beaneaters were in disarray, having only fifteen players on their reserve list, including three deemed to possess minor league ability.[87]

Pittsburgh Pirates manager Fred Clarke came to the rescue on December 15. Clarke immediately searched out William Conant when he arrived at the league meetings and told him he was deeply interested in acquiring Willis. When Fred offered $5,000 in exchange for the hurler, Conant countered by saying he preferred players. The two men eventually hammered out an agreement. Boston shipped Vic to Pittsburgh for first baseman George "Del" Howard, infielder David "Dave" Brain, and pitcher Vivan "Vive" Lindaman.[88] After striking this deal, Clarke claimed he based his interest in securing an agreement on the elongated slab artist's strong performances against Pittsburgh in 1905.[89]

Amid suspicions, suppositions, and rumors that he was all in or had seen better days as a player, Vic Willis set the record straight before the 1906 campaign started. Vic was confident he would enjoy immense success, pitching for a top-flight team like the Pirates.

"Many a time," said Willis, "I have worked my head off to win a game, and just when I thought I had things sewed up, someone would commit some error, for which there was no excuse seemingly, and things would go up in the air. With a team like the Pirates behind me, I believe that I will win the big percentage of my games. At least, I will do my best. Those stories sent out from Boston about my being all in were mere pipes, started by someone jealous of my good fortune in getting away from the Hub."[90]

Playing for a contender worked wonders for Willis's psyche and statistics. Vic topped the 20-victory plateau with Pittsburgh four straight seasons in 1906 (23-13, 1.73 ERA), 1907 (21-11, 2.34 ERA), 1908 (23-11, 2.07 ERA), and 1909 (22-11, 2.24 ERA). Willis also received an opportunity to play in the only World Series of his career in 1909, when the Pirates defeated the Detroit Tigers in seven games. During his four seasons with Pittsburgh, Willis lost 46 games, while he suffered 54 defeats those final two years playing for Boston.

In the period before baseball's modern era took root in 1900, when exceedingly high innings pitched numbers and twirling every day were the norms, many individuals topped Vic Willis' 29 losses in 1905, with John Coleman's 48 defeats for the 1883 Philadelphia Quakers being the highest. Willis shattered

Dummy Taylor's modern-era record when he had fashioned a mark of 18-27 for the New York Giants in 1901.

Brooklyn Superbas pitcher George Bell came closest to breaking Vic's mark when he went 10-27 in 1910. Hurler Samuel Paul Derringer tied that exercise in futility in 1933, going 7-27 while pitching for the St. Louis Cardinals and Cincinnati Reds. Vic's long productive career, which eventually gained him entry into the Baseball Hall of Fame in 1995, certainly was a mixed bag at times. Although the elongated slab artist reached "20" on the downside on three occasions, the fact that Willis achieved or surpassed that number by celebrating victories in eight different seasons cements his legitimacy as one of the Deadball Era's premier pitchers.

During his rookie campaign in 1898, Boston Beaneaters pitcher Vic Willis became involved in a confrontation with catcher Marty Bergen. The incident occurred on July 28 in the dining room of St. Louis's Southern Hotel. Bergen threatened and then slapped Willis across the face after he sat down at the catcher's table for breakfast. A press member promised to keep the incident a secret until after Boston's season concluded due to the pennant race. In this 1899 team photo, Willis is standing in the middle of the top row, with Bergen directly to his right. (Photo in the Public Domain.)

CHAPTER 6

Frank Schulte – 1911

Achieving a New Standard Beyond Those Diamond Barriers

Throughout baseball's Deadball Era, the power dynamic acted as the exception rather than the rule. As the game's modern era gained footing, many considered it a grand accomplishment when a player reached double figures in the home run department. In 1902, the Pittsburgh Pirates' Tommy Leach led the National League with six home runs. Half of Leach's four-baggers that year resulted from utilizing his speed to scamper around the bases for an inside-the-park home run. While this method and the bounce home run were instrumental toward beefing up totals for major leaguers, who topped statistical categories in the long-ball department, the true fence buster was an anomaly. Pure sluggers like Socks Seybold, Buck Freeman, and Timothy "Tim" Jordan were a rare breed in the era of small-ball tactics and situational hitting.

The magical mark of 20 home runs seemed unattainable as baseball moved into the twentieth century's second decade. This premise quickly changed in 1911, thanks to a man who snuck up on rooters when it came to being a home run slugger. In 1910, Chicago Cubs outfielder Frank M. Schulte tied Frederick "Fred" Beck of the Boston Doves for National League honors, striking ten four-baggers. Although a hard-hitter before this year, Schulte had only been credited with 17 home runs since debuting in 1904. Of those 17, ten were inside-the-park home runs, while in 1910, eight of his blasts cleared a ballpark outfield barrier on the fly. After establishing power capability that season, Frank expanded this aspect of his game to even greater heights in 1911.

Frank Schulte was born on September 17, 1882, in Cochecton, New York.[1] When Schulte became interested in baseball as a youngster, his father,

John, attempted to persuade him to abandon the game, believing it to be an unsavory profession. At 17, Frank was offered $1,000 by his dad to burn his uniform and quit baseball.[2] Ignoring this plea, Schulte gained experience performing for several teams. Frank certainly made the rounds sharpening his skills, starting by playing baseball in Glen Aubrey, New York. Schulte matriculated to Poseyville, Poseytuck, and Hickory Grove before landing with a squad in Blossburg, Pennsylvania. In 1897, Frank played for a team in Waverly, New York, and remained there for two seasons. He then hooked up with Lestershire in his home state before joining the New York State League's Syracuse Stars in 1902.[3] Schulte batted .280 his first year with Syracuse and followed that up in 1903 by hitting .294.

Frank was even better in 1904, posting a mark of .307, playing left field for manager Tobias "Sandy" Griffin's Stars. One day that season, Schulte endeared himself to Troy's fans when Syracuse played a road contest against the Trojans at the Laureate Boat Club Grounds. While chasing a fly ball during a game, Frank jumped over an 18-inch wire fence in the outfield. He grabbed the sphere while sliding down an embankment into the Hudson River. A few innings later, Schulte blasted the baseball into that river for a home run.[4]

Unfortunately, Schulte's consistency at the plate hadn't attracted much attention from major league scouts. That changed due to some splendid fortune. Needing to replace aging outfielder Jack McCarthy, Chicago Cubs scout George Huff was dispatched to Syracuse by manager Frank Selee to look over outer gardener Jake Magee (or Magie). When Huff arrived to monitor Selee's suggestion, he became sidetracked by the play of two other Stars outfielders.[5] The scout telegraphed Chicago's pilot his recommendation to immediately purchase both Schulte and fellow outfielder Michael "Mike" Mitchell. Offered less money to play for Chicago than he was making at Syracuse, Mitchell rejected this overture, threatening not to give his best effort if purchased.[6] Mike remained in the minors until joining the Cincinnati Reds in 1907.

Besides scouting for the Cubs, Huff was also the athletic director at the University of Illinois. Schulte's purchase price was $1,500, and a promise to allow Syracuse to pocket all the gate receipts in an exhibition game between the two teams after the Stars won the league championship.[7] Frank made his major league debut on September 21, 1904, and batted .286 while appearing in 20 late-season games for Chicago. Frank offered a glimpse into his immense potential in 1905, hitting .274 in 123 games.

On August 1, 1905, Cubs' first baseman Frank Chance replaced Frank Selee as the team's manager. Health concerns forced Selee to walk away from baseball. Under Chance's leadership, Chicago breezed to a National League pennant in 1906 with a 116-36 record before losing the World Series to the Chicago White Sox in six games. The Cubs repeated as National League flag winners in 1907 and 1908 and then defeated the Detroit Tigers in each World Series clash. Although Schulte established himself as one of baseball's top players in his first four full seasons, this didn't preclude Chicago's outfielder from occasionally making boneheaded plays. One of these less flattering moments occurred in 1905 against the Brooklyn Superbas.

Holding down the third base spot for Brooklyn was local product Emil "Heinie" Batch. By day, Batch contributed to the diamond cause at Washington Park. At night, Heinie operated a saloon that he owned. Besides being a drinking emporium, Batch's establishment also conducted a booming business selling clams and oysters. That season, teammate and outfielder Harry Lumley constantly boasted to Heinie about his prowess when it came to enjoying the pleasures of an oyster bar. When Chicago played a series in Brooklyn, Batch confided to Frank Schulte that he wanted to bet Lumley, his teammate, couldn't eat 150 clams. The two Superbas players set conditions where if Harry successfully polished off 150 clams while eating in Batch's bar, the house would pay his bill. Lumley accepted these terms, requesting Schulte act as the official counter.

Harry and Frank arrived at Heinie's saloon that evening to partake in the clam exhibition. Lumley was a fantastic, devouring dynamo, as he consumed more than 200 clams before calling it quits. The following afternoon, Chicago and Brooklyn resumed their series at Washington Park. In his first two trips to the plate, the left-handed-hitting Schulte was retired by the opposing hurler. His third time up, Frank hit a twisting liner off the end of the bat. Unable to gauge the ball's trajectory, Batch failed to make the play down at the hot corner, as Schulte ended up at second base with a double, representing the potential winning run. Frank then moved over to third after an out.

When Schulte reached third base, an irate Heinie, still seething about losing that bet the previous night, started talking about clams. Suspicious about possible cheating, Batch played the role of inquisitor, asking Frank how Harry Lumley possibly could have gobbled down so many clams. Schulte had offered various plausible explanations when the Superbas' hurler threw a pitch to a Cubs batter that eluded the catcher and rolled to the stands. Unaware of this miscue because he was distracted, Frank remained cemented to the third-base bag, bloviating about clams to Heinie. Frank Chance, Johnny Evers, Joseph "Joe" Tinker, and others jumped up from the bench, screaming for Schulte to head home, but he didn't hear them. When Frank finally snapped out of his trance, the catcher was back at home plate, holding the baseball. On the next pitch, Chicago's batter hit a slow roller to the pitcher. Schulte was easily tagged out as he attempted to make amends by bolting for the plate. One of Frank's most brutally embarrassing baseball moments happened because he lost focus while talking about clams.[8]

For the most part, Schulte executed smart, heady plays. In 1908, Frank acquired his "Wildfire" nickname. Schulte received this moniker related to a stage play of the same name starring actress Lillian Russell and christening one of the trotting horses he owned, "Wildfire." Known as an intelligent and witty player, Frank diversified his interests in things other than baseball. When rain postponed a Cubs game early in the 1909 campaign, Schulte angered manager Frank Chance, almost to the point of issuing a suspension, when he said: "I hope it stays this way all season."[9] Chicago failed to capture their fourth consecutive National League pennant in 1909, although they posted a 104-49 record, as the Pittsburgh Pirates copped the flag by going 110-42.

The Cubs came roaring back in 1910, winning top honors with a mark of 104-50, placing them 13 games in front of the second-place New York Giants. Frank Schulte suffered a personal tragedy during the summer of 1910. On August 29, his brother, John Schulte, Jr., was found dead in his bed at a hotel in Lestershire, New York. According to the coroner, John committed suicide by drinking carbolic acid.[10] Besides tying for circuit honors in round-trippers that year, Frank also reached the heralded .300 batting mark for the first time in his major league career, hitting .301. In the 1910 World Series, Chicago's opponent was Connie Mack's Philadelphia Athletics.

At 7:30 p.m. on October 15, a special train, including three sleeper cars, left Union Station carrying Chicago's entourage. Thousands of passionate, baseball-hungry fans had packed the terminal and surrounding streets for hours, hoping to catch a glimpse of their heroes before giving the Cubs a rousing sendoff. The train's expected arrival in Philadelphia the following afternoon was around dinnertime. Chicago's players reached the hotel and were nestled in their beds at an early hour in anticipation of starting this titanic World Series battle. The hopes and aspirations of more than two million Chicago denizens rested on the shoulders of these players.[11] Those diamond desires were crushed, as Philadelphia outscored the Cubs 35-15 and claimed the World Series, four games to one. After the series concluded, Chicago manager Frank Chance was philosophical about his squad's disappointing performance.

"I have said often enough that we wouldn't do any squealing if the Athletics beat us in the World's Series, and I don't intend to do any now," declared

Chance. "We were beaten four games out of five, and I will let the figures talk for themselves. If anyone wants to say Connie Mack has a better ball club than I have, I will let him say it, and I won't try for a comeback. The Cubs were beaten. They have been beaten before, but I think they have made a record of which anyone would be proud. They demonstrated in Saturday's game [a Game Four victory on October 22] that they wouldn't quit, and that's a big comfort. There are other years to come, and we will be on hand next season to fight our hardest and strive for the National League pennant and what comes after. I hope the Athletics will win the American League pennant next year, for I want another chance at them."[12]

As Cubs fans licked their wounds following the pasting, their team suffered at the Athletics' hands; initial off-season scuttlebutt was devoted to opposing teams' complaints regarding the visitors' quarters at Chicago's West Side Grounds. In January 1911, Cincinnati Reds manager Clark Griffith claimed conditions at the ballpark were unsanitary. Cubs owner Charles Webb Murphy offered a blustery response, attacking Griffith. An article in the *Chicago Daily Tribune* joked that Murphy should purchase expensive Turkish rugs, pricey knickknacks, and valuable paintings selected by resident team poet laureate Frank Schulte and hang them on the visiting team's locker room walls.[13]

Pittsburgh manager Fred Clarke entered the fray, offering his opinion about the accommodations at West Side Grounds. He denounced the conditions and threatened to take up the matter with National League officials. This appeal to the league only came after what he believed were unsatisfactory responses to numerous complaints about its dangerous nature after addressing the matter personally with Murphy. Fred's main concern was related to defective plumbing. In one instance the previous season, numerous Pirates players were severely burned while using the showers. Cincinnati's players' most significant criticism surrounded the clubhouse's utilization as a chicken coop during the winter. Cramped conditions were also an issue because of the addition of 20 unsanitary wooden lockers in the dressing quarters following expanded rosters beyond the league's original 15 or 16-player limit. The alleged bathroom was a dark shed tucked into a corner of the room.[14]

On January 24, Charles Murphy announced the players' quarters would be remodeled, asserting it wasn't in response to these complaints but rather planned construction. Two critical parts of the modifications were eliminating a barn, which stabled the horse that pulled the grass mower, and the frame structure used by visiting teams that Griffith had admonished.[15]

Chicago sportswriter Irving E. Sanborn offered a sobering solution relative to the verbal barrage Murphy had received from league colleagues regarding this matter.

"The only way to stop the kicking against visiting clubhouses is to abolish them and go back to the former way of having the players dress at their hotels and travel to the grounds in buses or taxis," writes Sanborn. "The American League has clung to the old-fashioned way, and one of its most potent reasons is said to be the knowledge that no other way will prevent constant airing of the ball player's grouch in the public prints."[16]

A player's grouch acting as the narrative certainly helped offset any perception surrounding a cheapskate baseball magnate. Frank Schulte most likely didn't hold this opinion about Murphy, based on the news he had signed a three-year contract in February.[17] Inner harmony didn't seem to be a premium feeling at that time when it came to Frank Chance, amid rumors the skipper was pining for California orange groves, which he owned, and experiencing general misgivings about continuing his baseball career.

"I don't want to come back, and I wouldn't if I could help it," said Chance, "but I'm still under a two-years contract with Murphy, and I will be there when the bell rings. Say, by the way, you hear a lot about Murphy being a quarrelsome man, but he is the best man I ever saw to work under. He allows me to do what I think best, and he doesn't bother me."[18]

Chicago prepared for the 1911 campaign, doing diligent training in West Baden, Indiana, where the mineral baths soothed tight muscles, and New Orleans, Louisiana. Before players embarked on the first stage of this baseball voyage, holdout outfielder Arthur "Solly" Hofman finally agreed to contract terms. A sticking point in the negotiations was Hofman's demand to be paid $400 he claimed was a promised bonus from Frank Selee upon joining the Cubs following a tryout in 1904. Charles Murphy balked at this demand during a meeting in Chicago, creating a brief stalemate before Solly ironed things out with Chance hours later.[19]

Once spring training started, it seemed to be a foregone conclusion that one member of Chicago's infield not immortalized in Franklin Pierce Adams's poem "Tinker to Evers to Chance" ("Baseball's Sad Lexicon") would be moving on. Rooters believed that either Henry "Heinie" Zimmerman or recruit James "Jimmy" Doyle would take over at third base since the Cubs had waived Harry Steinfeldt.[20] Steinfeldt eventually was sold to the American Association's St. Paul Saints on April 5.

Frank Schulte was considered one of Chicago's revered veterans as he entered his seventh full season with the club. Chance's dependable three-hole hitter was a quiet, modest, reserved individual who preferred spending downtime alone. On occasion, Schulte could be outspoken when a situation demanded a direct approach. Frank never boasted about his accomplishments and sarcastically chastised players who did. He always referred to himself in the third person as "Frank" or "Schulte" when he gave a locker room speech. He also assumed the mantle as an elder statesman during spring training, helping teach unrefined rookies proper table manners. Advice could be blunt, as was the case one time when a recruit started eating his mashed potatoes with a knife.

"What're you doing, pal," protested Schulte, "learning to plaster?"[21]

The Cubs finished their spring exhibition tour with games in the Indiana cities of Evansville and Terre Haute before jettisoning to Illinois to appear in Danville and Champaign. Chicago then returned to West Side Grounds' friendly confines, playing a few contests against college squads in preparation for hosting the season opener against the St. Louis Cardinals on April 12.[22] Schulte was in peak condition as the curtain on this season was ready to be raised. The consensus throughout the league was that Frank would vigorously beat back all challengers to his home run title this upcoming summer while also surpassing his total from the 1910 campaign.[23]

Nothing was settled on opening day as 18,000 fans packed West Side Grounds to watch their beloved Cubs. Many rooters kept a close eye on Heinie Zimmerman, replacing Harry Steinfeldt at third base. Fans were also eager to see Schulte in action for the first time in 1911. During the training session games, his work had been speedy while he sizzled at the plate and was more robust in the field than usual.[24] In this thrilling opener, Chicago and St. Louis ended up playing a 3-3 tie that umpires called after 11 innings because of darkness. Mayor-Elect Carter Henry Harrison IV started the proceedings by throwing out the first pitch. After the Cardinals grabbed a 3-0 lead, the Cubs scored a tally in the bottom of the first inning, courtesy of two doubles. Chicago's second run occurred in the sixth when Frank blasted a home run over the right-field bleachers. The Cubs tied the game in the eighth after Frank Chance reached base on an error by St. Louis shortstop Arnold Hauser and scored on Joe Tinker's two-out triple.[25]

Schulte connected for the only home run on opening day in the seven games played between both leagues.[26] In their first completed game on April 14, Chicago lost to the Cardinals, 2-1, as Schulte went 3-for-3 at the plate with a double. These two squads finished their series on April 15 by playing a second extra-inning game, which ended in a 3-3 tie. The Cubs finally placed a victory on the board when they defeated Pittsburgh, 7-2, on April 17. Chicago made it two in a row over the Buccaneers, claiming a 3-0 decision on April 18. Schulte was held in check during both games, failing to record a hit. Frank's long-ball groove returned when his team hit the road for the first time in 1911, playing St. Louis at Robison Field on April 20. In the first frame, Schulte sent two teammates across home plate ahead of him with an inside-the-park homer off Cardinals hurler Roy Golden, helping set the stage for Chicago's 9-5 victory.[27]

Three days later, Frank connected for another home run against Golden. This one was a conventional, solo blast in the fourth inning, as the Cubs defeated St. Louis, 7-0. Early season returns indicated Schulte was determined to establish a new home run record in 1911. Frank's strong hitting had been instrumental in breaking up many games to his team's advantage. Schulte claimed his batting eye was sharper than when the previous season ended, and he was judging the baseball better than at any time in his career.[28] Fluidity to the Cubs' diamond machine became wrenched when first baseman Frank Chance sprained his ankle while sliding into home plate during the sixth inning of a game against Cincinnati at the Palace of the Fans on April 26.[29]

Chicago slumped a bit following Chance's injury, losing their way and dropping three straight games before beating Pittsburgh, 6-4, on April 30. Pitching had been erratic, with Edward "Ed" Reulbach exhibiting wildness as he always did when the season started. Adding to the mound problems was 1910 pitching phenom Leonard "King" Cole being unavailable due to recovering from malaria.[30] When April ended, the Cubs were in fourth place with a 9-6 record, 2 ½ games behind the league-leading Philadelphia Phillies. Although Frank Schulte was batting .365 and slugging at a .712 clip, this didn't mean he was exempt from angering his manager. Schulte was fined $50 by Chance following the game against St. Louis on April 22 for loafing running to first base after hitting a lazy fly ball and not reaching second when it was dropped by outfielder George "Rube" Ellis.[31]

The long-ball well ran dry for Frank as the season entered May, and Chicago exhibited a Jekyll-and-Hyde persona throughout the month. After winning consecutive games against Cincinnati on May 3 and 4, the Cubs dropped their next five contests. They embarked on a trip through the East in a crippled condition. A wrenched ankle sidelined Frank Chance while Heinie Zimmerman battled a cold he had contracted from playing games in frigid weather. Solly Hofman was also hobbling around after being struck with a pitched ball on his troublesome knee. These maladies paled compared to the unfortunate affliction bothering second baseman Johnny Evers. He suffered a mental collapse which forced him to leave a game against the Reds on May 4.[32]

In Troy, New York, rest at his home was prescribed for Evers to heal his frayed nerves hopefully. Over the past six months, concerns and worries over numerous things acted as a catalyst toward landing the discouraged star player sick at home in bed.[33] Johnny's main problem stemmed from issues surrounding his fledgling business venture, through ownership of shoe stores, compounded by being a high-strung individual who placed immense pressure on himself while performing at a lofty level on the diamond.[34] Evers had saved his money and invested in two shoe stores, one in Chicago and the other in Troy. In a year, this business venture wiped out his entire life savings of $16,000. Exacerbating this situation were other unfortunate events such as poor health, an injured ankle, figuring in a fatal automobile accident, and the death of Cleveland pitcher and close friend Addie Joss, who passed away from meningitis on April 14, 1911.[35]

On a positive note for the Cubs, Ed Reulbach concluded his wild streak on the mound. Reulbach reasoned that understanding each National League hitter's weaknesses was causing him to overthink rather than just firing the ball over home plate. Chance suggested Ed forget opponents' weaknesses and concentrate instead on throwing strikes.[36] Chicago ended their five-game losing streak on May 11, pounding New York, 9-3, at Hilltop Park, as Frank Schulte broke out of a minor slugging drought by hitting his first home run in more than two weeks.[37]

Chicago reeled off three more consecutive victories before losing two tight games to the Brooklyn Superbas, by scores of 3-2 on May 16 and 1-0 the next day. In the loss on May 17, Zimmerman was ejected from the game by umpire James "Jim" Johnstone for sitting on Jacob "Jake" Daubert after Cubs catcher John "Johnny" Kling made a wild throw when Brooklyn's first baseman attempted to steal second base.[38] Following this loss against the Superbas, Chicago was unstoppable throughout the remainder of May, going 8-1 the rest of the month. On May 18, the Cubs crushed Philadelphia at National League Park, 11-2. Phillies players Michael "Mickey" Doolin, Franz Otto Knabe, and Sherwood "Sherry" Magee were all ejected in the eighth inning by umpire John "Jack" Doyle for arguing his decisions.

Known as a rowdy individual during his playing days, Doyle was confronted by about 1,000 angry Philadelphians once the game ended. The quick deployment of police officers assisted the umpire's escape from the mob. Outraged fans hurled cushions at Jack, with two striking him but causing no injury before law enforcement escorted the arbitrator to a subway entrance behind the Phillies' bench.³⁹ Frank Schulte connected for a two-run blast in the eighth inning off pitcher William Edward "Eddie" Stack on May 19, as Chicago defeated Philadelphia, 7-2. Frank suddenly became locked in a clouting groove, for Deadball Era standards, as he went yard again a day later. Schulte blasted his sixth home run of the season off hurler Earl Moore, with no runners on base, as the Cubs prevailed over the Phillies, 7-4.

Despite the team playing solid baseball, everything wasn't rosy in Chicago's camp. Concern flourished over Johnny Evers's condition, which hadn't improved since his nervous breakdown. Mounting problems and suffering from a cold also caused Chance to almost collapse from exhaustion before the Phillies series began. Hot weather helped the cold break, and doling out fines was a tonic for his troubles. Chicago's manager forced King Cole to fork over $200, while fellow hurler Orville "Orlie" Weaver coughed up $100 for violating disciplinary rules. Chance then gave half of Cole's fine to pitcher Mordecai "Three Finger" Brown, who bailed out his teammate when King's booze-soaked body weakened in the game against Philadelphia on May 20. The Cubs' manager explained that Cole would receive a $600 bonus if he won sixty percent of his outings, so Brown deserved some of that money for helping him out.⁴⁰

Although he didn't smack a home run against the Boston Rustlers on May 24, Frank Schulte contributed to Chicago's 4-2 victory. In the top of the ninth inning, with the score tied 2-2, Heinie Zimmerman's single was followed by Jimmy Sheckard's double before Schulte drove home the winning runs, blasting a triple.⁴¹ Frank failed to record a round-tripper in the Cubs' final three games of the month. Schulte's home run total stood at six, while he was hitting .290 as the season entered June. Chicago currently was in third place with a 23-14 record, one game behind league-leading New York.

Schulte broke open another game as the Cubs battled the Giants in a contentious contest at West Side Grounds on June 3. Umpire Malcolm "Mal" Eason tossed Chicago's Heinie Zimmerman and Three Finger Brown, as well as David "Beals" Becker, Arthur "Bugs" Raymond, and John "Chief" Meyers from New York, for disputing calls.⁴² With the bases loaded in the eighth inning and the score tied, 4-4, Frank strode to the plate and crushed a pitch from Richard "Rube" Marquard into the right-field bleachers for a grand slam homer that secured an 8-4 Cubs victory.⁴³ His drive cannonaded off the ballpark's electric scoreboard.⁴⁴ While relaying opinions held by Philadelphia's players during a clubhouse fanning bee about National League performers, in his article for the *Philadelphia Times*, Chandler Richter claimed the Phillies characterized Schulte as the circuit's most indifferent man.⁴⁵

On June 11, Johnny Evers saw his first action in over a month as a defensive replacement at second base for Heinie Zimmerman, who smacked two homers and drove in nine runs.[46] After giving it the old college try as Chicago defeated Boston, 20-2, Evers didn't return to the lineup permanently until September 2. In Johnny's absence, rookie Jimmy Doyle had played good baseball at third base when Zimmerman shifted to second. Indeed, the winds of change were howling through the organization. Longtime catcher Johnny Kling had been involved in an eight-player deal with the Rustlers on June 10. After playing for Boston that day, Kling then balked at consenting to the transfer, although the decision to join his new squad circumvented that stance.[47] Kling accepted his fate a few days later.

Further changes were imminent due to the condition of the man known as the "Peerless Leader." After returning to his first base position on May 6, Frank Chance had been sidelined a second time since month's end. On June 12, an announcement came that Chance was dealing with two health issues. The first surrounded the effects of being beaned about 38 times throughout his career, forcing him out of the lineup due to headaches. During an examination one day earlier by team physician Dr. T. A. Davis, he discovered a second problem regarding a shooting pain in Frank's right foot. Dr. Davis prescribed treatment for this nerve issue, which had also plagued Chance two years earlier.[48] While Chance refused to believe his playing days could be over, Chicago's manager admitted that instances arose when his eyes could not see a pitched ball clearly.[49] The Cubs' skipper only appeared in two more games during the remainder of the 1911 campaign.

Frank Schulte's grand slam home run on June 3 was his only long hit of the month. This power outage didn't preclude Schulte from impacting games. Frank's mad dash for the plate in the eighth inning of a contest against the Phillies on June 18 sent the West Side Grounds' patrons home happy, as it gave Chicago a 4-3 victory. Trailing 3-2, the Cubs rallied on two singles, a double, and Frank's daring theft of home plate. Philadelphia objected to how Schulte pilfered home, claiming batter David "Dave" Shean interfered with the pitched ball.[50] The visitors vehemently complained about the decision in a rowdy fashion before manager Charles "Red" Dooin officially protested the game.[51]

On June 26, Frank engaged in a fulfilling endeavor that transcended diamond activities. Schulte married 29-year-old Mabel Kirby, who resided in Chicago.[52] The ceremony at 4:00 p.m. was performed by Reverend Walter H. McPherson at the bride's home at 4157 Indiana Avenue. That night, the groom left with his teammates on a 10:15 train bound for St. Louis. Mabel, figuring the Cubs players would subject her husband to kidding and ribbing because of the nuptials, planned on joining Frank the following day.[53] Schulte had met Miss Kirby two years earlier when she attended a box party at West Side Grounds. Frank traveled alone the morning of the wedding to secure a marriage license at the county clerk's office. Friend J. N. Bailey performed the duties as best man, while Mabel's aunt, Mrs. D. Dobson, acted as bridesmaid, with only immediate family attending the ceremony.

While discussing Schulte's wedding in his article for the *Chicago Daily Tribune*, a writer, who used the penname, Handy Andy, discussed a vital baseball matter related to the Chicago right fielder's long-ball prowess. This scribe declared that carelessness by umpires or official scorers had robbed Frank of three home runs in 1911.[54] Sidelined manager Frank Chance hoped his hard-hitting slugger would break the home run record with assistance from his new bride.[55] While Chicago was in Cincinnati for a series; Chance collapsed after playing in the game on June 30. The diagnosis was a small blood clot formed due to being plunked in the head earlier in the year by a pitch thrown by Reds hurler George Suggs. Chance ignored suggestions to take a relaxing three-week vacation, opting instead to continue managing his team. Frank did promise not to play until the pain in his head subsided.[56]

Schulte's one-month power slump finally ended in the morning game of a July 4 doubleheader at West Side Grounds against the Reds. Frank connected for a grand slam home run off of hurler Robert "Bobby" Keefe in the third inning as the Cubs cruised to an 8-3 victory.[57] The afternoon nightcap was called by agreement after ten innings, with the score tied 2-2, so both teams could catch a train.[58] Schulte didn't launch another four-bagger until July 15, when he smacked his ninth homer of the season, as Boston won a wild affair over Chicago, 17-12. Married life seemed to be agreeing with Frank as Chance had hoped. Chicago's right fielder belted his tenth home run of the season on July 18. Schulte connected for yet another grand slam as the Cubs beat the Rustlers, 14-6.[59]

Third baseman Jimmy Doyle was Chicago's long-ball hero on July 19. His two-run blast over South End Grounds' left-field fence in the eleventh inning secured a 5-3 win.[60] One day later, Frank assumed that role when his solo blast in the eighth frame was the deciding factor as the Cubs defeated Philadelphia, 4-3. Schulte also added a double and a triple to his resume.[61] Home runs 12 and 13 were smacked in a doubleheader against Boston on July 26 at West Side Grounds. Frank blasted a solo four-bagger in the first inning of game one off Rustlers pitcher William "Bill" McTigue, as Chicago prevailed, 4-1. This trip to the plate ended up being the only time Schulte utilized his bat, as he drew three passes. Frank launched a solo shot in the fifth against Herbert "Hub" Perdue in the second game, with the Cubs breezing to a 7-2 victory.

Schulte finished July with a total of six homers for the month. As the season entered August, his average stood at .318. Chicago was the league pacesetter with a 56-33 record, putting them 1 ½ games ahead of second-place New York. As the campaign entered its stretch drive, pundits pondered the possibility that Buck Freeman's mark of 25 home runs in 1899, while playing for the Washington Senators, was attainable by either Frank or Phillies first baseman Frederick "Fred" Luderus, who had smacked 14 round-trippers. One writer alleged the new cork-cored baseball contributed to an offensive influx in the National League. In assessing both players, this scribe said Schulte and Luderus utilized similar stances from the left side of the plate, laying back with the bat on their shoulders, before pouncing on an offering and pulverizing it with a heavy swing. The writer also believed Frank was more graceful than Fred.[62]

Luderus only hit two more home runs in 1911, while Frank Schulte continued his assault on Freeman's mark. Frank launched his fourteenth homer of the season during an 8-5 loss against Brooklyn on August 5.[63] The big story from this game was a confrontation between Frank Chance and shortstop Joe Tinker. Chance admonished Tinker after failing to pursue Jake Daubert's pop fly in the sixth inning, leading to two Superbas runners scoring. When he finished taking his oral medicine, Joe responded: "If you don't like my fielding, why don't you send someone else out there?" Chicago's manager obliged, replacing him with Dave Shean. Following consultation with owner Charles Murphy after the game, Chance announced he had fined Tinker $150 for insubordination and indifferent play. He also suspended him for the remainder of the season.[64]

Chance remitted the fine and lifted the suspension the following day after he and Tinker were brought together at team offices and aired their grievances. Frank announced that Joe would return to Chicago's lineup the following afternoon.[65] While local fans had some gossip to chew on, the Cubs were beaten by Brooklyn, 6-1, on August 6. The team averted a shutout when Schulte smacked the ball over the right-field fence in the third inning.[66] Tinker was an energetic dynamo upon returning to the lineup on August 7. Joe struck two singles, a double, a triple, stole home, and drove home four runs against Christy Mathewson as the Cubs prevailed over New York, 8-6.[67]

Schulte's hot home-run bat continued smoking in a 9-1 victory over St. Louis on August 12. His first blast, a two-run shot in the first inning off Cardinals hurler William "Bill" Steele, was categorized as the longest ever at West Side

Grounds, clearing an 80-foot signboard in right field. Frank's three-run moonshot in the second ascended above netting that protected the ballpark's right-field bleachers.[68] This round-tripper gave Schulte 17 homers in 1911, breaking the modern-era record of 16 held by Sam Crawford (in 1901 with the Cincinnati Reds) and Socks Seybold (as a member of the Philadelphia Athletics in 1902). When the Cubs played their next game on August 16, Schulte cleared the bases in front of him when he crushed a fourth-inning grand slam into the center-field bleachers.[69] Frank also smacked a double and finished with five RBIs for the second game in a row, after receiving a day off, as Chicago was victorious, 13-6.

On August 17, Schulte clouted his nineteenth home run of the year, a two-run, ninth-inning blast off Hub Perdue, although Chicago lost to Boston, 12-8.[70] One of the largest crowds at South End Grounds in more than two years witnessed the Cubs thrash the Rustlers, 16-8, on August 19. Frank connected for his twentieth home run when he crushed an offering from pitcher Alonzo "Al" Mattern in the fourth inning, with two teammates on base.[71] Having reached the heralded achievement of 20 home runs, expectations ran high that Schulte could surpass Buck Freeman's mark. While Frank received praise in many circles, Heinie Zimmerman was the latest player to feel Frank Chance's wrath, being suspended and fined $100 for listless play. Like the Joe Tinker situation, this threat lacked teeth, as Zimmerman was in the lineup the following day.[72]

A funny thing happened on the way to the forum in his quest to supplant Mr. Freeman. Frank Schulte fell short, only mustering two homers during the season's final six weeks. When the campaign entered September, Chicago held the second position in the standings with a 67-44 record, putting them 2 ½ games behind the Giants. In the first game of a doubleheader on September 7, Schulte's twenty-first home run of the season helped lead the Cubs to a 3-0 victory over Cincinnati. Frank connected for a two-run blast in the first inning against Reds hurler Harry Gaspar. In game two of the twin bill, Schulte's two-run single in the eighth sewed things up as Chicago triumphed, 4-2.[73] His gargantuan game one four-bagger careened off an advertising sign in the right-field bleachers. Johnny Evers, back in the lineup since the beginning of September, did excellent work at the plate and in the field.[74]

Although Frank cooled off over the next few weeks chasing history, newspaper articles proclaimed baseball fans across the country were rooting for the Cubs' outfielder. The topic regarding Schulte's favorite diversion away from the diamond also found its way into print. Even when Chicago played road games, Frank excitedly met with horse dealers, hoping to sell him beautiful trotters. Back in Syracuse, Schulte owned a stable of very fast trotters. He always enjoyed driving his favorites around the state fairgrounds racetrack in a racing sulky.[75] When it came to smacking four-bagger number 22 on September 27 against New York, Frank performed in grand style. The Cubs easily won the game at West Side Grounds, 8-0. Schulte hit a single and two doubles besides his home run. Frank's final round-tripper of the season occurred in the fourth inning after teammate Jimmy Sheckard singled and moved to second on a wild pitch.[76]

Chicago made it two in a row over the pace-setting Giants on September 28, 2-1, as King Cole outdueled Christy Mathewson.[77] This victory cut New York's lead to 5 ½ games. Possibilities of closing that gap further were dashed on September 30. The Giants' Lawrence "Larry" Doyle started things off nicely, connecting for a first-inning home run against Chicago's Three Finger Brown. New York went on to defeat the Cubs, 3-1.[78] Frank Schulte scored Chicago's only run in the fifth frame when he walked, moved to third on Joe Tinker's single, and scored on a double steal when Giants catcher Chief Meyers dropped the return throw from second baseman Larry Doyle.[79] New York pushed their lead back to 7 ½ games by defeating the Cubs, 5-0, on October 1.

Chicago never challenged again, finishing the season in second place with a 92-62 record, 7 ½ games behind the pennant-winning Giants. Schulte played his final contest of the campaign on October 9 against Pittsburgh at West Side Grounds. Frank went 3-for-4 at the plate and smacked a tenth-inning single that drove home Sheckard with the deciding run, as the Cubs claimed a 6-5 victory.[80] Schulte wasn't available for Chicago's last contest on the road against Cincinnati on October 12 because his automobile, which he was driving out in the country, broke down. While Frank's not arriving in time for the game caused some angst, he exhibited a calm, calculating demeanor surrounding the situation.

"Yes," said Schulte, "I was taking a spin in my machine, and it broke down on me. I was anchored up in the country, and it was the last game of the season. You didn't think I was going to get me a new machine just to get to the last game, did you?"[81]

A new automobile was in Frank's future, thanks to exciting news one day earlier on October 11. That night, an announcement confirmed that Schulte and the Detroit Tigers' Ty Cobb would be awarded vehicles from the Chalmers Motor Company after being voted as the players in each league most valuable to their team by a committee of newspapermen.[82] Commission chairman Ren Mulford, Jr., revealed that Frank had secured 29 points in the voting, while Cobb was a unanimous choice, earning a perfect score of 64.[83] Chicago White Sox pitcher Ed Walsh finished as runner-up to Ty in the American League, while the Giants' Christy Mathewson placed second behind Frank in the National

League.⁸⁴ One day after learning the news, Schulte, in a gesture of civic pride, started a movement in favor of buying Walsh a car and immediately donated $25 to the fund.

The itinerary called for Frank to receive his automobile during the city series between the Cubs and White Sox.⁸⁵ Cubs owner Charles Murphy had kept his intentions regarding this series close to the vest until New York eliminated his team from pennant contention.⁸⁶ Things didn't go so well for Murphy's boys in this postseason clash, as the White Sox demolished the Cubs in four straight games, with Ed Walsh doing the honors securing the series for the White Sox on October 18.⁸⁷ Walsh's team cruised through the Chicago City Series, winning the fourth and final contest, 7-3.⁸⁸ Following the game, Ed's teammates agreed to chip in to purchase their star hurler a brand new car. Schulte's initial movement to start a similar fund had received a tepid response.⁸⁹ When Game Four originally began on October 16 but was called off in the first inning because of rain, Frank received his automobile before the contest started.⁹⁰

Schulte and his wife motored from Chicago to their Syracuse home in his new vehicle.⁹¹ The couple spent little time there since Frank had sold his business interest in that city and planned on making Chicago their permanent home.⁹² Schulte's final unofficial stat line for 1911 read that he had smacked 22 home runs, connected for 21 triples, and hit 29 doubles.⁹³ Schulte claimed statistics shorted him two home runs, one of which was witnessed by thousands of people in Chicago as the baseball sailed over the fence. When National League secretary John Heydler released the official numbers, Frank lost another four-bagger due to adjustments. A homer he had hit on May 11 against New York was changed to a double and an error, leaving him with a final tally of 21 round-trippers and 30 doubles.⁹⁴ Four of those homers were grand slams. Schulte also batted .300 for the season, knocked in 107 runs, and stole 23 bases.

Frank was unable to duplicate this historic year in 1912. Although he smacked 12 home runs, Schulte's average plummeted to .264. Chicago's season began under a pall of tragedy as crackerjack third baseman Jimmy Doyle passed away on the evening of February 1. Following an operation for acute appendicitis at St. Joseph's Hospital in Syracuse on January 29, Doyle succumbed when complications developed two days later, and his condition became quite serious.⁹⁵ Jim had done brilliant work for the Cubs in 1911, appearing in 130 games and batting .282.

An old nemesis caused problems for Frank Schulte during the 1912 season's latter stages. When Frank first broke in with the Cubs, he tended to drink too much. One time, Schulte was the object of Frank Chance's fury because some players were out partying while the team was in Cincinnati. Although he was only drinking in the hotel bar, Frank accepted his terse reprimand from Chance upon walking through the lobby. Never feeling that concealment of behavior was proper, Schulte had refused an offer from sportswriter Hugh Fullerton to whisk him away in a freight elevator, so the Cubs' player could avoid detection. Although Frank had curbed his drinking habits the past two years, a problem again arose in Cincinnati on September 7, 1912, while imbibing with some friends.[96] Trouble arose for Schulte when Chance encountered him at a late hour at the team hotel.[97]

The following day, after appearing on the field for practice, the Cubs' manager informed Frank he was suspended without pay for the remainder of the season for failing to observe the liquor clause in his contract. Schulte went to the clubhouse, took off his uniform, and prepared to return to Chicago.[98] There was no bitterness between the two, as the Cubs' outfielder admitted to his wrongdoing, acknowledging he deserved to receive such punishment.[99] As had been the case on many occasions in 1911 with other players, Frank Chance rescinded Schulte's suspension and reinstated him on September 17.[100] When discussing drinking, Schulte gave a unique explanation justifying that behavior. "My mother used to say to me: 'Frank, my boy, any time you want a little drink, you go out and take it,'" related Schulte. "And you know I could never have the heart to disobey my mother."[101]

Frank Schulte didn't reside at the top of the home run mountain for long. In 1915, the Philadelphia Phillies' Clifford "Gavvy" Cravath clouted 24 round-trippers, breaking Schulte's modern-era record for most home runs in a single season. George Herman "Babe" Ruth surpassed that mark in 1919, blasting 29 homers for the Boston Red Sox, before taking the standard for long-ball prowess to a new level in the 1920s with the New York Yankees. Other home-run hitters such as Roger Maris, Sammy Sosa, Mark McGwire, and Barry Bonds later surpassed Ruth when it came to being single-season, record-breaking power brokers.

Before Frank's grand 1911 season, Buck Freeman smacked 25 home runs in 1899, while Edward "Ned" Williamson of the Chicago White Stockings had swatted 27 in 1884. Schulte undoubtedly was one of the supreme heavy hitters from his era, breaking around fifty bats each season.[102] One time during his heyday, Frank felt unappreciated, seeing a newspaper headline that read–"Cubs Win 4-3, Tinker to Evers to Chance." Further down in the story, in small print, it mentioned that Frank Schulte had hit a home run with the bases loaded.[103]

Nobody could expect anything less from the slugger known as Wildfire.

Frank Schulte became the first modern era player to top 20 home runs in a single season when he smacked 21 four-baggers for the Chicago Cubs in 1911, establishing the single-season record in that category. According to unofficial statistics released at season's end, Frank had blasted 22 home runs, before National League secretary John Heydler adjusted that figure. Schulte claimed statistics shorted him two round trippers, including one that was witnessed by thousands of Chicago baseball fans. (Photo in the Public Domain.)

CHAPTER 7

John Owen "Chief" Wilson – 1912

Flying Under the Radar Into Baseball's Record Books

Throughout baseball history, there have been many individuals who didn't readily garner press attention, although they worked each day diligently, perfecting their diamond craft. Putting in maximum effort and accomplishing great things while quietly toiling in the background wasn't always the recipe for exposure when bombastic and eccentric players were at a writer's beckoning call, supplying material with their words or deeds. During baseball's Deadball Era, many earnest players, acting as catalysts for their respective teams, saw the game's characters gain headlines through their oddball or demonstrative behavior. Like Pittsburgh Pirates outfielder John Owen Wilson, some were quite content with silently lurking in the shadows, providing consistency each day. Doing so in 1912, Wilson mounted an assault establishing a new hitting mark for striking triples.

Attracting attention that season in Pittsburgh was challenging for any player looking to gain name recognition. Perennial batting champion Honus Wagner still played shortstop for the Pirates. Fred Clarke attempted to manage exclusively from the bench in 1912 without playing, and highly touted hurler Martin "Marty" O'Toole began his first entire season with the team after a highly publicized acquisition in 1911. Not being the center of attention was just fine with Wilson, a man of few words who methodically went about his business each day on the ballfield, coaxing Pittsburgh to victory.

Wilson, who answered to his middle name of Owen, was born August 21, 1883, on a farm about five miles from Austin, Texas. Like many Texas youngsters, Owen gravitated toward baseball. In 1903, Wilson started playing semi-professional ball near his hometown.

Standing six feet one inch and possessing a sturdy physique, Owen aspired to be a pitcher, but an injury forced him to alter those plans when he hurt his arm in 1904. Although Wilson was a reasonably good hurler, the strain to continue on the mound became impossible because his arm failed to round into shape following the injury. Although disappointed over his plight, Owen refused to sulk, switching to the outfield instead since he had always been an accomplished hitter.

Wilson began his professional baseball career in 1905, playing for the Texas League's Austin Senators. After spending about a month and a half with the Senators, Owen moved to that league's Forth Worth Panthers team. Wilson remained with Forth Worth until August 1907, when he made the jump to a higher minor league classification, joining the Southern Association's Little Rock Travelers. Owen's career with Little Rock only lasted about a week due to an odd circumstance unearthed through an opposing team's diligent observation.[1]

Shortly after Wilson became a member of the Travelers, managed by Michael "Mickey" Finn, they played a game against the Memphis Egyptians. In the eighth inning, with Memphis leading, 2-1, Finn sent Wilson up to bat with runners on first and second base. Owen connected against an offering, blasting a triple that cleared the sacks, as Little Rock won the game, 3-2. After the contest ended, Memphis management asked the simple question: "Who is this fellow Wilson, anyway?"

The Egyptians counted the players on Little Rock's team and found that with Owen Wilson included, the Travelers' roster stood one over the league limit at 21. Memphis lodged a protest, which the league rejected, but they still ordered Mickey Finn to reduce his roster by one player to comply with the 20-man limit. The man cut loose from the squad was Wilson when Finn farmed him out to the Western League's Des Moines Champs. Had Owen not blasted that triple against Memphis, costing him a place on the team, he possibly may have remained inconspicuous, continuing to earn a paycheck with the Travelers.[2]

This transfer ended up being a huge blessing in disguise. In September 1907, Pittsburgh Pirates star outfielder and manager Fred Clarke traveled to Des Moines, Iowa, to see his ill father. While visiting his former home, Clarke was approached by various baseball fans telling him about an outfielder on the local team possessing immense talent. Fred smiled politely as he always did when receiving such tips on players. Pittsburgh's manager finally decided to scout Wilson after receiving many glowing recommendations. One glance watching him perform on the diamond convinced Clarke, who wired Pirates owner Barney Dreyfuss, requesting he immediately make a deal to purchase J. Owen Wilson of Des Moines.[3]

Pittsburgh was able to procure Owen Wilson, even though Mickey Finn had attempted to hide him in Des Moines while looking for a way to bring the young outfielder back to Little Rock. As Wilson prepared to join the Pirates for spring training in 1908 at Hot Springs, Arkansas, he and veteran Tommy Leach were the team's final outfielders to sign contracts.[4] When Pittsburgh began the regular season, Fred Clarke penciled Owen into the lineup as the squad's starting center fielder. Wilson received a nickname during his rookie campaign, courtesy of Honus Wagner, that he carried with him throughout his major league career. While the Pirates were in Chicago, Owen and Honus attended a Wild West Show. Noticing that his well-tanned Texas teammate resembled one of the act's Indian chiefs, Wagner gave Wilson the moniker of "Chief."[5]

Besides possessing great potential, Chief Wilson also endeared himself to manager Fred Clarke for another reason. One day early in the season, Wilson picked up a rope during a rain delay and exhibited his proficiency with the lariat. Clarke stared with envious eyes, watching his young player display consummate skill with the lasso. Such ability impressed Pittsburgh's manager, who resided at his farm and ranch in Winfield, Kansas, in the off-season. Clarke had dressed as a rustler from the Old West's rough and wild days when participating in past team field days' events. In a baseball sense, diamond contemporaries viewed Owen as a level-headed young man. The basis for his inclusion on the roster was solid batting during spring exhibition games.[6]

Owen's work in the field was exemplary from the first moment he pulled on a Pirates uniform. Wilson was a solid ballhawk who possessed a cannon-like arm. Unfortunately, hitting was a problem throughout his maiden season in the National League, as Chief only batted .227 in 1908.[7] Owen primarily labored at the plate early in the campaign. Despite struggling, Wilson never pouted, moped, or insinuated terrible luck was the culprit. Clarke, deeply impressed with his young outfielder's positive, even-keel attitude, exhibited extreme patience.[8] Pittsburgh fans at Exposition Park weren't quite so forgiving. Before a game against the Brooklyn Superbas on May 20, Owen's batting average stood at .125. When Chief connected for a single during that contest, he received the usual derisive mock cheers from the right-field grandstand inhabitants.

Confidence in the rookie's ability aside, Clarke relegated Wilson to the bench for two games.[9] Owen's big turnaround occurred on June 4, when Pittsburgh's manager shifted him to right field. At the time this change happened, Chief was batting .150. Less pressure playing a less demanding outfield position helped elevate Wilson's hitting, as he raised his average out of the batting doldrums, reaching .209 on June 26. Although Owen only banged out 120 safeties in 1908, with a tiny 18 going for extra bases, he exhibited timely clutch hitting, driving in 43 runs. Chief was also well-liked by his teammates.[10] Such growing pains were more tolerable when playing for a talented pennant contender. Pittsburgh tied for second place in 1908 with a 98-56 record. This final mark put them one game behind the pennant-winning Chicago Cubs, who wrecked Pittsburgh's flag aspirations with a 5-2 victory on October 4 at West Side Grounds.

These two teams reversed spots in 1909, as the Pirates claimed the National League flag, finishing 6 ½ games ahead of the Cubs, with a record of 110-42. Pittsburgh then defeated Ty Cobb and the Detroit Tigers in the World Series, four games to three, as rookie phenom hurler Charles "Babe" Adams secured three victories for the Pirates. Owen Wilson's rapid development continued, batting .272 for the season, although he only hit .154 in the World Series. Pittsburgh fell to third place in 1910, as Wilson put together another solid season, hitting .276. Owen experienced a breakout year in 1911, as power became part of his repertoire. Wilson batted .300 and smacked 12 home runs, one more round-tripper he had hit in the previous three seasons combined. Chief also tied Chicago's Frank Schulte for the league lead in RBIs, with 107. Wilson led all National League right fielders with a .976 fielding percentage while being credited with 20 assists.

The Pirates placed third in 1911, with a mark of 85-69. One big reason the Pirates finished 14 ½ behind the pennant-winning Giants was their 6-16 record against New York. That year, star shortstop Honus Wagner won the eighth and final batting crown of his illustrious career, pacing the league with a .334 average. Before the campaign's closing series against the Cubs at West Side Grounds, manager Fred Clarke sent second baseman John "Jack" Miller home to Kearny, New Jersey, with instructions to undergo an operation and fix an ailment that had plagued him the entire season.

Miller, nicknamed "Dots," as well as "Jack," had burst brightly on the scene in 1909, hitting .279 in his rookie campaign. Jack suffered a sophomore slump in 1910, batting a paltry .227, before rebounding in 1911 with a .268 average while also driving home 78 runs. Although Clarke felt Miller was one of the greatest young players in major league baseball, Pittsburgh's manager understood that one major flaw hampered his second baseman.

"Jack has only one fault," said Fred at the end of the 1911 season, "and that is nervousness. By that I do not mean that he is afraid of anything, but he is young, and the importance of his task preys on his mind a bit. Of course, that will all wear off as he gets older, and he will be one of the greatest second basemen in the business."[11]

Although Clarke was one of Miller's most ardent supporters, this didn't prevent hot stove scuttlebutt over the winter from suggesting a change at second base could be in order; with Alexander "Alex" McCarthy or William "Bill" McKechnie as possible candidates. For whatever reason, Dots wasn't very popular with Pittsburgh's patrons, who believed he lacked class as a diamond performer and felt it would serve the team well to move him elsewhere.[12] Another topic for off-season discussion centered on Clarke's contract expiring when the campaign ended in October. Pirates owner Barney Dreyfuss had always treated his field general and friend generously regarding salary, thought to be the league's highest in past years. Confidence abounded among rooters that Fred would be back in 1912 because of this indispensable relationship.

Stories about Pittsburgh's favorite son were also plentiful throughout the off-season. Wagner, a native of the nearby municipality of Carnegie, was having a grand time driving around the area in his automobile. Honus was also spotted at Forbes Field watching the University of Pittsburgh football team play Pennsylvania State on Thanksgiving Day, November 30, 1911. At one point in the game, which Pennsylvania State won, 3-0, Wagner exclaimed, after a punt by one of the squads: "Oh, look at the guy hitting a Texas leaguer over the post."[13]

Pirates' fans received an early Christmas gift when reports on December 17 affirmed that Fred Clarke had signed a contract for the 1912 campaign. Of course, mixed feelings were present since the document called for Clarke to act exclusively as bench manager, meaning he would no longer be playing in the outfield. Although terms of the deal weren't released, the consensus was that Fred received somewhere in the neighborhood of $15,000. This dollar amount was what his contract had called for working in a dual capacity in 1911.[14] Near year's end, Dreyfuss received a letter from hurler Marty O'Toole, assuring the magnate that rumors related to his arm and shoulder being in bad shape were untruthful larks.[15] Pirates fans expected big things from O'Toole, whom

Pittsburgh's owner had purchased for a record price of $22,500 the previous summer from the American Association's St. Paul Saints.[16]

Over the winter, a conversation involving Dreyfuss turned to the dimensions of Brooklyn owner Charles Ebbets's new ballpark, for which construction was to begin shortly. Dreyfuss beamed with pride over the cavernous outfield of his ballpark, Forbes Field. It was 555 feet from home plate to the farthest corner of center field regarding Pittsburgh's ballpark dimensions. Over 485 feet covered the area from the dish to the right-field bleacher screen. Chief Wilson was the only player to this point who had the pleasure of smacking a drive that caressed that wire barrier.[17] Against the Philadelphia Phillies on June 3, 1911, Wilson had blasted an Earl Moore offering in the seventh inning to right field that bounced directly in front of the bleachers before skipping over the fence for a home run.[18] Every player on Pittsburgh's bench arose and greeted Owen when he reached home plate.[19]

Changes to Forbes Field had occurred while the Pirates were on a road trip through the East in May 1911. Every square foot of the property, recently obtained by the organization through the annexation of leased land, was utilized to expand the size of the ballpark's playing field rather than adding any seating capacity. This reconfiguration greatly expanded the dimension of the diamond's outfield area. Pittsburgh held the inaugural game commemorating the new Greater Forbes Field on May 26 against the Cincinnati Reds.[20] Outfielders needed to make significant adjustments to cover the obscene acreage created by this new layout. Sportswriter A. R. Cratty, who covered the team for *Sporting Life*, observed that the distance to the deep center-field fence was now 120 feet further from home plate compared to when the ballpark first opened in 1909.[21]

Barney Dreyfuss further expanded the spaciousness in Forbes Field's comfy confines before the 1912 season commenced. The ballpark's configuration in 1911 accounted for the outer end of the left-field bleachers being part of fair territory. The new plan called for changing the diamond's layout by shifting this entire section behind the foul lines. Such a move added more real estate to what already was considered the most expansive playing area of any ballpark in the league. In early February, Dreyfuss announced all Pirates player contracts for 1912 called for an abstinence clause prohibiting the consumption of alcohol, a requirement that had worked well one year earlier.[22] When it came to contracts, Jack Miller was classified as a holdout, although the player stated he was satisfied with the terms and planned on signing the document. Miller also failed to take care of the matter from 1911, which he had promised to address with surgery. Pitcher Lefty Leifield and outfielder Arthur Vincent "Vin" Campbell were the only true balkers.[23]

Campbell refused to sign his contract because he wasn't satisfied with the salary figure offered. Dreyfuss responded to this economic dissatisfaction by trading Vin to the Boston Braves on February 17, 1912, for veteran outfielder Mike Donlin.[24] A day or two after Barney consummated this deal, he called Donlin on the telephone to hammer out contract negotiations. When asked about the salary figure, Mike told Pittsburgh's owner to fix an amount that suited him. Anxious to prove his skills hadn't eroded, Donlin agreed to Dreyfuss's fair offer. The document was mailed out on February 20, while the signed contract was returned to Barney two days later, with a letter stating Mike was delighted to be wearing a Pirates uniform.[25]

On March 3, the advance guard under Fred Clarke's direction, consisting of a small group of battery men, left Pittsburgh for the first phase of spring training at West Baden, Indiana. Before this group left, Honus Wagner held a conference with Clarke and Dreyfuss at Pirates headquarters, asking for permission to skip the West Baden leg of the training session, joining the team instead when they arrived in Hot Springs. Barney persuaded Honus to accompany him when the second squad reached West Baden the following Sunday. Although carrying 15 more pounds on his frame than last season, pitcher Marty O'Toole declared his salary wing was fine and expressed confidence in having an excellent campaign. Modest but exuding strong resolve, O'Toole was determined to fulfill the immense promise expected from a player procured for $22,500.

"They've kidded Barney Dreyfuss so much about what he spent for me," said Marty, "that I want to prove to them that it was money well invested."[26]

The weather was uncooperative at West Baden, forcing Clarke to fashion a makeshift gymnasium for the players. Each day, two solid workouts involving basketballs, medicine balls, and other paraphernalia helped his players get into shape. Pittsburgh was greeted by excellent conditions when they reached Hot Springs on March 15, allowing for a practice game between the Regulars and Yanigans the following day. As Lefty Leifield finally relented after a stubborn holdout and agreed to contract terms, the Pirates were at full strength. Clarke also announced that since he no longer was an active player, Wagner would be taking over as team captain on the field.[27]

The schedule slated Pittsburgh to open the regular season against the St. Louis Cardinals at Robison Field on April 11. The Pirates played their final exhibition game of the spring training tour on April 9, beating the Western League's St. Joseph Drummers, 9-1. Illness forced Mike Donlin to retire after the third inning as a severe cold had settled in his back and legs. Owen Wilson had also missed time because of a stubborn cold, which didn't respond to treatment.[28] O'Toole was also in a weakened condition. While in Hot Springs, fearing Marty was experiencing a touch of rheumatism, Fred Clarke ordered his pitcher to partake in a battery of mineral baths. The water's temperature was 110 degrees, about 12 to 14 notches above the standard heat threshold. Clarke expected O'Toole's strength to return after a brief rest.

Pirates fans back in Pittsburgh were also probably happy when news reached the city that Alex McCarthy would be the team's starting second baseman on opening day. Excitement over the thought that Dots Miller may perform a utility role was tempered with the discovery he most likely would be the Pirates' first baseman in 1912. When Barney Dreyfuss returned to Pittsburgh before the campaign commenced, he understood that Miller had won the first base job. The owner seemed less than enthusiastic when announcing this to members of the local press.

"Jack Miller has been doing fairly well at first thus far," said the magnate. "But I am free to say that I do not know yet who will play the position. I do not believe that Fred will arrive at a definite decision until he reaches St. Louis Thursday morning. Hyatt [Ham Hyatt] has been playing first for the Yanigans, and has been doing it very well–better, I might add, than some other men who are holding down the job in the big leagues."[29]

First base had been a problem area for Pittsburgh since the Pirates traded William "Kitty" Bransfield to the Philadelphia Phillies after the 1904 season. The main obstacle regarding Miller's play at first base during the spring games was that he attempted to roam the entire infield. Fred Clarke worked diligently drilling Jack to remain somewhere near the bag.[30] The Pirates' season started ominously due to travel issues, making the trip from St. Joseph to St. Louis. Since trains from the west were running five hours behind schedule because of connection problems, the team left St. Joseph well past the scheduled time of 9 p.m. on April 10. This tossed Pittsburgh's initial arrival time into disarray. The Pirates didn't reach St. Louis's Planters Hotel until 11 a.m. the following morning. Team secretary William H. Locke attempted to secure a special train, but Burlington Railroad officials refused, citing no available engines. These administrators scoffed at Locke's attractive monetary offer that he proposed to expedite matters.[31]

There were two key takeaways from Pittsburgh's opening game against the Cardinals on April 11. First, the Pirates resembled a tired, ragged squad, as St. Louis's Robert "Bob" Harmon tossed a four-hit shutout and claimed a 7-0 victory. Honus Wagner and Mike Donlin each banged out two hits.[32] Owen Wilson played center field and was hitless in four trips to the plate. The second critical nugget of information related to Pittsburgh's opener was that Jack Miller indeed played first base. Although he connected for two singles, Donlin was a melancholy soul since he was nursing an injured leg and wasn't with his wife and vaudeville partner Mabel Hite on their sixth wedding anniverasary.[33]

St. Louis made it two in a row on April 13, defeating the Pirates, 6-5, in ten innings. Some lousy luck cost Pittsburgh a run that would've secured the game in regulation. In the second inning, Wilson drilled a triple that drove home Miller. After receiving the squeeze play sign, Owen broke for home plate. Unfortunately, Alex McCarthy's bunt attempt only grazed the baseball, right into the glove of catcher John "Jack" Bliss, who quickly tagged Wilson for the out. St. Louis's fans started yelling "bonehead" at Chief, although he had executed his end of the proposition perfectly.[34] Things didn't get much better when the team moved on to Cincinnati, as the Reds claimed the first two games of that series, 11-7, on April 14 and 3-2, in 11 innings, on April 15. Cincinnati secured the extra-inning affair after Babe Adams issued his only walk of the game to John Bates, who then scored after Pirates' third baseman Robert "Bobby" Byrne fielded Richard "Dick" Hoblitzell's bunt and threw to an uncovered first base, allowing the ball to roll to the grandstand. Owen was one of the game's batting stars, collecting three hits.[35]

Pittsburgh finally claimed their first victory of the season on April 16, beating the Reds, 8-2. Marty O'Toole was in fine form on the bump, allowing only five hits, limiting the damage due to wildness, despite yielding seven bases on balls. Honus Wagner's fielding and hitting were the day's showcase event.[36] The Pirates won their second consecutive game on a chilly, cloudy day when they opened the season at Forbes Field on April 18, defeating St. Louis in a tight affair, 4-3. Pittsburgh secured victory with two outs in the ninth inning when Chief Wilson blasted his second triple of the campaign and then scored after shortstop Arnold Hauser, in his haste to make a play, fumbled McCarthy's ground ball. Mike Donlin, forced to leave the game with an injury, was replaced by Tommy Leach.[37] The Pirates took a second game from St. Louis on April 20, as hurler Samuel Howard "Howie" Camnitz tossed a shutout, beating the Cardinals, 7-0.

Fred Clarke's team left behind the home cooking for a trek to Chicago. Days before Pittsburgh's arrival in the Windy City, innovative Cubs owner Charles Murphy did due diligence in the publicity department. Signs around the grandstand advertising the series contained slogans such as "Donlin, the slugger, here Sunday, Monday and Tuesday," "Honus, the great, comes with the Pirates," and "Marty O'Toole is here Sunday, Monday and Tuesday." West Side Grounds' fans ended up being disappointed, not witnessing Mike Donlin in action since the injured player remained in Pittsburgh.[38] When Murphy also gave his unsolicited opinion regarding the whys and wherefores behind the Donlin deal with Boston, Clarke offered a tongue-in-cheek response.

"The only reason I traded Campbell for Donlin," said Clarke, "is that we needed an actor on our team. The Giants and Cubs each have an actor, and we are entitled to one too."[39]

Besides offering comic retorts, Clarke also pitched batting practice to his players to break the monotony since he no longer was an active player. While Pittsburgh's batters usually smashed their manager's offerings, Fred occasionally slipped over a strike with his curveball.[40] Due to poor weather, Pittsburgh and Chicago only played two games, with each team securing a victory. The Cubs won on April 21, 6-0, while the Pirates claimed the game on April 23, 5-3.

Chief Wilson was the second game's hero, scoring Honus Wagner with a double in the second inning and tripling in the sixth to send Tommy Leach across home plate, giving Pittsburgh the lead. In the ninth, he saved the game, robbing Heinie Zimmerman of a home run with a spectacular catch as two Cubs runners occupied the bases.[41]

Mike Donlin remained on the sidelines thanks to dislocating a toe while rounding first base in the home opener. The injury forced Donlin to visit the famous muscle specialist, John "Bonesetter" Reese, in Youngstown, Ohio.[42] The Pirates experienced their best day at the plate against Cincinnati at Forbes Field on April 27, blitzing Reds pitchers for 27 hits while winning the game, 23-4. Bobby Byrne and Jack Miller recorded five hits apiece for the Pirates.[43] Owen also launched his fourth and fifth triples of the young campaign.[44] When April ended, Pittsburgh was in a tie for fourth place, with a 5-7 record. Wilson and second baseman Alex McCarthy, who followed each other in the batting order in the sixth and seventh slots, were dubbed the Mutt and Jeff of National League sluggers through the season's early stages.[45] McCarthy's stickwork particularly sizzled, as his batting average stood at .450 through the first ten games.[46]

Things started roughly for the Pirates in May. After driving in three runs in Pittsburgh's 6-0 victory over Chicago on May 2 at Forbes Field, Honus Wagner experienced an injury the following day. A sprained left leg he suffered while running the bases briefly sidelined Wagner.[47] Owen Wilson blasted a triple in that game on May 3, as Pittsburgh lost to Chicago in 11 innings, 9-8. In the third inning, Owen smashed a terrific drive over the head of center fielder Solly

Hofman, causing the baseball to roll to the fence. Wilson attempted to stretch the blast into an inside-the-park homer, but a series of excellent relay throws cut him down at the plate.[48]

Wilson smacked triple number seven of the year as the Pirates exacted revenge on May 4, beating the Cubs, 12-11. In the ninth inning, when Chicago manager Frank Chance, who only appeared in two games that year, started swinging two bats as an indication he might pinch hit for hurler King Cole, Fred Clarke picked up a pair of war clubs and began gyrating them back and forth, eliciting cheers from the crowd.[49] Donlin finally returned to the lineup on May 9, as the Brooklyn Superbas defeated Pittsburgh, 6-5. Mike gave a tremendous performance at the plate, smacking three hits. He also entertained the right-field bleacher patrons, known as "Gobblers' Knob," by talking to them, answering questions, and kidding the public. When Chief occupied that territory, he also responded to some patrons.[50] While Donlin made his return; Honus Wagner traveled to Youngstown so that Bonesetter Reese could work on his painful charley horse injury.[51]

In a 4-3 loss against the New York Giants on May 15 at Forbes Field, Owen misjudged a fly ball off the bat of catcher Chief Meyers in the second inning, which allowed him to complete the circuit for an inside-the-park home run. Wilson made amends in the bottom of that frame, repeating Meyers's performance, scoring Wagner and Jack Miller ahead of him.[52] One day later, a tremendously anticipated matchup between two pieces of high-priced baseball property occurred at Forbes Field. Marty O'Toole faced New York Giants star southpaw Rube Marquard. O'Toole gave a solid performance but was no match for Marquard's brilliance. Rube scattered four hits as New York won, 4-1.[53]

After playing mediocre baseball throughout the season's early weeks, Pittsburgh finally experienced a hot streak, going 7-1 from May 18 through May 26. Regarding the triples parade, Wilson smacked one against Boston on May 21 and two when the Pirates opposed Chicago on May 25. In a game versus the Braves on May 23, Owen swiped his second base of the season, which prompted Bill Twitmeyer to offer a compelling explanation surrounding the outfielder's low steal total while sitting in Section 10 at Forbes Field.

"You see," said Bill, "the Chief is so all-fired stuck on three-baggers, and home plate is such a blamed hard base to steal that . . ."[54]

Wilson's two triples off Cubs hurler James "Jimmy" Lavender on May 25 were tremendous shots; one to the far left corner of Forbes Field, while the other reached deep left-center.[55] On Sunday, May 26, Pittsburgh made a one-day trip to play Chicago. While a few Pirates players hung out in the team hotel's lobby around noon, an automobile in front of the hostelry backfired with a loud bang.

"Gee!" roared Honus Wagner, jumping to his feet. "Wilson hit another triple."

Chief grinned before answering: "No, that's the echo of Saturday's first triple."

The vehicle immediately emitted another unpleasant booming jolt.

"There is the echo of the second one, just arrived," chimed in Jack Miller.

Wagner then commented that each time Wilson hit a triple the previous afternoon, umpire Bill Klem thought Chief had knocked the cover off the baseball. "Notice how he examined the ball each time?" asked Honus. "Even McCarthy [Alex McCarthy] thought the pill was lopsided and asked Klem to take a look at it."[56]

Wilson connected for his eleventh triple of the season in the morning contest of a Decoration Day doubleheader on May 30 at Forbes Field. Pittsburgh lost to St. Louis, 8-3, before winning the afternoon game, 9-7. A blockbuster deal put forward that day with Chicago eclipsed diamond events. The Pirates shipped veteran Tommy Leach and pitcher Lefty Leifield to the Cubs for outfielder Solly Hofman and hurler King Cole. Leach had been a fan favorite since his arrival in Pittsburgh in 1900, while rooters never appreciated Leifield's solid work because they misinterpreted his deliberate approach on the mound for apathy and laziness.[57] This trade did not benefit the Pirates, as Cole was virtually useless, while Hofman only appeared in 17 games due to health problems.

As the campaign swung into June, Pittsburgh held fourth place in the standings with an 18-17 record, putting them ten games behind first-place New York. Although Chief Wilson slumped a bit smashing three-baggers, he continued offering critical offensive production. Chief blasted a home run at National League Park on June 1, as Pittsburgh defeated Philadelphia, 7-5, and then crushed a titanic wallop into South End Grounds' bleachers on June 7, when the Pirates topped Boston, 4-0. Sportswriter Ralph S. Davis wrote that Wilson likely would be one of the National League's most discussed players if he were savvy in working the publicity machine. Instead, Chief never craved the spotlight, trotting around the bases without demonstration following a home run before taking his seat on the corner of the bench.[58] In the final game of the Phillies' series on June 4, which Philadelphia won, 17-4, Pittsburgh's players accused their opponent of curtailing pitcher Marty O'Toole from loading up the baseball with saliva to throw his spitter by placing tabasco sauce on the sphere.[59]

While the Pirates were in Boston, an unfortunate incident occurred that possibly circumvented the grand return of an old baseball warrior. While practicing at first base, manager Fred Clarke fractured a finger on his right hand when attempting to catch the baseball. Clarke made a surprising revelation as a doctor attended to his injury in the clubhouse.

"That's tough luck," said Clarke, "especially coming just when I was about to help the boys out."

"What do you mean," asked a scribe, "that you are going to return to the game?"

"Well, I couldn't return now if I wanted to, could I?" responded the pilot.

Pittsburgh's baseball fans had been clamoring for Clarke's return, blaming the team's bad luck on his retirement as a player.[60] Before the season, Fred had made numerous wagers with friends for suits, hats, shoes, and socks to remain on the sidelines until June 1. When that date arrived, Clarke collected a bounty of clothing valued at over $500.[61] Regarding those Pirates who played the outfield, Pittsburgh's triples machine, Owen Wilson, finally connected for a three-bagger after a long drought. Wilson smacked a triple on June 17, as New York defeated Pittsburgh in 11 innings at the Polo Grounds, 5-4. The usually mild-mannered Owen exhibited surprising anger at one point in the game, arguing with home plate umpire Charles "Cy" Rigler over two pitches he believed were low, calling the arbitrator things like a "policeman" and a "cabbage head."[62]

Reacquainting himself with the majestic triple opened the floodgates for Wilson. He smacked another three-bagger as Pittsburgh defeated New York, 7-2, on June 18. Owen crushed a triple at Forbes Field the following day when the Pirates beat St. Louis, 8-1. Chief's proficiency in a Sunday doubleheader split with Cincinnati at Redland Field on June 20 knew no bounds. In the first contest, won by Pittsburgh in ten innings, 6-4, Wilson blasted two triples while adding another in the nightcap, which the Reds claimed, 5-3. Owen's three triples that afternoon gave him 17 for the campaign and propelled him into a tie with Chicago's Heinie Zimmerman regarding clouting extra-base hits.[63] Before the game against Cincinnati on June 23, when members of the team clowned around during pregame fielding practice, Wilson covered third base, attempting his best Bobby Byrne imitation.[64]

Although Chief's ability to produce triples the remainder of June dried up, he smacked a monstrous home run at Robison Field, in game two of a doubleheader against St. Louis, on June 25. Wilson drilled a mammoth bomb over the ballpark's right-field pavilion as Pittsburgh completed the twin bill sweep, beating the Cardinals, 19-3.[65] Records showed that only Tim Jordan, Harry

Lumley, and current teammate Mike Donlin had ever smacked a baseball out of Robison Field. None of those drives traveled to the far reaches where Owen's landed.[66] As the season entered July; National League pitchers feared no player more than Wilson.[67]

When June ended, Pittsburgh found themselves in second place with a 37-25 record, putting them 13 ½ games behind the pacesetting Giants. This rise in the standings was astounding, considering veteran outfielders Solly Hofman and Mike Donlin were on the sidelines. Doctors had advised Hofman to rest at his home in Akron, Ohio. Donlin missed part of the team's eastern swing to remain with his wife, Mabel Hite, who underwent an urgent operation for intestinal cancer at a New York hospital.[68] Mike returned at the end of June while the team was in Chicago since doctors perceived Mabel was out of danger.[69]

When Pittsburgh arrived home to play Chicago on July 1, Chief Wilson owned a .333 batting average. Wilson embarked on the triples cavalcade once again, smacking his first one in 12 days on July 2, as the Cubs smoked the Pirates, 9-2. Owen added another three-bagger in the first game of a holiday doubleheader on July 4, as Pittsburgh claimed the morning contest over Cincinnati, 11-5. Wilson smacked his twentieth triple in game two of a twin bill on July 8 when the Pirates crushed Philadelphia, 9-2. Chief's performance thus far in 1912 made him the fans' darling, even when making mistakes. He received a standing ovation while batting in game one's fifth inning, shortly after missing Mickey Doolin's drive to center field, allowing the Phillies' shortstop to travel the circuit for an inside-the-park home run. Although an angry Wilson had misplayed the ball in the top of the frame, some in the crowd cheered him on, while one fan yelled: "Don't let that bother you, old boy."[70]

Philadelphia was up to their old tricks again when Marty O'Toole opposed them on July 9, using a substance curbing his ability to fire the spitball. Phillies manager Red Dooin initially denied doctoring the baseball, saying his men were applying Vaseline to soften their gloves. After being called out by Fred Clarke for dangerous behavior and lack of sportsmanship, Philadelphia's skipper admitted his players administered disinfectant to the sphere since the use of the spitter was unsanitary. Dooin's troops had also tried this maneuver when fellow spitball hurler and staff ace Claude Hendrix pitched weeks earlier in Philadelphia but didn't go that route at Forbes Field, following a stern warning from Pittsburgh's hurler.

"If you fellows ever doctor the ball on me again," Hendrix said, "I'll bean the first man that faces me, and I'll put him out of business for a month."[71]

Owen Wilson slipped into a batting slump starting on July 9, going 4-for-23 over the next six games and not striking a three-bagger during that week. Wilson got back into the groove on July 16, smacking a triple as Pittsburgh defeated Brooklyn, 5-4, in ten innings. One day later, against Christy Mathewson, Chief's twenty-second three-bagger of the season in the ninth inning was his team's only significant hit as Pittsburgh fell to New York, 10-2. Over 26,000 patrons attended a doubleheader against the Giants on July 19, the largest crowd to view a game at Forbes Field since the 1909 World Series.[72] The two teams split for the afternoon, each winning by a 5-4 score. Owen was responsible for four of the Pirates' nine runs, accounting for two with a first-game triple and scoring two teammates with a double in the nightcap.[73]

Pittsburgh's fans lamented that Wilson was sometimes unable to play the right field position, where he was proficient, due to being Fred Clarke's best option in center.[74] On July 22, Chief rapped out his twenty-fourth triple of the season as Pittsburgh defeated Boston, 2-0. Owen reached a milestone when the Pirates beat Brooklyn, 8-7, in 14 innings on July 25. In the first frame, Wilson smacked another triple. In the fifth inning, when he stroked a two-run single, Chief became the first Buccaneers player to reach the century mark in hits. He then singled in the fourteenth inning and scored the deciding run.[75] Triple number 26 came on July 26, as Philadelphia defeated Pittsburgh, 4-1.

As had been the case throughout this campaign, there were ebbs and flows when it came to Chief Wilson's ability to swat triples. After not hitting a three-bagger in eight days and then connecting for a double in each game of the doubleheader split with Boston on August 3, Wilson sadly viewed this as tough luck when posing a poignant question at the team hotel that night. "Has anybody seen the batting averages for this week?" asked Wilson.[76]

As the Pirates trudged through the dog days of summer, an annual story regarding Fred Clarke's retirement from the game appeared on the scene. However, everyone expected Barney Dreyfuss to offer him a contract for 1913.[77] The transition from July into August didn't go smoothly for Wilson, as he went 0-for-23 in the next six games of an eastern swing after tripling on July 26.[78] Owen broke out of this funk by hitting safely in his subsequent five appearances. After not connecting for a triple in more than two weeks, Wilson finally struck gold against Brooklyn at Washington Park on August 10. Owen secured his twenty-seventh three-bagger in the sixth inning, driving the ball safely to deep center field. Pittsburgh lost the game, 7-5, as retired pitcher Vic Willis watched his former team from the grandstand. Willis severely critiqued Pirates' hurler Marty O'Toole's control.

"That young fellow O'Toole has been running too many bases," commented Vic, as Marty walked John Herbert "Herbie" Moran to start the sixth inning.[79]

Wilson blasted his twenty-eighth triple of the season against the Phillies at Forbes Field on August 16, as Pittsburgh lost, 5-3. Owen also recorded a single and a double while scoring two of the Pirates' runs.[80] In a doubleheader on August 20 against Brooklyn, stellar defense thwarted his bid at adding to that total when Superbas outfielders Zachariah "Zack" Wheat and Herbie Moran each made spectacular catches on drives off Chief's bat.[81] After struggling to crack long drives where he ended up tearing around the bases to garner prime real estate at third, the floodgates opened for Wilson as the month concluded. Owen connected for his twenty-ninth triple of the campaign in game two of a doubleheader on August 23, as New York beat the Pirates, 3-2.

Chief went triples crazy in a twin bill against the Braves at Forbes Field on August 26, when Boston and Pittsburgh split a doubleheader. Wilson poled a long triple in the first game, giving him 30 on the season. Owen added numbers 31 and 32 in the second contest. Chief attempted to make it a trifecta in the nightcap but failed when great relay throws from John Titus and William "Bill" Sweeney gunned him down at third, trying to stretch a double into a triple.[82] Wilson secured that thirty-third three-bagger the following day, as the Pirates beat Boston, 9-4.

When Honus Wagner smashed a triple against Cincinnati on August 29, a game in which Pittsburgh lost, 7-2, the Pirates established a new National League record for triples in one season with 107, eclipsing the mark they had set one year earlier. Chief Wilson had already obliterated the modern-era National League mark for most three-baggers in a single season regarding individual honors. This record belonged to Larry Doyle of the New York Giants, who hit 25 in 1911. Wilson still had some ground to make up to eclipse the major league record, which belonged to the Cleveland Naps' Napoleon Lajoie, who smacked 43 triples in 1903.[83] From a team perspective, Pittsburgh held down third place with a 71-50 record, heading into September.

A phenomenal 20-7 mark for Pittsburgh in September allowed the Pirates to make up eight games on the Cubs and pass them by month's end. This point of the season wasn't so glorious for Owen Wilson in the triples department, as the well ran dry for the Pirates' outfielder. In a doubleheader against Cincinnati on September 1, Reds center fielder Armando Marsans shaded Wilson deep toward Redland Field's flagpole, robbing him of two potential triples that afternoon.[84] On September 3 at Forbes Field, Chicago center fielder Ward Miller performed the same baseball burglary stunt at Owen's expense in game two of a doubleheader.[85] Against St. Louis at Robison Field on September 6, Wilson smacked three hard singles and scored two runs but didn't hit a triple.[86] Chief finally ended his three-bagger futility when he blasted his thirty-fourth triple in the sixth inning of a game versus the Cardinals on September 7.[87]

Owen didn't connect for another triple until the end of September. His power proficiency was still robust, as Wilson clouted six home runs during the month. One of those was smacked in Philadelphia on September 13, earning him a prize of seven bags of tobacco for the second time, awarded to players who homered at the Phillies' ballpark.[88] Two days earlier, Chief had netted $50 for hitting an advertising sign with his ninth-inning double at National League Park. Many speculated that if not for the fence containing this painted sign, Owen possibly would have bagged triple number 35.[89] Wilson didn't smack his thirty-fifth triple until September 29, as Pittsburgh defeated Chicago at West Side Grounds, 9-0.

As the season wound down, Pirates fans, disappointed over the team's failure to win a pennant, started striking proverbial hammers at the anvil, complaining over the outcome with comments like the players were quitters or the National League race was fixed in New York's favor.[90] Before leaving to play the final two series of the campaign in Chicago and Cincinnati, the press announced that Fred Clarke had signed to manage the Pirates in 1913.[91] Heading into the season's final game against the Reds on October 6, Chief Wilson's batting average stood at .300, while fellow outfielder Max Carey's was .299. Carey had three singles, while Wilson connected for two hits as the Pirates beat Cincinnati, 16-6.[92] One of Owen's two safeties ended up as a triple after the Reds' Andrew "Andy" Kyle threw him out at the plate attempting to stretch a blast to the scoreboard into an inside-the-park home run.[93]

Pittsburgh finished the 1912 season in second place, trailing New York by ten games, with a 93-58 record. Owen "Chief" Wilson had a sensational campaign, batting .300, with 19 doubles, 36 triples, 11 home runs, and 94 RBIs. Regarding a breakdown of three-baggers at home versus the road, Forbes Field's spacious outer garden impacted the outcome, as Wilson blasted 24 triples there and 12 in enemy territory. Once the final bell rang, Owen believed he had missed tying Nap Lajoie's record by seven triples. From a personal standpoint, an exciting moment in Wilson's life occurred on February 8, 1913, when he married Bernice Mosely in Austin.[94]

Shear power, rather than speed, accounted for Chief blasting 36 triples. At times, Wilson foiled the outfield shifts of opposing teams, by utilizing the entire ballpark, especially at Forbes Field. Almost half of his three-baggers on the home grounds were hit the opposite way to left field or left-center field. As baseball writer A.R. Cratty had pointed out in a September article for *Sporting Life*, most of those cascading bombs to the deepest reaches of major league grounds indeed weren't cheap.

"J. Owen Wilson's three-base shots are entitled to be credited as one of the wonders of 1912," writes Cratty. "Best of all, few of the smashes have struck in front of fielders. They have been over their heads or between the fields, all juicy jams. Ask any pitcher if Wilson hits a high ball very hard."[95]

For five months after the season ended, Wilson was under the impression he had fallen short of breaking Napoleon Lajoie's mark. Thanks to the diligent research of Ernest J. Lanigan, sportswriter and statistical expert for the *Sporting News*, that changed. According to Lanigan, it showed on page 331 of the *Record Book of 1913* that Napoleon had recorded 43 triples with Cleveland in 1903. Ernest examined old records and boxscores and found that Lajoie had only smacked 13 three-baggers that year (later adjusted to 11 triples). A typographical error in this record book led Owen to believe that the ultimate goal during his assault on history was reaching 43, which was factually incorrect.

In reality, Wilson had broken the modern record of 25 triples, achieved by Larry Doyle in 1911 and the Detroit Tigers' Sam Crawford in 1903, when he smacked his twenty-sixth three-bagger on July 26.[96] Before 1900, the top mark for triples in a single season was 31. This was accomplished by David "Dave" Orr of the American Association's New York Metropolitans in 1886 and the Baltimore Orioles' Henry "Heinie" Reitz in 1894. Concerning the typographical mistake, one must wonder if Lajoie was aware of this error in the records.[97]

After five long months, John Owen "Chief" Wilson received his rightful crown as the "Three Base King." In that same year of 1912, Cleveland's Joseph "Shoeless Joe" Jackson blasted 26 three-baggers. Crawford, in 1914, and Pittsburgh Pirates outfielder Hazen "Kiki" Cuyler in 1925 came closest to eclipsing Owen's incredible mark when they too smacked 26 triples. Over a century later, the quiet, unassuming Wilson still stands above all others regarding three-base knocks, a testament to an era when the triple was indeed king and baseball's most exciting play.

Pittsburgh Pirates outfielder Chief Wilson established a modern-era, single-season record in 1912 that possibly will never be broken, smacking 36 triples. When the season ended, Chief believed he'd fallen short of setting the modern era record. Excellent research work by baseball writer and statistical expert Ernest J. Lanigan found a typographical error in the *Record Book of 1913*, erroneously showing that Nap Lajoie had hit 43 triples in 1903. In this photo, Wilson (right) is loosening up alongside Pirates hurler Babe Adams (left). (Courtesy of the Library of Congress.)

CHAPTER 8

Rube Marquard – 1912

The Nerve-Wracking Journey to Fame and Glory

Whenever individuals decorate baseball players with boundless greatness and grandeur, even before pulling on a major league uniform for the first time, the possibility of crumbling under the magnificent weight of these expectations can be daunting. Throughout history, the road to diamond glory had become rockier when these bright prospects included the caveat of paying a large amount of money to secure that individual's services. The combination of great expectations and a high price tag could be lethally discouraging if things didn't work out, especially when fans quickly turned on a player who underperformed after being thrust under the bright lights on baseball's grand stage. For one Deadball Era pitcher, the path to fame was a dreadfully rough trip, which genuinely challenged his spirit and grit.

Hurler Richard William "Rube" Marquard lived on both sides of the street, facing adversity before diamond success came at a price, after his introduction into the world of major league baseball. In Cleveland, Ohio, Richard was born on October 9, 1886, to Fred and Lena Marquard. His father, who eventually became a city engineer, had journeyed to America by boat as a ten-year-old from Germany with his parents in 1874. The family name originally was "Marquardt" before they eliminated the last letter.[1] Besides enjoying visiting the fire station where his father worked for a few years and listening to firemen's tales, young Richard developed his powerful left arm throwing a baseball. During his youth, a constant sight in the local neighborhood was Marquard having a grand time tossing a ball in the air and catching it with his small glove. Tragedy dealt a severe blow to the family in 1899 when Richard's mother, Lena, died.[2]

Marquard's baseball skills were sharpened by practicing and playing at Cleveland's Brookside Park.[3] Although Richard's passion for baseball was evident, Fred Marquard initially told his son that those who played the game were no good and never would be. His father later experienced a transformation, exhibiting pride in Richard's achievements within that profession.[4] Enjoying playing baseball throughout Cleveland during his teenage years, Marquard eventually gained notice and recognition in 1905 at 18, pitching for a squad called the Colonials. One of two stories regarding the origin of Marquard's nickname was born that year, courtesy of a teammate who dubbed him "Rube," when the pitcher eagerly arrived early at the train depot for a road trip, toting a farmer's carpet satchel. Another possible derivation of this moniker came from a sportswriter, commenting years later on Richard's similarity in pitching ability to southpaw hurler Rube Waddell.

Pining to pursue a baseball life, Rube constantly argued with his father, who wanted his son to concentrate on getting an education and going to college. Richard's grandfather always sided with him during these discussions.[5] Rube's strong convictions won out, as he signed his first professional contract with the Ohio-Pennsylvania League's Lancaster Lanks in 1906. Aspiring to eventually reach the game's pinnacle by becoming a major leaguer, Marquard held one advantage not always afforded to others. Rube was exposed to the big league atmosphere, performing duties as a batboy for the American League's Cleveland Naps in 1904, 1905, and 1906.[6]

In 1907, Rube burst on the scene in a big way, pitching for the Central League's Canton Chinamen. Marquard posted a 23-13 record with a sterling 2.01 ERA. This solid performance earned him a promotion to Class A ball in 1908, twirling as a member of the American Association's Indianapolis Indians. Rube's mound brilliance attracted numerous major league scouts, as the southpaw went 28-19, bolstered by a 1.69 ERA while fanning 250 batters. On June 30, Marquard allowed three hits as Indianapolis defeated the Louisville Colonels, 3-0. Following this game, a spirited bidding war involving ten major league organizations began for the young pitcher's services. New York Giants manager John McGraw and owner John T. Brush came away victorious after a long evening, purchasing Rube for $11,000.[7]

Anticipation pulsated, and expectations ran high when Rube Marquard joined the Giants after the American Association campaign ended. Advance newspaper articles talked about Rube's reputation as a dominating pitcher who had suppressed all opponents, while no batter could solve his baffling curveball. New York certainly paid a considerable price above the standard to purchase

Marquard. When Rube joined the squad, McGraw was in a bind regarding rested pitchers. The Giants' skipper was reticent to throw a young hurler into the fire as his team battled the Chicago Cubs and Pittsburgh Pirates in a red-hot pennant race. Anxious to see the youthful prodigy make an appearance, Giants owner John T. Brush suggested using Marquard while discussing the pitching situation with his manager. "Don't you think Marquard would win?" asked Brush. "Can't you put him in?"

"I don't know," answered McGraw. "If he wins his first time out in the big leagues, he will be a world-beater, and, if he loses, it may cost us a good pitcher."

Brush remained persistent, despite McGraw's reservations. John finally relented, allowing Rube to pitch on the spur of the moment in game one of a doubleheader against the Cincinnati Reds on September 25 at the Polo Grounds. Things didn't go smoothly for the young southpaw in his inaugural game. Rube started the contest by hitting the Reds' John Kane with a pitch. Kane promptly stole second base. After retiring Richard "Dick" Egan, Marquard faced John "Hans" Lobert. Querying Rube about possessing talent or being just another bush-leaguer, Lobert quickly received his answer, connecting for a triple to the outfield's farthest reaches, scoring Kane. A fan yelled–"Take him out"–before Robert "Bob" Bescher followed up Hans' blast with another triple (a throw to the plate caught Bescher as he attempted to stretch the hit into an inside-the-park home run). Marquard only lasted five innings, producing a pitching line of five runs, six hits, two strikeouts, and two walks, as Cincinnati defeated New York, 7-1. Rube later explained to teammate Christy Mathewson that he had been overwhelmed by the situation.

"When I saw that crowd, Matty," he said, "I didn't know where I was. It looked so big to me, and they were all wondering what I was going to do and all thinking that McGraw had paid $11,000 for me, and now they were to find out whether he had picked up a gold brick with the plating on it very thin. I was wondering, myself, whether I would make good."

Over the next two seasons, following his only appearance with the Giants in 1908, Marquard failed to live up to the promise for someone carrying an $11,000 price tag. John McGraw slowly nurtured Rube, so he became comfortable in his surroundings, allowing him to finish some games and only start against the National League's weaker clubs.[8] In 1909, Marquard appeared in 29 games, started 22, and went 5-13 with a 2.60 ERA. He regressed in 1910, making only 13 appearances and crafting a 4-4 mark, supported by an uninspiring 4.46 ERA. Through August that year, Rube had only started four games. Although he possessed great speed and an adequate arsenal of benders, Marquard lacked control.[9]

Known as the "$11,000 Beauty" when he entered the league, disappointed fans now referred to Rube as the "$11,000 Lemon." Although his career stagnated, Marquard exhibited a good sense of humor during these challenging times. Rube responded with a snappy retort when the Giants opposed the American League's New York Highlanders in an interleague postseason series after the 1910 campaign concluded.

"Behold the $11,000 joke," yelled a rooter. "I can't understand why McGraw keeps him."

"Because I'm such a joke, I keep the rest of the club in good humor," a smiling Marquard shouted.[10]

Reaching a career crossroads was no joke, as a new baseball season beckoned. Before spring training in 1911, Rube deflected some blame for his problems and failure, placing them on his manager for advising him to use an unnatural motion while pitching.

"In the American Association, I used a side-arm ball," said Rube. "McGraw makes me pitch over-hand. I haven't been able to master the new style. I used to turn my back to the batter, lean back as though picking the ball off the ground, and shoot my right foot into the air. With that motion, I used all my strength. McGraw makes me face the batter. Sometimes I fall into my old style and go pretty good, but when I get back to the bench, the boss tells me to quit it and pitch his way. He ought to know the best way to pitch, and when I get accustomed to his way, I expect to win a lot of games."[11]

Shattered confidence could quickly end a career before it had an opportunity to flourish if a player wasn't willing to work hard and listen to instructions. Fortunately for Marquard, things came into focus thanks to the efforts of former Baltimore Orioles catcher Wilbert " Robbie" Robinson, who joined old friend John McGraw as a coach on his staff in 1911. Amid the Texas heat of spring training in Marlin Springs, Rube became Robinson's primary project. As the team trained, newspaper articles implored McGraw to trade the "$11,000 Lemon" for a competent batboy. To eliminate this stigma and turn him into a solid pitcher, Robbie privately tutored Rube for hours every day. Wilbert started each lecture with the same line of advice.

"Now, Rube," Robbie said each day, "you've got to start on the first ball to get the batter. Always have something on him, and never let him have anything on you. This is the prescription for a great pitcher."

According to Christy Mathewson, one of Marquard's worst habits was getting two quick strikes on a batter before letting up, digging himself a hole, and running into trouble. Besides nurturing Rube, Robinson also went to great lengths to build his confidence.

"Rube, you've got a lot of stuff today," Robbie advised in one instance, "but don't try to get it all on the ball. Mix it with a little control, and it will make a good blend. Now, this guy is a high ball hitter. Let's see you keep it low for him. He waits so you will have to get it over."[12]

Armed with added confidence and knowledge, Rube Marquard was ready when the time came to utilize Robinson's instructions. The pieces to the puzzle finally fell into place when the Giants opposed Philadelphia in an early July series at National League Park. The Phillies swept the first four games due to overwork and extreme heat taxing McGraw's staff. Before the series' final contest, the second game of a twin bill on July 5, Marquard, after collecting his thoughts, walked up to his manager and said: "Give me a chance." On a whim, McGraw concurred and gave him the starting assignment. Rube didn't disappoint, as he throttled a team that had feasted on Giants pitching. A star was born that sweltering Philadelphia afternoon, as Marquard made the Phillies' batters look foolish, cruising to a 10-1 win. Recalling his debut three years earlier while opposing the Phillies later that season, Rube exacted some revenge when Hans Lobert stepped up to the plate.

"Remember the time," howled Marquard, "you bow-legged Dutchman, when you asked me whether I was a busher? Here is where I pay you back. This is the place where you get a bad showing up."

Marquard proceeded to strike out Lobert by firing three consecutive pitches past him.[13] Rube finally achieved a breakout season in 1911, going 24-7 with a 2.50 ERA and fanning a league-leading 237 batters. John McGraw received credit for exhibiting the wisdom and patience to stick with Marquard through rough times, although some believed New York's manager already would've cast him adrift if not for that $11,000 purchase price.[14] When it came to Rube's newfound ability to utilize all parts of the plate while working against a batter, Chicago Cubs shortstop Joe Tinker declared that old-fashioned, blazing heat always caused tremendous damage.

"You can't hit what you don't see," said Tinker. "When he throws his fast one, the only way you know it's past you is because you hear the ball hit the catcher's glove."[15]

Marquard was also quite proficient in throwing the fadeaway pitch, made famous by teammate Christy Mathewson, which broke away from left-handed batters. Rube's solid work in 1911 earned him two bumps in salary by McGraw totaling $1,000. He also promised Marquard a $500 bonus if the Giants won the pennant. Before the season started, a loyal rooter had told Rube he would present him with a $5,000 car if New York topped the league. A stage career through a local theatrical company was also in his future.[16] The critical condition for earning money and prizes were achieved when the Giants copped the flag by going 99-54. The Philadelphia Athletics then defeated New York in the World Series, four games to two.

Rube Marquard was tagged with the loss in Game Two on October 16 at Shibe Park, 3-1, as Athletics' third baseman John Franklin "Frank" Baker took the first step toward earning his nickname of "Home Run" when he belted the winning two-run blast in the sixth inning. Marquard also had a no-decision start in Game Five at the Polo Grounds on October 25, which the Giants won in ten innings, 4-3, before a mop-up relief appearance one day later in the final contest. This championship clash, delayed a week at one point because of rainy weather, contained some controversial moments. Philadelphia first baseman Harry Davis verbally attacked Detroit Tigers manager Hugh "Hughie" Jennings, accusing him of being a traitor to the American League cause by categorizing Baker as the Athletics' weak link to former Baltimore Orioles teammate John McGraw. According to Davis, Jennings advised New York's skipper to go after him hard, through verbal abuse from the coaching box and sliding into him with sharpened spikes.

Outfielder Frederick "Fred" Snodgrass followed that second suggestion twice, with the most egregious and flagrant maneuver occurring on a play at third base in the tenth inning of Game Three at the Polo Grounds on October 17. Snodgrass catapulted his body at Frank while attempting to advance from second on a passed ball, spiking him in the arm before being called out by the umpire. An unnamed baseball player was a lone dissenting voice, stating Baker should have bailed and pulled away from the bag. Even the Polo Grounds' patrons were disgusted over the play, jeering Fred as he walked off the field after Philadelphia's third baseman recorded the out.[17] Frank had enjoyed some sweet revenge a second time, for the first incident involving Snodgrass three days earlier in Game One, by crushing a solo home run off Mathewson in the ninth. This course of events prompted one fan to question Jennings's capabilities as an intelligence agent. "Say, Hughey," shouted the fan, "either you mixed your signals, or you're double-crossing McGraw."[18]

Tigers star player Ty Cobb believed the first of these two incidents afforded him vindication over the accusation he had spiked Frank intentionally back in 1909. Cobb contended Baker was susceptible to spiking due to how he blocked the bag.[19] The tough loss aside, New York experienced a very successful campaign despite being defeated by Philadelphia. Shortly after the World Series ended, McGraw and many of his players took a trip to Cuba for a series against teams of talented athletes from that country. On November 15, the Giants left New York on a train bound for Jacksonville, Florida, where the team planned on playing some practice games before journeying to Cuba by boat.[20]

The Giants went 9-3 during this series on foreign soil. Christy Mathewson praised the people of Cuba for the kind treatment afforded his team. Mathewson also declared it was the destiny of these Cuban players that he faced to become magnificent performers in a few years.[21] After New York returned home, John McGraw submitted his opinion regarding the Cuban baseball player. On a positive note, McGraw believed they were lightning quick on the bases, possessed powerful throwing arms, and were excellent fielders. John's criticism centered on the Cubans' poor batting and the fact they didn't practice a key tenant he preached to his players; playing brainy, inside baseball, and combining mind with athletic talent.[22] Former Giants outfielder Mike Donlin, currently a member of the Boston Rustlers, batted .375 in the Cuban baseball tour's first five games.[23]

Rube Marquard didn't make the trip, opting instead to launch his stage career. After signing a contract with his theatrical manager to perform on the vaudeville stage, Rube refused to appear in an engagement booked in a cheap moving-picture show. Marquard contended the obligation was beneath him and couldn't fulfill it because he deemed it necessary to retain his dignity as a leading pitcher on a championship baseball team. Appearing in established venues was especially critical for him since Athletics hurlers John "Jack" Coombs, Charles "Chief" Bender, and Harry "Cy" Morgan were performing in first-class houses.[24] The only contract that mattered to Giants fans was the signed document proclaiming him to be in the fold for 1912. Rumors abounded that Rube possibly could be a holdout, although many believed such an ungrateful stance implausible since the hurler had been carried on the roster for two years when he was useless.[25]

Although Marquard didn't sign a contract while chatting with Joseph "Joe" O'Brien for an hour at team headquarters near the end of January, the team secretary felt Rube likely would come to terms with the club. O'Brien was the second person to hold this position in the organization after longtime team secretary Frederick "Fred" Knowles tendered his temporary resignation and moved to Denver, Colorado, hoping the climate would benefit his health problems, including tuberculosis.[26] Everyone connected to the organization was saddened and shocked when news reached New York on February 1, 1912, that Knowles had passed away.[27] Fears were allayed over a Marquard holdout when the southpaw hurler signed a three-year contract in early February. Money hadn't been the issue, as John McGraw initially was reluctant to give the hurler a long-term deal. Rube's persistence that such an agreement was in the best interest of all parties concerned eventually convinced New York's manager. These terms also guaranteed Marquard a good pay advance.[28]

Some spring training concerns cropped up related to the Giants' location on getting in their preseason work. In January, a meningitis outbreak ravished Texas and spread to Marlin Springs. Groundskeeper John Murphy, who had been there most of the winter setting up quarters in anticipation of the players' arrival, kept John McGraw abreast of the situation. In late January, one of Murphy's letters to McGraw offered assurances that the epidemic likely wouldn't wreak havoc in Marlin since conditions were improving while reported cases had been isolated and contained. Although New York's concerned skipper hadn't indicated a venue change would be considered, many believed he privately selected an optional location.[29]

Things ended up proceeding as planned. On Saturday night, February 17, a group of 17 recruits, along with McGraw and coach Wilbert Robinson, boarded a special train in St. Louis. Their destination was the Giants' standard spring training facility since 1908 in Texas.[30] When New York's second group of players joined these youngsters in Marlin Springs, sportswriter William J. McBeth proclaimed that Rube Marquard didn't size up quite correctly in his eyes, appearing less sturdy than when the previous campaign closed. While McBeth remarked the lanky hurler hadn't lost any weight, there seemed to be no added pounds to Rube's frame. The scribe concluded that a body for a player Marquard's age should still fill out and pack on added muscle weight.[31]

As the spring campaign progressed, it quickly became evident that Marquard was determined to continue improving following his splendid 1911 season.[32] The Giants were a diverse group of players possessing contrasting personalities. *New York Globe* sportswriter Sid Mercer ordained Rube's roommate, outfielder Joshua "Josh" Devore, as the squad's most fastidious dresser during the early stages of camp. The basis for this honor was Mercer's contention that Devore packed 53 articles in his suitcase—a deck of cards and a change of one necktie.[33] As his team's spring itinerary wound down, McGraw offered some wise baseball counsel. "Forget the World's Series last fall," advised McGraw, "and win another pennant. Maybe next time we can put the rollers under the American League champions."[34]

John McGraw afforded Marquard the honor of pitching on opening day. New York started the campaign against their crosstown rivals, the Brooklyn Superbas, at Washington Park, on April 11. A vast multitude, estimated at 30,000, crammed their way into the ballpark as an overflow crowd surged toward the diamond. It looked as though this chaos might force Brooklyn to forfeit the game since special police were ill-equipped to handle the swelling crowd. Superbas owner Charles Ebbets appealed to New York mayor William Jay Gaynor, who was on hand to throw out the first pitch, for assistance. Gaynor instructed his deputy police commissioner to use regular officers to clear the grounds. These police officers successfully pushed the swarm away from the infield. Despite their diligent efforts, some sitting in the stands couldn't see the diamond action due to being blocked by people standing on the field. Special rules were adopted, stipulating that any baseball hit into the outfield's overflow crowd count as a double.

The Giants took full advantage of this ground rule, swatting 12 doubles and claiming an 18-3 victory, as umpires called the contest after six innings because of darkness. Marquard was solid on the bump in every inning but the third, when he allowed three runs.[35] Rube also went 3-for-4 at the plate and blasted two doubles. After cruising to an easy opening-day victory, New York dropped two straight to the Superbas before losing the series' first game against the Boston Braves, 3-0, on April 15 at South Ends Grounds. Marquard stopped the brief skid on April 16, defeating Boston 8-2. Rube tossed a complete game, allowing no earned runs, striking out five, and walking one batter. The Braves' two runs came courtesy of errors by center fielder Fred Snodgrass and catcher Arthur "Art" Wilson.[36]

New York kicked off the home portion of their schedule with a 6-2 victory over Brooklyn at the Polo Grounds on April 19. Cold weather suppressed attendance below what hardy patrons considered normal regarding an opening day crowd. Christy Mathewson was presented with an automobile from admirers before the contest started. Although touched up for 12 hits, Mathewson was strong on the mound and benefitted from many defensive gems by his teammates. In the fourth frame, umpire William "Bill" Finneran banished John McGraw to the bench before ordering him to the clubhouse one inning later.[37]

Assessed a five-day suspension for his actions, McGraw missed the fireworks one day later when the Giants defeated the Superbas, 4-3. Brooklyn manager William "Bill" Dahlen bumped into umpire Cy Rigler when he ran up to the arbitrator to argue a call. Rigler punched Dahlen in the face, initiating a scrap between the two men. After the game, Superbas owner Charles Ebbets sent a message to league president Thomas Lynch, demanding that Rigler receive punishment for his unwarranted attack. In the ninth inning, New York secured victory when Art Wilson drove a two-run homer into the right-field grandstand.[38] After starting pitcher Charles "Jeff" Tesreau had given up two runs in the top of that frame, allowing Brooklyn to grab a 3-2 lead, Marquard came on in relief and stemmed the tide. Although Rube finished the ninth for his team, Tesreau was awarded the victory under the rules of that time.

On Wednesday, April 24, Marquard raised his record to 3-0 on the young season, defeating the Philadelphia Phillies, 11-4, in an affair shortened to seven innings. Rube performed steadily on the mound, while Phillies pitcher Grover Cleveland Alexander was wild and ineffective.[39] Giants officials were extremely unhappy over Philadelphia ownership arbitrarily canceling the first two games of this series. Monday's contest was postponed before noon since it was raining in the morning, but the weather cleared before the game's scheduled start time. The following sunny day, Phillies president Horace Fogel called off that game due to cold and windy conditions, which weren't outside the norm of typical spring weather.[40]

A seven-game winning streak allowed New York to finish April with an 8-3 record, placing them second, one game behind the Cincinnati Reds. Rube was brilliant against Philadelphia on May 1 at the Polo Grounds. The Giants cruised to an easy 11-4 win, as second baseman Larry Doyle went 4-for-4 at the plate, hit a double, smacked a homer, and drove in five runs. When New York increased their lead to 11-0 in the fifth, McGraw allowed several substitutes to enter the game.[41] Marquard pitched shutout ball and fanned nine batters before Louis Drucke took over in the eighth inning. Rube made his second relief appearance of the season on May 3, tossing a perfect ninth, as the Phillies claimed an 8-6 victory in ten innings. Marquard won his fifth consecutive game of the campaign on May 7, defeating the St. Louis Cardinals at Robison Field, 6-2. Rube rolled along unscathed until the ninth, when a walk to Edward "Ed" Konetchy, Ennis "Rebel" Oakes's single, and a double by Elmer Miller plated two tallies.[42]

Marquard pushed his record to 6-0 on May 11, beating Chicago at West Side Grounds, 10-3. Rube didn't allow an earned run while his teammates battered the offerings of Cubs pitchers Elwood "Lew" Richie and King Cole all over the lot. Marquard faltered in the final two innings as a drizzle decorated the field.[43] A stretch of 16 victories in their last 17 games had propelled the Giants atop the standings with a 17-4 record. Winning certainly was a recipe for a loose and happy ball club. After taking a whirl in teammate Christy Mathewson's new car, Josh Devore declared that the people from his hometown of Terre Haute, Indiana, wouldn't even buy him a drink, much less present him with an automobile.[44]

Rube Marquard received an honor previously bequeathed to Mathewson. For years, Christy possessed a watch that once belonged to fellow Giants pitcher Hooks Wiltse. Supposedly, Wiltse had fallen into a swamp and retrieved a gold watch as he climbed out of the bog. Hooks eventually lent the good luck charm to friends, with Mathewson gaining possession of the gold watch. In 1912, Rube secured temporary ownership of this item, causing his teammates to refer to him as "Watch" Marquard.[45] With the gold watch in tow, Rube took the mound in a highly anticipated matchup against the Pittsburgh Pirates at Forbes Field on May 16. Marquard locked horns with Marty O'Toole, who had been purchased by the Pirates the previous summer for a new record price of $22,500.[46]

O'Toole was good, but Rube was superb. Marquard held the Pirates to four scattered singles, allowed an unearned run, and only walked one batter as New York prevailed, 4-1.[47] Both pitchers put up goose eggs through five innings before the Giants broke through in the sixth. Many New York sportswriters claimed this effort was Rube's best since joining the team.[48] Marquard secured his eighth consecutive victory against Cincinnati on May 20, defeating the Reds, 3-0. He was untouchable, allowing only six hits, as his teammates scratched out single runs in the fourth, fifth, and seventh innings.[49] Rube was forced to work out of more jams in his next outing versus Brooklyn on May 24. Although Marquard exhibited signs of wilting on different occasions, solid fielding behind him helped save the day, as New York claimed a 6-3 victory. Third baseman Charles "Buck" Herzog was the Giants' hitting star, smacking a double, a triple, laying down two beautiful sacrifice bunts, and driving in three runs.[50]

Rube raised his record to 10-0 on May 30, defeating Philadelphia in the morning game of a Memorial Day doubleheader, 7-1. While Marquard was batted hard for nine hits, he did fine work in the pinches, allowing only a single run.[51] As the season moved into June, it was quickly becoming apparent that the only actual battle in the National League would be to see who finished second behind New York. The Giants stood at the top with a 28-7 record, 7 ½ games ahead of second-place Cincinnati. For Rube, a new month meant the same results, as he secured his eleventh straight win on June 3, breezing to an 8-3 victory over St. Louis. This contest was never in doubt, as the Giants placed a seven-spot on the scoreboard in the third inning, with catcher Chief Meyers's grand slam homer into the Polo Grounds' left-field bleachers acting as the highlight moment.[52]

In his first 13 appearances, Rube Marquard was a perfect 11-0, with a 1.44 ERA. The star southpaw certainly benefitted from solid run support thus far in 1912, as New York scored 89 runs and rapped out 115 hits in games he started. The man who at one time was an abject failure now was the toast of baseball. John McGraw could rest easily every four days when Rube took his turn on the mound. Vindication was sweet for the Giants' manager, who had always expressed supreme faith in Marquard's potential, even when detractors criticized him for keeping the hurler on his roster.

"I'll keep him because I know he is 'there,'" McGraw had said when Marquard experienced rough patches early in his career. "Any youngster with the 'stuff' he has needs time. When he does come, he will be a world-beater."[53]

When New York opposed Cincinnati at the Polo Grounds on June 8, another pitcher nicknamed Rube proved a worthy adversary. The Reds' John "Rube" Benton matched the Giants' star hurler pitch-for-pitch, giving up a single run in the first inning before his teammates tied the game in the sixth. Benton weakened in the seventh, allowing four runs, and giving New York a 6-2 win, as Marquard notched his twelfth consecutive victory. After a foul tip severely lacerated umpire Cy Rigler's ear in the fifth inning, he was forced to leave the contest and be relieved by substitute arbitrator Robert "Bob" Emslie.[54]

Good fortune helped Rube keep up his hot pace. He was credited with the victory on June 12, as the Giants defeated Chicago, 3-2. When John McGraw pulled Marquard in the bottom of the eighth for pinch hitter Arthur "Tillie" Shafer, New York trailed in the contest, 2-1, before plating two tallies that inning.[55] Although some doubt initially existed over whether James "Doc" Crandall, who hurled the ninth, should be recognized as the victor, Rube received credit with his thirteenth triumph of the season.[56] Round two of Rube Marquard versus Marty O'Toole occurred on June 17 at the Polo Grounds. Rube needed every ounce of guile and strength at his disposal to secure a hard-fought, 5-4 victory over Pittsburgh in 11 innings. The game was played between thunderstorms and delayed by umpires for about 15 minutes in the fifth frame.[57]

Accolades poured in from all areas of the baseball landscape. Cincinnati baseball scribe Ren Mulford, Jr., wrote that Rube Marquard was now a star attraction in New York that rivaled Christy Mathewson. Mulford also opined that while Marquard was a sensational drawing card, his performance kept the Giants so far in front as the pacesetters that the National League race may be over by the Fourth of July.⁵⁸ Earlier in the month, when New York opposed St. Louis, Cardinals manager Roger Bresnahan fantasized about potential glory if Rube were a member of his mound corps. "If I had Marquard," Bresnahan said, "the Cardinals would be at or near the top of the heap. The Rube is the best left-hander I ever saw, and I wouldn't be at all surprised if he won 30 games or more."⁵⁹

Marquard gained his first victory as a relief pitcher in 1912, defeating Boston on June 19 at South End Grounds, 6-5, in extra innings. Rube relieved Leon "Red" Ames in the eighth when the Braves tied the contest and extinguished their rally. After New York took the lead with a run in the tenth, Marquard shut the door in the bottom of the frame, fanning George Jackson to end the game as Bill Sweeney occupied third base.⁶⁰ By capturing his fifteenth consecutive victory of the year, Rube had now established a new modern-era, single-season mark. Marquard's feat surpassed fourteen straight wins in a single season, set by Joe McGinnity and Jack Chesbro in 1904, as well as Ed Reulbach in 1909.⁶¹

Before the modern era, muddled records alleged that in 1886, James "Jim" McCormick had won 24 straight games for the Chicago White Stockings, while John "Pat" Luby secured 20 in a row for the Chicago Colts in 1890, and Old Hoss Radbourn 18 in 1884, with the Providence Grays.⁶² Radbourn's mark, along with Timothy "Tim" Keefe winning 19 straight as a member of the New York Giants in 1888, were the only two positively accurate records.⁶³ Efforts to surpass all records continued for Rube against the Braves on June 21. Although Boston's Hub Perdue outpitched Marquard, the Giants' star southpaw won his sixteenth consecutive game, defeating the Braves, 5-2.⁶⁴ Based on his recent performances, members of the Pittsburgh Pirates believed a colossal fall from the top awaited Rube. Fred Clarke's team felt Marquard should've already been tagged with a loss, claiming an incorrect decision by umpire Cy Rigler against them on June 17 allowed New York to win that game.⁶⁵

Following this victory, the *New York Herald* wrote that Rube jokingly declared he had now reached the pinochle of fame.⁶⁶ Marquard engaged in a spirited battle for the ages on June 25, facing Phillies star pitcher Grover Cleveland Alexander. New York scored their only two runs of the game in the third inning, while the single blemish to Rube's day was a solo home run by catcher William "Bill" Killefer in the sixth, as the Giants prevailed, 2-1.⁶⁷ Marquard's record now stood at 17-0, with a 1.58 ERA. Rube had a tough time against Boston on June 29 but still secured his eighteenth consecutive victory, equaling Old Hoss Radbourn's achievement from 1884. The Giants defeated the Braves in a wild affair, 8-6. New York had won 12 consecutive games while defeating Boston

11 straight times.⁶⁸ When June ended, the Giants were on top of the league with a phenomenal 50-11 record, 13 ½ games ahead of second-place Pittsburgh.

In the first game of a doubleheader against Brooklyn on July 3 at the Polo Grounds, Marquard joined Tim Keefe, defeating the Superbas, 2-1, and winning his nineteenth straight game. Although Brooklyn hurler George "Nap" Rucker outperformed Rube, the staunch southpaw was strong in the clutch, working his way out of numerous situations. The Superbas stranded eight base runners in the first three innings, as Marquard surrendered nine hits.⁶⁹ During a time when a player's success was community-based, a day didn't go by in Cleveland without someone shouting, "Rube is certainly showing them this year," or, "I'll bet Rube just about owns New York this year," while walking past the Marquard household on 3180 West Forty-Sixth Street. Rube's 78-year-old grandmother was an ardent baseball fan, while his stepmother felt he was the greatest pitcher ever and a good boy. Marquard's father was prouder than his son regarding the young man's performance.⁷⁰

When it came to being thrust into baseball's limelight and pushing New York's fans to a fevered pitch, Rube gave credit for his massive success to manager John McGraw, coach Wilbert Robinson, and his teammates playing behind him. After striving to strike out batters when first reaching the majors, experience and wisdom made him realize that he could achieve better results depending on those teammates. Marquard also credited a new pitch in his arsenal, a slow ball he referred to as the "turkey trot," which broke unusually while using the same motion as when tossing a fastball.⁷¹ Offering advice to kids interested in pitching, Rube counseled the need to obtain control first and not worry about throwing curveballs until after mastering this capability. He also warned against straining the arm through overwork and recommended remaining healthy by getting as much sleep as possible while also not drinking or smoking.⁷²

Rube Marquard put all these principles into practice, striving to grab consecutive victory number 20 against the Chicago Cubs on July 8 at West Side Grounds. While anxious fans wondered if they would be crowning this king with more glory, a new conquering hero was born, who extinguished the record flame in one afternoon. Following a few jitters at the game's outset, Cubs rookie hurler Jimmy Lavender was brilliant for Chicago, handing Marquard his first defeat of the 1912 campaign, 7-2. Rube was pulled for pinch hitter Josh Devore in the seventh inning after the Giants' pitcher allowed six runs, five earned tallies, and eight hits.⁷³ Lavender had been locked in a strong groove of his own, tossing shutouts in his past three starts.⁷⁴

Feeling immense pressure certainly was evident in this contest. At second base, rookie Henry "Heinie" Groh, subbing for Larry Doyle, seemed flustered by the sheer magnitude of the moment.[75] Groh committed one of the Giants' three errors in the game, while his unsteadiness and nervousness were apparent on every play involving him.[76] It seemed that Rube had experienced more stress and burden in his recent starts, losing 12 pounds since the season opened.[77] Adding to this angst while suffering his first defeat were the antics of a woman, later identified as Mary Porter, who had taken up residence in a tree overlooking Chicago's ballpark. Fans and players could hear her piercing shrieks throughout the game. Besides yelling things such as, "Take him out," "Knock the cover off the ball," and "Come on, you Cubs," Porter also waved a big shawl.

When manager John McGraw replaced Marquard in the seventh, the hurler trudged dejectedly to the clubhouse, a path that required him to walk near the location where this woman was perched. Mary stared down at the beaten hurler as he walked by and shouted: "Oh, you big bum. I'm certainly glad you got yours." When the game concluded, a large crowd gathered at Polk and Wood streets, where this woman in a tree was entertaining the masses with her roasts, catcalls, and jabs. The fire department was alerted, and Mary Porter was eventually forcibly removed, carried down on a ladder, and returned to the nearby detention hospital for the insane, where she was a resident. After the contest, Rube commented in the clubhouse on the negative karma this woman and her derisive comments had projected. "That poor woman certainly proved to be a jinx," said Marquard. "Her shrill shrieks affected me more than the cries of all the fans inside the park."[78]

While talking with reporters, Marquard also stated he was sorry over not winning his twentieth consecutive game and would be a fool to deny it. Rube said he felt strong and confident before the game and never had more zip on his pitches in his career, working against the Cubs. Marquard wasn't willing to blame his teammates' shoddy defensive work, exhibiting consummate humility while informing the public this record couldn't have been achieved without them.

"But I want to say that my fellow players of the Giants are entitled to just as much credit for my record as I am myself, and perhaps more," said Marquard. "I would not have been able to win as I did if I had not been fortunate in having such a great team behind me and McGraw as my manager."

Rube Marquard also declared the ending of this streak lifted a massive strain that had started to permeate, and his mind now felt at ease.[79] Experiencing such pressure certainly had been noticeable to members of opposing teams in recent weeks. Days after the streak ended, while Brooklyn was playing in Pittsburgh, a member of the Superbas offered his assessment regarding Marquard's fragile state of mind.

"Had he won a few more games, Marquard would have been a fit candidate for the bughouse," said Brooklyn's player. "He was almost a physical wreck when we met him in the East before the present trip. It is true that he defeated us [2-1 on July 3], but he was so nervous that the slightest untoward happening upset him. His mates were at his side almost every inning, trying to take his attention from himself. Every time a fly ball was raised, Rube stood there with clenched fists and shaking limbs until it was caught."

Rube frankly admitted he had been deeply distressed and anxious throughout its latter stages when asked directly about his feelings and impressions regarding this long streak. "Did you ever work at a given task until you felt that it was 'getting' you–that you couldn't think of anything else when you were awake and that your sleep was troubled with dreams of it?" pondered Marquard. "Of course, I want to win every game I pitch, just as does every pitcher who has the good of his team at heart, but to be candid, I'm glad that streak is over.

"It was getting on my nerves. Why, several nights, I went to bed, and the moment I closed my eyes, the air became full of baseballs, gloves, and bats. I could see players running to me as though they were going to annihilate me. When I would finally get to sleep, I was pitching ball all night.

"When I awoke in the morning, I felt as if I hadn't been rested a bit. I want to tell you that the strain of such a performance is awful. It isn't so bad when you're out there pitching. It's after the games and at nights when it gets you. When you are on the mound, your mind is taken up with your work, and you don't worry. Why, when I had my eighteenth straight game, I wanted to go back the next day and try it again. I couldn't get away from the feeling that I ought to pitch at once for fear something might happen to me."[80]

One day after securing his nineteenth consecutive victory, Rube Marquard purchased a stunning stickpin with opal clusters, which he happily showed to his teammates. On the evening following his first defeat, Marquard chucked this trinket that had plagued him with bad luck into the Chicago River on the advice of these baseball brothers.[81] Following his defeat at the Cubs' hands, Rube took the loss in a relief appearance in game one of a doubleheader against St. Louis on July 14, before starting the nightcap and succumbing against the Cardinals, 4-2. Marquard achieved his twentieth victory in the first contest of a twin bill on July 19 at Forbes Field, beating Pittsburgh, 5-4.

When Rube's winning streak reached 19 games on July 3, a 1.63 ERA supported his perfect record through 21 trips to the mound. Marquard's hurling was mediocre in his next 22 appearances, starting with that run ending on July 8, as he went 7-11 with a 3.70 ERA through the remainder of the season. Rube finished the 1912 campaign at 26-11, bolstered by a 2.57 ERA. When Marquard took the bump against Chicago on July 8, the Giants' record stood at 56-13. As Rube stumbled, finding his way throughout the campaign's final three months, New York went 47-35 after their blistering, torrid start. Performing at a .812 percentage throughout an entire season certainly wasn't sustainable. A baseball campaign in its totality is what mattered most, as the Giants claimed the National League pennant with a 103-48 record while finishing ahead of the second-place Pittsburgh by ten games.

The opinion that John McGraw could only count on hurlers Christy Mathewson and Jeff Tesreau was a consensus reached by many as the season wound down. One critic believed Marquard's problems correlated with him attempting to be a foxy twirler who fooled batters with numerous pitches and deliveries rather than rearing back and blazing away with the fastball.[82] A false rumor surrounding Rube's marriage to actress Shirley Kellogg, whom he had appeared alongside in a vaudeville sketch the previous winter, rose to the surface in September while she starred in Broadway's *The Passing Show of 1912*.[83] Although New York was beaten in eight games by the Boston Red Sox in the 1912 World Series (Game Two on October 9 was declared a 6-6 tie after 11 innings), Marquard proved the Giants could count on him at crunch time.

Rube evened the series at one victory apiece in Game Three on October 10, at Fenway Park, tossing a masterpiece and defeating Boston, 2-1. When Marquard reached the bench after finishing each inning, he received attention from a few teammates. One individual took off Rube's cap and mopped his face and head with a towel. A second teammate bundled up his left arm in sweaters, while a third handed Marquard a fresh piece of chewing gum.[84] The Giants' meal ticket helped his team stave off elimination on October 14, defeating the Red Sox in Game Six at the Polo Grounds, 5-2. In the World Series, Rube tossed two complete games, went 2-0, and posted a 0.50 ERA. Following their defeat in the decisive contest at Fenway Park on October 16, the Giants returned to New York the next day without any fanfare, and each player went to team offices to receive their check for $2,566.46; the losers share for each individual.[85]

Days after the World Series ended, Rube Marquard signed a deal to perform on the stage with popular vaudeville actress Blossom Seeley, brokered by her husband, entertainer, and manager, Joe Kane.[86] At the end of the month, advertisements proclaimed Marquard and Seeley would be performing the musical skit *The Nineteenth Straight* at Hammerstein's Victoria Theatre.[87] While these two found immediate chemistry on the stage and in their personal lives, manager John McGraw performed at the Colonial Theatre.[88] When Giants outfielder John "Red" Murray arrived from Elmira, New York, on October 27, he expressed no desire to play favorites between the two, intending to view his teammate's matinee show and watch his boss perform at night.[89]

On October 29, with Rube by her side, Blossom appeared in New York's Jefferson Market Police Court, obtaining a summons against Joe Kane for abuse and physical assault. Seeley claimed her husband had made threats because he was suspicious of her and expressed a jealous streak toward Marquard. Blossom alleged Kane threw a mirror at her and punched her the previous night at their Hotel Hermitage residence. Offering support with Seeley on his arm, Rube proffered that he had heard Kane threaten to "shoot her up onstage." When asked who would be acting as Blossom's new manager, the star pitcher responded: "Mr. Marquard!"[90] Two days later, Seeley announced she had entered into a legal separation from her spouse. When Kane appeared before Magistrate Keyran J. O'Connor in response to the abuse and assault charge, the judge announced that a letter he received from Blossom, who wasn't in attendance, requested a withdrawal of her complaint since the two had agreed to live apart.[91]

Seeley's husband's real name was Joseph Cahen, with Joe Kane being his stage persona.[92] No matter the name, he failed to live up to his end of the agreement, promising not to bother his estranged wife. At 2 a.m. on November 8, the jealous husband and hired New York detectives W. K. Carter and George Kenzie broke down the door and burst into a room lodging Rube and Blossom at the Hotel Dunlop in Atlantic City, New Jersey.[93] Marquard and Seeley evaded detection, climbing down a fire escape to exit the premises, before fleeing in an automobile, with help from hotel proprietor Bob Delaney and manager Frank Bowman. Kane possessed a warrant sworn out by him before local Magistrate Joshua Jagmetty for alienation of affections against Rube. Joe had received credible information that his wife and the pitcher were engaging in a romantic dalliance by the seashore before gathering his goon squad and arriving in Atlantic City days earlier.[94] Kane alleged that when he burst into the room, his wife was under the bed, while Marquard was hiding in a closet, trembling.[95]

The booking agent opted to hit Rube where it hurt, in his pocketbook. Kane filed suit under his real name of Cahen on November 13 in the New York City Supreme Court. He wanted $25,000 in damages relevant to Marquard alienating Blossom Seeley's affections. Cahen alleged the pitcher had persuaded his wife that he wasn't good enough for Blossom.[96] Six days later, in filing his response, Rube denied all the allegations other than a mention in the initial affidavit that he was a famous baseball pitcher.[97] One person expressing extreme disgust over this matter was Giants manager John McGraw.[98] Those who broached the subject with McGraw affirmed the pilot was profoundly bitter in denunciating Marquard's behavior.[99]

Rube offered numerous responses upon hearing about his manager's reaction to the affair with Seeley. Marquard alleged McGraw was jealous of his success as an actor.[100] While performing in Chicago in December, he threatened to remain in vaudeville full-time unless the Giants paid him a salary of $10,000 yearly.[101] Exhibiting a swelled head while discussing his superiority as a playhouse icon over his manager, Rube reasoned that earning $1,500 a week performing on a vaudeville stage was pretty good money, and farming was an option if the Giants didn't recognize his baseball value.[102] Marquard also claimed McGraw had minimized his World Series workload because the pilot was afraid Rube would hog all the glory.[103] Rube said he planned on marrying Blossom Seeley once she became divorced from her husband.[104] That hurdle was officially cleared when Cahen obtained a divorce from his wife on January 15, 1913.[105]

McGraw responded to these remarks by saying that kind of talk made him tired. John vowed Marquard would report for spring training since he had signed a three-year contract before the 1912 campaign. Regarding not using him more often in the World Series because it would justify his demands for a higher salary, McGraw claimed he left it up to Rube about pitching a third game, who had declined.[106] Such drama seemed relatively trivial when considering a profound tragedy related to the Giants. On November 26, 1912, owner John T. Brush passed away while traveling by train from New York to the Pacific Coast. Brush had been ill for several years, suffering from locomotor ataxia.[107]

In the end, Rube got the girl and returned to the diamond. On March 12, 1913, Marquard married Blossom Seeley while the couple performed in San Francisco, California.[108] Later that month, Marquard and McGraw patched up their differences. Rube attached his signature to a contract in San Francisco after new team secretary John B. Foster negotiated a deal. The pitcher left immediately to join his teammates in Houston, Texas.[109] In respect to the suit put forward by Blossom's ex-husband, on October 15, 1913, New York City Supreme Court Justice Joseph E. Newburger signed an edict discontinuing Joseph Cahen's suit to recover $50,000, accepting Marquard's compromise settlement instead. That amount was $2,254.78, Rube's losers share from participating in the recent World Series against the Philadelphia Athletics.[110]

Rube Marquard's modern-era record of winning 19 consecutive games in a single season still stands today. In the campaign that Marquard established this mark, Joe Wood of the Boston Red Sox and the Washington Senators' Walter Johnson won 16 straight games. After this, four other hurlers matched that 16-game threshold until Pittsburgh Pirates reliever Elroy "Roy" Face came closest to besting Rube's record in 1959. Face started that season 17-0 before losing his first game on September 11. Marquard had packed a large amount of living into one glorious year in 1912. While Rube's achievement pushed his mental state to the limit due to the stress and strain he experienced accomplishing this outstanding baseball achievement, the record still endures today as his lasting legacy.

Rube Marquard started out the 1912 campaign by winning 19 consecutive games and establishing a new modern-era, single-season record in that category. The streak ended on July 8 when the Chicago Cubs defeated Marquard and the New York Giants, 7-2, at West Side Grounds. Throughout the game escapee Mary Porter, who resided at a nearby detention hospital for the insane, heckled Rube while perched up in a tree overlooking the ballpark until he exited the contest for a pinch hitter in the seventh inning. In this photo Marquard (right) is warming up alongside teammate Tillie Shafer (left). (Courtesy of the Library of Congress.)

CHAPTER 9

Tris Speaker — 1912

The Model of Consistency and a Two-Bagger Machine

The notion of putting a square peg in a round hole certainly had applied to baseball history when it came to one-dimensional players who only possessed skill or talent in a single area of the game. A batter sustaining a healthy appetite at the plate but bored in the field fell into this category. The same holds for the expert gloveman whose stickwork earned praise when it was mediocre or the slugger desiring to put a charge into the baseball and swinging at nothing but air. Teams have always possessed different pieces that needed to be appropriately aligned to bring positive results. Problems arose when managers attempted to assign roles that didn't fit a particular player or expected an individual to perform beyond their capabilities. Fortunate was the pilot with a roster loaded with players that broke out of the one-dimensional mold, excelling in all aspects of the game.

Baseball's Deadball Era produced its share of well-rounded performers, which scouting experts could classify with the five-tool designation, which is common while rating players today. When separating the wheat from the chaff, adding the qualities of leadership and a winning spirit, and being proficient at hitting, running, throwing, and fielding, one person, gained supreme status as a diamond icon during the second decade of the twentieth century. Outfielder Tristram E. Speaker was an exceptional individual in every department and a two-base record-setter who played on two pennant-winning teams over those ten years.

Tristram Speaker was born on April 4, 1888, in Hubbard, Texas. Little Tristram was a rare breed, expressing a strong desire to play baseball at a young age, which his parents, Archery and Nancy Jane, didn't readily understand. As a boy, Speaker devoted every spare moment of his day to playing ball while sometimes attempting to abandon essential responsibilities so that he could engage in his life's passion. Work on the family ranch, school, and other tasks interfered with those diamond ambitions. Tristram preferred playing baseball to eating and missed meals on many occasions. In Speaker's mind, performing chores on the ranch was insignificant compared to his aspiration of becoming a baseball player.[1]

Speaker also started being called "Tris" when he was a kid, as his parents eliminated the last syllable from the old English name Tristram.[2] When Tris was nine years old, his father, Archery Speaker, passed away.[3] Tristram experienced a busy life as a youth, hunting and fishing, roping cattle, and breaking in horses, besides playing baseball.[4] Speaker threw right-handed until he was propelled from a bronco at ten and broke his right collarbone. Rather than being sidelined because of his useless right limb, Tris continued playing by throwing with his left arm.[5] It was also at this stage of the young baseball virtuoso's life, he started envisioning himself someday becoming a peer among diamond performers and a hero to thousands of adoring baseball fans.[6]

Speaker, an excellent student, enrolled at Fort Worth Polytechnic Institute upon completing his general studies. Tris quickly exhibited more interest in playing football and baseball than in his academic lessons.[7] At 16, Speaker received his first opportunity to play semi-pro baseball with the Hubbard town team. Tris was a pitcher for the squad in a league that received scant notice from those searching for baseball talent. Speaker could throw pitches with blazing speed but lacked control. Tris' manager stuck with him, recognizing his potential until the number of opposing players sent to local hospitals by the hurler became too concerning that he had to release him. One year later, Speaker returned to try out as an infielder and made the squad. Tris' play was so remarkable that it attracted attention outside Hubbard.[8]

In 1906, after Texas League president J. Doak Roberts saw Speaker playing for Hubbard, the eighteen-year-old signed his first professional contract with that organization's Cleburne Railroaders, which the executive owned.[9] Cleburne happened to be the location for league headquarters in 1906. Roberts took Tris under his wing, converting him to an outfielder and using the youngster as a pitcher.[10] Speaker went an uninspiring 2-7 on the bump in 11 appearances and batted .268 while playing 75 games in the outfield. The following year, Tris was a member of the Houston Buffaloes in the reorganized Texas League, which now held a Class C designation, one level above the old institution's minor league status. Used solely as an outfielder, Tris exhibited excellent proficiency as a hitter in 1907, batting .314 in 118 games for the Buffaloes.

Speaker's performance attracted Boston Americans scout George Huff's attention, who signed him to a contract.[11] Huff was able to secure the young man's services from Houston for a modest price of between $750 and $800. Tris made his major league debut as a replacement in right field against the Philadelphia Athletics on September 12, 1907, and went 0-for-2 at the plate. Rough around the edges and insecure, Speaker was reticent on the field while also being intimidated by the major league environment and living in a big metropolis. After drawing his release from the Americans when the season concluded, Tris attempted to find employment with other teams. He was rejected by each one, including John McGraw's New York Giants. Although not under contract for 1908, Speaker arrived at Boston's spring training facility in Little Rock, Arkansas, and was permitted to practice with the squad.[12]

Before the 1908 campaign, Boston farmed Tris out to the Southern Association's Little Rock Travelers, where it would be manager Mickey Finn's task to bring the young outfielder's potential to the surface.[13] Boston president John I. Taylor brokered an agreement with the Travelers' front office, turning Speaker over in exchange for not paying anything for the unrestricted use of Little Rock's training grounds for his team's spring session.[14] The arrangement was finalized, although Taylor had failed to mail out a contract to Tris by the mandated date of March 1. Although Speaker technically was a free agent, he still signed to play for Little Rock, who forwarded all the proper paperwork to baseball's National Commission.

This little twist made things interesting, as Tris led the association in hitting with a .350 average, and his all-around play improved dramatically. Finn, sensing a massive windfall from potentially selling Speaker to interested parties throughout the year, attempted to purchase his release from Boston, now known as the Red Sox, but was continuously rejected by Taylor.[15] The foresight of Little Rock's manager was accurate, as offers poured in from major league teams. An undisclosed amount was proposed by the Brooklyn Superbas' Charles Ebbets, while an agent representing the Cincinnati Reds stated owner Garry Herrmann was willing to pay $7,500 to acquire Tris. The Pittsburgh Pirates were close behind, proffering $6,000 to buy Speaker.

At the end of August, Little Rock's directors announced that out of loyalty to John I. Taylor and due to the previous gentleman's agreement, they were selling Tris Speaker to Boston for a paltry $500.[16] In the middle of September, New York Highlanders owner Frank Farrell informed Taylor that former Red

Sox manager Deacon McGuire, whom Boston had fired at the end of August, approached him. Farrell explained that McGuire had alerted him to the technicality of Speaker not being offered a contract by March 1. Frank refused to listen to this deceitful business perpetrated by a vindictive former employee. McGuire then made a trip to Cleveland, attempting to convince Naps' ownership to subvert Boston purchasing the outfielder. Such tactics became moot when Tris signed a contract to play for the Red Sox in 1909.[17]

Exhibiting thoughtful courtesy, Taylor informed Ebbets and Pirates owner Barney Dreyfuss that he had exercised his option on Speaker and then rejected an offer of $5,500 from Brooklyn's owner to purchase the young player.[18]

Motivated by his plight surrounding the past year's circumstances, Tris Speaker made his triumphant return to Boston, exhibiting an assertive and self-assured demeanor when undertaking any diamond task.[19] While he only batted .224 in 31 games for the Red Sox, Speaker handled every chance that came his way in the outfield without committing an error. Months after the 1908 season ended, Tris philosophically laid out the next step of this natural progression, in his eyes, to becoming one of baseball's greatest players. "We speak of a fellow as a coming man when he makes a go of it," said Speaker.[20]

In 1909, Tris boldly transformed into manhood as a diamond performer. Speaker earned a starting berth in Boston's outfield and served notice that he would be a key cog, influencing games with both a bat and a glove. Tris appeared in 143 contests for the Red Sox, batting .309, smacking seven home runs, and driving in 77 runs. Speaker also established his credentials as a proficient ballhawk in center field, leading the American League in putouts (319), assists (35), and fielding percentage (.973). Tris was adept at reaching fly balls that eluded others and participating in more chances because he played a very shallow center field, standing 30 to 40 feet, or less on occasion, behind second base. Through undertaking this transformative, aggressive style, Speaker sometimes acted as an extra infielder, who became involved in pickoff maneuvers and double plays at second.[21] The premise behind such defensive positioning was that it allowed Tris to move in on chopped hits, while his sturdy legs permitted him to run toward the fence and snag long drives.[22]

Speaker's ascension as a great player continued in 1910. The sophomore jinx was an oxymoron, as Tris appeared in 141 games, batted .340, and stole 35 bases for the second consecutive campaign. Speaker followed that up with a beautiful encore in 1911, playing in 141 contests and hitting .334. Through his first three full major league seasons, Boston had finished third (1909), fourth (1910), and fifth (1911). Although the Red Sox seemed to regress each year as

Tris climbed the stardom mountain, the pieces fell into place to allow this team to become a solid competitor in the American League race. Flanking Speaker in Boston's stacked outfield was George "Duffy" Lewis and Harry Hooper. William Lawrence "Larry" Gardner anchored the third base position, while Charles "Heinie" Wagner played shortstop, and Arthur Clyde Engle expertly performed the utility role. Hurler Howard Ellsworth "Joe" Wood, known as "Smoky Joe," seemed poised to take the next step toward greatness after going 23-17 with a 2.02 ERA in 1911.

Changes to Boston's management structure came swiftly after the 1911 campaign ended. News from Chicago in early November indicated that a long-discussed deal regarding the Taylor family, selling half their interest in the team, had been finalized. Former player James "Jimmy" McAleer, who managed the Washington Senators in 1911, and Robert McRoy, right-hand man to American League president Ban Johnson, joined the organization. Jake Stahl, who had played for the Red Sox in 1903, and from 1908 through 1910, was also part of this group. Stahl's father-in-law, Henry W. Mahan, and entrepreneur C. H. Bandle, both from Chicago, rounded out this coalition. The deal was consummated, with a forthcoming organizational meeting expected to formally elect McAleer club president and McRoy team secretary.[23] Stahl promised Boston's new team president he would manage and play first base in 1912 if his family consented, meaning permission needed to be granted by his wife.[24] Mrs. Jennie Stahl was amenable, and Jake signed a two-year deal to be the Red Sox's player/manager.[25]

With the on-field hierarchy in place, John I. Taylor could now devote all his attention to overseeing the construction of Boston's new baseball palace, Fenway Park. Taylor promised Red Sox fans that this brand new ballpark would be one of the finest ever erected in the country. In November, when John inspected progress on the work, which had started at the end of September, he was amazed at how far the building project had advanced in such a short time. Within a half-mile of the Charles River, the sterling ballpark would be pretty accessible due to the addition of new streetcar lines to accommodate the massive crowds expected at the new grounds.[26]

As team president, Jimmy McAleer's first official act was to forward circular letters and contracts from his Youngstown, Ohio, home to each of Boston's players. Robert McRoy, who was already very adept at interacting positively with the press and the paying public, immediately built a strong relationship with baseball correspondents. McAleer announced that manager Jake Stahl and catcher William "Bill" Carrigan would leave for Hot Springs, Arkansas, on

February 20, 1912, to engage in early workouts and prepare for spring training. Jimmy planned on arriving at the training grounds with a group of Red Sox players on March 10. When talking to reporters for the first time, McAleer intimated it was the destiny of Connie Mack's defending champion Philadelphia Athletics to receive a stiff rebuke from a few other teams.

"All great clubs come back," said McAleer, "and this looks like the year, as Detroit, Cleveland, Chicago, and Boston look much stronger, and with a good start, we can make a great race this year."[27]

Boston's team president refuted a ridiculous rumor that he planned on trading Tris Speaker to reacquire third baseman Harry Lord, whom the Red Sox had shipped to the Chicago White Sox in 1910. Such a proposition seemed to be pure fabrication since Larry Gardner was doing a fine job at the hot corner, while the idea of dealing one of baseball's top outfielders for a player the team didn't need seemed to border on ludicrously insane.[28] When the time arrived for spring training to commence, McAleer decreed that all players report to Hot Springs. However, Harry Hooper, second baseman Stephen "Steve" Yerkes, pitcher Thomas "Buck" O'Brien, and Speaker still hadn't signed contracts.[29]

Boston management didn't seem concerned that their gifted center fielder wasn't in attendance when the training session started.[30] Tris finally arrived at Hot Springs on Saturday night, March 16. McAleer immediately went into conference with Speaker to see if the two could hammer out contract terms.[31] On March 19, Tris was the final player to come into the fold when he signed a one-year contract, presumably including a salary increase.[32] Although the weather hadn't always been cooperative during the training session, Jake Stahl's boys were relatively well-conditioned, thanks to the benefits of long hikes along mountain roads and the area's hot mineral baths.[33] Each player believed pitcher Smoky Joe Wood was in excellent shape and ready to embark on a sensational season.[34]

The Red Sox broke camp and traveled to Nashville for an exhibition game on April 2. Before opening the regular season against the New York Highlanders at Hilltop Park, on April 11, Boston had a slate of games scheduled against the Cincinnati Reds on three consecutive days, starting on April 5 at that team's new baseball grounds, Redland Field.[35] Having received harsh criticism over his team's past performance, John I. Taylor was anxious to see if local fans would appreciate the new stockholders' diligent efforts to produce a pennant-contending team.[36] Rabid Red Sox baseball patrons were giddy with anticipation over Fenway Park's inaugural major league game, scheduled for April 18, resplendent with all the pomp and circumstance usually afforded such a monumental event.

An official dedication, with Ban Johnson, Reds owner Gary Herrmann, and White Sox magnate Charles Comiskey as honored guests, was planned for later that spring.[37]

A large crowd was on hand at Hilltop Park to witness the opening-day game between Boston and New York on April 11. Trailing 2-1, heading into the ninth inning, the Red Sox exploded for four runs and held on to defeat the Highlanders, 5-3. Joe Wood tossed a complete-game victory, recovering after allowing two runs during a shaky first inning.[38] Tris Speaker went 0-for-3 at the plate and drew one walk. Boston made it two in a row over New York on April 12, beating the Highlanders, 5-2. Jake Stahl starred at the plate, going 4-for-4 and reaching on a base on balls. The Red Sox rolled out of the gate strong in the first inning by scoring three tallies, with Speaker's two-run homer supplying the critical jolt of energy.[39] Boston finished off their sweep over the Highlanders with an 8-4 win one day later, before losing their first game of the season against the Philadelphia Athletics, 4-1, on April 15. The Red Sox returned to a winning frame of mind on April 16, defeating Philadelphia, 9-2, as hurler Joe Wood fanned 11 batters.[40]

The weather thwarted Boston in its effort to build on this solid start. Rain canceled the final contest of the Athletics series and then wreaked havoc on the grand plans to christen Fenway Park. Team officials canceled the game against New York on April 18, while the Red Sox also didn't play a doubleheader commemorating Bunker Hill Day the following day. When the Boston organization called off these contests about two hours before festivities were to commence, at least 10,000 patrons milled around or near the new ballpark, exhibiting disappointment as the sun broke through the clouds for a few minutes. Many of these people had traveled great distances for an opportunity to watch a baseball game at the new ballpark. Red Sox management was frustrated that horrible weather had cost them a windfall at the gate.[41]

Boston finally played a game at Fenway Park on April 20, as a large crowd of around 24,000 passionate rooters watched the Red Sox claim a thriller over the Highlanders in 11 innings, 7-6. Buck O'Brien was ineffective on the mound for Boston before giving way to Charles "Charley" Hall, allowing five runs in the first three innings, and dodging more trouble in the fourth, when he escaped unscathed as New York stranded three runners. The Red Sox clawed their way back into contention and secured victory in the eleventh frame when Steve Yerkes reached first base on an error by Highlanders' third baseman Albert "Cozy" Dolan and eventually scored on Tris Speaker's single.[42] Tris also smacked his first double of the season. Following this thrilling victory, Boston lost two out of three games in their next series against the Washington Senators while anointing their new baseball palace.

The defending champion Athletics arrived at Fenway Park on April 26 and were throttled by the Red Sox, 7-6. Substitute first baseman Hugh Bradley was the day's hero, going 2-for-4 at the plate, with one double and one home run, while knocking in five runs. Bradley launched a wind-aided round-tripper over the left-field fence with two teammates on base and Philadelphia leading 6-4 in the seventh inning. Hugh's homer went down in the record books as the first-ever hit at Fenway Park.[43] Speaker was the featured artist the following day, receiving acclaim for his batting, fielding, and throwing as Boston beat the Athletics, 6-5.[44] Tris went 3-for-4 at the plate, scored three runs, and smacked his second double of the campaign.

Philadelphia gained some revenge on April 29, blitzing the Red Sox, 7-1, before Boston claimed the final game of the series the next afternoon, 6-1. Hugh Bedient did excellent work on the mound after replacing Charley Hall, who arbitrator Silk O'Loughlin ejected in the fourth inning for kicking over the home plate umpire's calls. Newspapers commended Speaker for making one of the contest's three spectacular running catches in the outfield.[45] He also went 3-for-4 at the plate and scored twice. As April ended, the Red Sox were in second place with a 9-4 record, ½ game behind Chicago. Through the campaign's early stages, Tris's batting average was .333.

Boston sportswriter Tim Murnane wrote that while the Red Sox were winning, they still hadn't started playing the high-class style of baseball expected from them. Murnane felt this would be remedied once the days became warmer while claiming the primary reason for Fenway Park's disappointing attendance to date was because of poor weather.[46] He also believed that secondary factors other than cold and rain contributed to the small crowds. Tim stated the new ballpark wasn't as readily accessible as the old Huntington Avenue Baseball Grounds. The bleacher inhabitants weren't thrilled over Fenway Park's configuration, which pushed their section further back to make room for the big grandstand. Murnane also found the relaxed, friendly attitude of the past no longer possible due to the new ballpark's immense size and entrances at opposite ends.[47]

As the 1912 baseball campaign entered May, Tris Speaker's name was in the news, thanks to a *Houston Chronicle* interview involving J. Doak Roberts, the man responsible for starting the outfielder on his path to a major league vocation. While discussing how detractors could be highly effective in derailing the careers of even talented ballplayers, Roberts cited Tris. He related that when major league teams courted Speaker, a Texas League umpire had expected a commission for his sales pitch to Chicago magnate Charles Comiskey. When Roberts chastised the arbitrator for his behavior and remarked he had already brokered a deal for Tris' sale to the White Sox, this umpire went back to Comiskey and knocked the outfielder's ability. Chicago's owner then wired Doak a message: "We can't use Speaker."

When Roberts finally helped finalize the deal with Boston scout George Huff, he needed to convince Tris' mother, Nancy Jane Speaker, that playing baseball was in her son's best interests. Mrs. Speaker, not understanding the game, felt the buying and selling of players was akin to bartering over slaves.

"I saw that I had to overcome Mrs. Speaker's objections," said Roberts. "So I made a trip to Corsicana [Texas], where a kinsman of hers and a good friend of mine was in business, and I explained the case to him. I told him that if Tris made good, he would earn a salary of four or five thousand dollars. I told him that in his winter profession, he could hope to earn but $40 or $50 a month and that he risked his life every time he climbed a telegraph pole. And I added that Speaker was expected to report at Boston at once. If he did so, traveling with the Red Sox, he would have an opportunity to see the big cities of the country—New York, Chicago, Philadelphia, St. Louis, Washington—places that would be an education for him to see. And I added, 'Let him go on this fall trip. And then let Mrs. Speaker decide next year whether he is to go back or not. And then I will not say a word one way or the other to influence her.'

"Mrs. Speaker came over to Corsicana the next day, and her relative put the case to her as I had explained it to him. So Tris got his fall tryout, and next year there was no dissenting voice from Mrs. Speaker. And I am satisfied that she has never regretted our influence in gaining her first consent."[48]

Red Sox fans were indeed ecstatic that Mrs. Speaker had acquiesced over her son continuing his baseball career. Patrons displayed some disappointment as Boston lost against Washington, 2-1, on May 1, with Joe Wood's wild pitch sending home the game's winning run in the ninth inning.[49] When the Red Sox turned the tables one day later, beating the Senators, 6-5, Tris was commended for making four difficult catches in center field and recording three timely singles.[50] Boston lost their second game in a row against Washington on May 4, 8-7, despite Speaker going 4-for-4 at the plate, scoring three runs, and connecting for a double and a home run.[51] On May 8, an astonishing rumor was perpetrated in the lobby of New York's Hotel Somerset, where the St. Louis Browns were staying while playing the Highlanders. Pondering over New York first baseman Harold "Hal" Chase's mysterious illness, baseball scribes exchanged hot gossip resembling fantasyland fiction, claiming the Highlanders would execute a trade in the next few days, swapping him for either Senators hurler Walter Johnson or Tris Speaker.[52]

After smacking only three doubles in the season's first month, Tris delved into the two-bagger genre in back-to-back games, smashing one each day as the Red Sox defeated St. Louis, 14-9, May 13, and 6-5, the following afternoon. Speaker kept that hot streak going when he blasted his sixth double of the campaign on May 15, as Boston beat the Browns, 2-1. On May 17, a huge crowd witnessed the official dedication of the Red Sox's new $650,000 baseball plant. Before the contest, White Sox skipper Nixey Callahan was presented with a beautiful floral arrangement, courtesy of admiring fans. Although Chicago secured the game with four runs in the ninth inning to defeat Boston, 5-2, Callahan missed the comeback, having been ejected in the eighth by umpire Frederick Westervelt for arguing a decision too vociferously.[53]

Tris Speaker smacked his seventh double on May 22, as the Red Sox crushed the Cleveland Naps, 9-0. The next day, Tris played the hero role when Boston secured a ten-inning victory over Cleveland, 6-5. Speaker fired his first salvo by hitting a three-run homer in the fifth. Trailing 5-2 in the ninth, the Naps scored three runs to tie the game. After Joe Wood retired the side in the top of the tenth, Tris scored the winning run in the bottom of the frame. Following his single, Speaker moved to second on Duffy Lewis's sacrifice bunt. Tris kept running to third since nobody covered the bag, as his teammate was being retired at the initial sack. He scored when Cleveland's first baseman, Edward "Eddie" Hohnhorst, made an ill-advised, late throw to the unoccupied hot corner area.[54] On May 27, Tris went 3-for-4, swatted two doubles, and scored three runs as Philadelphia walloped Boston, 12-6.[55]

The Red Sox occupied second place when May ended with a 25-13 mark, placing them two games behind league-leading Chicago. Baseball scribes hinted that Speaker was tossing his hat into the ring as a challenger for the American League batting title with Ty Cobb of Detroit and Cleveland's Shoeless Joe Jackson.[56] Tris' average currently stood at .386, while Cobb was hitting .374, and Jackson lagged at .308. Speaker's doubles total stood at nine heading into the new month. In June, Tris elevated his game in that department, becoming a two-bagger machine, initially receiving credit for 15 doubles over 30 days.

Speaker started this blistering extra-bases parade by smacking doubles on consecutive days at League Park, as the Red Sox defeated the Naps in ten innings on June 2, 5-4, and then were beaten the following day, 4-3. Although he didn't drill a double on June 4, Tris went 3-for-4 at the plate when Cleveland triumphed over Boston, 5-1, as "Lajoie Day" was celebrated at the ballpark in honor of the 10th anniversary of Nap Lajoie joining that team. Lajoie was presented with a horseshoe containing 1,009 silver pieces from fans, while teammates gave him $125 in gold.[57] In the Red Sox's 5-2 victory over Detroit on June 6, spectacular catches by Speaker and Harry Hooper helped snuff out Tigers rallies.[58] The following afternoon, Tris belted his twelfth double of the season as Boston succumbed to Detroit, 4-3.

On June 9, Tris Speaker hit for the cycle as the Red Sox obliterated St. Louis, 9-2.[59] Speaker added doubles number 14 and 15 to his resume in back-to-back games, as Boston was victorious over the Browns, 3-2, on June 10, and 4-0, the following afternoon. When the Red Sox arrived in Chicago to begin a series on June 13, they held a one-game lead over the second-place White Sox. Boston lost the series' first game before catching fire and claiming the final three contests. Before the first contest, played on a diamond saturated by rain, Jimmy McAleer and Robert McRoy were honored. McAleer received a chest of silver, while McRoy was gifted a watch by local admirers. Admiring fans presented manager Jake Stahl with floral tributes. Umpire John "Jack" Sheridan also banished eight Boston team members from this game for protesting one of his decisions.[60] After receiving floral arrangements before the first contest, Stahl was given a case containing silver two days later, similar to McAleer's.[61]

Tris continued adding more two-base gold nuggets to his treasure chest. In the final game of the Chicago series on June 17, Speaker blasted two doubles. Tris procured two more on June 22, smacking a single two-bagger in both ends of a doubleheader against New York at Hilltop Park. The Red Sox cruised to a duo of easy victories, outscoring the Highlanders in the twin bill, 23-5. In the first game of a doubleheader against Washington at National Park, on June 26, Tris struck his twentieth double of the season while the Senators claimed a 3-2 victory in ten innings. Boston won the nightcap, 3-0, as Joe Wood and Walter Johnson engaged in a classic pitchers' duel. Speaker plated two critical insurance markers with a triple in the sixth inning.[62] Tris added another two-bagger on June 27, when the Senators defeated the Red Sox, 8-4, as the game was shortened to eight innings so that Boston could catch their train home.[63] Speaker eventually lost this double due to an official scoring change.

Boston's star outfielder finished up the month by recording two doubles in the first game of a doubleheader against New York on June 28, which the Red Sox won, 5-4, and then connected once again the following afternoon in the second show of a twin bill. Joe Wood tossed a one-hitter as Boston won that contest, 6-0, which umpires reduced to seven innings because of darkness.[64]

As the month ended, a newspaper article broached the subject surrounding a theory that players didn't necessarily like teammates who were popular with the fans. The piece concluded that Tris Speaker was the exception, adored by the public and Boston's other players. There wasn't any doubt Tris was the team's most popular player, revered for his humble and modest demeanor. For good measure, this article also declared Speaker possessed the best throwing arm in baseball.[65]

The Boston machine looked unstoppable as it roared with proficiency and powerful momentum into July. The Red Sox were atop the standings with a 46-21 record, six games ahead of second-place Philadelphia. Tris' average stood at a lofty .393, while the great Ty Cobb was batting .366. Speaker's two-bagger barrage continued in July, as he blasted 12 doubles that month. Consistency was the catchphrase in the month's first week, with Tris connecting for five two-base hits in eight games from July 1 through July 6. Boston also secured four out of six contests in a critical series against the Athletics that started on July 3 at Shibe Park. Before the first game, fireworks and a band concert began the celebration, which concluded by raising a pennant to the top of the Philadelphia ballpark's flagpole, commemorating the Athletics winning the 1911 World Series.[66]

A question arose over whether 24-year-old Tris Speaker was baseball's new king. Boston manager Jake Stahl tamped down such discussion, expounding upon a teamwork philosophy while telling his players: "This is not a one-man team; you are all entitled to the credit." Since he had no connection to this organization and wasn't concerned about keeping players happy and focused while fighting to win a pennant, Pittsburgh Pirates scout Billy Murray offered his opinion regarding Tris without any reluctance.

"You can praise Ty Cobb, Joe Jackson, and other great outfielders in the big leagues," said Murray, "but none of them is in the class with Tris Speaker of the Red Sox. Speaker is the best player on the diamond today. As a hitter, fielder, thrower, and baserunner, he has Ty Cobb and others beaten. I have seen all of the stars of 25 years, and Tris is the king."[67]

While Speaker received warranted praise and adoration, Jimmy McAleer explained the subpar performance thus far of young hurler Buck O'Brien. After showing promise during his late-season debut in 1911, O'Brien's record dropped to 7-8 following a loss to Philadelphia in game one of a doubleheader on July 5. McAleer blamed Buck's poor performance on the pitcher suffering from a stomach problem.[68] O'Brien eventually turned things around, finishing the 1912 campaign with a 20-13 record and a 2.58 ERA. Following a few games where hitting doubles eluded him, Tris got back on track against St. Louis on

July 10, smacking his twenty-ninth two-bagger of the season, as the Browns defeated Boston, 9-2. Speaker added another double in the second game of a doubleheader on July 12, with the Red Sox beating Detroit in an 11-inning thriller at Fenway Park, 1-0. Tris scored the winning run when his hit went through the legs of left fielder Jim Delahanty for three bases and then came home on Duffy Lewis's single.[69]

Tris regained that two-bagger he had lost on June 27, when official scorers changed his eleventh-inning safety to a double and a one-base error on Delahanty. As Boston prepared to play the Tigers on July 15, Jimmy McAleer expressed supreme confidence that his team would claim the league pennant and increase their current 6 ½ game lead over second-place Washington. Jimmy explained that a simple recipe for success instilled him with such a high level of confidence. "Our pitchers are working like machinery," said McAleer, "and our hitters are landing on the ball just when most needed. The whole team is working in harmony, and, honestly, I think we have that flag right now."[70]

In each game that Tris Speaker smacked his final four doubles of the month, the Red Sox were victorious. Boston defeated Chicago, 3-2, on July 20, beat Cleveland, 8-3, two days later, and then handled the White Sox, 5-4, on July 28 and 7-5, the following afternoon. Proving he wasn't a one-trick pony, Speaker had launched a tenth-inning, two-run homer off Ed Walsh into White Sox Park's left-field bleachers on July 27. This four-bagger proved to be the difference in a 5-3 victory.[71] When the month concluded, the Red Sox's record stood at 67-30. After briefly topping the .400 mark in the middle of July, Tris was currently hitting .392, while Ty Cobb sizzled at .422, and Joe Jackson was batting .369. According to Senators manager Clark Griffith, Speaker and pitcher Joe Wood were the two players most responsible for Boston building up a strong lead in the American League. Griffith added that while he didn't expect Tris to experience a slump, he felt it was Wood's fate to be plagued by a rough patch on the mound.[72]

Regarding legging out doubles, Speaker's production tailed off slightly to ten in August. Tris bolted out of the gate, swatting four two-baggers from August 1 through August 7. When Speaker connected for a two-base hit on August 9, while Boston defeated Detroit at Navin Field, 6-1, it was double number 40 in 1912. Some concerns arose when the Red Sox kicked off a long homestand on August 14 against St. Louis. Potential worries existed for team management and fans when a report claimed that Tris' mother, who had arrived in Boston to watch him play, might attempt to convince her son to quit baseball and return home.⁷³ A newspaper article presented an interview where Nancy Jane Speaker appeared quite forthcoming while expressing her feelings on this subject.

"I am pleased with his success," she said, talking about Tris, "and proud of him always. But–he is my baby. I want him for myself–and he belongs to everybody. We have a quiet little home down in Texas. It's a little home with sunflowers in the backyard and morning glories over the porch at the side. I want Tris to give up baseball and come and live there quietly like we used to live before he began to play. I never wanted him to play.

"His father died when Tris was nine years old, and my boy has taken care of me since then. He always was a smart boy. Why, at 17, he ran an oil mill all by himself. Now he is only 23 [24-years-old], and I want him to come home. He should have been a mechanic."⁷⁴

One individual connected to the press believed this tale to be embellished melodrama perpetrated by scribes needing to hunt up a story on a day that Boston played no game due to rain. The dissenting writer from El Paso, Texas, Norman M. Walker, surmised Mrs. Speaker was probably doing nothing more nefarious than wishing her son good luck, continuing his magnificent pace throughout the year.⁷⁵ Regardless of which account passed muster, Speaker remained with the Red Sox, while his mother eventually returned to Texas. Following a brief drought, Tris slammed his forty-first double of the campaign on August 19, as Boston defeated the Tigers at Fenway Park, 4-3. With 78 wins now on the team's ledger, manager Jake Stahl expressed his determination to reach 100 victories since that total assuredly guaranteed a pennant.⁷⁶ Philadelphia second baseman Edward "Eddie" Collins provided bulletin board material for Boston's clubhouse, stating that the Red Sox players were starting to weaken and feel the strain from leading the pack.

Sportswriter Tim Murnane proclaimed Tris Speaker as baseball's most remarkable player. Murnane said Speaker's importance to his team was commensurate with Detroit's Ty Cobb and Honus Wagner of the Pittsburgh Pirates.⁷⁷ Tris smacked double number 42 on August 26, as Chicago defeated the Red Sox, 4-2. Umpires called the game on August 27 after 12 innings with the score tied 8-8. Speaker stroked a triple and blasted his eighth home run of the year in the fourth off former teammate Edgar "Eddie" Cicotte, whom Boston had sold to the White Sox in July.⁷⁸ Tris added two more doubles on August 28, hitting one in each game, as Boston swept Chicago by scores of 5-3 and 3-0. Speaker recorded his forty-fifth two-bagger of the season on August 30, with the Red Sox beating the Athletics, 7-4.

Jake Stahl's boys didn't seem to be wilting as Eddie Collins had suggested, holding an 11-game lead over second-place Washington as the season entered September. Although he no longer controlled the team's day-to-day operations, John I. Taylor received credit and praise for procuring the talent Stahl had developed into a pennant winner.[79] Many fans believed Tris Speaker was a better all-around player than Cobb, although they weren't quite willing to accede every inch of ground regarding Ty's proficiency as a hitter.[80] On September 5, Speaker blasted double number 46, as Boston expanded their lead over Philadelphia and Washington to 14 ½ games, with a 4-3 victory over the Senators.

Over 30,000 fans packed Fenway Park on September 6 to watch staff aces Joe Wood and Walter Johnson face each other in the series' third game. Stahl arranged this challenge after Senators skipper Clark Griffith claimed Wood was a coward if he didn't pitch against Johnson, who at one point had won 16 consecutive games in 1912.[81] On top of this historical pitching clash, Joe came out on top, beating Walter, 1-0, and winning his fourteenth in a row. Tris accounted for the contest's only run when he smacked his forty-seventh double into the left-field overflow crowd in the sixth inning and scored on Duffy Lewis's two-bagger.[82] Speaker's forty-eighth two-base hit of the season occurred in the first game of a doubleheader on September 15, as Boston was defeated by St. Louis, 5-4, at Sportsman's Park. Smoky Joe recorded his sixteenth consecutive victory in the nightcap, securing a 2-1 win, as umpires shortened the game to eight innings.[83]

Speaker's mother, who had joined her son on the early leg of the Red Sox road trip, returned to Texas when the games in St. Louis concluded. During a recent interview, while his squad played in Detroit, Browns manager George Stovall had declared that Boston was the best team ever developed in the American League and should effortlessly smother John McGraw's New York Giants in the upcoming World Series. Stovall also stated that Tris was better than Ty Cobb and Wood superior to Walter Johnson.[84] Washington's star hurler also weighed in, ordaining Speaker as the organization's best hitter.

"Speaker has absolutely no weakness at the bat," said Johnson. "You might just as well pass him as to try to coax him to offer at bad balls. When Tris comes up, all I do is to put everything I have on the ball and pray that he does not hit it on the nose."[85]

Tris clouted his forty-ninth double as the Red Sox lost the first game of a doubleheader against Cleveland on September 17 in 11 innings, 4-3. The Naps also secured the second contest shortened by umpires to five frames, 3-2. Although Boston was idle the following day, they clinched the American

League pennant after Chicago defeated the Athletics, 9-1, in the first game of a doubleheader.[86] When Cleveland swept the Red Sox in a second twin bill on September 19, it marked the first time they had lost four consecutive games in 1912. The proceedings were quite bizarre, as the first game was shortened to five innings because of rain, while umpires had to call the second contest after six stanzas due to darkness. Speaker and Jake Stahl were also ejected in game one by umpire Tommy Connolly for arguing over one of his decisions.[87] Joe Wood's sixteen-game winning streak ended on September 20, when the Tigers defeated him, 6-4.[88]

While the team was in Cleveland, Jimmy McAleer offered that in the hunt to secure the American League flag, Tris Speaker and Joe Wood acted as executioners for Boston's opponents while commending Bill Carrigan and Heinie Wagner for their brainwork.[89] McAleer also spoke admiringly about Speaker's strong commitment to the team-first concept. "I consider Tris Speaker a far more valuable player than Cobb," said McAleer while discussing his team. "This Speaker fellow is a wonder. I rate him the best player in the country today, and that doesn't exclude Cobb. He's a valuable man because he's in there every day doing his best to win—not necessarily to swell his own average but to obtain more runs for his team than the other fellow gets.

"And with all his success, he's a grand boy. He isn't a bit swell-headed because he has made a great name for himself. That's another great thing in his favor."[90]

Boston resumed strutting their winning stride with an 11-4 victory over the Tigers on September 21. Speaker went 2-for-3, scored three runs, and legged out an inside-the-park home run.[91] Three days later, when the Red Sox lost game one of a twin bill versus New York, 5-2, Tris connected for his fiftieth double of the campaign. Tris clubbed another two-bagger on September 25, as Joe Wood pushed his record to 33-5 on the year (he finished the season at 34-5), defeating the Highlanders, 6-0. Without any fanfare or mention in publications, Speaker established a new modern-era record in a 3-2 loss against Washington on September 28. Tris launched his fifty-second double of the season, shattering the modern-era mark established by Nap Lajoie in 1910 when the record books credited him with 51 two-baggers. Speaker finished the campaign with 53 doubles, smacking his final two-base hit on October 4, as Philadelphia defeated Boston, 4-3.

The Red Sox surpassed Jimmy McAleer's goal of winning 100 games, going 105-47, and finishing 14 games in front of the second-place Senators. Performing the role as Boston's catalyst, Tris Speaker experienced a monumental season. Speaker batted .383, stole 52 bases, and tied the Athletics' Frank Baker for the league lead in home runs with ten, besides pacing the circuit in doubles. Regarding defensive categories for center fielders, Tris led the organization in assists (35), double plays (12), and fielding percentage (.957). Speaker finished third in the American League batting race behind Ty Cobb (.410, later adjusted to .409) and Joe Jackson (.395).[92] On October 3, Tris received validation for his performance. On that date, the voting committee announced that he, along with New York Giants' second baseman Larry Doyle, were the winners of automobiles awarded by the Chalmers Motor Company to the player deemed most valuable to their team in each league.[93] Speaker fell five points short of unanimous selection with 59, while Doyle garnered 48.[94]

Tris' magnificent season was topped off grandly when the Boston Red Sox defeated the Giants in the World Series, four games to three. Before the World Series started, Detroit manager Hughie Jennings stated New York needed to stop Speaker if the Giants were to achieve their desire to be crowned world champions.[95] Some of McGraw's players may have taken Jennings's advice too literally. With one out in the tenth inning of Game Two at Fenway Park on October 9, which ended tied 6-6, Tris blasted an offering from hurler Christy Mathewson to center field and started tearing around the bases. When Speaker reached the hot corner sack, intending to head home, Giants third baseman Buck Herzog deliberately tripped him. Tris had to fight past Herzog to arrive at home plate and score as catcher Art Wilson muffed the relay throw. As his Texas temper kicked in, Speaker threatened to settle the matter with Buck after receiving no satisfaction from umpires Cy Rigler and Silk O'Loughlin.

A doctor and a trainer attended to Tris that night, wrapping hot bandages on his sore ankle.[96] When Boston had their turn, taking batting practice the following day before Game Three at Fenway Park, Speaker entered the fray with his foot shrouded in bandages. Although Tris made a remarkable catch in the outfield, robbing New York's Arthur "Art" Fletcher of a potential triple, his face exhibited agony and pain as he limped throughout the contest.[97] This tight post-season series came down to a scintillating Game Eight at Fenway Park on October 16, which went into extra innings. After New York scored a run in the top of the tenth to take a 2-1 lead, Boston responded with two markers in the bottom of the frame off Mathewson to claim the game and the title.

Pinch hitter Clyde Engle reached second base when the Giants' Fred Snodgrass dropped his fly ball to center field. Snodgrass made amends with Harry Hooper at the plate, making a sensational grab on the batter's blistering drive to center. Steve Yerkes followed by drawing a walk. Speaker stepped to the plate and promptly hit a pop foul between home and first that inexplicably dropped between two New York players. Given a second chance, Tris singled, driving home Engle with the tying run, as both runners moved up a base on the attempted throw home. Mathewson then intentionally passed Duffy Lewis to load the bases before Larry Gardner lifted a sacrifice fly to right field that knocked in the winning run and gave Boston their first World Series title since 1903.[98]

Speaker appeared in all eight games of the series, batting an even .300. Tension ran high throughout this colossal clash between two baseball titans. Before starting Game Seven at Fenway Park on October 15, Joe Wood and Buck O'Brien engaged in a fistfight in Boston's clubhouse. The altercation resulted from Wood making a derogatory remark about O'Brien committing a balk during Game Six the previous afternoon.[99]

Tris Speaker's 1912 season acted as the springboard for his long and productive major league career. Although he achieved star status that season, Tris' new modern-era standard smacking doubles largely went unnoticed due to him being a model of consistency in all facets of the game. Before the modern era, Ed Delahanty of the Philadelphia Phillies had hit 55 two-baggers in 1899. Speaker's mark of 53 in 1912 endured until he surpassed that by swatting 59 for the Cleveland Indians in 1923. Indians teammate George Burns broke Tris' record when he stroked 64 doubles in 1926 before Earl Webb of the Red Sox established the lasting standard with 67 in 1931. While playing for Boston, teammates dubbed Tris with the nickname "Spoke."[100] When it came to the 1912 season, Speaker's performance spoke volumes toward placing him on baseball's highest pedestal, next to the game's all-time greats.

In 1912, Tris Speaker established a new modern-era, single-season record for hitting doubles as he smacked 53 two-baggers. This feat largely went unnoticed because of Speaker's versatility as an all-around baseball player. Besides pacing the American League in doubles, Tris tied Frank Baker of the Philadelphia Athletics' for top honors in homeruns. Speaker also finished third in the league with a .383 batting average. Tris acted as the catalyst behind the Boston Red Sox claiming the pennant and defeating the New York Giants in the World Series. (Courtesy of the Library of Congress.)

CHAPTER 10

Hubert "Dutch" Leonard – 1914

Master of Precision and a World Beater on the Bump

Throughout the Deadball Era, teams religiously employed the time-tested tactics of stealing bases, bunting, and the hit-and-run, hoping to scratch out runs. As a result, it was good practice for managers to possess as many hurlers on their staff who didn't turn around and immediately give away gains on the scoreboard. When runs were at a premium, it stood to reason that pitchers who used guile, speed, and savvy to keep games close would be a hot commodity during baseball's Deadball Era. While a hurler's winning percentage was the critical barometer evaluating an individual since it correlated with leading his team to victory, the earned run average statistic grew in importance over time. During the first decade of the twentieth century, pitchers such as Jack Taylor, Christy Mathewson, Three Finger Brown, Addie Joss, Rube Waddell, and Harry Krause put together minuscule single-season marks in this department.

Brown's 1.04 ERA in 1906 acted as the trendsetter in the National League during the Deadball Era, while over in the American League, Walter Johnson's 1.14 ERA in 1913 was tops for that organization. These two solid performances, preventing opponents from crossing home plate with expert aplomb, didn't stand the test of time very long, as a young southpaw hurler established the standard in this statistical category, which no pitcher surpassed for more than a century. Pitching in his second season at the major league level, Hubert Benjamin Leonard tailored a campaign for the ages with the Boston Red Sox in 1914, which was the envy of any hurler.

On April 16, 1892, Hubert Leonard was born to Ella and David, a carpenter in Birmingham, Ohio.[1] Hubert enjoyed life in this Ohio town until he was nine, when the family moved to Fresno, California, due to David Leonard's health. Leonard acquired the nickname "Dutch" while attending the area's public school system since his classmates believed he resembled a Dutchman.[2] As a youngster, Leonard became enamored with the pitching side of baseball, although most of his siblings were accomplished musicians. Dutch dedicated himself to following the family path and contemplated working professionally in an orchestra before being smitten by his love for baseball.[3] After completing general school requirements, Dutch enrolled at St. Mary's College in Moraga, California, a suburban community near Oakland. Leonard established stellar credentials as a hurler for St. Mary's, quickly exhibiting the type of ability indicating a professional baseball career was in his future.[4]

Dutch's pitching at St. Mary's caught the notice of a Philadelphia Athletics scout and Boston Red Sox president, John I. Taylor. Leonard received a tryout with the Athletics during spring training in 1911 but failed to make the grade. He then pitched for an independent squad in the San Joaquin Valley League that year.[5] The Boston Red Sox secured Leonard, who joined the team for spring training at Hot Springs, Arkansas, before the 1912 campaign.[6] Following his purchase, some fans suggested Boston hurler Joe Wood's crown as the team's "Boy Wonder" would be claimed by Dutch. Since Leonard was the latest acquisition from St. Mary's College, expectations were high among rooters because that school had previously produced star outfielders Harry Hooper and Duffy Lewis. Many fans expected Dutch to remain on the Red Sox roster the entire season based on his previous work.[7]

Boston manager Jake Stahl had different plans, farming out Leonard to the New England League's Worcester Busters in May for more seasoning. Former major league outfielder Jesse Burkett managed Worcester. Dutch only pitched one game for the Busters. Although the opposing team freely knocked his offerings all over the lot in that single outing, Leonard felt better defensive support might have minimized the damage. Dutch was particularly irked over his left fielder's slowness while chasing balls.[8] This plodding individual manning left field was the 43-year-old Burkett. When Jesse failed to reach a hit Leonard believed he should have caught, the pitcher's anger boiled to the surface.

"What's the matter with you!" the pitcher yelled. "Are your feet tired? Why don't you cover some ground?"

When Worcester's players came to the bench after the inning ended, Burkett unleashed a blistering tongue lashing toward Dutch about his comments before the hurler's teammates informed him he had reprimanded the manager.

"I didn't know he was the manager," said Leonard, "but my remarks go just the way I said them."

While Dutch didn't hesitate to offer a straightforward opinion, he realized his brief time playing for Worcester had ended due to scolding Jesse Burkett. Leonard caught the first train out of Worcester, traveling to Boston. After meeting with team president Jimmy McAleer upon his arrival, the Red Sox sent Dutch to the Western League's Denver Grizzlies under pilot John "Jack" Hendricks's tutelage.[9] Leonard was phenomenal for Denver in 1912, appearing in 35 games, hurling 241 innings, striking out 236 batters, and posting a 22-9 record. Dutch also showed proficiency at the plate, hitting .299. Since Boston had turned Leonard over to the Grizzlies on a provisional agreement, the organization recalled him in September. He didn't make an appearance with the Red Sox. Besides receiving praise for his performance on the bump, many within baseball commended Dutch for possessing excellent habits that would help him earn a job with Boston.[10]

When Leonard arrived home in Fresno after the season ended, he pitched a game for his hometown team against Lemoore, the San Joaquin Valley League champions. Dutch was brilliant, tossing a no-run, no-hit game. The only Lemoore batter who reached base drew a walk and then stole second. The contest was called after nine innings due to darkness, with the score tied 0-0.[11] Based mainly on his strong performance in Denver, Leonard earned a roster spot with the Red Sox in 1913. The club was American League pennant winners in 1912 and had claimed the World Series over the New York Giants.[12] Boston failed to repeat in 1913, falling back to the fourth position with a 79-71 record, placing them 15 ½ games behind first-place Philadelphia. Dutch's rookie season contained high and low points, as the young southpaw posted a 14-17 record, supported by a 2.39 ERA.

About one month after the season concluded, news started circulating, alluding to possible changes within the organization's ownership hierarchy. On November 2, a report disclosed that John I. Taylor and his father, General Charles H. Taylor, possibly would be interested in selling their half interest in the Red Sox after overseeing the organization since 1904. While John's pursuits seemed to be branching out beyond baseball, the suggestion was that General Taylor, now in his mid-sixties, didn't want to act as a counterbalance to his son's sometimes extravagant approach to hobnobbing within the sports world.[13] Interestingly, things took a significant shift in a different direction. On November 29, the announcement came that Joseph Lannin, real estate mogul and proprietor of the Garden City Hotel in Long Island, New York, had finalized a deal to purchase half of the Boston team's stock for roughly $200,000. It turned out that the Taylors weren't walking away from baseball, as Lannin obtained the shares held by Jimmy McAleer, Robert McRoy, and former manager Jake Stahl.[14]

Born in Quebec, Canada, Lannin eventually made his home in Boston, getting his first job as a teenager working as a bellboy, door boy, and head bellboy at the Adams House, about 32 years before purchasing the Red Sox. Joseph amassed his great fortune through numerous real estate ventures. He directed Lannin Realty Company and owned the Arborway Court at Jamaica Plain and the Fordham Court in Forest Hills, located in those Boston neighborhoods, besides possessing the Garden City Hotel. Lannin previously had attempted to place a bid to buy the National League's Boston club but was rebuffed.[15] Before the 1912 campaign, McAleer, McRoy, Stahl, and two other individuals had paid $170,000 to purchase their stake in the team.

That year, the organization made $400,000 as the Red Sox won the World Series. Still, a chasm developed when Robert McRoy displaced members of the passionate "Royal Rooters Club," selling their seats to other patrons for Game Seven at Fenway Park. Boston mayor John "Honey Fitz" Fitzgerald, sensing possible political gains, sided with the Royal Rooters and demanded McRoy's termination. Discontentment continued in 1913, as friction developed between Jimmy McAleer and Jake Stahl due to the team's horrible performance. McAleer fired Stahl in mid-season and replaced him with catcher Bill Carrigan. This development, and Jake being publicly humiliated by Boston's team president, didn't please league head Ban Johnson.

When Johnson met with the Taylors before Lannin bought his interest in the franchise, the two men still had hoped to gather the necessary capital to allow them to be sole owners.[16] When news broke about a possible sale, Ban claimed such speculation was false while adding a change was necessary regarding Boston's ownership.[17] Shortly after finalizing the deal, transferring the stock on December 10, a decision was made related to front office titles.[18] Joseph Lannin was elected team president, replacing Jimmy McAleer, while General Charles H. Taylor became team treasurer. John I. Taylor remained vice president, and Edwin L. "Eddie" Riley, employed within the organization for the past decade, was named team secretary.[19] When the vice president first introduced Lannin as negotiations entered the stretch run, a reporter asked if Carrigan would be relieved of his managerial duties.

"Oh, no," hastily said Lannin. "Let me tell you that I am not in sympathy with those who want to change over everything that they get their hands on. I believe that Bill Carrigan is one of the brainiest men in baseball today. He has the respect of his players and of everyone who has ever known him personally."

Lannin also believed the Red Sox would be pennant contenders in 1914 while adding that the team couldn't obtain decided results without the suitable material and tools.²⁰ The schedule for cultivating the appropriate material and tools during the spring training session at Hot Springs was announced in January. Under the guidance of Eddie Riley, expectations were that the first party of players would leave for the Arkansas town on March 6. Bill Carrigan planned on going to Hot Springs early with some Red Sox members who required extra work.

The itinerary called for Boston to remain at the training site until March 31 before embarking on their exhibition tour leading up to the opening game against the Washington Senators on April 14. Star center fielder Tris Speaker would be a late arrival since he was touring the world playing baseball with individuals from the New York Giants, Chicago White Sox, and other players. The boat bringing this team back to the states, if arriving on time, was scheduled to dock in New York on March 6. Upon his return, Speaker planned on leaving immediately for the West to visit family and friends in Texas before joining his teammates at Hot Springs.²¹

When Tris arrived at spring training, he signed a contract making him the highest-paid player in baseball. Speaker inked a deal paying him $18,000 for the 1914 season. Fellow outfielders Harry Hooper and Duffy Lewis joked that Tris might have to play the entire outer garden if they didn't receive a cut of that money. Although Speaker was a shrewd, calculating negotiator when it came to placing a financial price on his ability, he always gave his employer every ounce of energy on the diamond after signing a contract. Carrigan declared that Tris was the easiest man to handle in the world. As Boston's players readied themselves for the upcoming baseball campaign, they would be without the services of star hurler Smoky Joe Wood, expected to be sidelined until May while recovering from an operation for appendicitis.²²

Due to the absence of his meal-ticket pitcher, the Red Sox skipper turned to others, offering praise for southpaw hurlers Dutch Leonard and Ray Collins as the training session progressed. Boston sportswriter Francis Eaton claimed Leonard was only weak in preventing a runner from possibly stealing home. Eaton then added the qualifier that the way Dutch was pitching thus far, he couldn't envision an opposing runner reaching third base.²³ When Joseph Lannin arrived at Hot Springs to watch his team, he was so impressed with the first-rate condition of the famous resort that he renewed the club's lease on Majestic Park for five more years, although John I. Taylor had indicated a trip to the Pacific Coast might be a possibility in the future due to being enamored with California.²⁴

As the season opener approached, Bill Carrigan emphatically informed Joe Wood that he wouldn't be permitted to pitch in a game until June. Carrigan also stressed the importance of taking proper care of himself and delegated this responsibility to Joe's wife, Mrs. Laura O'Shea Wood, ensuring he obeyed the pilot's directive.[25] It was also apparent following the spring training session Boston's players exhibited a substantial degree of esteem and friendship toward Lannin. This sentiment was critical for team harmony since baseball players tended to perform to their capabilities while employed by an owner they respected and trusted. In his many other enterprises, those who worked under Joseph characterized him as a prince of a boss.[26]

Tris Speaker contracted a severe cold after leaving the warmth of Hot Springs and traversing through chilly weather playing exhibition games in Ohio and Indiana. Speaker, along with injured teammates Joe Wood and shortstop Heinie Wagner, arrived in Boston before the remainder of the team.[27] Tris was in the starting lineup when Boston opened the 1914 season against Washington at Fenway Park on April 14. Weather conditions were perfect as a large crowd gathered for the proceedings. Boston mayor James M. Curley threw out the first pitch to Bill Carrigan. Unfortunately, Senators' hurler Walter Johnson tempered this festive atmosphere by tossing a complete-game shutout and defeating the Red Sox, 3-0.[28] Boston won their first game of the year on April 15, with George "Rube" Foster besting Washington's Yancey "Doc" Ayers, 2-1.

Dutch Leonard was handed the baseball in this series' rubber match on April 17. Leonard and Senators hurler John Joseph "Joe" Boehling pitched exceptionally, as neither team scored a run through eight innings.[29] The Senators finally broke this logjam in the ninth. With one out, Washington's Raymond "Ray" Morgan lined an offering over second base. Running at full speed, Tris Speaker almost made one of his patented impressive catches, just failing to secure the baseball by mere inches. Howard "Howie" Shanks stepped up to the plate and hit a smash that Boston shortstop Lewis Everett Scott couldn't handle, leaving runners at second and third. Morgan scored the game's only tally when he slid across home plate, beating the throw on John Henry's infield chopper.[30] Boehling allowed one hit in the game; a single by Steve Yerkes.

The defending champion Philadelphia Athletics strolled into town for a series at Fenway Park. After Hugh Bedient snuffed out the Athletics, 1-0, on April 18, the Red Sox lost both ends of a doubleheader on April 20, falling in the first game that lasted ten innings, 8-2, before being shut out in the nightcap, 6-0. Leonard made his second start of the campaign on April 21, opposing Philadelphia's James Robert "Bob" Shawkey. Once again, Dutch was exceptional but couldn't place a game in the win column. Both men battled gallantly through 13 innings without any outcome. Leonard fanned Frank Baker on two occasions when a hit by Philadelphia's third baseman would've driven home a run. In the twelfth frame, Baker finally connected solidly against one of Dutch's offerings but was robbed by Harry Hooper, who made a circus catch in right field.[31] After 13 innings were completed, with the score tied, 1-1, umpire Tommy Connolly called the contest since he no longer could follow the curves of these two twirlers due to darkness descending upon the field.[32]

In his first two appearances of the season, Leonard had pitched 22 innings without allowing an earned run. Boston played a second consecutive tie game against the Athletics on April 22, as umpires called the contest after eight innings, with the score knotted, 9-9. The Red Sox hit the road for the first time and took two out of three games from Washington. Boston's players received their fair share of scrutiny, with mediocre baseball being the norm through the season's first two weeks. Newspaper gossip suggested the team might be prepared to pay big money to bring a first baseman who could cover ground and hit into the fold. There was also concern over the dependability of third baseman Larry Gardner, who suffered from a digestive disturbance. Tris Speaker seemed to be pressing to warrant his hefty salary, while Harry Hooper's overall defensive work wasn't achieving its usual glowing standards. These same critics viewed shortstop Everett Scott as a life-saving epiphany for the team.[33]

Although Red Sox fans certainly couldn't be upset with the fine work exhibited by Dutch Leonard, the southpaw pitcher had every reason to be perturbed with his teammates over the lack of run support. On April 29, he took the mound against Ray Fisher of the New York Yankees at the Polo Grounds. Fisher was sensational for New York, tossing a shutout and scattering seven hits.

Leonard was also solid but made one mistake in the fourth inning when Yankees left fielder James "Jimmy" Walsh launched a pitch into the left-field bleachers that accounted for the contest's only run. Hugh Bedient was sharp in two innings of relief work after Bill Carrigan pulled Dutch for a pinch hitter in the seventh frame.[34]

When April ended, Boston was mired in seventh place with a 4-6 record, leaving them four games behind the first-place Detroit Tigers. Leonard finally received some help from his friends in his next start against Philadelphia at Shibe Park on May 4. The Red Sox connected for 12 hits, ending a four-game losing skid by drubbing the Athletics, 9-1. Leading this hitting barrage was Hooper, who banged out two singles and a triple, and Gardner, who smacked a duo of one-base hits and a double. Dutch was untouchable, scattering six hits while fanning eight.[35] Leonard was magnificent once again versus New York on May 8, winning the game, 3-0. He tossed a complete game, allowed only three hits, and struck out at least one Yankees batter in each inning, recording 11 for the game.[36]

Dutch exhibited excellent speed and control working in the fog and rain while also baffling New York's hitters with his moist pitch. Boston scored all three runs in the eighth off hurler Raymond "Ray" Keating. Bill Carrigan opened the frame with a single to center field and moved over to second base on Leonard's sacrifice bunt. Clyde Engle reached first on an infield single to third. He made it to second, and Carrigan scored when Yankees' third baseman Frederick "Fritz" Maisel fell to the ground while fielding the baseball and then threw wildly, making the peg over to first. Harry Hooper beat out a roller to Keating, pushing Engle over to third. Tris Speaker drove Clyde home with the second run by lashing a single out to center as Hooper motored to third. After Duffy Lewis was retired on a fly ball, Harry scored the final run on Larry Gardner's single to right.[37]

After going 3-5 on their recent eastern road swing, the Red Sox split their four-game series with New York at Fenway Park. Lackluster hitting looked to be the culprit behind Boston's tepid start, although storms and wet grounds throughout these early-season games didn't allow for sufficient practice time, while pitchers who thrived under a heavy workload were also affected.[38] Leonard's prowess on the mound continued in his next outing against the St. Louis Browns on May 14. Dutch tossed his second consecutive shutout, defeating the Browns and hurler Earl Hamilton in a tight contest, 1-0. Leonard scattered four hits and struck out nine batters as league president Ban Johnson watched the proceedings. Umpire John "Jack" Egan banished St. Louis manager Wesley Branch Rickey and catcher Samuel "Sam" Agnew from the game for protesting a call.[39]

Dutch Leonard had only allowed two earned runs through his first six starts, while his record stood at 3-2. Sportswriter J. Ed Grillo proclaimed that no young pitcher in the American League was making a better showing than Leonard. Grillo stated that Dutch was securing victories with splendid consistency after offering occasional flashes of talent one year earlier and pitching better than any other southpaw hurler in the circuit. The writer concluded that Leonard's superb work would force critics to include Boston in pennant discussions.[40]

Big news made a splash in Boston on May 18, announcing that Joseph Lannin was now the sole owner of the Red Sox organization's common stock, which elevated him to majority magnate status, giving him supreme voting power and authoritative control. John I. Taylor and his father, General Charles

H. Taylor, would no longer be involved in the club's management. General Taylor still controlled most of the shares of preferred stock while also being the largest single holder of the bonds for the Fenway Realty Company, related to Fenway Park. The total price tag for Lannin purchasing all the common stock was $450,000. Concerning General Taylor stepping away from baseball, various wearisome events over time had caused him to become disgusted with the game. These feelings tore away at the elder Taylor for some time as he wrestled over limiting his investments or continuing out of affection for his son. The latter wanted to remain connected to baseball since it gave him so much pleasure.

The revelation also surfaced that before Lannin entered the picture as a potential buyer, both the Taylors and Jimmy McAleer's investment faction had requested Ban Johnson's permission to sell their baseball team stock. Moreover, when Joseph joined the ownership hierarchy, General Taylor was still determined to retire from baseball.[41] One day after these revelations about notable changes to Boston's front office, Dutch secured his fourth victory of the campaign against Detroit after coming on in relief for starter Hugh Bedient in the seventh inning. Although Boston had grabbed the lead with two runs in the sixth, Leonard received credit for the win before adding a single tally in the seventh to claim a 6-4 victory. Dutch allowed no hits in his three innings of work. Leonard again performed relief duty on May 21, as Boston fell to the Chicago White Sox, 5-2. Dutch allowed a single run in one inning on the bump after replacing starter Adam Rankin Johnson.

Leonard started the game at Fenway Park two days later, defeating Chicago, 6-2. Dutch scattered eight hits and aided his cause at the plate by driving home two runs in the second inning with a single. White Sox utility player Thomas "Tom" Daly received a tribute from admirers before the game and was presented with the gift of a gold watch. Daly had gained fame by smacking a home run in the presence of King George V when the world touring baseball team played a game in England.[42] On May 26, Red Sox hurler Rube Foster saw his string of pitching 42 ⅔ consecutive shutout innings snapped when the Cleveland Naps secured the first of their two runs in the fifth frame. Leonard finished the game in relief, fanning two batters in the ninth, as Cleveland was victorious, 3-2.

The following afternoon, Smoky Joe Wood made his first appearance of the season versus the Naps. Although Wood was shaky at the start, walking three batters in the first inning, he settled down, tossed a complete game, and defeated Cleveland, 5-4.[43] Bill Carrigan gave Dutch the starting assignment in the second game of a doubleheader against Washington on May 29. Leonard only lasted four stanzas and received a no-decision, as Boston won the ten-inning affair, 6-5. Dutch allowed two unearned runs before being pulled for pinch hitter Walter "Wally" Rehg. Leonard didn't pitch very deep into the contest the following morning after receiving the ball from his manager in game one of a Memorial Day doubleheader. Dutch gave up two earned runs on three hits before yielding mound duties to Ray Collins in the third inning and being charged with the loss as the Senators prevailed, 6-4.

Heading into June, the Red Sox found themselves in fifth place with a 17-19 record, leaving them five games behind pacesetting Philadelphia. Leonard raised his record to 6-3 with a tight, 3-2 victory over the Athletics in the first game of a twin bill on June 2. Dutch tossed a complete game, allowing two earned runs, five hits, walking three, and fanning three batters. After Leonard's strong performance gave Boston a leg up in this crucial series against Philadelphia, the Red Sox would lose the next three contests against the league leaders. As the team embarked on a long trip away from home, Joseph Lannin joined the boys, making his inaugural road swing with his squad. Lannin was ecstatic while enjoying his first boat ride at night from Cleveland to Detroit on June 9, since Boston had just completed a four-game sweep over the Naps.[44]

After not pitching for almost two weeks, Dutch Leonard received the nod against St. Louis at Sportsman's Park on June 14. Leonard stifled the Browns, allowing only three hits, while his teammates feasted on offerings from three different hurlers as Boston claimed a 10-1 victory. Dutch's only mistake of the afternoon occurred when Clarence "Tillie" Walker blasted a home run in the seventh inning.[45] Dutch won his eighth game of the season on June 18, breezing to an 8-0 victory over Chicago at Comiskey Park. Although the White Sox hitters connected for eight solid safeties, Leonard was impenetrable in the clutch. Boston's batters had an easy time routing hurler James "Jim" Scott.[46] Collecting 14 hits on the afternoon against Chicago was encouraging for a team whose batting had been generally weak and was bouncing around between the American League's first and second divisions. After tossing a three-hit shutout in his previous start against St. Louis, Joe Wood had a rough outing against the White Sox on June 20.[47]

Leonard's victory was the only one claimed by Boston in the five-game series with Chicago. Lannin blamed lack of focus for the four defeats due to some of the team's best players mulling generous offers from the upstart Federal League, as the squad resided in a city that was a hotbed for such activity related to this organization. Rumors also alleged that relations had become strained between the owner and two players. Joseph also usurped Bill Carrigan's authority when he revealed during an interview that changes might be forthcoming without consulting his manager on the subject. One potential deal perpetrated by the press was a straight transaction involving the Tigers' Ty Cobb and Tris Speaker.

Since Cobb was friends with Red Sox's third baseman Larry Gardner, such a trade made sense to sportswriters. Ty also had a good relationship with Carrigan and likely would feel that playing for Boston enhanced his chances of winning a World Series. A change of scenery also looked suitable for all parties involved. Cobb was involved in a recent altercation with the owner and an employee at a Detroit butcher shop. The quarrel resulted from how the proprietor had earlier treated Ty's wife. Of course, such a trade didn't seem feasible from the Red Sox's standpoint since Cobb had injured his thumb in the fray while using the gun he was carrying as a blunt instrument. The outcome of this physical engagement ended up sidelining him for a month.[48] Throwing cold water on this fallacy were statements by Lannin and Tigers owner Frank Navin that they wouldn't trade their respective players for each other.[49]

Dutch Leonard halted Boston's losing streak, tossing a four-hit shutout in the first game of a doubleheader against New York on June 24. Leonard secured a 3-0 victory, as the Red Sox scored all their runs in the fifth inning, with Steve Yerkes's two-run homer off Yankees hurler Martin "Marty" McHale being the critical hit. Dutch retired 20 of New York's batters on fly balls or popups.[50] Leonard pushed his record to 10-3 on June 26, performing damage control in relief, as Boston prevailed over New York in ten innings, 2-1. Dutch tossed three shutout frames while allowing only one hit. The Red Sox secured the win in the tenth when Harold "Hal" Janvrin started the inning by beating out an infield single, moved over to third base on Larry Gardner's base hit, and scored after hurler Ray Fisher threw a wild pitch.[51] Dutch was masterful against Philadelphia in game one of a doubleheader on June 29 at Shibe Park, allowing only five hits and fanning six, as Boston cruised to a 7-1 victory. Duffy Lewis exited the contest after a pitch struck him in the hand.[52]

When June concluded, the Red Sox found themselves in fifth place with a 35-32 record, leaving them five games out of first in the very tight American League race. Leonard attempted to weave his magic against the Athletics in the first game of a doubleheader on July 2 but was batted freely in eight innings of work and left with his team trailing, 4-3. Boston scored four runs in the ninth on a walk, sacrifice bunt, two singles, and a two-run homer by Tris Speaker and then held off a Philadelphia rally, claiming a 7-6 victory.[53] Dutch was credited with another no-decision while pitching against Chicago in game one of a twin bill at Fenway Park on July 8, allowing one earned run in seven innings of work. The White Sox secured victory in the tenth when catcher Ray Schalk's two-run double broke a 2-2 tie. Earlier in the game, Harry Hooper had to be carried off the field when he collided with Speaker as both men chased a fly ball.[54]

Amid injury concerns related to the Red Sox's pitching staff, since a lame arm sidelined Joe Wood and Rube Foster couldn't play because of a twisted knee, Joseph Lannin swung a colossal deal that brought in mound reinforcements. On July 9, Lannin brokered an agreement with Baltimore Orioles manager and owner John "Jack" Dunn to purchase pitchers George Herman "Babe" Ruth and Ernest "Ernie" Shore and catcher Arthur "Ben" Egan from that International League team for $25,000. Ruth, the centerpiece of this transaction, was the man Joseph and Bill Carrigan had strongly desired to bring into the fold.[55] George made his major league debut on July 11, pitching seven innings and securing a 4-3 victory over Cleveland. Dutch Leonard hurled the game's final two frames, striking out four of the six men he faced.[56]

On July 15, Leonard's performance completed a four-game sweep over Cleveland at Fenway Park. Dutch was exceptional, scattering seven hits and whiffing nine batters as he defeated the Naps, 4-0. Leonard held the visiting team hitless and fanned five players in the first four innings. Umpire Tommy Connolly asked eight members of the Red Sox to leave the bench and retire to the clubhouse for directing rude and disparaging remarks at Cleveland's players.[57] Three days later, Dutch tossed two shutout innings of relief but didn't figure in the outcome, as Detroit scored two runs in the thirteenth inning to claim a 4-2 victory. Leonard did marvelous work as a reliever once again versus the Tigers on July 20. Dutch threw eight shutout, hitless frames, and fanned nine, as Boston prevailed in 16 innings, 3-2. Bill Carrigan led off the sixteenth with a base on balls and was forced at second by Leonard. Harry Hooper recorded his fourth hit of the game, a single to left, before a pitch hit Everett Scott to load the bases. Dutch crossed home plate with the winning run on Tris Speaker's single to left-center field.[58]

Leonard experienced his worst outing of the year in a start against Cleveland on July 25. Dutch only lasted one inning, allowing four runs; three earned, and gained a no-decision when Boston secured an 8-6 victory in 11 innings. Leonard made quick work of the Naps two days later, tossing a complete-game shutout and allowing eight hits, as the Red Sox prevailed, 3-0. Dutch fanned seven batters, while Cleveland was only retired twice on infield ground balls. Tris Speaker made eight putouts in center field and starred at the plate, smacking two singles and a triple.[59] Pitcher Sylveanus "Vean" Gregg, acquired from Cleveland on July 28 for hurlers Rankin Johnson and Frederick "Fritz" Coumbe, received his first start for Boston one day later against Chicago.[60] Boston trailed 4-2 when Gregg exited after seven innings of work. A single run that frame, one tally in the ninth, and four more in the tenth gave Hugh Bedient and the Red Sox an 8-4 lead, which held firm, with Leonard closing out the proceedings in the bottom of that inning.

Dutch pushed his record to 15-3 as Boston gained their third consecutive victory over the White Sox on July 31, grabbing a 5-1 decision. Leonard tossed a complete game, scattered four hits, and struck out seven batters.[61] As the season moved into August, the Red Sox's record stood at 54-41, putting them second, 6 ½ games behind first-place Philadelphia. Joseph Lannin made a prudent business venture in the front office to give Boston an excellent minor league club to send young players for development. On July 31, with the assistance of Ban Johnson and International League president Edward "Ed" Barrow, Lannin purchased the Providence Grays and their home grounds, Melrose Park, from Detroit's ownership group.[62] Pitching prospect George Herman Ruth, whom the Tigers had savaged in his second start of the year on July 16, was farmed out to Providence for more seasoning in August.[63]

Leonard's overpowering performance was too much for St. Louis to handle when the southpaw took the bump for his next start on August 5.[64] Dutch tossed a shutout, allowed five hits, and whiffed eight batters as the Red Sox claimed a 6-0 victory. Leonard shut the door in relief on August 8 against Detroit at Navin Field after starter Joe Wood hurled seven frames. Dutch only gave up one walk in two innings of work, preserving Boston's 5-2 triumph. Leonard was credited with his seventeenth win of the season one day later due to his stellar performance, tossing three shutout innings in relief. Horrendous fielding by the Tigers in the top of the seventh inning allowed the Red Sox to score five runs and grab an 8-6 lead.[65] Dutch was crowned as the winning pitcher since his solid outing surpassed the performances of Ernie Shore and Rube Foster, who preceded him on the mound.

After the series in Detroit ended, concluding Boston's road trip, manager Bill Carrigan praised Dutch Leonard's splendid work. Carrigan declared that if his team did capture the American League pennant, much of the credit would deservedly go to Leonard, whose steadiness was a beacon of light when other hurlers on the team exhibited inconsistency.[66] The Red Sox's manager further expounded upon why he believed Dutch was the most improved pitcher in major league baseball.[67] "I never saw a pitcher who improved so greatly in one season, as long as I have been in baseball—and I have been connected with the national pastime for quite a while," said Carrigan.

"Last season, Leonard was considered only a fair pitcher. Now he is hailed as a world-beater all over the circuit. He has all the stuff in the world and knows how to use it. Then he also has good control, which is lacking in so many southpaws.

"Take, for instance, the game he pitched against the Browns. He passed only two batters—Ivan Howard drawing the base on balls each time. Well, this year, in all the contests he has worked for me, I don't think he has issued more than five passes in any of them."

Carrigan also marveled at some of Leonard's battles when working in tight games against other pitchers. Every member of Boston's squad echoed their manager's sentiment, believing at season's end Walter Johnson would be a distant memory when Dutch assumed the mantle as "King of the Pitchers."[68] Leonard was involved in another one of those great battles, against New York's Ray Fisher at Fenway Park, on August 13. Fisher came out the victor in this instance, winning 1-0. Dutch lasted seven innings before being pulled for pinch hitter Olaf Henriksen. The Yankees scored the game's only run in the third when Fritz Maisel drew a walk, was sacrificed to second on a bunt by Fisher, moved to third on Leonard's wild pitch, and scored on Lute "Luke" Boone's double to left field.[69] This defeat ended Dutch's 12-game winning streak. During that run of consecutive victories, Leonard had beaten every team in the American League except Washington.[70]

Dutch raised his record to 18-4 with a 3-1 win against Chicago in game one of a doubleheader on August 19. Leonard exhibited efficiency on the mound and at the plate, tossing a complete game and striking out six while going 2-for-3 and knocking in a run.[71] Dutch added another notch to his win total on August 24, besting Cleveland, 7-3. Leonard lasted six innings and left the contest with the Red Sox ahead, 7-2. Attempting to win his twentieth game of the season, Dutch came up empty versus Detroit on August 28. Locked in a pitcher's duel with the Tigers' Tillar "Pug" Cavet, Leonard blinked first, allowing the contest's only three tallies in the seventh inning, as Ty Cobb doubled home two teammates and then scored when shortstop Everett Scott muffed a pop fly off Sam Crawford's bat.[72] Before the month ended, Joseph Lannin jettisoned a few players from the roster he considered to be a harmful element regarding team cohesion who weren't earning their salaries. Steve Yerkes and Clyde Engle were both handed their unconditional releases by Boston's owner.[73]

As the baseball campaign swung into September, the Athletics' lead over second-place Boston stood at 13 games. Then, on the month's first day, Dutch Leonard's fantastic season reached an unexpected conclusion. Two different narratives arose regarding Leonard suffering an injury to his right arm. The first explanation claimed Dutch had been roughhousing in the dugout with a teammate during the doubleheader at Fenway Park on September 1 against St. Louis. The other player twisted Leonard's wrist, which resulted in a tendon being pulled loose.[74] Dutch entered the first contest in the eighth inning that day and faced two batters.

The other story alleged Leonard suffered his injury in the clubhouse after a game while participating in a little good-natured wrestling match with about six other Red Sox players. Dutch's hand was damaged when he ended up underneath six bodies at the bottom of the pile. Boston's club physician only discovered the injury two days later, as Leonard went about his business, not realizing anything was wrong.[75] The diagnosis was a broken bone in the back of his right hand, near the wrist.[76] A doctor placed splints around the hand, which forced Dutch to wear a sling. The initial prognosis was for Leonard to be out of commission for three or more weeks.[77] Leonard didn't play in another game for the remainder of the season. Washington manager Clark Griffith expressed a novel solution for those who engaged in such childish antics, placing their health at risk. Griffith recommended that any player taking part in one of these clubhouse bouts should receive a fine of two weeks' pay, while a forfeiture of the remaining season's salary was the proper punishment for its ringleader.[78]

The Red Sox finished strong without their staff ace in tow, concluding the 1914 season 8 ½ games behind the pennant-winning Athletics with a 91-62 record. Team management allowed the Boston Braves to use Fenway Park in the World Series, who claimed the world championship by sweeping Philadelphia in four games. Although he missed the campaign's final five weeks, Dutch Leonard experienced a breakout season. Leonard went 19-5, made 36 appearances, started 25 games, completed 17, and comfortably paced the squad with 176 strikeouts. Official records at the time charged the southpaw pitcher with an average of 1.01 earned runs per game against him in 1914.[79] This figure was adjusted to 0.96 many decades later. For over a century, it stood as the litmus test for the lowest modern-era qualifying earned run average for a single season. In his 25 starts, Dutch hurled seven shutouts and gave up one earned run in ten of those games. Opponents touched up Leonard for three and four earned runs each on only one occasion.

Joseph Lannin was tremendously pleased with his team's performance in 1914. He also believed Boston could contend for the pennant in 1915.[80] Red Sox management felt Smoky Joe Wood had overexerted himself too soon following his operation, despite orders to proceed slowly. Bill Carrigan believed Dutch was one of the game's premier pitchers, who likely would experience continued improvement in 1915. Carrigan also said that the team physician made an interesting admission during the previous spring training session. Upon administering Leonard's physical, the doctor commented: "I have been practicing a long time, but in all my experience, I have never seen a more perfect physical specimen for an athlete than you." Bill also shared that on one occasion in 1914, when Dutch fanned Ty Cobb, umpire and former pitcher Bill Dinneen marveled that he had never seen a curve as good as the one that retired Detroit's star player.[81]

Leonard seemed poised to continue his progression with Boston, where he was indeed happy, having signed a two-year contract in the summer of 1914.[82] Unfortunately, things started badly for the southpaw hurler in 1915. Dutch couldn't pitch the first ten days of the season due to a lame arm caused by working in cold weather during the spring exhibition tour. Joseph Lannin was highly disappointed that Leonard couldn't answer the bell.[83] Dutch received rough treatment when he finally pitched against Philadelphia on April 24 and was relieved in the fourth inning. Leonard performed much better in a relief appearance and two starts which he won, but his unreliability posed a severe problem. Lannin rectified that dilemma while Chicago swept the Red Sox in a series that started on May 21 at Comiskey Park. Boston's owner suspended Dutch without pay for his failure to keep in condition and sent him home to Boston.

There was no mention of whether drinking and keeping late hours was the basis for Leonard's suspension.[84] When Dutch reached Boston, he wasted no time firing a vicious verbal broadside in Lannin's direction. Leonard unequivocally asserted he had never touched a drop of liquor in his life and that Boston's team president was killing the club through constant interference.[85] Dutch also alleged that Joseph refused to pay for his train fare upon being ordered to return to Boston and needed to borrow the money from Bill Carrigan.

Leonard then unleashed his harshest criticism, declaring Lannin was running the squad, using methods he employed on the current road trip. At the same time, Carrigan was only a figurehead with no input into the team's direction. Dutch claimed Boston's players avoided eating at the hotel after a road loss, preferring to pay for their meals rather than encountering the owner and enduring his fury and criticism. Lastly, Leonard charged that Joe Wood was fined half a month's pay for allowing Chicago's Ray Schalk to record a hit as the hurler attempted to walk him with opponents on base in the game on May 23.[86] When pressed for a comment on his pitcher's allegations, Carrigan refused to discuss the matter.[87] Lannin refuted Dutch's statements, saying: "Leonard's whole story is absurd and false, and his action that of a spoiled, sore-headed kid."

Boston's owner quickly squelched the pitcher's claim that he wasn't receiving a fair salary for his services. Joseph explained that to fend off Federal League overtures in 1914, he had extended to Leonard a new contract for the balance of last season and 1915, paying him $5,000 a year, a $2,000 per season increase over what the two parties had agreed upon in the original document.[88] Sportswriter Tim Murnane corroborated Lannin's claim that Dutch still owed the owner $1,500 advance money which he had borrowed.[89] In early June, Leonard intimated he would be happy with a trade after reading the owner's comments.[90]

Dutch eventually realized his impulsive response was problematic, leading him to work diligently to get back into management's good graces.[91] After returning from suspension in June, Leonard reclaimed his status as one of baseball's top hurlers, going 15-7 with a 2.36 ERA, as Boston garnered the American League pennant. Dutch then topped off his comeback by besting Phillies staff ace Grover Cleveland Alexander in Game Three of the World Series at Braves Field, 2-1, as Boston claimed the title, winning four out of five games.

Hubert "Dutch" Leonard had played for a world championship squad. He had also established a modern-era pitching feat that no hurler most likely would ever break. Both accomplishments occurred within the span of three seasons as a major leaguer. Until 2021, it seemed no other pitcher during the modern era would ever post an ERA under 1.00 in a single season while pitching the prerequisite innings necessary to be recognized as leading that category. Robert "Bob" Gibson of the St. Louis Cardinals appeared to be the closest in 1968 when he crafted a 1.12 ERA. Although New York Giants pitcher Ferdinand "Ferdie" Schupp fashioned a 0.90 ERA in 1916, he only tossed 140 ⅓ innings, splitting time as a starter and a reliever. New York played 155 games that year. In 1880, rookie hurler Tim Keefe posted a 0.86 ERA while pitching 105 innings, as his Troy Trojans played 83 games.

Two men retroactively surpassed Dutch Leonard's mark when Baseball-Reference issued its statistical findings in June 2021 regarding the Major Negro Leagues. In 1932, hurler Roy Parnell of the Negro Southern League's Monroe Monarchs posted a 0.83 ERA. Leroy "Satchel" Paige established the new record in this pitching category in 1944. Hurling for the Negro American League's Kansas City Monarchs that year, Paige fashioned a 0.72 ERA. In 1937, pitcher Eugene Bremer had crafted a 0.71 ERA while playing for the Negro American League's Cincinnati Tigers. However, when following the Ferdie Schupp standard, also used as the formula, Bremer falls short of qualifying since his innings pitched (50 ⅔) were less than the number of games played by Cincinnati (54).

In 2021, New York Mets starting hurler Jacob DeGrom posted a 1.08 ERA but didn't reach the prerequisite innings.

When Leonard passed away on July 11, 1952, the record books still listed his ERA as 1.01 in 1915.[92] Diligent research in the 1970s and 1980s shaved off .05 percentage points to the recognized figure today.[93] For the man who once dressed down Jesse Burkett in his only game wearing a Worcester uniform, the number 0.96 garners Dutch continued admiration for his achievement and a place in baseball's record books as the first modern-era pitcher to establish such a single-season record.

In his second season as major leaguer in 1914, southpaw hurler Dutch Leonard rose to star status as one of the American League's premier pitchers. Leonard went 19-5 while records from that time showed he posted a 1.01 ERA. Decades later, researchers adjusted this figure to 0.96. Following his breakthrough campaign, Dutch fell into disfavor with team management in 1915. After being suspended by Boston Red Sox owner Joseph Lannin, Leonard harshly criticized how the magnate's constant interference ruined the club. (Courtesy of the Library of Congress.)

CHAPTER 11

Ty Cobb – 1915

Baseball's Top Player Sets the Standard for Swiping Bases

Receiving the honor as one of baseball's greatest players in history during the Deadball Era was no small feat. Nap Lajoie established his credentials to enter this elite ballplayer class at the beginning of the twentieth century. In 1901, when he batted .426, Lajoie's record-breaking season launched his phenomenal American League career. It also helped that new organization achieve serious recognition as a viable alternative to the established National League. Over in the Senior Circuit, Honus Wagner of the Pittsburgh Pirates threw his hat into the ring for the title of greatest by performing every facet of the game with expertise and brilliance while winning eight batting titles during that time. These two men enjoyed the breathtaking view from atop baseball's mountain alone until a spunky individual from Georgia, who possessed unassailable grit and determination, quickly earned his place standing among these two icons.

Tyrus Raymond "Ty" Cobb became the game's most recognizable name from baseball's Deadball Era. A man who was misunderstood and misinterpreted at times, Cobb's drive to excel as a ballplayer and robust work ethic helped him attain eminent status in the sport during his baseball career. Raw talent, an unbridled passion for succeeding, and a keen analytical approach to all aspects of the game constituted the recipe that reaped immense success and endless reward. As a result, baseball fans gorged on this enjoyable meal of diamond achievement and unparalleled batting numbers. While Ty reached lofty heights in the hitting department, his speed and cunning on the base paths may have supplied the most entertainment for fervent patrons. It was within the statistical category of stolen bases, where one could best judge an adept runner, that Cobb shattered the modern-era record for pilfering bags in a single season.

Tyrus Cobb was born on December 18, 1886, in the rural Georgia farming community of Narrows. Tyrus' birth came three years after his parents, Amanda Chitwood and William Herschel Cobb, married. An educated man, William acted as a teacher in different small farming towns until 1893, when the family moved to Royston, where he served with honor and distinction as a local school's principal. Ty's father also purchased 100 acres of land for farming when school wasn't in session during the summer. William Cobb's political career began in Royston through his election as the city's mayor.[1] The elder Cobb was also an esteemed professor within the realm of mathematics, eventually became a Georgia State Senator, and was founder and editor of the democratic *Royston Record* newspaper.

As a youngster, Ty Cobb realized he was a swift runner who usually was victorious, engaging in town races with other kids. Ty was also a natural when it came to playing baseball. He first garnered attention at 14 as a shortstop for the "second nine" on Royston's town team. Initially, Cobb was too small and skinny to break into the squad's "first nine." When the two units played against each other in practice, Ty always ensured the older boys hustled. One day, the Royston team traveled to the peach country to play a contest in Elberton, Georgia. The center fielder for the "first nine" couldn't make the trip since he would be away purchasing cattle. This circumstance opened the door for young Ty, selected as a last resort, to go in his place.

William Cobb vehemently protested his son traveling out of town to play baseball. Robert McCreary, Royston's first-team manager, spoke to William and persuaded him to allow Ty to make just this one journey as a player. Based on the promise of McCreary, a fellow Mason, to look after the welfare and conduct of his son, Senator Cobb granted permission. Spindle-legged Tyrus made a grand impression in his first opportunity as a starter in an actual game. He slashed out one hit after another and landed the huge safety that clinched victory for his team, crowning him the boy hero of Royston. Years later, after achieving major league success, Ty reminisced about this moment while being interviewed by sportswriter Bozeman Bulger.

"And let me tell you something," said Cobb in 1912, "once an athlete feels that peculiar thrill that goes with victory and public praise, the fascination holds him for life. He can never get away from it. On the way back home from that game, I made up my mind that I would try and be a great ballplayer, and I worked at it by day and dreamed of it by night."

Ty became the team's regular center fielder following his performance in Elberton. Away from home attending a state senate session, William Cobb heard stories of his son's phenomenal diamond exploits. This praise didn't alter William's opinion about the game. He continued objecting to his son playing baseball and mapped out a path where the lad would attend the University of Georgia. When Senator Cobb returned to Royston, passionate fans convinced him to watch Tyrus play against a team from Commerce, Georgia. For several days, William secretly inquired about whether his son possessed the actual ability to succeed, also asking if baseball was an honorable profession or would he see Ty involved in a sport dominated by rowdies.

When the day arrived for the big game, Tyrus was determined to shine on the field, knowing his father would be watching. Cobb's copious opportunity came in the eighth inning when Commerce had the bases loaded with two out. The batter smacked a long drive to left-center field that seemed destined to land safely for a double. Ty recollected over what happened next in his discussion with Bulger.

"Somehow," said Tyrus, "I felt that the left fielder was going to miss it, and I ran behind him. He backed up on the ball and barely managed to touch it with the tips of his fingers. I was running at full speed and, by a dive, managed to scoop the ball with one hand when it was a foot from the ground. The catch saved the game, and I can truthfully say I never made a better one in my life.

"When I came in, the spectators were crazy with joy, and they began tossing me money. I picked up $11 in quarters and half dollars. My father was so carried away with my performance that he immediately became a fan. More than that, he went back to the office and wrote a full account of the game in his paper. It was the first baseball story that the town of Royston had ever read, and it made a great hit."

Ty briefly paused before concluding his account of this early moment from his baseball career. "So you see," laughed Tyrus, "that one catch made a baseball player out of me and a baseball writer out of my father."[2]

An opportunity arose for Ty Cobb to branch out beyond his home environment to play baseball. In the winter of 1903-04, a Royston teammate, who had failed in a tryout with the Southern Association's Nashville Volunteers the previous summer, told Cobb that he had mentioned some Georgia players to manager Isaac Newton "Newt" Fisher, including him. Buoyed by this news, Ty started mailing out letters to teams from the South Atlantic League. This correspondence acted as a publicity mechanism that included critical information and clippings related to his diamond conquests. Cobb was ecstatic when he received a response from that organization's Augusta Tourists. Augusta would pay Ty $50 a month if he made the team, although they required him to cover traveling expenses independently for spring training. Cobb didn't tell his father the news until the night before he was supposed to report for training. Although William Cobb lectured Ty about the importance of getting an education and disparaged baseball, he acquiesced since he couldn't convince his son to abandon his dream and gave him money for necessary expenses.

Cobb and friend Stewart Brown left by train the following day to begin this baseball odyssey.[3] The rambunctious Ty didn't last very long in Augusta's camp, drawing his release after only two games. Luckily, Cobb immediately received an invitation to join a team from Anniston, Alabama, in the Tennessee-Alabama League, an independent organization. When Ty asked for advice from the man whose opinion mattered most, William Cobb offered tough love, telling his teenage son not to return home a failure. Anxious to gain his father's approval when it came to playing baseball, Tyrus took the suggestion to heart and dazzled with Anniston, leading to his recall by Augusta. Cobb batted .237 for the Tourists for the remainder of 1904.

Ty's assertive and forceful attitude on the diamond didn't go unnoticed when the Detroit Tigers played two exhibition contests against Augusta in the spring of 1905. Cobb's overall play made quite an impression on Tigers' management.[4] Ty started slowly with Augusta in 1905 until catching his stride when the team temporarily dismissed Andy Roth as manager and replaced him with George Leidy. Cobb's game developed dramatically under Leidy's stewardship after the new manager had a long conversation with him regarding the virtues of hard work and dedication in response to a listless approach to playing the outfield.[5] With George's help, Ty, who batted .326 for the Tourists in 1905, became a well-rounded player.

This rise to prominence received a severe jolt in the summer when a deadly tragedy occurred back home in Royston. State Senator William Herschel Cobb was shot to death around midnight on August 8 by his wife, Amanda. Initial newspaper stories stated Mrs. Cobb shot her husband because she believed he was a burglar lurking outside the house. Amanda Cobb alleged that William, a somnambulist for many years, must have been sleepwalking when she mistook him for a prowler. Aroused by a noise near her bedroom window, Amanda looked in that direction. She saw a man moving about on the outside veranda.

Amanda grabbed a pistol from under her pillow, firing twice, as one bullet struck Senator Cobb in the head while the other penetrated his abdomen.[6]

Authorities, believing a different chain of events occurred, quickly arrested Mrs. Cobb following her husband's funeral and burial. Further developments came to the forefront two days after the tragedy occurred. This new information indicated that William Cobb had led his wife to believe he was traveling to Atlanta on August 8. He instead remained in Royston on the advice of a close friend who alleged she was being unfaithful and entertained a gentleman when he went out of town. In planning to prosecute Amanda Cobb for murder, the state theorized her husband arrived back at the house around midnight to spy before she killed him on a porch adjacent to the window of his wife's room. They alleged a man was also in the room, whose identity authorities didn't release.[7] Exhibiting a salacious slant in reporting, newspaper articles mentioned that Amanda Cobb was a beautiful woman much younger than her deceased husband.[8]

On March 31, 1906, a jury acquitted Amanda Cobb on the charge of manslaughter related to her husband's death.[9] Amid the turmoil surrounding the passing of a man he revered and held in the highest esteem, Ty Cobb's dream of reaching the major leagues became a reality when Detroit purchased his option from Augusta on August 24, 1905. Cobb made his major league debut on August 30, going 1-for-3 against New York, as the Tigers defeated the Highlanders, 5-3.[10]

Compounding being affected by events at home was Ty's sudden exposure to a different environment, where hazing by some veteran players was a common practice when a rookie joined a baseball team. Cobb batted .240 in 1905 while appearing in 41 games. Ty exhibited marked improvement for the Tigers in 1906, participating in 98 contests and hitting .316. All the hard work, dedication, and perseverance paid off in 1907 when Cobb claimed the American League batting title by batting at a .350 clip while also leading the circuit in hits (212), RBIs (119), and stolen bases (53). Detroit won the American League pennant under first-year skipper Hughie Jennings, who had replaced Bill Armour, before the Chicago Cubs swept them in the World Series. Ty claimed another hitting crown in 1908, with a mark of .324, as the Tigers triumphed in a very tight pennant race, culminating with another postseason defeat against Chicago.

Cobb dominated the baseball conversation in 1909, winning the league's Triple Crown in batting with a .377 average, nine home runs, and 107 RBIs. He also paced the circuit with 76 stolen bases, establishing a new modern-era single-season record. Detroit claimed their third consecutive American League pennant and faced the Pittsburgh Pirates in the World Series. When Ty arrived in Pittsburgh before Game One on October 8, he received a warm, loving reception from the city's residents while traversing about in the company of his wife Charlotte "Charlie" Lombard Cobb, whom he had married in 1908, and his mother. As reporters interviewed baseball's newest sensation two hours after reaching Pittsburgh, one writer asked Cobb if he believed he could outhit the great Honus Wagner in this World Series.

"Oh, you mustn't compare us," replied Cobb. "He is a baseball veteran, and I am only a youngster. He has had years of experience and is up in all the tricks of the trade. I have never seen him play, but from what I have heard of him, he must be a wonder. I don't know whether I will make a single hit in the series, but I don't care if Wagner hits .400 and I only bat .100, if the Tigers win out."[11]

Cobb and Wagner expressed mutual admiration for one another. In the World Series, the Pirates were victorious over the Tigers, four games to three, as Honus batted .333 while Ty hit .231. After the series ended, Wagner heaped praise on Detroit's young outfielder, declaring Cobb was the fastest man he had seen and a perfect baseball player.[12] Cobb's path to baseball grandeur over the next few years was a rocky one. During the 1909 season, he received vilification in some circles for spiking Philadelphia Athletics third baseman Frank Baker. However, later evidence related to the 1912 World Series indicated Connie Mack's player possibly was prone to such treatment due to blocking base runners.[13] In 1910, St. Louis Browns manager Jack O'Connor hoped to prevent Ty from winning the batting title. O'Connor ordered third baseman John "Red" Corriden to play very deep when challenger Nap Lajoie batted during a doubleheader against the Cleveland Naps on the season's final day. This strategy gave Lajoie carte blanche to record seven bunt singles in the two games.[14]

Ty Cobb's 1911 campaign was his best since breaking into the major leagues in 1905. Cobb paced the circuit in batting average (.419), hits (248), doubles (47), triples (24), runs (147), and RBIs (127). He also led the league with 83 stolen bases, establishing a new single-season mark, surpassing the 81 thefts achieved by the Athletics' Eddie Collins in 1910. Washington Senators outfielder Jesse Clyde Milan shattered that record one year later when he swiped 88 bags. Before the 1912 season, Tigers manager Hughie Jennings wrote an article about baseball's undisputed top player for *Baseball Magazine*. Although Jennings readily admitted Ty was a bit too heady when he first joined Detroit, he declared the great outfielder was one of the most trouble-free players to manage ever under his charge, while his demeanor on and off the field was a source of gratification. Hughie stated Cobb was a dashing player who always took chances to exert himself to the utmost extreme, played within baseball rules, and was legitimately sorry over spiking a player while making a lightning dash for the bases.

"There used to be a rumor," writes Jennings, "which has fortunately died out now, that Cobb was reckless and inconsiderate of opposing players on the diamond. This rumor was aroused by several unfortunate accidents in which Cobb was mixed up, particularly in Philadelphia. I say at this time what I have stated before, that Cobb has never intentionally spiked another player in his life. He is particularly fast on the bases and always plays the game for everything there is in it. But he is a considerate and likable player in every way, and I know from my own personal knowledge that he would never be guilty of such an unsportsmanlike act. If anyone will take the pains to examine the records, he will find that Cobb has spiked fewer players than several other prominent stars who have been criticized in the slightest degree or accused of unnecessary roughness. I am sure the average critic nowadays is ready to admit there is nothing whatever of rowdyism or dirty tactics in the playing of Tyrus Cobb."

Jennings stated that Ty Cobb was an individual everybody enjoyed watching on the field while also ordaining his star outfielder as the most outstanding player baseball had ever known.[15] Before the 1912 season began, Cobb offered a technical, scientific assessment related to the analytical aspect of the game, regarding his approach on the base paths being unpredictable rather than reckless. "They say," remarked the Georgian, "that I run wild and use no judgment or little judgment in picking my start. It may look that way, but I figure ahead on every base-running move I make. I start when I have an opening, and there are times when I start without one, but it's all part of a system.

"When I start at the wrong time, I call it advertising. You'll often see a poker player stand put on a king-high nothing and then show down his hand when no one has called. He does that for strictly advertising purposes. There are times I run when it is against all baseball law and judgment to make the attempt. But it's part of my system. They have no basis then to figure when I am going. They figure 'this crazy mutt is likely to start any time,' which does its part in helping to keep a catcher worried and guessing. There is no foundation for him to build on."[16]

When assessing a situation on the diamond or plotting a strategic maneuver, Cobb's mind was always numerous chess moves ahead of his counterparts. Although two other players supplanted Ty as the league's base-stealing king for three consecutive seasons, he still topped the organization in batting, with averages of .409 in 1912 and .389 in 1913. In 1914, an injury that didn't occur on the field sidelined Cobb. After Detroit defeated Washington on June 20 at Navin Field, 1-0, Ty invited Senators manager Clark Griffith, pitcher Walter Johnson, and a few other players to his home for dinner.[17] Upon arriving at his domicile, Cobb found his wife Charlie distressed, following an argument on the phone with the proprietor of a market over three perch she had recently purchased for twenty cents. These fish happened to be spoiled as she prepared to cook them.[18]

Following a phone conversation with the individual who had disrespected his wife, Ty immediately set out for this establishment located on Hamilton Boulevard, with a revolver in his possession. When Cobb entered the butcher shop, he encountered owner William L. Carpenter and demanded the proprietor apologize to his wife for insulting her. 20-year-old employee Howard Harding intervened when he saw the baseball player draw his weapon while arguing with Carpenter. The two men became involved in a fistfight, with Ty breaking his right thumb in the scuffle. Cobb was arrested, taken to the police station on Bethune Avenue, and held before being released the following morning. Harding refused to press charges, while Carpenter claimed Ty had rushed into his establishment, made an accusation, and started trouble. When Cobb talked to the press, offering his account of the incident, he claimed Carpenter grabbed a meat cleaver when the two started quarreling. "I have a permit to carry a revolver, and I told Carpenter I had the means to protect myself," said the outfielder. "Our little affair was practically over when Harding butted in. He seemed to want trouble, and I was so angry I gave him what he was looking for."

A new revelation came to the forefront about Cobb having permission to carry a weapon for some time in response to receiving threatening letters. Carpenter enlisted counsel to consider filing suit against Ty.[19] The situation was quickly resolved, as Cobb paid a $50 fine, thus concluding the criminal side. At the same time, Carpenter dropped his threat to seek damages on the civil angle when the Tigers organization gave the butcher a pass to watch games at Navin Field.[20] On July 14, Ty briefly returned to the lineup and then only saw action as a pinch-runner on one occasion before taking his permanent place in the outfield on August 7. Cobb, who batted .368 in 1914, only appeared in 98 contests, the lowest amount of games played since his first entire season in 1906. Detroit finished fourth in the standings with an 80-73 record.

The opportunity to begin preparing for vindication and marked improvement in 1915, as per schedule, would commence later than the customary date. At the end of November, Tigers management announced that spring training would launch two weeks later than usual at the camp in Gulfport, Mississippi. The time spent in Gulfport would be the same, reducing exhibition games as the team headed north to open the regular season.[21] During the off-season, Ty Cobb spent many days golfing on a course in Georgia.[22] On the hot-stove league front related to the Tigers, rumors abounded that pitcher George "Hooks" Dauss and shortstop Owen "Donie" Bush would be the targets of the Federal League's Indianapolis team since both players hailed from that city.[23] A big story related to Detroit's baseball scene surrounded Jacob Ruppert. The latter had just purchased the New York Yankees with partner T. L. Huston.

The two men desired that Hughie Jennings join the organization to manage their team. Jennings quickly rebuked the suggestion that he might be heading to New York. "I do not want to go to New York," said Hughie. "Why should I? Frank J. Navin has always treated me with the very best consideration in Detroit. He pays me well and shows his appreciation keenly for whatever I may have done in behalf of his club."[24]

Such a move seemed a distinct possibility since William H. Yawkey, Frank Navin's partner in the Detroit club's ownership, supposedly hadn't been enamored with Jennings's work as a field leader for years. According to team secretary Charles A. Hughes, Ban Johnson contacted Navin about Hughie joining the Yankees. When Frank asked Yawkey for his opinion, the man who had wanted to dismiss Jennings many times gave a surprising response. "Tell them to take a jump in the lake," was Yawkey's unexpected reply. "They couldn't get Jennings for love or money."[25]

Shortly before a new year dawned, a *Washington Star* sports writer claimed the Tigers' success in 1915 hinged on Ty Cobb. The scribe reasoned that if Cobb realized he owed it to his club and teammates to give consummate effort, chances became greatly enhanced that Detroit would play a more prominent role in the pennant race. This writer believed Ty's absence from the lineup, as was the case in 1914, proved detrimental to the Tigers and the entire league.[26] Weeks before the beginning of spring training, Cobb candidly stated he didn't believe Detroit would win the pennant and that the Boston Red Sox should have things wrapped up by September 1. Ty added he was staying in shape by hunting and golfing. Cobb also said that Federal League agents hadn't interviewed him over the winter, hoping to convince the star player to join their organization.[27] On a sad note, pitcher Marcus "Marc" Hall, who had gone 4-6 with a 2.69 ERA in 25 games for the Tigers in 1914, passed away on February 24, 1915, following a nine-month illness with Bright's disease.[28]

Hughie Jennings, trainer Harry Tuthill, and outfielder Sam Crawford greeted the advance squad when they arrived in Gulfport on February 28.[29] An earlier press release placed the number of players participating in spring training at 29, which was considered a small group compared to other years.[30] Cobb, who usually didn't participate in the spring barnstorming tour leading up to the opener, initially had promised to report with the regulars and appear in every exhibition game.[31] Ty ended up arriving on his revised date of March 20, as Detroit prepared to play the Southern Association's Mobile Sea Gulls, managed by former Tigers catcher Charles "Boss" Schmidt. Cobb donned a uniform and smacked a single that helped Detroit secure victory.[32] Ty was a delighted individual, having just agreed to a three-year contract with Frank Navin, calling for a salary of $20,000 per season, which made him baseball's highest-paid player.[33]

While his team trained in Gulfport, Jennings said during an interview the Tigers didn't look any better than they did the previous year; before adding the caveat that a pennant would have been achieved in 1914 if Ty Cobb had played the entire season.[34] When Detroit played an exhibition game in Jackson, Mississippi, Cobb encountered people attached to a convention related to "Votes for Women." Ty pledged himself to the cause, leading an admiring Mississippi woman to pin a rose on him, thus ordaining him as a member of the suffragette party.[35]

As the spring training session progressed, Cobb warned fans there would be no three-cornered race for the base-stealing title involving him, Clyde Milan of the Washington Senators, and New York's Fritz Maisel. Ty indicated he was willing to allow the other two gentlemen to battle for honors, realizing there was great danger in taking chances on the bases, with risk now outweighing reward. He still planned on stealing bases when such a strategy was prudent but would no longer take needless chances.[36] While engaging some newspapermen in Gulfport at the end of March, Cobb picked up a copy of *Richter's History of Base Ball* and started consuming the game's batting records throughout its history. Ty was particularly intrigued by Honus Wagner's mark of topping the National League in hitting eight times, which he had tied in 1914 as a member of the American League.

"There isn't anything I wouldn't give to lead the league just two years more," said Cobb. "I don't know whether I can do it or not, but to be the best batter in a major league for ten years would be enough to satisfy any man. It sure would suit me. If there is anything more for which I would give almost anything, it would be to beat Lajoie's batting average of .422 [.426] in 1901.

I got .420 [.419] in 1911, and there were two games in which I didn't play that I might have. I don't know that they would have boosted my average, but I can't help thinking that I passed up a big chance. I certainly was a fortunate batter that year."

Ty came across an intriguing entry, which offered him plaudits as a batter but questioned his durability compared to bigger men like Wagner, Adrian "Cap" Anson, Dennis "Dan" Brouthers, and Nap Lajoie. Although Cobb realized many people expected him to break under the strain of playing baseball, he felt his winter training regimen helped him conserve strength during the season.[37] The opportunity to face new diamond challenges finally arrived on April 14, as Detroit opened the 1915 campaign at Navin Field against the Cleveland Indians. The Tigers opposed hurler William "Willie" Mitchell, whom sportswriter Ring Lardner had selected as his left-handed twirler on an All-American team for his article in *American Magazine*.[38] Solid pitching by Mitchell and extremely poor fielding by Detroit, including a first-inning error by Ty, spelled doom and defeat, as five unearned runs gave Cleveland a 5-1 victory.

Cobb tallied the Tigers' only marker in the fourth inning when he singled and eventually scored on Robert "Bobby" Veach's fly ball.[39] After reaching first, Ty motored over to third on a single to left field by Sam Crawford, barely beating a strong throw by Indians left fielder John "Jack" Graney. Cleveland's players were upset with umpire Silk O'Loughlin's safe call, especially Mitchell, who became tremendously peeved. "I wish I was a star," said Mitchell, "and could get all those close ones. I'd just like to see how it feels."

"You want to be a star, eh?" shot back Cobb with loud emphasis on the 'want.' "Why don't you buy a copy of the *American Magazine*!"[40]

Snappy banter was replaced by better fundamental baseball as Detroit won their first game of the season on April 15, beating the Indians, 5-4. Cobb went 2-for-4 at the plate, legged out an inside-the-park home run in the sixth inning, and stole a base. The following afternoon, while playing in temperatures barely above freezing, a Tigers lead quickly evaporated when Cleveland scored six runs in the seventh inning and secured a 9-6 victory.[41] Ty recorded one single and pilfered two bases. Cobb added two more hits and stole his fourth bag of the season on April 17, as hurler Jean Dubuc shackled the Indians, 5-0. In the first game of the series against the Chicago White Sox on April 18, Ty saved the day by firing a bullet from deep center field and cutting down John "Shano" Collins at the plate, preserving an 8-7 victory.[42] Cobb also went 2-for-3 and scored three runs.

Hurler Bernard "Bernie" Boland snuffed out Chicago one day later, 6-1. The White Sox's only run came in the fourth frame, as Shano Collins eventually scored after reaching base when Ty muffed his fly ball.[43] Detroit's slugging trio of Cobb, Crawford, and Veach did heavy damage in a 6-3 victory over the White Sox on April 20. The three players had two hits apiece and combined to score five of the Tigers' runs.[44] Ty scored a critical tally in the eighth inning one day later when he doubled after Detroit had just tallied their first run and then came home on Crawford's two-bagger, as the Tigers secured a 4-3 victory over Chicago.[45] Cobb added one stolen base in each of the first two games against Cleveland at League Park, as Detroit prevailed, 5-3, on April 22 and 8-4, the following afternoon. On April 25, Indians hurler Guy Morton snapped the Tigers' eight-game winning streak, claiming a 3-1 victory.[46] Ty drove home Detroit's only run and swiped his seventh base of the year.

Cobb added two more thefts in games against the St. Louis Browns on April 26 and 28, giving him nine for the month. He swiped home on April 28 during the front end of a triple steal. When the month concluded, Detroit found themselves atop the standings with a 12-5 record, 1 ½ games ahead of second-place New York. Ty's batting average stood at .389 heading into May. When the man known as the "Georgia Peach" flirted around the .500 mark during the season's early days, *Sporting Life* scribe Chandler D. Richter pondered if this possibly could be the season that Cobb might realize his desire to hit .450.[47] When Ty left the bench, he prepared by swinging three bats before taking his turn at the plate. Cobb picked up his cudgel, slender and light in the handle, Donie Bush's long, wispy, thin bat for luck, and Sam Crawford's formidable war club for positive karma and weight. Once in the batter's box, Ty gripped his slim, light bat firmly with his right hand before sliding the left paw two inches above that.[48]

A newspaper article forced Ty Cobb to refute a statement quoting him that players who jumped to the Federal League and attempted to rejoin their former teams were undesirables. Cobb clarified this error, affirming he commented that players who hopped back and forth had made mistakes and acted foolishly.[49] When it came to exerting his will on the base paths, statistics initially credited Ty with 13 stolen bases in May (later changed to 14). Ty turned the trick on four occasions pilfering one bag, swiped two sacks three times, and was daring in a contest against the Yankees on May 19 at Navin Field, stealing four bases. In that game, which Detroit won, 3-1, Cobb smacked a single that sent pitcher Harry Coveleski home with the Tigers' first tally in the third inning.

The fleet-footed Ty then stole second and third before the frame concluded. In the eighth, Cobb was passed for the third time, stole second, went to third on a wild pitch, and scored on Ralph Young's single.[50]

Three days before Ty's superb performance, former Tigers pitcher William "Bill" Donovan, who now managed New York, was honored on a Sunday afternoon billed as "Wild Will Day." Although the original estimation was that 25,000 patrons might jam Navin Field to pay tribute to Donovan, cold, dreary weather knocked the attendance down to about 12,000, with rain falling in Detroit the next two days.[51] The Yankees' manager was given several gifts by local friends and organizations before the contest started.[52] At one point in May, a reporter told Ty that Federal League star Benjamin "Benny" Kauff had claimed that if he could break into Organized Baseball, he would make the Georgia Peach look like a busher. "Who's Kauff?" was Cobb's simple comeback. Ty also cautioned those writing epitaphs regarding hurler and friend Walter Johnson, citing a game from earlier that month as proof he wasn't losing any speed. "Johnson breezed a couple under my chin that nobody in the world could have walloped," Cobb said. "He's just as fast as ever; don't let anybody tell you different."[53]

When May ended, the Tigers were perched in second place with a 25-16 record, putting them 1 ½ games behind Chicago. After unofficially being credited with 23 thefts through May, Ty Cobb, whose average stood at .418, went on a rampage running the bases in June. Cobb stole an astounding 28 bases that month, turning the trick on multiple occasions in a game eight times while claiming home plate through the pilfering gambit in four instances. Ty participated in base thievery once in a 4-1 loss against Chicago on June 1. Cobb recorded two steals the following day as Detroit returned the favor with a 4-1 triumph. Leading 1-0, heading into the bottom of the eighth, White Sox pitcher Joseph "Joe" Benz became so unnerved after Ty smacked a single that he lost his composure, allowing Sam Crawford, Martin "Marty" Kavanagh, and Ralph Young to connect for safeties that put the Tigers in front, and sent him to the showers.[54]

Cobb took matters into his own hands in a 3-0 victory over New York on June 4. Ty drove home Oscar Vitt with a triple in the first inning and then scored on Sam Crawford's Texas League single over second base.[55] It remained 2-0 until Ty started the ninth by smashing a single that Luke Boone knocked down behind second. Yankees pitcher Ray Caldwell kept Cobb at bay as he retired Crawford and Veach before baseball's most outstanding player decided to use his legs to push the defense.[56] Ty bolted for second base and kept moving to third when catcher Les Nunamaker's throw skipped through to center field. Cobb teased New York's players as Marty Kavanagh batted, running halfway toward the plate on each pitch, before finally dashing homeward. Baseball and player arrived at home plate amid a cloud of dust.[57] Umpire Silk O'Loughlin remained silent, prompting Ty to rise, walk over, and touch the dish with his foot, which elicited a safe call.[58] The Yankees vehemently protested the decision. Caldwell became so miffed over this call that he threw his glove into the air, causing O'Loughlin to eject him.[59]

On June 9, the Tigers connected for 17 hits and bombarded Boston, 15-0. Cobb stole home once again in the third inning, one of his three thefts on the day, and went 3-for-5. Red Sox shortstop Everett Scott left the game in the first after he was spiked when Ty attempted to steal second base.[60] Cobb added two more pilfers the following day as Boston defeated the Tigers, 6-5. Ty ran wild against Philadelphia at Shibe Park on June 12, grabbing four stolen bases as the Athletics defeated Detroit, 7-6, in 13 innings. Before the game, local admirers presented Cobb with a hunting gun.[61] A contingent of Shriners, headed by Philadelphia receiver of taxes W. Freeland Kendrick, was on hand to honor Ty.

Detroit's baseball scribes estimated that Ty Cobb's brilliance had been directly responsible for one-third of the Tigers' victories through this point in the season.[62] Some national writers started referring to Detroit as the Tygers in their articles since Cobb was the most significant factor behind the team's success and should receive just accolades through spelling the team nickname this way.[63] When discussing Ty's ability to run to first base with incredible velocity, Grantland Rice wrote that his blazing speed even placed pressure on infielders who handled the ball cleanly. Domination on the base paths resulted, where players would have recorded easy outs on mere mortals. One baseball fan didn't comprehend that Cobb benefitted by pushing the opposing defense beyond its limits. "This Cobb is a lucky guy," remarked this fan. "The infielders are always fumbling his hits."[64]

Tyrus seemed to be bitten by the pennant bug more than any of his teammates, who then became believers because of his awe-inspiring play, and infectious enthusiasm.[65] Amidst all the happy talk and joyous bonding, Cobb became embroiled in a controversy in mid-June, connected to a syndicated baseball article containing his byline. The prose claimed that an American League squad was notorious for stealing opposing teams' battery signs during games on their home grounds. In the article, the author, presumed to be Ty, wrote that he wouldn't mention the organization's name since he didn't possess irrefutable proof. It seemed this particular squad was proficient at home but struggled when they played games on the road. Cobb also declared that all members of Detroit's team would take an oath alleging something funny was going on while claiming signal stealing was unfair and dangerous and that baseball was too big for petty larceny.[66]

After people read this account in newspapers across the country, many believed Ty had insinuated the Chicago White Sox and manager Clarence "Pants" Rowland were the culprits. The basis for this conclusion was a statement in the piece that the manager in question "owed his success as a bush-league boss to grab signals."[67] President Ban Johnson threatened Ty with expulsion from the league if he wrote the article, which surprised Detroit's outfielder since he believed people shouldn't make such declarations without knowing the facts.

"I never said or wrote that the White Sox are stealing signals," said Tyrus Raymond. "Lots of players have told me that such is the case, but I would not make such charges unless I saw for myself that this is being done, and I have not seen it. It seems to me that Johnson ought to make sure he is in the right before he threatens to drive me out of baseball."[68]

Although the article didn't mention the White Sox by name, it was common knowledge among those in the circuit that Rowland and his boys were circumventing the rules. In a recent series, members of the Yankees complained about Chicago even pulling their signal tipping chicanery at New York's home ballpark of the Polo Grounds. Since Cobb's name was connected to this column and received payment for his services, this acted as an adequate admission to the charge in Johnson's eyes. Ban was adamant over Ty pronouncing he was writing about the White Sox.[69] Johnson expressed his dissatisfaction about the situation upon arriving in Washington on June 16 while reiterating his call to banish Cobb from baseball.

"Cobb will have to see me about that story," said Johnson, "and in addition, he may have to come before the National Commission. If it is proved that he himself wrote the story and that he meant the White Sox when he spoke about a 'certain team' whose players have been stealing the signals of rival clubs, it will go hard with him.

"If he is guilty on both counts, I will drive him out of baseball. I don't care if he is a great ballplayer. No player or anyone else amenable to the discipline of the American League can pull anything like that and get away with it."

Ban also avowed that he wasn't in favor of any players lending their names to stories about baseball. Johnson alerted the press that he had spoken to Chicago owner Charles Comiskey about this allegation. Regardless, Ty wasn't concerned over the league president bloviating about things that weren't true.[70] Never one to be submissive when challenged, Cobb continued pushing back against the threats, leading Ban to retreat swiftly. On June 25, Johnson announced he was misquoted and had never threatened to banish Cobb. He always believed Ty hadn't written the story and surmised Detroit's star player wasn't aware of its contents until appearing in print. Ban also suggested the Baseball Writers' Association may investigate the Detroit reporter who penned this column.[71] Lastly, Johnson said if Cobb had written the article, he wouldn't consider driving him from baseball.[72]

Any turmoil perceived by others certainly didn't affect Ty Cobb's performance. Cobb's average stood at .397 when June ended while being unofficially credited with 51 stolen bases. The Tigers held the third position with a 39-26 record, putting them 5 ½ games behind first-place Chicago. Expectations ran high that Clyde Milan's modern-era and American League record 88 steals in 1912 was likely to fall.[73] Ty slowed somewhat in July pilfering bags, only getting credit for 11 that month. Cobb experienced a brief drought before stealing two bases on July 9 as Detroit beat Boston, 15-4. In his push to establish high marks in many offensive categories, Ty was commended daily for his natural talent, speed, precise batting eye, and a brain that allowed him to think quicker than most baseball players.[74] Always willing to pass on advice or suggestions to younger players, Cobb had recently tutored one of his favorite pupils, Fritz Maisel, on batting and base running when the Tigers played New York a month earlier.[75]

When the topic came up regarding sons of major leaguers following in their father's footsteps, Ty offered an opinion that differed from that of New York Giants hurler Christy Mathewson and his encouraging Christy, Jr., to play baseball. Cobb hoped that Ty, Jr., would become a good lawyer or physician rather than an athlete.

"I would hate to see a son of mine go through some of the things ballplayers have to put up with," said Cobb. "Baseball is the greatest game in the world. But I do not believe boys should go into it blindly and thinking that it is a bed of roses."[76]

On July 10, Johnson decreed that all American League players must immediately discontinue writing syndicated articles for newspapers. Cobb voluntarily agreed to quit this practice, with three more installments as a contributor slated to appear in newspapers. Johnson's organization had taken a strong stance several years ago against players moonlighting as writers. Still, the rule was permitted to lapse so these athletes could earn extra money due to the Federal League muscling their way into the picture.[77] As the pennant race proceeded into the stretch drive, baseball followers offered a plausible reason for Ty's assault on the game's base running records. In 1912, a Cleveland fan had told Cobb: "Joe Jackson says he will hit .400 this year." Ty smiled and responded: "If he does, I'll hit .450." That year, Jackson hit .395 while Cobb batted .409. The motivating factor behind swiping bases in 1915 seemed to be the contention that Fritz Maisel was the fastest man in baseball.[78]

Near the end of July, a potential chink in the armor regarding Ty's outstanding campaign was brought to the forefront by Tigers pilot Hughie Jennings. While discussing how excessive throwing before games could be detrimental to young players, Jennings stated the habit of pitching for hours each day might have possibly shortened his career by five years. Hughie also revealed that Cobb was experiencing problems with his throwing arm because of this practice. "Cobb has spoiled his arm by pitching before each game and doing a lot of unnecessary throwing," said Jennings. "Ty had one of the greatest arms I have ever seen when he came to Detroit, but he overtaxed the cords and the muscles and lost much of his strength."[79]

Before the season swung into August, Ty changed his position about playing golf during the baseball campaign. Cobb declared he was quitting the links until the off-season, except for a scheduled match when Detroit played in Washington, since golfing indeed interfered with the batting eye.[80] Heading into August, the Tigers were still in the thick of the pennant hunt, holding down third place with a 57-36 record, putting them two games out of first. Ty was batting .398 and had stolen 62 bases. Cobb added 14 more thefts to the vault in August but tailed off after a blistering start due to a scenario that was foreign to the great hitter. Ty grabbed three steals in a doubleheader sweep over the Athletics at Shibe Park on August 7 and laid down a beautiful bunt single in the tenth inning of game two, giving Detroit a 3-2 victory.[81]

Cobb went dry on the base paths for over a week before stealing three bases in the first game of a doubleheader on August 16, as the Tigers defeated Cleveland, 6-2. He swiped another trio of bags in game one of a twin bill against the Indians one day later, when Detroit claimed a 10-3 victory. Ty kept the momentum rolling toward surpassing 88 thefts when he stole single bases in back-to-back games versus Philadelphia on August 19 and 20.

American League umpire William "Billy" Evans explained why Cobb was so adept at beating throws to the bag on a steal attempt. "I doubt if there is a man in baseball who is harder to touch than Ty Cobb," said Evans. "Time after time, Cobb is declared safe when the ball beats him to the bag by several feet.

Often it looks as if the umpire has rendered a bad decision, but it is usually the old, old story, the baseman failed to touch him."[82]

When Detroit defeated the Athletics, 11-1, on August 20, it was the team's ninth consecutive victory. That solid stretch ended on August 22, as Washington beat the Tigers, 8-1, in the first game of a doubleheader. Between those two days, a monumental story hit newspapers, claiming that Ty Cobb's throwing arm was dead. Trainer Harry Tuthill worked diligently on Cobb's right arm daily without gaining the desired results. Some suggested a visit to muscle specialist and doctor Bonesetter Reese in Youngstown, Ohio, may be necessary. A minor batting slump resulted from Ty feeling anxiety over his damaged wing. Cobb noticed a change in early July when his throws from the outfield became less powerful. As manager Hughie Jennings had alluded to, the belief was that the root cause was related to when Ty warmed up tossing curveballs with Detroit's pitchers before games as a babe breaking into the major leagues.[83] On August 26, Cobb celebrated the tenth anniversary of becoming a major leaguer as the Tigers defeated Boston at Navin Field, 7-6, in 12 innings.[84]

A minor batting slump was nothing compared to what Cobb experienced at the end of August. After going 2-for-3 in game one of a doubleheader against New York on August 27, Ty went hitless in 14 official trips to the plate over the next four games. Initially, when Cobb was credited with a weak single in the eighth inning of the contest with Chicago on August 31, it was the first time he had hit safely in 20 at-bats. Ty proceeded to take the collar the following day, facing the White Sox.[85] A later scoring change gave Cobb another hit earlier in the game on August 31, while he also stole bases number 74, 75, and 76 off catcher Ray Schalk.

Sportswriter Grantland Rice asked Ty to account for how a batter could average two hits a contest for over 100 games while flirting with .400 and then go up to the plate so many times without landing one safely. "I haven't tried to account for it," said Ty. "But I'm going out there tomorrow and knock the cover off that ball or break my doggoned back."[86]

Even when times were tough and fretfulness entered the picture, Cobb remained focused and never lost his confidence. While Ty experienced the worst batting funk of his storied career, a laughable rumor emerged claiming the fledgling Federal League planned on offering Cobb $100,000 in salary, spread over three years. The story was ridiculous since Ty had never received this offer, while the outlaw organization couldn't afford such a pricy stipend, even if they were eager to sign him to a contract. Because of personal pride and the desire to play in front of large crowds, Cobb most likely would accept a pay cut to remain in a league that included classy competition rather than go to a place where the diamond standards were much lower.[87]

Following the worst batting slump of his major league career, Ty hit safely in 17 straight games from game two of a doubleheader on September 5 through September 24. When it came to chasing Clyde Milan's record, steady and consistent ruled the day for Cobb. Ty added single steals in nine different contests through the first half of September, bringing his season total to 85. In the first game of a crucial series against Boston at Fenway Park with pennant implications, Detroit's aggressive style of play helped secure a 6-1 victory for the Tigers on September 16. Cobb was jeered and heckled by Red Sox fans the entire afternoon.[88] In the eighth inning, Boston hurler Carl Mays chucked two pitches near Ty's head. On the third offering, an angry Cobb allowed the bat to fly out of his hands toward Mays, who ducked to avoid the projectile. After Ty berated Carl while walking out to recover the bat, the hurler responded by plunking him in the elbow with the next pitch. When the game concluded, a squad of police officers escorted Cobb off the field as a mob of bleacher fans descended upon him.[89]

This victory pulled Detroit to within .012 percentage points of first-place Boston.[90] Unfortunately for Ty and his teammates, the Red Sox won the final three games of this series.

Because statistics tended to be unofficial at a particular moment in time during the Deadball Era, the *Washington Times* credited Cobb with breaking Milan's record of 88 steals in a single season during a game against the Athletics on September 22.[91] The *Washington Herald*, using the unofficial figures of statistician George Moreland, claimed that when Ty swiped second base in the sixth inning against Washington on September 24, it was his eighty-seventh steal of the campaign. He was then gunned down at third, attempting to add to that total.[92] The *Detroit Times* declared Cobb tied the record against the Senators that afternoon.[93] In reality, through making the necessary statistical adjustments where stolen bases were added or taken away, Cobb tied Milan's mark on September 22, when the Tigers beat Philadelphia at Shibe Park, 13-9. Ty broke the record with his eighty-ninth steal one day later, as Detroit defeated the Athletics, 6-5.

Cobb's ambition as the 1915 season progressed was to steal 100 bases.[94] He fell a few short, finishing the year with 96. Detroit's star outfielder could have added to that total if teammate Donie Bush wasn't occupying third base when he took off from second in a game versus Washington on September 27. Ty quickly retraced his steps, was called out at second, and ejected by umpire, and former St. Louis Browns great, Bobby Wallace, for strenuously arguing the decision.[95] The Tigers had a fantastic season, going 100-54 and finishing in second place, 2 ½ games behind pennant-winning Boston. Cobb paced the league in a host of categories other than stolen bases, including batting average (.369), hits (208), and runs (144). In his effort to steal 96 bases, opposing catchers threw out baseball's gambler on 38 other attempts.

Ty's modern-era record of 96 stolen bases in a single season stood for 47 years until the Los Angeles Dodgers' Maurice "Maury" Wills swiped 104 in 1962. Louis "Lou" Brock of the St. Louis Cardinals topped that mark with 118 in 1974, before Rickey Henderson set the standard as a member of the Oakland Athletics by stealing 130 bases in 1982. Before the Deadball Era, Billy Hamilton, Walter "Arlie" Latham, and Charles Comiskey were a few who had surpassed the 100 plateaux in steals. Hugh Nichol of the American Association's Cincinnati Red Stockings stood above all others, with 138 stolen bases in 1887.

Summing up the Georgia Peach's majestic excellence in all facets of life was done eloquently by an article in the September 1915 issue of *American Boy* magazine. "Ty Cobb is called the greatest ballplayer that ever lived," stated the article's author. "He did not earn that title easily. No man works harder than does Cobb, and only a part of his efforts take place on the ball field."[96]

Tyrus Raymond Cobb indeed had traveled a great distance on this fruitful journey since making an electrifying outfield catch as a youngster, prompting his father to write that first baseball article in Royston.

In 1915, Ty Cobb broke the modern-era, single-season record for stolen bases previously held by Clyde Milan of the Washington Senators. Cobb stole 96 bases, a mark that stood until the Los Angeles Dodgers' Maury Wills swiped 104 bags in 1962. The worst batting slump of Ty's career at the end of August thwarted his efforts to top the century mark in stolen bases. Cobb became concerned over suffering from a dead throwing arm that didn't respond to treatment. (Courtesy of the Library of Congress.)

CHAPTER 12

Jack Nabors – 1916

A Season of Futility, Pitching for a Wretched Team

For those fortunate enough to reach the major leagues in past eras, being exposed to the proper environment has allowed many baseball players to blossom, flourish, and reach their full potential. Favorable circumstances, achieved through either an immediate opportunity arising to perform to the best of one's ability or watching and learning on a pennant contender before finally bursting onto the scene, helped enhance that development. In direct contrast to players fortunate enough to hook up with a good team, some individuals joined an organization defined by second-division finishes and flirtation with the cellar's mistress each season. Compounding matters for a performer joining a lousy team was when that organization rushed a minor leaguer to the big show, well before being prepared to perform at that level.

As baseball's Deadball Era neared its conclusion, a young hurler, greener than the decor in an Irish pub on St. Patrick's Day, was called upon to join what used to be one of the game's most storied franchises. In 1915, pitcher Herman John Nabors became a member of a Philadelphia Athletics team that had won four American League pennants and three World Series' from 1910 through 1914. Unfortunately, when he boarded the Athletics' ship, it was pitching, swaying, and taking water, as past glory quickly became replaced by diamond ineptitude and incompetence. One year later, while playing for a team that quite possibly might have been one of the worst in baseball history, Nabors established a modern-era, single-season record that no pitcher would be proud to have attached to his name.

Herman Nabors was born on November 19, 1887, in Montevallo, Alabama. Both of John's parents, James Nabors and Sarah Matilda Foster Nabors, had relatives from the city of Piedmont in that state. His family referred to him as John Jackson, which they then shortened to the nickname "Jack." Nabors's interest in baseball was due to his older brothers, who played for amateur and community teams in and around Montevallo.

One of his brothers, Dr. Arthur H. Nabors, who practiced medicine in Decatur, Alabama, talked about those early days in a 1968 interview with *Anniston Star* sportswriter Bill Plott. "Jack was probably influenced by our brother Bill Nabors more than anyone else," said Dr. Arthur Nabors. "Bill played community baseball in Dogwood, Ala. He was 6' 4" tall and played center field, and they beat nearly every team in the country."

Through watching Bill Nabors, young Jackson understood baseball's fundamentals, leading him to start pitching for community teams in Shelby County. "Later, he went up to Walker County where some of those industrial teams would pay him if he pitched and won," recalled Dr. Nabors.

After spending time on the industrial and community league circuit, Jack Nabors signed his first professional contract with the Georgia-Alabama League's Selma River Rats in 1914. One year later, after the organization was contracted from eight teams to six, with Selma being one of the squads eliminated, Jack cast his lot with the Talladega Tigers. In early June, Talladega traded Nabors to the Newnan Cowetas of that league.[1] As Jack bounced around the Class D minor league environment, a team that had dominated the major league baseball scene throughout the decade was going through a significant transformation.

In 1914, the Philadelphia Athletics claimed the American League pennant by going 99-53. Hoping to win their fourth World Series title in the past five years, the upstart Boston Braves of the National League swept manager Connie Mack's squad. Shortly after the Athletics were slaughtered in Game One on October 9 at Shibe Park, 7-1, behind the brilliant performance of Braves hurler Richard "Dick" Rudolph, the scribe working with Philadelphia third baseman Frank Baker on the syndicated column bearing the player's name, offered insight about the article related to that contest. The writer described his brief interaction with Baker about the game, causing him to pen a fake column related to the Athletics' defeat.

"Hello, Bake?" gently queried the scribe.

"Howdy?" responded Baker.

"Well, what did you think of it, Bake?" asked the writer.

"We got licked plenty," replied Philadelphia's third baseman. "Pretty good pitcher, that fellow. Gowdy [Braves catcher Henry "Hank" Gowdy] hit the ball on the snoot. Don't knock anybody else."[2]

Weeks after the World Series concluded, Connie Mack made a bombshell announcement regarding three hurlers who had been a massive part of the team's success for many years. He only did so after Detroit Tigers manager Hughie Jennings unprofessionally broke league protocol by exposing that the Athletics had asked for waivers on pitchers Eddie Plank, Chief Bender, and Jack Coombs. Jennings' revelation forced Mack to make a statement regarding the matter.

"Yes, waivers have been asked on Plank, Bender, and Coombs," replied Mack when queried by reporters. "Before releasing a player unconditionally, all clubs of the American League must waive on him. While I have no intention of retaining any one of the three players named for 1915, I would not have asked waivers on them at this time, but for the fact that one of the three told me he had been talking business with the Federal League. He said that he was offered big money and did not suppose that we would be willing to meet the offer."[3]

After meeting with Baltimore Terrapins treasurer Harry Goldman, Plank signed a general contract on December 2 to join the Federal League in 1915. The expectation was that he would suit up for the St. Louis Terriers.[4] Three days later, after negotiating with Goldman, Bender inked a deal to play for Baltimore in the rebel league. Mack wasn't surprised or concerned over the news regarding Chief. A renewal didn't seem likely for Bender once his contract expired after the 1914 campaign.[5] When a baseball writer informed Connie that Eddie had signed to play with the Feds, he offered a mixed opinion about the hurler, who had been a mainstay on his staff for many years.

"I wish him the best of luck," said Connie Mack.

"Are you sorry to see him go?" asked a writer.

"Oh, no," replied Connie. "I was through with him. He was after the money and was quite willing to go to the Federals. He was a wonderful pitcher, and he is a good one yet."[6]

The release of three veteran pitchers was just window dressing compared with the next step of dismantling an outstanding baseball team. On December 8, the Chicago White Sox purchased star Athletics second baseman Eddie Collins for $50,000.[7] Mack brokered the deal after he, Collins, league president Ban Johnson, and Chicago owner Charles Comiskey had held a secret conference at Philadelphia's Bellevue-Stratford Hotel two days earlier. The first of two reasons why Connie decided to move Eddie over other players was that his second baseman had dictated terms for a lucrative, ironclad contract signed the previous year in response to Federal League overtures.[8] Besides forking over $50,000 to purchase Collins, Comiskey inherited an agreement that called for paying the second baseman $60,000 over the next five years.[9]

A second critical motivation for moving Collins was his love of writing newspaper columns over the past few seasons. Eddie had developed a strong reputation as an excellent writer with rare abilities during that time.[10] In the end, this authoring caused discord with Collins's teammates.[11] Friction emerged between Eddie and catcher Ira Thomas, who acted as the Athletics' team captain. A quote attributed to Thomas expressed displeasure that Collins's newspaper and magazine articles revealed secrets about strategy and other things related to the team.[12] Shortly after the deal was consummated, the *Chicago Daily Tribune* suggested Eddie discontinue his literary endeavors so the writings didn't alienate his new teammates. Ban Johnson also stated that he would forbid Collins from continuing to write for publications.[13] Although it appeared Collins had been at loggerheads with some connected to the Athletics organization, he exhibited consummate class, closing the chapter on a very successful portion of his baseball career.

"I want to say," said Collins, "that Connie Mack and I part the best of friends. There was talk of friction on the team last season, but it wasn't true. I count every member of the Athletics a friend. I see there was a report that Ira Thomas had the hammer after me, but I don't believe he ever gave out that interview. I haven't a single kick in Philadelphia and was treated royally by fans and press. I leave wishing Mack and the Athletics the best of luck. I certainly will miss playing alongside Barry [shortstop John "Jack" Barry] and McInnis [first baseman John "Stuffy" McInnis], but in baseball, sentiment cuts little figure."[14]

Another intention behind Eddie Collins's sale to Chicago was for it to serve as an object lesson for Philadelphia's baseball fans, that had grown fickle and apathetic. Connie Mack hoped roster upheaval might supply shock treatment for those who hadn't supported the team in 1914. Bored over watching a near-perfect squad perform on the diamond for years that conquered all challengers, fans stopped attending games. Such low attendance put a crimp in Mack's pocketbook, giving him a valid reason for eliminating high-priced talent and rebuilding the team. Not once during their championship run in 1914 did a crowd large enough to fill all 21,000 seats in Shibe Park make the trek to Philadelphia's baseball grounds. Management realized this group had peaked, and despite its immense skill, it no longer captured local fans' hearts. Internal dissension and ridiculous salary demands acted as the final nails in the coffin toward starting from scratch to build a new baseball dynasty.[15]

Mack announced another change when he attended the eleventh annual dinner of the Philadelphia Sporting Writers' Association on February 16, 1915. While speaking from the dais, Connie shocked banqueters when he proclaimed Athletics third baseman Frank Baker planned on retiring from baseball. "I can't say I've had as good a time this year as I have in years gone by at this banquet," said Mack, "for I've bad news on my mind. Frank Baker wrote me tonight that he would not play with the Athletics the coming year. I got the letter just as I sat down to this banquet table. Frank has decided to quit the game for good. No, he's not going with the Federals now nor with any other team. He's just sick of traveling, and he wants to settle down for good on his Maryland farm. His wife has been at him for years to quit, and it's been a tussle to make him sign for each season.

"I've had to go down to that farm and plead with him. The last time I went down, I said, 'Frank, I can't keep on coming down here; sign up for three years,' and he did. That was last year, and he has two more seasons contracted for, but he wants to quit. I shall wish him luck and say OK"[16]

Baker had expressed a desire to walk away from baseball before sending this correspondence to Connie Mack. After Philadelphia clinched the 1914 pennant, Frank told Mack he wanted to quit immediately, feeling his best days were behind him. Concerned over losing a critical member of the team and a giant drawing card for the World Series, Connie begged Baker to reconsider retiring. Frank only agreed to participate in the World Series to please his manager.[17] Baker's retirement from baseball was short-lived, as he signed a contract to play for Upland of the Delaware County League of Pennsylvania, an outlaw organization. This news prompted Mack to announce on April 26, 1915, that he was through with Frank, who would never appear in an Athletics uniform as long as Connie had any connection to the team.[18]

As Philadelphia traveled through the uncharted waters of despair and mediocrity as a revamped squad in 1915, the paths of the Athletics and pitcher Jack Nabors eventually intersected. Shortly after joining Newnan, Nabors gained national prominence when he faced his former Talladega team on June 15, 1915. Jack was artful on the mound for 13 innings, not allowing a hit, a run, or a walk, as the Cowetas won the game, 1-0, thanks to W. C. Edmonson's home run in the final frame. Nabors faced 40 batters in the game, as two Tigers runners reached first base on errors. A failed steal attempt eliminated one of those runners. Jack's performance established a new record, as no minor league player had advanced beyond 11 innings, tossing no-hit baseball. In comparison, two twirlers had gone ten innings in the majors, with New York Giants hurler Hooks Wiltse most recently turning the trick against the Philadelphia Phillies on July 4, 1908.[19]

Decades later, Dr. Arthur Nabors offered insight regarding his brother's no-hitter against his former team, days after being traded by Talladega. "Jack wasn't scheduled to pitch," Dr. Nabors reminisced, "but he went to the manager and asked to be allowed to pitch against his former teammates. The manager was reluctant but finally let Jack pitch. He pitched a no-run, no-hit game that lasted 13 innings."[20]

Nabors's sensational performance quickly caught the attention of scouts from every major league team, possibly hoping to sign the Class D pitcher.[21] Connie Mack ended up winning the sweepstakes for Jack's services when he secured the youngster on July 13 for $500, a price believed to be the highest ever paid for a player from that minor league level. Newnan manager Harry Matthews, a catcher, declared that Nabors possessed the best curveball he had ever witnessed in any minor league. At the same time, there was no hurler currently in the loop with better control. While Mack was hoping Newnan could deliver Jack at once, he likely would be permitted to remain with them until the middle of August.[22]

Pitching for two Georgia-Alabama League teams thus far in 1915, Nabors had won ten games, lost one, and tied one.[23] The deadlocked contest was a 15-inning, 0-0 affair against the Anniston Moulders, where Jack only allowed three hits and averaged better than one strikeout per inning.[24] On July 26, Jack, along with fellow pitcher Dana Fillingim and outfielder Wilborn Everett "Bill" Bankston, joined the Athletics in yet another wave of untried and untested youngsters added to the organization.[25] A constant influx of promising talent was necessary due to Connie Mack continuing the gutting-out process regarding his roster. On June 28, the Athletics sold pitcher Bob Shawkey to the New York Yankees for $3,000. The Boston Red Sox purchased stalwart shortstop Jack Barry's release on July 2 for the speculated price of $8,000.[26] Outfielder John Edward "Eddie" Murphy packed his bags and moved on to Chicago after the White Sox obtained him for $11,500 on July 15.

Jack Nabors made his major league debut against Chicago on August 9, as "Eddie Murphy Day" was celebrated at Shibe Park.[27] Before the game, Murphy received a handsome traveling bag as a gift from adoring Philadelphia fans.[28] As Nabors prepared to pitch his first game in the big show, the Athletics were solid cellar-dwellers with a 33-66 record. The White Sox gave Jack a rough ride. He allowed five earned runs and 12 hits as Chicago secured an 8-4 victory. Wildness was an issue as Nabors walked seven batters while going the distance. Over his next three starts, Jack went 0-2 and saw his ERA balloon to 7.77. On September 1, Jack Barry received honors and accolades as Boston played Philadelphia at Shibe Park. Councilman Louis Hutt presented Barry with a magnificent chest of silver valued at $500 before the contest started.[29] Red Sox pitcher Rube Foster tossed a three-hitter and defeated Philadelphia, 6-0. Nabors hurled six innings of relief, allowing two earned runs, five runs, and five hits.

Although Nabors had taken his lumps, consensus indicated he possessed the potential to be a grand hurler, given his tangible improvement since debuting in August. Upon returning home at the beginning of September following a long western swing, receiving news that Frank Baker might join the Federal League didn't shake manager Connie Mack's resolve.[30] Utilizing a new side-arm delivery, Jack fashioned his best performance of the season on the bump as a reliever in a 7-5 loss against the Detroit Tigers on September 21. Nabors tossed four scoreless innings, scattering two hits, fanning five, and walking no batters. Jack also connected for a single and made it over to second when Tigers center fielder Ty Cobb, understanding the hurler possessed the speed of a plow horse, made a robust peg to first, which eluded George Burns due to something else on the diamond diverting his attention.[31]

Nabors made ten appearances in 1915, started seven games, and went 0-5, supported by a 5.50 ERA. The Athletics finished last, with a 43-109 record, putting them 58 ½ games behind pennant-winning Boston. Despite his team's atrocious year, Mack expressed confidence that things were moving in the right direction. He believed this current aggregation would hit their stride in the middle of the 1916 campaign after gaining some vital experience. Philadelphia's devoted followers understood that patience was essential while rooting for this group of players. Connie, who wasn't concerned over low attendance at Shibe Park under these circumstances, felt rooters would return in droves when the Athletics eventually started trending upward.[32] After the dreadful 1915 season concluded, first baseman Stuffy McInnis, the only remaining member of the famed "$100,000 Infield" still on Philadelphia's roster, offered a unique perspective on the completed campaign.

"It was the best year I ever had," said McInnis.

"I mean that I never had so much fun. When Collins and Baker and Murphy and Bender and Plank and Coombs were with us, it wasn't any sport. All we could do was feel sorry for the other team. Now I suppose I ought to feel sorry for my own team, but we're so bad that I can't do anything but laugh. If you could have seen us day in and day out this season, you would have wondered why we happened to pick out baseball as a profession.

"I was lucky in not having much to do. The only people that got to first base were the ones that walked. The rest of them never hesitated at my station."33

Off-season hot stove scuttlebutt focused on one key point related to Philadelphia. All discussion centered on the Frank Baker affair and whether he would continue playing for the Athletics or move on to another organization after deciding to leave behind the retired life. This past summer, so many rumors had been bantered about that Mack stated he never wanted to hear Baker's name mentioned again. The rumor mill had dissected possible destinations since spring training in Jacksonville, Florida. In the fall, gossip pointed toward Philadelphia shipping Frank to the Yankees for fellow third baseman Fritz Maisel.34 In December, rumors indicating Baker could be joining Eddie Collins in Chicago prompted him to refute this claim.35

"The Chicago yarn is a pipedream," said Baker during a long-distance phone call with a Philadelphia sportswriter, who had inquired if the stories were true about accepting terms with the White Sox. "I have not seen or talked to any representative of the Chicago club and don't expect to. I expect to play ball in the American League again and am now considering an offer from New York."36

On February 15, 1916, Connie Mack peddled Home Run Baker to New York for $37,500. In respect to selling the slugger, Mack declared it had become a matter of principle with him, or he likely would have declared Frank a free agent long ago. Connie never considered bringing Baker back into the fold at the salary he would earn with the Yankees, or the terms of his old contract, due to mudslinging and chicanery that occurred in the spring of 1915. On the day the deal was consummated, Mack claimed he hadn't intended to do a complete housecleaning until Frank announced his retirement before offering his feelings of joy over disposing of this individual.

"The sale of Frank Baker brings greater satisfaction to me than winning pennants," declared Mack. "I do not care particularly about the money involved in the transaction but am glad to get rid of the responsibility which was placed on my shoulders through the whole affair."37

Worry and apprehension over the old guard quickly were replaced with hope and optimism regarding those who would lead the new Philadelphia Athletics. Pitchers and catchers left the Quaker City on March 7 for the spring training session in Jacksonville.38 This group traveled to Florida by boat on the steamship Comanche. At the same time, Mack, his wife Katherine, Ira Thomas, pitcher Leslie Ambrose "Bullet Joe" Bush, and team vice-president Thomas Shibe used the railroad for transportation. Promising backstop Ralph "Cy" Perkins, who had been ill since the steamship left New York, was diagnosed as suffering from typhoid fever.[39] Infielders and outfielders, under the charge of Harry Davis, started their trek south ten days later.[40]

Once the second group arrived, Connie planned on putting his players through their paces down in Florida for three weeks, with two exhibition games scheduled against the Boston Braves in Jacksonville, two in Miami, and one in Palm Beach.[41] When the training session commenced, Mack was pleasantly surprised over the rapid development of Jack Nabors, who had reported to camp in excellent shape.

"We drilled Nabors mighty hard last summer," said Mack. "I have never in my life seen a ballplayer as green as he was when he joined us. Ordinarily, I would have passed him up at once, but he naturally interested me. I have had plenty of green ones, but he was the limit.

"I took a liking to the youngster because he realized that he knew absolutely nothing about the game. All he could do was throw the ball. He did not even know how to wind up, much less have a delivery which was permitting him to get the maximum amount of speed out of his pitches.

"The curveball he used was of the back-lot variety, and no one had shown him what to do with it or his fastball. I was first attracted to the youngster because of his wonderful natural fastball. It did not break as much as it will before the summer is over, but it surely had something on it.

"Finally, I could not withstand the temptation to send him into a game. I felt sorry for the lad when the opposing team (it was Detroit, I think) started bunting on him. Nabors was tied into knots, and if they had not taken pity on him, they would have been beating out bunts yet. I knew then that there was absolutely nothing Nabors could do but throw the ball.

"Ira Thomas also felt that the youngster might be developed because of his ambition, so I turned him over to Ira. He is still a miserable fielder, and he is going to be one of the main pupils in my little school to perfect fielding among the boxmen."

Mack, who was incorrect about which team mauled Nabors in his debut, which happened to be Chicago, admitted he hadn't even possessed a stable of solid fielding pitchers during the Athletics' glory days.[42] Preparations for the season began on March 12, rather than two days earlier as planned. Due to travel complications related to a storm on the Atlantic Ocean that had damaged the steamship on its most recent trip before Philadelphia used it as a transportation mechanism to Florida, this caused a late departure of 24 hours.[43] Many of Connie Mack's hurlers developed sore arms shortly after training started due to the brisk practice pace.[44] Philadelphia sportswriter Chandler D. Richter felt Nabors displayed more natural ability than any member of the pitching staff but would be of little use in 1916 because of his inexperience. Mack planned on regularly sending Jack to the mound, feeling there was no better way to learn than by benefitting from making mistakes. Connie also had no intention of farming Nabors out since he wanted to tutor the pitcher personally.[45]

Philadelphia opened the 1916 season against Boston on April 12 at Fenway Park, as more than 5,000 patrons attended the contest on an unseasonably cold afternoon. Jack Nabors got the opening-day starting assignment against Red Sox hurler Babe Ruth. Nabors lasted four innings, allowing no runs, two hits, and walking three. Ruth scattered four hits before being relieved by Rube Foster in the ninth, as Boston claimed a 2-1 victory. The Red Sox scored unearned tallies in the sixth and seventh innings thanks to errors by third baseman Charles "Charlie" Pick and Bullet Joe Bush, who relieved Jack.[46] Although Boston swept all three games of this series, Mack was optimistic rather than discouraged. Connie told his players he was satisfied with their performance and believed the Athletics would finish in the first division.[47]

Nabors made his second start of the season against New York at the Polo Grounds on April 18. Jack lasted six innings, allowing three runs on ten hits, and was charged with the loss as the Yankees claimed a 4-2 victory. Former Philadelphia third baseman Frank Baker was sensational in the field, making impressive one-handed grabs down at the hot corner on two occasions with the bases loaded, converting one into a double play, and possibly saving four potential runs.[48] The Athletics lost their first six games before rookie pitcher Elmer Myers halted the skid on April 21, beating the defending champion Red Sox, 3-1, at Shibe Park.

Philadelphia made it two in a row over Boston on April 22, behind Jack Nabors's solid performance. Nabors tossed a complete game, scattered eight hits, and fanned four batters as the Athletics defeated the Red Sox, 6-2.[49] Rube Foster was knocked around freely and wild on the mound, leading to Philadelphia scoring three markers in the first frame. Rube surrendered two more runs in the third before giving way to Ernie Shore as James "Shag" Thompson and Amos Strunk drew walks and then came home on Reuben "Rube" Oldring's double. The Athletics scored their final run one inning later on back-to-back two-baggers by Stuffy McInnis and William "Billy" Meyer. The Red Sox produced their only two unearned tallies of the contest in the second frame.[50] Fans were deeply impressed with the performances of Nabors and Myers in this series, who had trimmed Boston in fine fashion.[51]

Jack experienced a tough time in his next outing against the Washington Senators on April 28 at National Park. After Philadelphia scored six runs in the top of the fifth inning to grab a 6-1 lead, Nabors eventually frittered away the game. Ahead 6-3 entering the ninth, Jack plunked Ray Morgan before walking John Henry and Howie Shanks to load the bases. Minot "Cap" Crowell relieved Nabors, and Washington secured a 7-6 victory on an infield out, an error, and two singles.[52] Although the deciding run was allowed by Crowell, Jack took the loss based on rules from that time. When April concluded, the Athletics found themselves in the basement with a 3-10 record, placing them five games behind first-place Boston.

On May 3, New York thwarted Nabors's quest to record his second victory of the season. Jack gave a solid effort on the mound versus the Yankees, allowing one run in seven innings, but earned a no-decision. Bullet Joe Bush replaced Nabors in the eighth after Walter "Wally" Pipp singled and moved to third on Roger Peckinpaugh's one-base hit. Bush proceeded to whiff Les Nunamaker and Ray Caldwell, who pinch-hit for pitcher Ray Keating. Bullet Joe then made a brilliant play when Peckinpaugh started for second base on an attempted steal, intercepting the throw from catcher Walter "Wally" Schang and firing to third to retire Pipp.[53] Nap Lajoie's long drive into the left-field bleachers in the eighth, with Rube Oldring on first, put Philadelphia in front 3-1.[54] Bush held on in the ninth to secure a 3-2 victory.

Jack's next outing against Detroit on May 9 at Shibe Park was an absolute disaster, with his fielding weaknesses proving to be a brutal albatross around his neck. Nabors started the game by walking Donie Bush. Jack then threw wildly to first base on a pickoff attempt, allowing Bush to move over to second. Oscar Vitt laid down a bunt to push Donie over to third. Nabors, who was slow fielding the ball, heaved the sphere wildly to the right-field fence when he reached it, allowing Bush to score and Vitt to go to third. Stuffy McInnis helped his teammate end the inning when he grabbed a relay from the outfield and gunned down Oscar, who fell asleep at third. Although Jack wriggled out of a tight jam, the Tigers' players had discovered the hurler's flaw in fielding bunts.

The floodgates opened at the top of the second. Harry Heilmann attempted to bunt Nabors's first pitch, causing the twirler to get into a hole, working carefully to prevent the batter from further utilizing that strategy. Heilmann eventually singled. George Burns stepped up to the plate and easily legged out a bunt that Jack fielded too slowly. Visibly shaken at this point, Nabors walked Ralph Young to load the bases. Heilmann scored when shortstop Lawton "Whitey" Witt couldn't handle a hot smash off Oscar Stanage's bat. Witt was out of position on the play since Jack hadn't allowed him time to shift back over before tossing a pitch after the shortstop had moved toward second in an attempt to pick off Burns.

Connie Mack pulled Nabors from the game after he walked pitcher George Cunningham to force in a third marker.[55] Eight runs crossed the plate that inning as the Tigers crushed Philadelphia, 16-2. Hurlers allowed an unbelievable 30 base on balls in the game, as Detroit's pitchers walked 12 batters. At the same time, Athletics' twirlers passed 18 opposing players, with Carl Ray leading the assault against control on 12 occasions in seven innings of work.[56] Free passes again dominated the conversation one day later when the Tigers defeated Philadelphia, 9-3. The Athletics' Thomas "Tom" Sheehan walked seven batters in seven innings, while Jack passed four in two frames of relief work. Detroit's George Boehler issued seven walks but was able to work out of jams brought about by this inaccuracy, unlike his opponents.[57]

Although fans and writers criticized Connie Mack's hurlers for their inability to throw the baseball across home plate, pitcher Elmer Myers received accolades for winning three consecutive games during the second week of May. The first in that string was a 4-2 victory over Walter Johnson and the Senators on May 8.[58] Myers ran the streak to five games before suffering a 2-1 loss against Washington on May 26. Following his rough treatment at the hands of Detroit, Jack Nabors remained idle for more than two weeks before receiving another opportunity to pitch on May 27. Such inactivity was curious since the release of several players had reduced Mack's pitching staff to six men until recently purchased collegiate hurlers arrived in Philadelphia.[59]

Nabors started the second game of a doubleheader against the Senators on May 27, who had beaten Bullet Joe Bush, 5-3, in the first contest. Jack pitched seven innings and absorbed a 3-1 loss, as Washington secured all their runs in the fourth. Edward "Eddie" Foster walked, and Clyde Milan singled before Charles "Charlie" Jamieson's one-base hit drove in the first tally. Milan scored when Joseph "Joe" Judge was retired, and Jamieson scampered home on a wild pitch. The Athletics recorded their only run off Walter Johnson in the ninth inning.[60] The large, noisy crowd heartily celebrated this sweep, which had allowed the Senators to move ahead of Cleveland into first place.[61] Jack relieved Tom Sheehan on May 29 and pitched three innings as Washington and Philadelphia battled to a 5-5 tie. The Senators scored two runs in the ninth to deadlock the contest before umpires called the game so Washington could catch a train to Boston.⁶²

Nabors started versus the Yankees in game one of a doubleheader on May 31, tossed three innings, allowed one run, one hit, three walks, and received a no-decision as the Yankees beat the Athletics, 8-7. Heading into June, Philadelphia was in a last-place tie with a 14-24 record, leaving them 9 ½ games behind pace-setting Cleveland and Washington. As Connie Mack's team embarked on a new month and an unprecedented stretch of baseball futility, the Athletics' manager announced eight collegians would be joining the squad in three weeks upon returning home from their current road trip.⁶³ Thus far, Jack Nabors secured one victory against four losses with a 3.96 ERA. Nabors received another extended hiatus from taking the bump until consecutive relief appearances against the Indians on June 11 and 13. Over the two games, Jack pitched eight innings and allowed only one run.

Mack started Nabors in the game versus Detroit on June 16 at Navin Field. Jack gave a commendable performance, outpitching the Tigers' Jean Dubuc while allowing no earned runs in seven innings. Unfortunately, five errors behind him led to four unearned runs being the difference in Detroit's 4-3 victory. Rain fell throughout most of the contest, causing problems for Philadelphia's fielders, although the conditions didn't seem to bother the Tigers.⁶⁴ Nabors's subsequent two appearances were against Washington, as he pitched one inning of shutout relief on June 20 at Shibe Park and started against the Senators two days later. A nagging injury that wasn't responding to treatment forced Jack to leave the contest on June 22. New information became public knowledge claiming that Nabors had been dealing with floating cartilage in his pitching hand for the entire season. Jack's exit from this game became necessary after a line drive struck that hand, and he could not grip the baseball.⁶⁵ When Elmer Myers defeated Washington, 4-2, in game one of this twin bill, it snapped an 11-game losing streak.

Although Philadelphia's poor play justified many of these defeats during this tough stretch, bad breaks certainly influenced some outcomes. In two June contests, Athletics' hurlers allowed five total singles and lost both games.⁶⁶ Nabors was brilliant in game one of a doubleheader against Boston at Fenway Park on June 24, carrying a 2-1 lead into the ninth inning. Jack wilted under pressure, allowing two runs and giving the Red Sox a 3-2 victory, with the winning tally scoring on a wild pitch.⁶⁷ The losses started piling up fast and furious for Nabors. He only pitched one inning on June 29 and took the defeat, allowing three runs as the Yankees cruised to a 5-0 victory. The Red Sox were very economical with their nine hits against Jack on July 3, scoring four runs, two earned before Connie Mack pulled him for a pinch hitter in the eighth inning. Boston won the game, 6-4.[68]

Reporting from July 3 confirmed that Connie Mack and Harry Davis conducted clinics with aspiring youngsters every morning at Shibe Park when Philadelphia played at home. This instruction lasted two hours in the morning before a break for lunch and continued in the afternoon until the Athletics took the field for pre-game practice.[69] Jack was strong on the mound versus the Tigers on July 8 but still saw his record plummet to 1-9, as Detroit claimed a 3-2 victory. After dropping 12 consecutive contests, the Athletics defeated the St. Louis Browns, 3-0, in game two of a doubleheader, on July 11. This much-needed win wasn't without controversy, as Browns' manager Fielder Jones protested the game. Jones contended that umpire Tommy Connolly incorrectly ruled when he allowed Philadelphia outfielder Jimmy Walsh, who had been ordered off the grounds in the first clash by arbitrator Clarence "Brick" Owens for bench jockeying, to participate in the nightcap.[70]

St. Louis victimized Nabors on July 13, with the hurler allowing two runs in five innings. Tom Sheehan and George Hesselbacher combined to give up five more tallies in relief as the Browns claimed a 7-3 victory. Jack received a no-decision working out of the bullpen on July 18, as Chicago pummeled Philadelphia in game one of a doubleheader, 9-2. Nabors allowed six runs, four earned, on ten hits in four innings on the bump. In the seventh, Athletics left fielder Wally Schang suffered a broken jaw and contusions to his right shoulder and arm when he crashed into Shibe Park's concrete wall while chasing a foul ball off Joe Jackson's bat.[71]

On July 21, Jack went down to defeat again, as Cleveland bunched nine of their 12 hits in three different innings and secured a 7-2 win.[72] After taking three out of four games in the series from Philadelphia, Indians manager Leo "Lee" Fohl filed an interesting grievance with league president Ban Johnson, complaining that Shibe Park's grass was too long. In response to Fohl's demand that someone cut the grass, Connie Mack replied that proper groundskeeping would happen when the Athletics hit the road since he wanted to use every spare moment to instruct his young players while the team played at home.[73] Jack was the recipient of insufficient support in the clutch by his teammates against St. Louis on July 27 at Sportsman's Park. Although Philadelphia smacked seven singles and four doubles, while the Browns connected for one two-bagger and five feeble one-base hits, including two that didn't leave the infield, Nabors lost the game, 3-2.[74]

Continuous abysmal play set in stone the Athletics' station in life as the campaign moved into August. Philadelphia's record stood at 19-71, leaving them languishing in the cellar with no hope of climbing, trailing seventh-place St. Louis by 25 ½ games. While some loyal fans pondered the possibility of their favorite team establishing a record for losing games (the Cleveland Spiders lost 134 times in 1899), the organization seemed committed to setting a new mark in the department of players receiving trials. It appeared that Mack gave anyone who knew how to hold a bat or wear a glove an opportunity.[75] The team's combined record in June and July was an unfathomable 5-47. Jack Nabors carried a 1-12 mark through this point in the season, supported by a 3.52 ERA. Jack had suffered 11 straight defeats since beating Boston on April 22. Nabors was conquered for the twelfth consecutive time in the first game of a doubleheader on August 1, as Chicago defeated the Athletics, 3-0.

While Jack didn't lose his start against Cleveland at Dunn Field on August 6, he wasn't around long enough to shape an outcome, hurling three shutout innings as Philadelphia fell to the Indians, 5-2. Nabors tossed a complete game versus the Tigers at Navin Field two days later but was liberally pounded by Detroit, 9-0. Jack's stat line was seven earned runs, nine runs, 16 hits, two walks, and four strikeouts. On August 9, teammate Bullet Joe Bush snapped the Athletics' 20-game losing skid by defeating Detroit, 7-1.[76] Nabors was sharp in his next appearance after a rough first inning against New York at the Polo Grounds on August 14.[77] Unfortunately, the damage done in that stanza was enough to lead the Yankees to a 4-3 victory. New York scored four runs before a man was retired on the strength of three hits, two errors by Athletics second baseman Nap Lajoie, and a successful double steal.[78] In his article for the *New York Tribune*, Grantland Rice joked that Philadelphia had a two-game winning streak from 1:30 p.m. Saturday until it ended at 5:15 p.m. on Monday.[79]

On the day this brief winning streak ended, Connie Mack wasn't with the team, opting instead to scout a player with a friend at the ballpark of the International League's Newark Indians. As this contest progressed, Connie's friend brought up the subject of his Athletics.

"Let's go to the press box and see what the Athletics are doing," suggested the friend.

"No, no; you go," said Mack. "You go look at 'em. I'm afraid I might suffer a nervous shock."

The friend walked to the press box and found out Philadelphia was losing in a manner befitting their horrible season. Armed with this information, he returned to his seat and gently broke the news to Mack, who seemed relieved upon hearing this baseball bulletin.

"That's all right," replied Mack. "I was afraid the boys had lost their heads. Now I know everything's all right again."[80]

Jack dominated the Browns during the early stages of his next start on August 18, not allowing a hit through the first five innings. As had been the case on many occasions in 1916, one lousy frame hurt Nabors. Two walks, two singles, and a sacrifice fly led to three St. Louis runners crossing the plate in the sixth.[81] Jack didn't figure in the outcome, as the Browns claimed a 4-3 victory in 11 innings. Nabors also received no-decisions in his final three appearances in August. Two were back-to-back starts versus Cleveland in the first games of doubleheaders on August 24 and 25, and the other was a relief outing against Chicago on August 31. In the game against the Indians on August 25, Jack walked four batters in the first inning, forcing in a run. When Nabors passed Raymond "Ray" Chapman to start the second, Mack had seen enough and yanked him from the game.[82] On August 26, fellow hurler Bullet Joe Bush tossed a no-hitter at Shibe Park, defeating Cleveland, 5-0.[83]

In game one of a doubleheader on September 1, Jack Nabors lost a heartbreaker to Washington at National Park, 3-1. Although Jack allowed 11 hits, he only gave up one earned run in his duel with Walter Johnson. Nabors's record dropped to 1-17 when he was beaten again by the Senators, 2-0, in the front end of a Labor Day twin bill on September 4. Jack lost by the same 2-0 score against Boston at Shibe Park three days later. In these three defeats, Nabors had tossed complete games in each, hurled 25 innings, and allowed three earned runs.

A very sparse crowd watched Wally Schang orchestrate a magnificent performance at Shibe Park on September 8, as Philadelphia defeated New York, 8-2. Only 25 people were in attendance due to a severe thunderstorm engulfing the city before the game. Despite the horrendous weather, Mack went forward with the contest. This select group of patrons, most of who utilized coupons to enter the premises, witnessed the switch-hitting Schang homer from each side of the plate. Wally blasted a first-inning grand slam over the right-field wall off right-handed hurler Allen Russell and then connected for a solo shot against southpaw Edward "Slim" Love in the second that bounced over the center-field barrier.[84]

Jack Nabors received a no-decision as a reliever in game two of a twin bill against the Yankees on September 9. Nabors's record dropped to 1-19 when he was mauled by Cleveland, 9-1, on September 14. Jack pitched seven innings, giving up eight runs, five earned, and ten hits. Connie Mack expressed the firm conviction that he would still develop Nabors into a great, first-class pitcher who only required more experience and self-confidence.[85] Another no-decision was added to Jack's resume versus Chicago on September 19 at Comiskey Park. Philadelphia grabbed a 4-2 lead after Mack pulled him for a pinch hitter in the eighth inning. The White Sox claimed the game, 5-4 when they scored three runs off Tom Sheehan in the ninth. Former Athletics second baseman Eddie Collins was the hero, driving in two teammates with a double to left field.[86]

Regarding game statistics, some publications tagged Nabors with the loss. Everything became uniform concerning the numbers when a committee headed by sportswriter Cliff Kachline made the necessary change in 1963, rightfully charging the defeat to Sheehan.[87] Jack made a solid effort in his next start against Washington at Shibe Park on September 28. Nabors allowed two runs in eight innings before Leland "Lee" McElwee batted for him, as the Senators led at the time, 2-1. That score ballooned to 4-1 when Philadelphia's Raymond "Rube" Bressler allowed two runs, one hit, and four walks in the ninth.[88] That score stood, leaving Jack with a 1-20 record in 1916.

Nabors didn't make another start in the season's final week, only appearing two more times in relief. Jack finished the campaign with 40 appearances, 30 starts, 11 complete games, 212 ⅔ innings pitched, a 1-20 record, an ERA of 3.47, and led all American League hurlers with 13 errors. The going was also rough for fellow innings-eating hurlers Bullet Joe Bush (15-24, 2.57 ERA), Elmer Myers (14-23, 3.66 ERA), and Tom Sheehan (1-16, 3.69 ERA). Philadelphia, who employed 50 players in 1916, finished last with a dreadful 36-117 record and 54 ½ games behind pennant-winning Boston. Regarding the discrepancy in Nabors's won-loss mark, a February 1917 article in the *Buffalo Sunday Times* naming him baseball's worst twirler claimed he had gone 1-21 in 1916 and lost 20 consecutive games.[89] That same month, *Sporting Life* mentioned the correct mark of 1-20 when talking about Nabors.[90]

By losing 19 consecutive games in 1916, with assistance at times from a porous defense and lackluster offense, Jack Nabors established the new modern-era, single-season record, surpassing the 18 consecutive times that Boston Doves' hurler Clifton "Cliff" Curtis suffered defeats in 1910. Roger Craig of the New York Mets came closest to topping Jack's record when he also lost 18 consecutive contests in 1963.[91] After appearing in two games in 1917, Connie Mack shipped Nabors and cash to the American Association's Indianapolis Indians for fellow pitcher Frederick "Cy" Falkenberg.[92] Jack didn't remain with Indianapolis very long, moving on to play for the Western League's Denver

Bears. On July 22, 1917, Nabors tossed a 1-0 no-hitter against the Sioux City Indians. Jack became a member of Sioux City's team in 1918 and then enlisted in the army when the season ended.

While stationed at Camp Dodge, Iowa, that winter, Nabors was afflicted with the Spanish influenza scourge, coming down with a severe case of the illness that carried a heavy death toll in the United States. This influenza settled near his heart and eventually developed into tuberculosis. Nabors never played baseball again, spending the remainder of his life in and out of a sickbed. On October 29, 1923, Jack passed away in Montevallo at 35. Dr. Arthur Nabors believed that his brother might have made the baseball world forget that he debuted with one of the worst teams in baseball history if not for influenza.

Dr. Nabors quoted New York Giants manager John McGraw during his 1968 interview regarding the aura surrounding hurler Jack Nabors. "John McGraw told him he had a million-dollar arm and a 15-cent head for trying to win games all by himself," said Dr. Nabors.[93]

Jack Nabors most likely could be forgiven for possessing a 15-cent head while playing for a major league team victorious 36 meager times in 1916.

Fans gathering outside the Philadelphia Athletics' home grounds of Shibe Park on October 9, 1914, before Game One of the World Series. Philadelphia claimed the American League pennant that year with a 99-53 record before the Boston Braves swept them in the World Series. Two years later, the Athletics finished the 1916 campaign firmly entrenched in the basement with a 36-117 mark. On April 22, pitcher Jack Nabors defeated the Boston Red Sox at Shibe Park, 6-2. Nabors didn't win another game in 1916, losing 19 straight and finishing with a 1-20 record. (Courtesy of the Library of Congress.)

CHAPTER 13

Deadball Era Pacesetters Writing Baseball History

Genuine numbers and concrete statistics have always acted as the bridge, connecting one era of baseball history with another. These numbers offer insight into victory and achievement, along with failure and defeat from different periods of baseball history. Ardent fans, absorbing information, facts, and figures like a giant sponge, have come to know and understand some of the game's greatest players by dissecting their statistics. Volumes of data and firsthand accounts make it possible to compare and contrast these diamond icons over many different stages and chapters throughout baseball's storied history. The game has changed immensely since Ty Cobb graced the diamond. Compared to men like Josh Gibson, Ted Williams, and Anthony "Tony" Gwynn, who later also established their credentials as lethal hitters, palpable, real numbers allow baseball devotees to formulate opinions about the greatest or the best of all time.

Baseball is constantly in flux when it comes to establishing new marks or records. On an opening day each year, as a new season dawns with endless promise and potential, a chance exists that some historical achievement could fall at any given time. As is the case with anything, a fickle, two-edged sword also exists, where the prospects for surpassing records in futility are also a distinct possibility. Regarding single-season records of the modern era, the group of players chronicled in this book from baseball's Deadball Era acted as diamond pioneers who set the standard for others to follow. The old saying: "Records are made to be broken," doesn't necessarily have practical application to the men covered on these pages since many of the 12 single-season marks discussed still stand today.

Before 2021, eight of these records still received acceptance as the standard. A change occurred in June of that year when a new statistical analysis by

Baseball-Reference included the numbers of Negro League players added under this umbrella following their organization rightfully receiving status as a major league institution at the end of 2020. Consequently, the modern-era records for highest single-season batting average and lowest single-season qualifying earned run average fell retroactively.

When utilizing numbers and figures, discrepancies do exist. While most statistical institutions, including the Baseball Hall of Fame, recognize Nap Lajoie's batting average in 1901 as .426, Major League Baseball considers it to be .421, based on him smacking three fewer hits that season. The "What If" scenario also applies, digging deeper into some of these single-season records. What if Jack Chesbro hadn't jumped to the American League in 1903? Would he ever have achieved 41 victories in a season pitching for the Pittsburgh Pirates? Chesbro came close to remaining with Pittsburgh before finally joining the New York Highlanders in 1903. Since the Pirates had a pitching staff at the time, which included Deacon Phillippe and Sam Leever, it's doubtful Jack would have received the kind of workload with Pittsburgh he did in 1904 while winning 41 games for the Highlanders.

Would John Owen "Chief" Wilson have smacked 36 triples in a single season, as he did with the Pirates in 1912, if he had played for another team? Wilson certainly benefitted from the spacious outfield at Pittsburgh's home ballpark of Forbes Field. During his three seasons with the St. Louis Cardinals from 1914 to 1916, Chief hit 20 triples. If Fred Clarke hadn't visited his sick father in Des Moines in 1907, the Pirates' manager possibly wouldn't have been tipped off to Wilson's diamond exploits playing in that city. Could hurler Vic Willis have avoided the stigma of losing 29 games in 1905 if he wasn't forced to remain with the team as a ledger asset related to the Boston Beaneaters' potential sale?

What if Ty Cobb didn't suffer through an August 1915 batting slump due to concern over an injury to his throwing arm? Would extra times on base have translated into him swiping more bags in a season when he stole 96 bases? Weeks before baseball's most outstanding player slipped into this temporary funk at the plate, Philadelphia sportswriter James C. Isaminger of the *North American* had responded to a hypothetical query. The question posed was, "Is it true that Ty Cobb went one month without making a base hit? If so, when?" Isaminger retorted that it was true and had occurred in January that year.[1]

Beyond the numbers, all these magnificent accomplishments are enhanced and enriched through stories and tales surrounding the individuals who established their record-setting achievements during baseball's Deadball Era.

Lending credence that Ty Cobb was a man of the people was an incident that occurred when the Detroit Tigers played a mid-June series against the Washington Senators in 1915. While in Washington, Ty visited Detroit friend Robert Clancy, a private secretary to Department of Commerce Assistant Secretary Edwin F. Sweet. Clancy was the president of the Woodrow Wilson Club of Detroit. Cobb acted as that organization's vice president.

When Ty arrived to visit his friend, a wide-eyed employee, giddy over meeting baseball royalty, started walking the halls of the building, alerting others to the star player's presence. From that point forward, a constant stream of visitors flocked to Clancy's office. Excited government employees arrived and gathered in the room. Robert's attempts to open a door that allowed people to enter that way, shake Cobb's hand, and move on were futile. These individuals lingered, soaking in the moment, sharing baseball stories with Ty, who politely listened to every word. As Clancy escorted Cobb while giving him a tour of the entire building, employees held impromptu receptions for the baseball icon on every floor.

Work in the Department of Commerce ceased throughout the entire time Ty visited his friend. When Cobb finally left the building, workers hung out every window to catch one final glimpse of him as he entered a waiting taxicab with Clancy. "Wave to them, Ty," said Clancy.

Ty Cobb waved, eliciting the people's loud, resounding cheer as the taxicab disappeared down the avenue.[2] The human side of diamond performers, cheered for their great exploits, adds to the mystique behind some of these record-breaking moments. The imperfections of human nature can also be brought to the forefront when mind-numbing anxiety and pressure result from chasing a record or setting a diamond standard. When it comes to being superstitious, baseball players tend to be in a class of their own, avoiding certain practices that tempt the gods of fate. New York Giants southpaw hurler Rube Marquard's one pet superstition was that he didn't like photographers snapping pictures of him on days he was scheduled to pitch. This feeling manifested after the 1912 season when his 19-game winning streak and off-season vaudeville tour thrust him front and center into the limelight.

On one occasion in 1913, when a photographer sneakily attempted to snap a picture of Marquard before pitching, he threw a baseball at the man. Before a game against the Chicago Cubs at the Polo Grounds on July 9 that year, Rube politely explained to another cameraman why he wouldn't allow him to snap his picture. "I never could pitch winning ball after having my picture taken the same day," said the eccentric southpaw, "and I'm not going to make an exception of the rule. Come around tomorrow, and you can snap me as much as you like."³

Superstition aside, pitching winning baseball was a foreign concept for the 1916 Philadelphia Athletics' mound staff members. While dissecting diamond futility, this squad ruled the day, thanks to a 36-117 record that season. Regarding this hapless, hopeless aggregation, Connie Mack was later philosophical about the prospect that his team avoided added failure, courtesy of a gift. According to Mack, odds were good that a game not completed in 1916 would likely have ended up in the loss column.⁴

When it came to losing games that season, hurler Jack Nabors was a master, fashioning a 1-20 record. The symmetry connected to being defeated 19 straight times in 1916 is intriguing since that beautiful number is the same as Rube Marquard's 1912 record for winning the most consecutive games in a campaign. Of course, just as the strain of winning 19 straight games caused Marquard mental duress, constantly losing took its toll on Nabors in 1916. Lack of support stretched Jack's patience while pitching game one of a doubleheader against the Boston Red Sox at Fenway Park on June 24. Boston outfielder Harry Hooper led off the first frame with a single and eventually stole home to make it 1-0. Nabors rolled along, allowing no more hits through the eighth inning, as the Athletics plated two tallies in the fourth to grab a 2-1 lead.

Everything imploded in the ninth, as Boston got men to second and third on singles by Hooper and Hal Janvrin, and Jack's error.⁵ The Red Sox tied the game when Wally Schang caught a fly ball and made a powerful throw to the plate, which caromed off the heal of catcher Michael "Mike" Murphy's glove, allowing Hooper, who had tagged up from third, to score. With runners now occupying second and third, Nabors, extremely disgusted with this course of events, threw his first pitch to the next batter high and wide to the screen behind home plate. Janvrin trotted home with the winning run as Boston claimed a 3-2 victory.

When Connie Mack scolded Jack about his wild pitch, the pitcher was ready with a snappy retort upon reaching the dugout. "I knew we never could score another run," he grumbled. "And I sure didn't feel like trying to pitch another no-hitter out there in that hot sun today."⁶

When establishing a record in baseball futility, individuals sometimes tended to become testy. Whether marks leading to eternal baseball glory or ventures into the record books that brought about shame, twelve players from the Deadball Era acted as the standard-bearers since 1900 within the realm of single-season diamond endeavors. Obviously, due to how baseball has evolved and changed, Jack Chesbro's 41 victories in 1904 and Chief Wilson's 36 triples in 1912 probably will never be topped. Raw numbers, unique personalities, fascinating characters, and important stories were the key ingredients in the baseball stew that pleased fans from long ago. These critical components supply current rooters with the necessary material to continue discussing and debating the magnificent game's illuminating history for many more generations.

Notes

CHAPTER 1

1. David L. Fleitz, Napoleon Lajoie: King of Ballplayers, (Jefferson, N.C.: McFarland & Company, Inc., 2013), 3-5.
2. "Baseball By-Plays," *Sporting News*, April 25, 1912, 4.
3. "Fall River Facts: The Team Practically Made Up Now by Manager Marston," *Sporting Life*, February 15, 1896, 2.
4. F.C. Richter, "Quakers Quashed: The Present Philadelphia Team Won't Do," *Sporting Life*, August 22, 1896, 6.
5. F.C. Richter, "Philadelphia Points: Lajoie's Fall from Grace and Punishment," *Sporting Life*, September 4, 1897, 13.
6. "The World of Base Ball: The League Race–Games Played Friday, August 27," *Sporting Life*, September 4, 1897, 2.
7. Richter, "Philadelphia Points: Lajoie's Fall from Grace and Punishment," 13.
8. Fleitz, *Napoleon Lajoie: King of Ballplayers*, 59.
9. "Base Ball: Caught on the Fly," *Sporting News*, October 6, 1900, 5.
10. Fleitz, *Napoleon Lajoie: King of Ballplayers*, 20.
11. Ibid., 64.
12. "Napoleon Lajoie's Case Is Heard: The Philadelphia National Base Ball Club Tries to Restrain Baseman," *Scranton Tribune*, April 20, 1901, 1.
13. "Tips by the Managers," *Sporting News*, December 29, 1900, 2.
14. "Base Ball Notes, *Evening Star*, January 5, 1901, 7.
15. "Base Ball: Caught on the Fly," *Sporting News*, February 2, 1901, 5.
16. "In Base Ball World: A Pretty Good Guess," *Evening Star*, February 9, 1901, 7.
17. "Hallman May Come West: Scrap Between the Different Leagues Likely to Result in Better Accommodations for the Public," *St. Paul Globe*, February 19, 1901, 3.
18. "Base Ball: Caught on the Fly," *Sporting News*, March 2, 1901, page 5.
19. "Lajoie Signs," *New-York Tribune*, March 21, 1901, 9.
20. Ernest J. Lanigan, "Badly Balanced: But American League Teams Have Good Managers," *Sporting News*, March 30, 1901, 2.
21. Fleitz, *Napoleon Lajoie: King of Ballplayers*, 64.
22. "Tips by the Managers," *Sporting News*, March 9, 1901, 2.
23. Chuck Kimberly, *The Days of Wee Willie, Old Cy and Baseball War: Scenes from the Dawn of the Deadball Era, 1900-1903*, (Jefferson, N.C.: McFarland & Company, Inc., 2014), 117.
24. "Baseball in Court: First Battle on the Option Clause in Contracts Soon to Begin," *Evening Times* (Washington, D.C.), March 27, 1901, 3.

25. "To Sue Deserting Players: Brooklyn National League Will Go After Contract Jumpers," *Topeka State Journal*, March 25, 1901, 2.

26. "Baseball in Court: First Battle on the Option Clause in Contracts Soon to Begin," 3.

27. Ernest J. Lanigan, "Legal Battle On: Injunction Suit Commenced at Philadelphia," *Sporting News*, April 6, 1901, 4.

28. "Players to Be Sued: Philadelphia Magnate Will Be First to Test the Option Clause," *Evening Star*, March 28, 1901, 9.

29. "Lajoie Bill Amended: Second Inning of the Legal Battle in Philadelphia," *Evening Star*, April 3, 1901, 7.

30. "Lajoie's Case in Court: Trial of Injunction Suit in Philadelphia," *Evening Star*, April 20, 1901, 2.

31. "Lajoie Answers Phillies' Legal Claim," *Evening Star*, April 20, 1901, 7.

32. "Base Ball Notes: National League Had a Bad Week for Opening," *Waterbury Democrat*, April 22, 1901, 7.

33. Quaker, "Eligible To Play: No Decision Reached in the Lajoie Case," *Sporting News*, April 27, 1901, 6.

34. "The Financial Prospects of Baseball for This Summer," *Waterbury Democrat*, April 22, 1901, 7.

35. "American League: The Opening–Games Played Friday, April 26," *Sporting Life*, May 4, 1901, 6.

36. "Senators' Victory: Washington Wins First Game of the Season from Athletics," *Evening Star*, April 27, 1901, 7.

37. "American League: The Opening–Games Played Saturday, April 27," *Sporting Life*, May 4, 1901, 6.

38. "American League: The Opening–Games Played Monday, April 29," *Sporting Life*, May 4, 1901, 7.

39. "American League: The Expanded Organization's First Campaign–Games Played Thursday, May 2," *Sporting Life*, May 11, 1901, 6.

40. "Base Ball: Caught on the Fly," *Sporting News*, April 13, 1901, 5.

41. G. S. D., "First with Fans: Athletics Have Best Crowds in Philadelphia," *Sporting News*, May 4, 1901, 3.

42. "Base Ball Booming: Great Crowds Attending the Games in All Leagues," *Waterbury Democrat*, April 29, 1901, 7.

43. "Base Ball: Caught on the Fly," *Sporting News*, May 11, 1901, 5.

44. "Lajoie Leads All the Great Hitters: The Big Captain of the American League Philadelphia Club Has Broken All Batting Records–Heidrick Is Doing Well," *St. Louis Republic*, May 12, 1901, 3.

45. "American League: The Expanded Organization's First Campaign–Games Played Thursday, May 9," *Sporting Life*, May 18, 1901, 6.

46. "American League: The Expanded Organization's First Campaign–Games Played Saturday, May 11," *Sporting Life*, May 18, 1901, 6.

47. "American League: The Expanded Organization's First Campaign–Games Played Tuesday, May 14," *Sporting Life*, May 25, 1901, 6.

48. "Decision in Baseball Case," *Alexandria Gazette*, May 17, 1901, 2.

49. "One-Sided Contract," *Minneapolis Journal*, May 17, 1901, 14.

50. "American League Wins: The Injunction Proceedings Brought by the National League Dismissed," *Waterbury Democrat*, May 17, 1901, 5.

51. "Lajoie Wins His Case: The Philadelphia National League Club's Bill Dismissed," *The Times* (Washington, D.C.), May 18, 1901, 1.

52. G. S. D., "Lajoie Decision: Court Refuses an Injunction against the Player," *Sporting News*, May 25, 1901, 5.

53. "Baseball: Rogers Will Go to the Law," *Philipsburg Mail*, May 17, 1901, 7.

54. "Base Ball Notes," *Evening Star*, May 23, 1901, 9.

55. "American League–The Expanded Organization's First Season–Games Played Saturday, May 18," *Sporting Life*, May 25, 1901, 6.

56. "American League–The Expanded Organization's First Season–Games Played Sunday, May 26," *Sporting Life*, June 1, 1901, 6.

57. "Base Ball Notes," *Evening Star*, May 30, 1901, 9.

58. "American League: The Expanded Organization's First Campaign–Games Played Friday, June 14," *Sporting Life*, June 22, 1901, 6.

59. "Base Ball Caught on the Fly," *Sporting News* June 22, 1901, 5.

60. "In the Baseball World," *The Times* (Washington, D.C.), June 17, 1901, 3.

61. "Baseball: Diamond Dust," *Lincoln County Record*, June 14, 1901, 3.

62. "Base Ball: Caught on the Fly," *Sporting News*, July 13, 1901, 5.

63. "American League: The Expanded Organization's First Campaign–Games Played Wednesday, June 3," *Sporting Life*, July 13, 1901, 6.

64. "The Sporting World: Lajoie's Good Work," *Bourbon News*, July 19, 1901, 1.

65. "Sporting News: Napoleon Lajoie the Star of American League," *Topeka State Journal*, July 20, 1901, 2.

66. "Base Ball Notes," *Evening Star*, July 3, 1901, 9.

67. "American League: The Expanded Organization's First Campaign–Games Played Tuesday, July 23," *Sporting Life*, August 3, 1901, 4.

68. "American League: The Expanded Organization's First Campaign–Games Played Wednesday, July 24," *Sporting Life*, August 3, 1901, 4.

69. "American League: The Expanded Organization's First Campaign–Games Played Thursday, Aug. 1," *Sporting Life*, August 10, 1901, 4.

70. "American League: The Expanded Organization's First Campaign–Games Played Wednesday, Aug. 7," *Sporting Life*, August 17, 1901, 4.

71. "American League: The Expanded Organization's First Campaign–Games Played Thursday, Aug. 8," *Sporting Life*, August 17, 1901, 4.

72. "American League: The Expanded Organization's First Campaign–Games Played Friday, Aug. 9," *Sporting Life*, August 17, 1901, 5.

73. "Senators Win and Lose: The Local Players Surprise Spectators by Capturing a Game," *Washington Times*, August 11, 1901, 5.

74. "Lajoie Is Leading: Quaker Hitter Best in American League–Heidrick Leads National," *Topeka State Journal*, August 12, 1901, 2.

75. G. S. D., "Pirates Checked: Phillies Won Opening Game of the Series," *Sporting News*, September 14, 1901, 6.

76. "Base Ball: Caught on the Fly," *Sporting News*, August 31, 1901, 5.

77. "Baseball Gossip," *Washington Times*, September 5, 1901, 3.

78. "American League: The Expanded Organization's First Campaign–Games Played Sunday, Sept. 1," *Sporting Life*, September 7, 1901, 5.

79. "Base Ball Figures: Heidrick Leads the National League Batters, and Lajoie the American," *St. Paul Globe*, September 16, 1901, 5.

80. "American League: The Expiring Hours of the New League's First Campaign–Games Played Thursday, Sept. 19," *Sporting Life*, September 28, 1901, 4.

81. W. R. Hearst, "Human Skill Powerless to Save Him: Autopsy Showed President McKinley Died of Blood-Poisoning–Gangrene Did Its Deadly Work," *Pittsburg Press*, September 15, 1901, 1.

82. "American League: The First Campaign as a Major League Is History–Games Played Tuesday, Sept. 24," *Sporting Life*, October 5, 1901, 4.

83. "Lajoie Is the King of American League Sluggers: Big Frenchman Finishes Season in a Class All by Himself," *St. Louis Republic*, September 30, 1901, 4.

84. "King of Batsmen: Lajoie Led American with .413 Percentage," *Sporting News*, October 5, 1901, 5.

85. "Baseball: Diamond Glints," *Silver Messenger*, October 15, 1901, 7.

86. "Lajoie a Great Batter: Finished the Season with an Average of .422," *St. Paul Globe*, October 21, 1901, 5.

87. "Base Ball: Caught on the Fly," *Sporting News*, October 12, 1901, 5.

88. "Tom Daly Not to Blame for Withdrawal of League Players: Worked Hard for the Success of the California Trip–American Leaguers Still His Friends," *Brooklyn Daily Eagle*, October 28, 1901, 8.

89. "Baseball," *St. Paul Globe*, November 10, 1901, 7.

90. "Tom Daly Not to Blame for Withdrawal of League Players: Worked Hard for the Success of the California Trip–American Leaguers Still His Friends," 8.

91. "Base Ball: Caught on the Fly," *Sporting News*, November 2, 1901, 5.

92. "Lajoie on Batting: Champion Gives Some Pointers on How to Work with the Stick," *Houston Daily Post*, November 10, 1901, 15.

93. "Connie Mack's Team: Has Hartzel and Flick Signed for the Outfield," *Topeka State Journal*, December 4, 1901, 2.

94. "Brief Comments on the Day's News," *Brooklyn Daily Eagle*, January 27, 1902, 17.

95. "Gossip of Players," *Sporting News*, February 8, 1902, 2.

96. Mark S. Halfan, *Tales from the Deadball Era: Ty Cobb, Home Run Baker, Shoeless Joe Jackson, and the Wildest Times in Baseball History*, (Lincoln, Neb.: Potomac Books–University Of Nebraska Press, 2014), 9.

97. "Playing Schedule for National Teams: Has Comparatively Few Conflicting Dates," *Washington Times*, April 5, 1902, 4.

98. "Spurns $30,000: Agent of the Giants Failed to Induce Lajoie to Jump," *Evening Star*, April 5, 1902, 22.

99. "Gave Agent the Laugh: Napoleon Lajoie True to His Colors–Offered $7,000 a Year," *Washington Times*, April 5, 1902, 4.

100. "Gossip of the Players," *Sporting News*, April 12, 1902, 2.

101. "National League Wins; Reserve Clause Valid: Decision May Affect All Base Ball Players Who Have Jumped to Rival Association," *Brooklyn Daily Eagle*, April 21, 1902, 2.

102. "Base Ball Injunction Cases: A Temporary Injunction for Five Days against Lajoie," *Waterbury Democrat*, April 24, 1902, 7.

103. "Dictum Opposed: American League Magnate on the Court's Judgment in the Lajoie Case," *Rock Island Argus*, April 24, 1902, 1.

104. "Keystone Courts Enjoin Lajoie and Two Others: Bernhard and Fraser, Both Pitchers, Are Permanently Under Ban," *Washington Times*, April 29, 1902, 1.

105. "Appeals of the Players Are Denied," *Evening Times*, May 6, 1902, 1.

106. "Lajoie May Play: Great Second Baseman Badly Wanted by Detroit Club," *Washington Times*, May 10, 1902, 4.

107. "Lajoie Plays Next Tuesday," *Evening Star*, May 30, 1902, 9.

108. "Current Comment," *Semi-Weekly Messenger*, June 6, 1902, 2.

109. "Cleveland, 4; Boston, 3: Lajoie Makes a Big Hit with Cleveland Fans," *Evening Star*, June 5, 1902, 9.

CHAPTER 2

1. "Two Young Ball Players Signed by Brooklyn for Next Year," *Brooklyn Daily Eagle*, November 26, 1901, 13.

2. "Johnny Gochnaur Dies at Hospital: Former Baseball Star and Widely Known Altoona Umpire Succumbs Early Today, Death Due to Pneumonia," *Altoona Mirror*, September 27, 1929, 22.

3. Filip Bondy, *Who's on Worst: The Lousiest Players, Biggest Cheaters, Saddest Goats and Other Antiheroes in Baseball History*, (New York: Anchor Sports–Anchor Books–Random House LLC, 2013), 13.

4. "Johnny Gochnaur Dies at Hospital: Former Baseball Star and Widely Known Altoona Umpire Succumbs Early Today, Death Due to Pneumonia," 22.

5. "New England League: News and Gossip," *Sporting Life*, August 5, 1899, 9.

6. David L. Fleitz, *Napoleon Lajoie: Kings of Ballplayers*, (Jefferson, N.C.: McFarland & Company, Inc., 2013), 86.

7. "Another Game: Won from the Columbus Team after a Hard Fought Battle–Gochnaur Injured," *Dayton Evening Herald*, April 29, 1901, 6.

8. "Two Young Ball Players Signed by Brooklyn for Next Year: Charles F. Fuller–John Peter Gochnaur," 13.

9. "Base Ball: Caught on the Fly," *Sporting News*, November 9, 1901, 5.

10. "Star Scintillations," *Sporting Life*, February 8, 1902, 3.

11. "New York Will Be Invaded Next Season: American League Plans to Locate a Team in the Metropolis in 1903," *St. Louis Republic*, March 7, 1902, 4.

12. "News and Gossip," *Sporting Life*, March 15, 1902, 7.

13. John B. Foster, "Brooklyn Bulletin: Reasons Why the League Factions Must Get Together–Both Sides Sincere in Their Convictions As to What the Welfare of the Game Demanded," *Sporting Life*, March 22, 1902, 8.

14. Henry P. Edwards, "Lost First Game: But Blue Birds Keep Patrons' Confidence," *Sporting News*, April 5, 1902, 3.

15. "Base Ball: Caught on the Fly," *Sporting News*, April 5, 1902, 5.

16. "Gossip of the Players," *Sporting News*, December 27, 1902, 2.

17. "Diamond Chips," *Brooklyn Daily Eagle*, July 26, 1902, 15.

18. Henry P. Edwards, "Best of Recruits: Armour Loses Pitchers Hickey and Stovall," *Sporting News*, February 28, 1903, 6.

19. H.P. Edwards," Blues' Prospects: Figure to Finish First This Season," *Sporting News*, February 7, 1903, 6.

20. Henry P. Edwards, "Patrons Protest: Cleveland Cranks Opposed to Foul-Strike Rule," *Sporting News*, March 7, 1903, 4.

21. "Base Ball: Caught on the Fly," *Sporting News*, March 7, 1903, 5.

22. Henry P. Edwards, "Ducked Hard Ones: Lajoie Was Cautious in Field and at Bat," *Sporting News*, March 28, 1903, 4.

23. Henry P. Edwards, "Are in Fine Shape: Clevelands Come North Ready for Business," *Sporting News*, April 11, 1903, 4.

24. "American League: The Official Record of the 1903 Pennant Race–Games Played Wednesday, April 22," *Sporting Life*, May 2, 1903, 8.

25. "American League: The Official Record of the 1903 Pennant Race–Games Played Thursday, April 23," *Sporting Life*, May 2, 1903, 8.

26."American League: The Official Record of the 1903 Pennant Race–Game Played Saturday, April 25, 1903," *Sporting Life*, May 2, 1903, 8.

27. Henry P. Edwards, "Blues' Bad Start: Unable to Win a Game from New Detroits," *Sporting News*, May 2, 1903, 7.

28. "American League: Large Crowd at Cleveland," *St. Paul Globe*, April 29, 1903, 5.

29. "Blues' First Victims Were the Browns: Captured Initial Victory of Season by Score of Six to Three," *St. Louis Republic*, April 29, 1903, 9.

30. "American League: The Official Record of the 1903 Pennant Race–Games Played Friday, May 1," *Sporting Life*, May 9, 1903, 8.

31. "American League: The Official Record of the 1903 Pennant Race–Games Played Saturday, May 2," *Sporting Life*, May 9, 1903, 9.

32. Henry P. Edwards, "Bring Up the Rear: Blues Have Made a Sorry Showing So Far," *Sporting News*, May 9, 1903, 3.

33. "American League: The Official Record of the 1903 Pennant Race–Games Played Thursday, May 7," *Sporting Life*, May 16, 1903, 8.

34. "American League: The Official Record of the 1903 Pennant Race–Games Played Saturday, May 9," *Sporting Life*, May 16, 1903, 8-9.

35. "American League: The Official Record of the 1903 Pennant Race–Games Played Tuesday, May 12," *Sporting Life*, May 23, 1903, 8.

36. "American League: At Cleveland," *Topeka State Journal*, May 15, 1903, 2.

37. "Cleveland 9, New York 2: Winners Take the Columbus Game in Hand from the Start," *St. Louis Republic*, May 18, 1903, 8.

38. "Senators Fall Easy Prey to Cleveland: The Cripples Could Not Hit Bernhard's Delivery," *Washington Times*, May 22, 1903, 8.

39. "Sports of All Sorts: Senators Dropped Third Game to Cleveland," *Evening Star*, May 22, 1903, 9.

40. "American League: The Official Record of the 1903 Pennant Race–Games Played Monday, May 25," *Sporting Life*, June 6, 1903, 8.

41. "Passed Balls," *Washington Times*, June 1, 1903, 8.

42. "American League Notes," *Sporting Life*, June 6, 1903, 5.

43. Henry P. Edwards, "Roast the Blues: Knockers Got after Armour's Players," *Sporting News*, June 6, 1903, 4.

44. "American League: The Official Record of the 1903 Pennant Race–Games Played Friday, June 5," *Sporting Life*, June 13, 1903, 8.

45. Henry P. Edwards, "Hitting the Ball: Lajoie and His Teammates Are Batting Well," *Sporting News*, June 13, 1903, 7.

46. "American League: The Official Record of the 1903 Pennant Race–Games Played Thursday, June 11," *Sporting Life*, June 20, 1903, 8.

47. "American League: The Official Record of the 1903 Pennant Race–Games Played Friday, June 12," *Sporting Life*, June 20, 1903, 8.

48. "American League: The Official Record of the 1903 Pennant Race–Games Played Saturday, June 13," *Sporting Life*, June 20, 1903, 8.

49. Henry P. Edwards, "West Outclassed: Eastern Teams Are Stronger Than Rivals," *Sporting News*, July 4, 1903, 5.

50. "American League: The Official Record of the 1903 Pennant Race–Games Played Wednesday, June 24," *Sporting Life*, July 4, 1903, 8.

51. Edwards, "West Outclassed: Eastern Teams Are Stronger Than Rivals," 5.

52. "American League: The Official Record of the 1903 Pennant Race–Games Played Tuesday, June 30," *Sporting Life*, July 11, 1903, 8.

53. "Delahanty Mourned by Fellow Players: Deep Gloom Settles over the Entire Team, Which Is Stunned by the News of the Big Fellow's Untimely Death," *Washington Times*, July 8, 1903, 4.

54. "American League: The Official Record of the 1903 Pennant Race–Games Played Saturday, July 4," *Sporting Life*, July 11, 1903, 9.

55. "American League: The Official Record of the 1903 Pennant Race–Games Played Friday, July 10," *Sporting Life*, July 18, 1903, 10-11.

56. "American League: The Official Record of the 1903 Pennant Race–Games Played Saturday, July 11," *Sporting Life*, July 18, 1903, 11.

57. "American League: The Official Record of the 1903 Pennant Race–Games Played Thursday, July 16," *Sporting Life*, July 25, 1903, 10.

58. "American League: The Official Record of the 1903 Pennant Race–Games Played Monday, July 20," *Sporting Life*, August 1, 1903, 10.

59. "American League: The Official Record of the 1903 Pennant Race–Games Played Saturday, July 25," *Sporting Life*, August 1, 1903, 11.

60. "Heavy Stick Work Beat the Browns: Cleveland Players Solve Big Jack Powell's Curves for Ten Hits," *St. Louis Republic*, July 26, 1903, 7.
61. "American League: The Official Record of the 1903 Race–Games Played Thursday, July 30," *Sporting Life*, August 8, 1903, 10.
62. Henry P. Edwards, "Garrison Finish: Blues Are Well Equipped for Closing Brush," *Sporting News*, August 8, 1903, 1.
63. "American League: The Official Record of the 1903 Pennant Race–Games Played Friday, August 7," *Sporting Life*, August 15, 1903, 10.
64. "American League: The Official Record of the 1903 Pennant Race–Games Played Saturday, August 8," *Sporting Life*, August 15, 1903, 11.
65. "American League: The Official Record of the 1903 Pennant Race–Games Played Wednesday, August 19," *Sporting Life*, August 29, 1903, 8.
66. "American League: The Official Record of the 1903 Pennant Race–Games Played Tuesday, August 25," *Sporting Life*, September 5, 1903, 10.
67. "Athletics Batted out Victory," *Indianapolis Journal*, August 26, 1903, 6.
68. "American League: The Official Record of the 1903 Pennant Race–Games Played Tuesday, August 25," 10.
69. "American League: The Official Record of the 1903 Pennant Race–Games Played Saturday, August 29," *Sporting Life*, September 5, 1903, 10.
70. Henry P. Edwards, "Blues Are Second: Only One Defeat in 13 Straight Games," *Sporting News*, August 29, 1903, 4.
71. "Wild William Changed Luck: Sprinkled Ten Strikeouts in Cleveland Game–Bad Work by Gochnaur Only Marring Feature," *Detroit Free Press*, September 3, 1903, 10.
72. "American League: The Official Record of the 1903 Pennant Race–Games Played Sunday, September 6," *Sporting Life*, September 12, 1903, 11.
73. Henry P. Edwards, "On Disabled List: Trio of Cleveland Club's Best Pitchers," *Sporting News*, September 12, 1903, 4.
74. "American League: The Official Record of the 1903 Pennant Race–Games Played Thursday, September 17," *Sporting Life*, September 26, 1903, 8.
75. "American League: The Official Record of the 1903 Pennant Race–Games Played Wednesday, September 23," *Sporting Life*, October 3, 1903, 6.
76. "Clevelanders Lose by Stupid Playing: Bemis and Bradley the Principal Offenders," *Washington Times*, September 24, 1903, 8.
77. Henry P. Edwards, "Both Handicapped: Neither Blues nor Reds in Good Shape," *Sporting News*, October 10, 1903, 1.
78. Jay Knox, "Cleveland Changes: Will Be Few and Far Between–The Only Debatable Places Now Are at First Base and in Centre Field," *Sporting Life*, October 31, 1903, 7.
79. "H.P. Edwards, "Outplayed Reds: Blues Made Better Record in All Respects," *Sporting News*, October 17, 1903, 4.
80. "Base Ball: Caught on the Fly," *Sporting News*, October 24, 1903, 5.
81. Jay Knox, "Cleveland's Change: Will Train Next Spring in Texas Instead of New Orleans–Infielder Gochnaur to Be Let Out," *Sporting Life*, November 14, 1903, 2.

82. "Base Ball: Caught on the Fly," *Sporting News*, January 9, 1904, 5.

83. Henry P. Edwards, "Goes to Detroit: Killian Will Be on Barrow's 1904 Payroll," *Sporting News*, January 9, 1904, 2.

84. "Baseball Notes," *Pittsburg Press*, February 6, 1904, 10.

85. "Base Ball Chat: Manager Carpenter's Team Will Be One of the Best This Season," *Morning Tribune*, February 16, 1904, 6.

86. "Base Ball Briefs," *Morning Tribune*, September 24, 1904, 3.

87. "Caught on the Fly," *Sporting News*, November 19, 1904, 6.

88. "Baseball Stories of the Great and the Near Great," *Buffalo Evening Times*, December 12, 1910, 8.

89. "Carpenter Issues Tri-State Bulletin: Shows That Fourteen Men Have Been Secured for the Altoona Team," *Morning Tribune*, January 22, 1910, 10.

90. "Caught on the Fly," *Sporting News*, March 4, 1905, 6.

91. "Notes of Sports: Nuggets of Base Ball News and Mention of Other Games," *Morning Tribune*, January 28, 1905, 8.

CHAPTER 3

1. Jim Reisler, *Before They Were the Bombers: The New York Yankees' Early Years, 1903-1915*, (Jefferson, N.C.: McFarland & Company, Inc., 2002), 78.

2. David L. Fleitz, *Ghosts in the Gallery at Cooperstown: Sixteen Little-Known Members of the Hall of Fame*, (Jefferson, N.C.: McFarland & Company, Inc., 2004), 48.

3. Reisler, *Before They Were the Bombers: The New York Yankees' Early Years, 1903-1915*, 78.

4. Fleitz, *Ghosts in the Gallery at Cooperstown: Sixteen Little-Known Members of the Hall of Fame*, 48-50.

5. "News and Comment," *Sporting Life*, July 15, 1899, 5.

6. Circle, "Proud Pittsburg: Elated Over the Pirates' Unnatural Gait," *Sporting Life*, July 29, 1899, 7.

7. Circle, "Pittsburg Points: Another Superb Week for the Pirates," *Sporting Life*, August 5, 1899, 5.

8. Circle, "Pittsburg Points: Likely That Few Moves Will Be Made Until the League Has Decided on the Circuit Matter," *Sporting Life*, January 13, 1900, 8.

9. Pirate, "Gigantic Deal: Star Colonels Sold to Pittsburg Club," *Sporting News*, December 16, 1899, 3.

10. "Jack O'Connor: Accused of Being an Agent for the American League," *Youngstown Vindicator*, August 21, 1902, 8.

11. "Base Ball News: Pitchers Want $17,000 for Two Years Work," *Waterbury Democrat*, September 10, 1902, 7.

12. Duquesne, "Saved His Stars: Dreyfus Gives List of His 1903 Players," *Sporting News*, October 11, 1902, 5.

13. "Pittsburg Players Turn Down Chesbro: Star Pitcher of National League Clashes with His Fellow-Pirates," *St. Louis Republic*, October 10, 1902, 7.

14. "Comments of the Day in the Realm of the Rooter," *Pittsburg Press*, October 11, 1902, 12.

15. "Pittsburg Players Turn Down Chesbro: Star Pitcher of National League Clashes with His Fellow-Pirates," 7.

16. W.M. Rankin, "Is Not Credited: Report That Pittsburg Has Signed Joe Corbett," *Sporting News*, November 14, 1903, 6.

17. "Gossip of the Players," *Sporting News*, January 30, 1904, 2.

18. "American League Notes," *Sporting Life*, January 2, 1904, 3.

19. "Base Ball: Caught on the Fly," *Sporting News*, January 23, 1904, 5.

20. "American League Notes," *Sporting Life*, January 23, 1904, 5.

21. "Base Ball: Caught on the Fly," January 23, 1904, 5.

22. "O'Loughlin Talked English," *Waterbury Evening Democrat*, February 11, 1904, 9.

23. Wm. F.H. Koelsch "New York Nuggets: The Latest Schedule Clash a Matter of Regret in the Metropolis," *Sporting Life*, March 12, 1904, 3.

24. Jacob C. Morse, "Boston Briefs: Brief Chats with Jack Chesbro and Fred Tenney," *Sporting Life*, March 19, 1904, 5.

25. Ted Leavengood, *Clark Griffith: The Old Fox of Washington Baseball*, (Jefferson, N.C.: McFarland & Company, Inc., 2011), 71.

26. "Practicing a New Delivery: Elmer Stricklett, of the Brooklyn Superbas, Has a Slow Floating 'Spit-Ball' among His Curves," *Pittsburg Press*, February 15, 1907, 18.

27. "Sporting Talk of Interest: Origin of the 'Spit Ball,'" *The Sun*, February 10, 1908, 8.

28. MacLean Kennedy, "First 'Spit Ball': Matthews Used Weird Twister in the Early Days," *Sporting News*, February 23, 1911, 8.

29. Wm. F.H. Koelsch, "New York Nuggets: Both Local Clubs Almost Ready for the Start," *Sporting Life*, April 2, 1904, 6.

30. W.M. Rankin, "Sorely Need Rest: Talkative Magnates of Major Leagues," *Sporting News*, April 9, 1904, 6.

31. Wm. F.H. Koelsch, "New York Nuggets: Successful Opening of American League Club's Season," *Sporting Life*, April 23, 1904, 9.

32. "Highlanders Win Their First Game with Champions: American League Park, Where the Baseball Season on Manhattan Island Was Inaugurated To-Day, Thronged by a Crowd of 20,000 Fans," *The World*, April 14, 1904, 1.

33. Koelsch, "New York Nuggets: Successful Opening of American League Club's Season," 9.

34. "Highlanders Win Their First Game with Champions: American League Park, Where the Baseball Season on Manhattan Island Was Inaugurated To-Day, Thronged by a Crowd of 20,000 Fans, 1.

35. "American League: Championship Record–The Season Opening," *Sporting Life*, April 23, 1904, 8.

36. W. M. Rankin, "Two Great Teams: Highlanders and Giants Better Than in 1903," *Sporting News*, April 16, 1904, 3.

37. "American League: Championship Record–Games Played Monday, April 18," *Sporting Life*, April 30, 1904, 8.

38. "American League: Championship Record–Games Played Friday, April 22," *Sporting Life*, April 30, 1904, 8.

39. "Shut Out by the Clevelands: Visitors Get After Chesbro Hard in Two Innings, *The Sun*, May 13, 1904, 5.

40. "American League: Championship Record–Games Played Saturday, May 14," *Sporting Life*, May 21, 1904, 9.

41. W. M. Rankin, "Only One Pitcher: M'Ginnity Is Mainstay of the Giants," *Sporting News*, May 28, 1904, 6.

42. "American League Championship Record–Games Played Friday, May 20," *Sporting Life*, May 28, 1904, 8.

43. "American League Championship Record–Games Played Tuesday, May 24," *Sporting Life*, June 4, 1904, 8.

44. "American League Championship Record–Games Played Saturday, May 28," *Sporting Life*, June 4, 1904, 9.

45. "The Highlanders Lose to Tigers: Detroit's Turn the Tables on Griffith's Men, Winning out in Another Close Contest at End of Long Game," *The World*, June 3, 1904, 2.

46. "American League Championship Record–Games Played Saturday, June 4," *Sporting Life*, June 11, 1904, 8.

47. Fleitz, *Ghosts in the Gallery at Cooperstown: Sixteen Little-Known Members of the Hall of Fame*, 53-54.

48. "American League Championship Record–Games Played Thursday, June 9," *Sporting Life*, June 18, 1904, 8.

49. Wm. F.H. Koelsch, "New York Nuggets: Cyclonic Enthusiasm Continues in Manhattan," *Sporting Life*, June 18, 1904, 4.

50. "National League News," *Sporting Life*, June 25, 1904, 7.

51. "Powell Got Revenge and Howell Suffered: Highlanders' Pitcher Put It on the Team That Let Him Go, While Former New Yorker Was Trying for Same Thing," *The World*, June 20, 1904, 9.

52. "American League: Championship Record–Games Played Tuesday, June 21," *Sporting Life*, July 2, 1904, 8.

53. "American League: Championship Record–Games Played Saturday, June 25," *Sporting Life*, July 2, 1904, 9.

54. Wm. F.H. Koelsch, "New York Nuggets: The Highlanders Gradually Forcing Their Way to the Top Despite Many Handicaps," *Sporting Life*, July 2, 1904, 3.

55. "American League Notes," *Sporting Life*, July 9, 1904, 9.

56. "American League: Championship Record–Games Played Monday, July 4," *Sporting Life*, July 16, 1904, 8.

57. "Bitter Boss Brush: Still Retains Extreme Hatred for Rivals," *Sporting Life*, July 9, 1904, 4.

58. "American League: Championship Record–Games Played Thursday, July 7," *Sporting Life*, July 16, 1904, 8.

59. "Highlanders 3, Clevelands 16: Griffith Is Knocked Out of Box in Second Inning, Chesbro Lasts to Fifth, Then Clarkson Goes In," *The World*, July 13, 1904, 1.

60. "American League Notes," *Sporting Life*, July 16, 1904, 9.

61. "Highlanders–9 the Detroits–8: First Game of Series with the Tigers at American League Park Developed Into a Slugging Game toward End," *The World*, July 16, 1904, 1.

62. Wm. F.H. Koelsch, "New York Nuggets: As to McGraw's Attack Upon the American League," *Sporting Life*, July 30, 1904, 5.

63. Wm. F.H. Koelsch, "New York Nuggets: Griffith's Busy Days," *Sporting Life*, August 13, 1904, 5.

64. "American League: Championship Record–Games Played Thursday, Aug. 11," *Sporting Life*, August 20, 1904, 6.

65. W.A. Phelon, Jr., "Chicago Gleanings: White Sox Fall before Athletics, but Rally and Soak Griffith's Gang," *Sporting Life*, August 20, 1904, 5.

66. "American League: Championship Record–Games Played Monday, Aug. 15," *Sporting Life*, August 27, 1904, 8.

67. W.M. Rankin, "Howl from Press: When Rules against Rowdyism Are Enforced," *Sporting News*, August 27, 1904, 6.

68. Wm. F.H. Koelsch, "New York Nuggets: The Highlanders Ho'ding on to First Place by the Skin of Their Teeth While the Giants Are Enjoying a Triumphal March Through the Wild West," *Sporting Life*, September 3, 1904, 3.

69. "American League: Championship Record–Games Played Friday, Aug. 26," *Sporting Life*, September 3, 1904, 7.

70. "American League: Championship Record–Games Played Saturday, Sept. 3," *Sporting Life*, September 10, 1904, 7.

71. "American League: Championship Record–Games Played Thursday, Sept. 8," *Sporting Life*, September 17, 1904, 8-9.

72. W.M. Rankin," Had a Close Call: M'Graw's Admirers Send Him to Hospital," *Sporting News*, September 17, 1904, 6.

73. "Miller Gets His Release: Pirates' Hard Luck Pitcher Is Turned Loose Unconditionally," *Pittsburg Press*, August 28, 1904, 20.

74. A. Yager, "Army of Players: Brooklyn Club Claims Title to 57 Men," *Sporting News*, September 17, 1904, 1.

75. "American League: Championship Record–Games Played Monday, Sept. 12," *Sporting Life*, September 24, 1904, 10.

76. Wm. F.H. Koelsch, "Metropolitan Mention: A Week of Great Ball by the Contenders for the Amer'can League Pennant," *Sporting Life*, September 24, 1904, 5.

77. "American League Notes," *Sporting Life*, September 24, 1904, 11.

78. Koelsch: "Metropolitan Mention: A Week of Great Ball by the Contenders for the Amer'can League Pennant," 5.

79. "American League: Championship Record–Games Played Tuesday, Sept. 20," *Sporting Life*, October 1, 1904, 10.

80. "American League: Championship Record–Games Played Monday, Sept. 26," *Sporting Life*, October 8, 1904, 8.

81. "American League: Championship Record–Games Played Tuesday, Sept. 27," *Sporting Life*, October 8, 1904, 8.

82. "American League: The Complete Championship Record–Games Played Tuesday, Oct. 4," *Sporting Life*, October 15, 1904, 4.

83. "American League: The Complete Championship Record–Games Played Friday, Oct. 7," *Sporting Life*, October 15, 1904, 5.

84. "Highlanders Win, Now Lead in Race: In the First Game of the Final Series Griffith's Men Play like Pennant Winners and Win out by a Score of Three to Two," *The World*, October 7, 1904, 1.

85. "American League Notes," *Sporting Life*, October 8, 1904, 9.

86. "Boston Forges Into the Lead: Supporters of Highlanders Groan When Champions Capture the Double-Header," *San Francisco Call*, October 9, 1904, 39.

87. "Boston Won Both Games Decisively from New Yorks: Chesbro Taken from Slab after Allowing Six Runs," *Washington Times*, October 9, 1904, 11.

88. "Baseball: Boston Takes Pennant from Highlanders–Games Divided," *New-York Tribune*, October 11, 1904, 9.

89. "Baseball Glory for Boston: American League Pennant Not for New York," *The Sun*, October 11, 1904, 10.

90. "Baseball: Boston Takes Pennant from Highlanders–Games Divided," 9.

91. Francis C. Richter, "New York Nuggets: Brush Unshaken," *Sporting Life*, October 8, 1904, 5.

92. Francis C. Richter, "The 'Spit Ball': Sharing Odium with the Foul-Strike Rule," *Sporting Life*, October 15, 1904, 12.

93. F.P. O'Connell, "Famous Spit Ball: Leaves the Fingers First and Thumb Last," *Sporting News*, January 28, 1905, 1.

94. "Practicing a New Delivery: Elmer Stricklett, of the Brooklyn Superbas, Has a Slow Floating 'Spit-Ball' among His Curves," 18.

95. W. J. M'Beth, "Farrell Cuts Knot: Red Tape That Blocked Building Plans Is Unwound," *Sporting News*, July 25, 1912, 1.

CHAPTER 4

1. J.G. Taylor Spink, "Waddell: Madcap Mound Marvel–Rose to Fame under Mack's Kindly Hand," *Sporting News*, October 9, 1946, 10.

2. Dave Anthony and Gareth Reynolds, *The United States of Absurdity: Untold Stories from American History*, (Danvers, Mass.: Ten Speed Press–The Crown Publishing Group, 2017), 33.

3. Spink, "Waddell: Madcap Mound Marvel–Rose to Fame under Mack's Kindly Hand," 10.

4. Pirate, "Gigantic Deal: Star Colonels Sold to Pittsburg Club," *Sporting News*, December 16, 1899, 3.

5. Circle, "Pittsburg Points: Early Enthusiasm Certain in the Smoky City," *Sporting Life*, January 27, 1900, 6.

6. Circle, "Pittsburg Points: Big Rube Suspended," *Sporting Life*, July 14, 1900, 10.

7. Spink, "Waddell: Madcap Mound Marvel–Rose to Fame under Mack's Kindly Hand," 10.

8. Ibid., 12.

9. "News and Comment," *Sporting Life*, September 1, 1900, 3.
10. Alfred A. Cratty, "Needless Alarm: The Pirates Certain to Secure Second Place," *Sporting Life*, October 13, 1900, 6.
11. A.R. Cratty, Pittsburg Points: Fred Clarke in Line for Next Year," *Sporting Life*, November 3, 1900, 6.
12. "Rare 'Rube': The Eccentric Waddell Makes His 'Debutt' as an Actor and Scores Heavily," *Sporting Life*, December 15, 1900, 3.
13. "Rough Waddell: The Big Pitcher Makes a Show of Himself in a Foot Ball Game," *Sporting Life*, December 1, 1900, 2.
14. A.R. Cratty, "An Annual Meet: Pittsburg Club's Yearly Session Next Week," *Sporting Life*, December 8, 1900, 8.
15. "News and Comment," *Sporting Life*, May 4, 1901, 4.
16. Frank McParthin, "Morley's Methods: To Boom 'Rube' Waddell and Keep That Eccentric Pitcher in California for the Coming Season," *Sporting Life*, April 5, 1902, 5.
17. "Waddell's Egotism," *Sporting Life*, April 12, 1902, 16.
18. "Sad Experience: The Former Mrs. Waddell Repents of Hero Worship," *Sporting Life*, April 26, 1902, 12.
19. Spink, "Waddell: Madcap Mound Marvel–Rose to Fame under Mack's Kindly Hand," 12.
20. "Base Ball: Caught on the Fly," *Sporting News*, September 5, 1903, 5.
21. W.M. Rankin, "Minors' Threats: Are Fighting Mad over New Agreement," *Sporting News*, September 12, 1903, 6.
22. "The Stain of Guilt," *Public Daily Ledger Maysville Republican*, September 25, 1903, 1.
23. "Will Welcome 'Rube' with Produce Shower: Chicago Ball Players Plan to Give Waddell a Warm Reception," *Washington Times*, October 5, 1903, 8.
24. "The Theaters: Melodrama at the Park," *Indianapolis Journal*, October 9, 1903, 3.
25. "Rube Waddell in His Great Drama: Baseball Player Has Mansfield, Bellew and the Rest of Them All Going," *Butte Inter Mountain*, October 20, 1903, 7.
26. "The Diamond: Other Interesting Base Ball News," *Waterbury Evening Democrat*, October 20, 1903, 9.
27. "Kelley Can't Get 'Rube' Waddell," *The World*, November 18, 1903, 12.
28. "Base Ball: Caught on the Fly," *Sporting News*, November 28, 1903, 5.
29. J. Ed. Grillo, "Wants Waddell: Herrmann Makes Offer for Erratic Pitcher," *Sporting News*, November 21, 1903, 1.
30. "Mrs. 'Rube' Waddell Sues for Support: Wife of the Eccentric Baseball Pitcher Brings an Action against Him," *St. Paul Globe*, December 7, 1903, 7.
31. "National League Meeting Promises to Be Interesting: Athletics to Keep the Eccentric Rube Waddell," *St. Louis Republic*, November 29, 1903, 8.
32. "How Mack Holds Rube: Waddell Must Pitch Forty Games or No Salary–Last Year It Was $25 a Game," *Salt Lake Herald*, December 6, 1903, 4.
33. "Waddell to Pitch Again," *The World*, December 12, 1903, 6.

34. "Rube Waddell Leaves the 'Stain of Guilt,'" *Washington Times*, December 4, 1903, 8.

35. "Rube Waddell Is No Longer an Actor Man: George Edward Quit Work When His Catcher Was Barred from Stage," *St. Paul Globe*, January 1, 1904, 5.

36. "Base Ball Notes," *Evening Star*, January 20, 1904, 9.

37. "Base Ball: Some Items of Interest to Lovers of the Game," *Richmond Daily Paladium*, January 20, 1904, 4.

38. "Rube Waddell Again Starting Trouble: Pitcher with Peculiar Thoughts Wants to Play with Homestead Team," *St. Paul Globe*, January 27, 1904, 5.

39. "'Rube' Waddell Has Become a Butcher: Ex-Pitcher, Ex-Actor, Ex-Bartender Has Gone to Work in Brother John's Butcher Shop," *Washington Times*, February 2, 1904, 8.

40. "American League Notes," *Sporting Life*, March 26, 1904, 5.

41. F.C. Richter, "Quaker Quips: Preparations for Rebuilding Philadelphia Ball Park," *Sporting Life*, February 27, 1904, 5.

42. "Gossip of the Players," *Sporting News*, March 19, 1904, 2.

43. Veteran, "Are in the South: Quaker City Rivals of This Season," *Sporting News*, March 19, 1904, 2.

44. Veteran, "Are in Fine Shape: Phillies' Recruits Make Good Showing," *Sporting News*, April 2, 1904, 1.

45. "Baseball Doings: Rube Waddell," *Lewiston Evening Teller*, April 15, 1904, 2.

46. "American League: Championship Record–Games Played Saturday, April 16," *Sporting Life*, April 23, 1904, 8.

47. "Failure to Hit Ruined Senators: Athletics Run Away with Game by 12 to 2," *Washington Times*, April 17, 1904, 8.

48. "Pitchers Learn New Delivery: Cy Young Studies Style of Tossing Ball to Waiting Batsmen," *St. Louis Republic*, April 17, 1904, 2.

49. "American League: Championship Record–Games Played Wednesday, April 20," *Sporting Life*, April 30, 1904, 8.

50. "Americans Lead the Athletics: Great Crowd Turns Out in the Quaker City to Witness the Opening of the American League Season," *The World*, April 21, 1904, 1.

51. "American League: Championship Record–Games Played Thursday, April 21," *Sporting Life*, April 30, 1904, 8.

52. F.H. Koelsch, "New York Nuggets: Base Ball Enthusiasm Rampant in the Metropolis," *Sporting Life*, April 30, 1904, 4.

53. "Base Ball: Caught on the Fly," *Sporting News*, April 30, 1904, 4.

54. "American League: Championship Record–Games Played Monday, April 25," *Sporting Life*, May 7, 1904, 6.

55. "American League Possesses Many Noted Speed Merchants: Young Organization Has More Fast Pitchers Than the National League–Waddell Is King of the Fast Ball," *St. Louis Republic*, May 1, 1904, 1.

56. Jacob C. Morse, "Hub Happenings: Some Details of the Great Pitching of Waddell and Cy Young in the Recent Boston-Athletic Series," *Sporting Life*, May 14, 1904, 4.

57. "Other American Games: Boston, 3; Athletics, 0," *Evening Star*, May 6, 1904, 9.

58. "American League: Championship Record–Games Played Thursday, May 5," *Sporting Life*, May 14, 1904, 8.

59. "American League: Championship Record–Games Played Wednesday, May 11," *Sporting Life*, May 21, 1904, 8.

60. "American League: Championship Record–Games Played Saturday, May 14," *Sporting Life*, May 21, 1904, 8.

61. "American League: Championship Record–Games Played Thursday, May 26," *Sporting Life*, June 4, 1904, 8.

62. "American League: Championship Record–Games Played Monday, May 30," *Sporting Life*, June 11, 1904, 8.

63. "American League: Championship Record–Games Played Sunday, June 5," *Sporting Life*, June 11, 1904, 9.

64. "American League: Championship Record–Games Played Tuesday, June 7," *Sporting Life*, June 18, 1904, 8.

65. W.A. Phelon, Jr., "Chicago Gleanings: Rube Waddell's Four-Game Bluff Didn't Go Through," *Sporting Life*, June 18, 1904, 7.

66. "Waddell's Hallucination: Rooters Make Him Think He Is Fishing and He Pitches Well," *St. Louis Republic*, June 19, 1904, 6.

67. "Good Short Stories," *Condon Globe*, June 9, 1904, 4.

68. "American League: Championship Record–Games Played Monday, June 13, 1904," *Sporting Life*, June 25, 1904, 8.

69. "American League: Championship Record–Games Played Friday, June 17, 1904," *Sporting Life*, June 25, 1904, 8.

70. "American League: Championship Record–Games Played Wednesday, June 22, 1904," *Sporting Life*, July 2, 1904, 8.

71. "Sports of All Sorts: Athletics Defeated Senators in an Interesting Game," *Evening Star*, June 27, 1904, 9.

72. "American League: Championship Record–Games Played Monday, July 4," *Sporting Life*, July 16, 1904, 8.

73. "Sports of All Sorts: Senators Broke Even with Athletics in Double-Header," *Evening Star*, July 11, 1904, 9.

74. "Attendance Good at Early Game: Would It Be Better to Begin at 3 P.M.?" *Washington Times*, July 8, 1904, 8.

75. Veteran, "Play Grand Ball: Athletics Won Every Game Last Week," *Sporting News*, July 23, 1904, 6.

76. "American League: Championship Record–Games Played Thursday, July 14," *Sporting Life*, July 23, 1904, 8.

77. "American League: Championship Record–Games Played Tuesday, July 19," *Sporting Life*, July 30, 1904, 8.

78. "American League: Championship Record–Games Played Wednesday, July 27," *Sporting Life*, August 6, 1904, 8.

79. Francis C. Richter, "Philadelphia News: The National Game Booming in Its Stronghold," *Sporting Life*, August 6, 1904, 1.

80. "American League: Championship Record–Games Played Saturday, July 30," *Sporting Life*, August 6, 1904, 9.

81. "Harry Gleason Badly Injured by One of Waddell's Inshoots: Missouri Baptist Sanitarium Physicians Say Browns' Utility Infielder Sustained Concussion of the Brain When Struck by Ball Pitched with Big Twirler's Greatest Speed," *St. Louis Republic*, August 3, 1904, 5.

82. "American League: Championship Record–Games Played Tuesday, Aug. 2," *Sporting Life*, August 13, 1904, 8.

83. "Harry Gleason Badly Injured by One of Waddell's Inshoots: Missouri Baptist Sanitarium Physicians Say Browns' Utility Infielder Sustained Concussion of the Brain When Struck by Ball Pitched with Big Twirler's Greatest Speed," 5.

84. "Base Ball Notes," *Evening Star*, August 20, 1904, 9.

85. "American League: Championship Record–Games Played Sunday, Aug. 7," *Sporting Life*, August 13, 1904, 9.

86. "Base Ball: Caught on the Fly," *Sporting News*, August 13, 1904, 6.

87. "Personal Comment on Men and Things in the Field Of Sports," *Washington Times*, August 17, 1904, 8.

88. "American League: Championship Record–Games Played Thursday, Aug. 11," *Sporting Life*, August 20, 1904, 6.

89. "American League: Championship Record–Games Played Monday, Aug. 15," *Sporting Life*, August 27, 1904, 8.

90. "American League: Championship Record–Games Played Friday, Aug. 19," *Sporting Life*, August 27, 1904, 8.

91. "Waddell Landed in Wrong Town: Took Train for Allentown and Thought He Had Reached Philadelphia, Sent Back Home," *Washington Times*, August 31, 1904, 10.

92. "American League: Championship Record–Games Played Monday, Aug. 29," *Sporting Life*, September 10, 1904, 6.

93. "American League: Championship Record–Games Played Thursday, Sept. 1," *Sporting Life*, September 10, 1904, 6.

94. "American League: Championship Record–Games Played Monday, Sept. 5," *Sporting Life*, September 17, 1904, 8.

95. "American League: Championship Record–Games Played Thursday, Sept. 8," *Sporting Life*, September 17, 1904, 8-9.

96. "American League: Championship Record–Games Played Monday, Sept. 12," *Sporting Life*, September 24, 1904, 10.

97. "American League: Championship Record–Games Played Thursday, Sept. 15," *Sporting Life*, September 24, 1904, 11.

98. "Base Ball Notes," Evening Star, September 17, 1904, 9.

99. "Some Gossip of the Big Leagues: Tales Told on Well Known Players," *Salt Lake Tribune*, September 18, 1904, 4.

100. Francis C. Richter, "Philadelphia Pointers: The Two Local Teams Jointly Enjoy a Good Week," *Sporting Life*, September 24, 1904, 22.

101. "Athletics Win One Browns the Other: McAleer's Men Return to Their Old Habit of Breaking Even in Double-Header," *St. Louis Republic*, September 30, 1904, 8.

102. "American League: The Complete Championship Record–Games Played Friday, Oct. 7," *Sporting Life*, October 15, 1904, 5.

103. "Senators Lose Rics: Fire Destroys Carriages–Rube Waddell a Hero," *St. Paul Globe*, October 10, 1904, 1.

104. "Waddell a Hero: Erratic Twirler Dashed Into a Burning Building at Washington," *Topeka State Journal*, October 12, 1904, 2.

105. "American League: The Complete Championship Record–Games Played Monday, Oct. 10," *Sporting Life*, October 15, 1904, 5.

106. "Season Closes With a Victory: Senators Take Fast Game from Athletics," *Washington Times*, October 11, 1904, 8.

107. Alan H. Levy, *Rube Waddell: The Zany, Brilliant Life of a Strikeout Artist*, (Jefferson, N.C.: McFarland & Company, Inc., 2000), 161.

108. Clifford Kachline, "Statisticians Still Fanning Figures over Bobby Feller's Whiff Mark: Experts Place Waddell Total Between 347 and 352; Evidence Supports 349," *Sporting News*, October 9, 1946, 12.

CHAPTER 5

1. David L. Fleitz, *Ghosts in the Gallery: Sixteen Little-Known Members of the Hall of Fame*, (Jefferson, N.C.: McFarland & Company, Inc., 2004), 177.

2. Ibid., 177-178.

3. "Star Scintillations: No Discord in the Team–Harry Raymond Signed, Etc.," *Sporting Life*, August 8, 1896, 9.

4. Fleitz, *Ghosts in the Gallery: Sixteen Little-Known Members of the Hall of Fame*, 178.

5. G. Whiz, "Syracuse Sayings: Further Light Shed on the Dispute over Bill Eagan," *Sporting Life*, November 6, 1897, 5.

6. Fleitz, *Ghosts in the Gallery: Sixteen Little-Known Members of the Hall of Fame*, 178.

7. Lois P. Nicholson, *From Maryland to Cooperstown: Seven Maryland Natives in Baseball's Hall of Fame*, (Centreville, Md.: Tidewater Publishers, 1998), 29.

8. J.C. Morse, "Hubs Happenings: Preparing for the Final Tussle with the Orioles," *Sporting Life*, September 25, 1897, 7.

9. "Slapped His Face: Sensational Incident at the Southern Hotel," *Sporting News*, October 15, 1898, 2.

10. Patrick R. Redmond, *The Irish and the Making of American Sport, 1835-1920*, (Jefferson, N.C.: McFarland & Company, Inc., 2014), 209.

11. Harold Kaese, *The Boston Braves, 1871-1953*, (1948; reprint, Boston: Northeastern University Press, 2004), 97.

12. "Cried Like a Child: Queer Actions of the Great Catcher While in Cincinnati," *Sporting News*, January 27, 1900, 3.

13. Kaese, *The Boston Braves, 1871-1953*, 97.

14. Fleitz, *Ghosts in the Gallery: Sixteen Little-Known Members of the Hall of Fame*, 180.

15. "Pitcher Willis Married," *Sporting Life*, March 31, 1900, 2.

16. Redmond, *The Irish and the Making of American Sport, 1835-1920*, 209-210.

17. "Bergen Tragedy: Terrible Deed of the Demented Catcher," *Sporting News*, January 27, 1900, 3.

18. "His Married Life: Not as Pleasant as Mrs. Bergen Declared It to Be," *Sporting News*, January 27, 1900, 3.

19. "News and Comment," *Sporting Life*, May 26, 1900, 3.

20. Norman L. Macht, *Connie Mack and the Early Years of Baseball*, (Lincoln, Neb.: University Of Nebraska Press, 2007), 224.

21. "Victor G. Willis: Pitcher of the Boston National League Club," *Sporting Life*, December 10, 1904, 3.

22. Hal, "Better Grounds: Champions' Playing Field Will Be Improved," *Sporting News*, October 29, 1904, 1.

23. Frederic P. O'Connell, "Will Keep Stars: Boston Recruits Must Show Jim Collins," *Sporting News*, December 3, 1904, 1.

24. "Tips by the Managers," *Sporting News*, January 14, 1905, 4.

25. F.P. O'Connell, "Famous Spit Ball: Leaves the Fingers First and Thumb Last," *Sporting News*, January 28, 1905, 1.

26. Jacob C. Morse, "Boston Briefs: The Boston National Club Appoints Billy Rogers as Business Manager and Fred Tenney as Team Captain," *Sporting Life*, February 11, 1905, 3.

27. Frederic P. O'Connell, "Are Working Hard: Practice Pointers from Both Boston Camps," *Sporting News*, April 1, 1905, 8.

28. Frederic P. O'Connell, "Worked All Week: Collins' Champions Played Five Games," *Sporting News*, March 25, 1905, 3.

29. "Caught on the Fly," *Sporting News*, April 8, 1905, 6.

30. "Caught on the Fly," *Sporting News*, April 29, 1905, 6.

31. "Baseball Teams Know Value of Star Players: Presence of Scintillating Performers Always Felt At the Box Office," *Brooklyn Daily Eagle*, April 9, 1905, 11.

32. Frederic P. O'Connell, "Started Upward: Collins' Team Breaks Losing Streak," *Sporting News*, April 29, 1905, 4.

33. "National League News," *Sporting Life*, May 13, 1905, 5.

34. "Rain Plays Havoc with Baseball Games: Home Coming of Superbas Marred and Openings in Other Cities Spoiled," *Brooklyn Daily Eagle*, April 22, 1905, 5.

35. "New England News: Rogers at Rest–Sudden Death of Boston's Business Manager," *Sporting Life*, April 29, 1905, 3.

36. "Notes of the Game," *Brooklyn Daily Eagle*, April 23, 1905, 5.

37. Sheckard Revival at Washington Park: Brooklyn Captain Displays Some Old Time Form and Team Wins Handily," *Brooklyn Daily Eagle*, April 26, 1905, 13.

38. "National League: The Championship Record–Games Played Tuesday, April 25," *Sporting Life*, May 6, 1905, 4.

39. "National League: The Championship Record–Games Played Saturday, April 29," *Sporting Life*, May 6, 1905, 4.

40. J.C. Morse, "Boston Briefs: The Hard Luck Start of the Champions–The Nationals Improving," *Sporting Life*, April 29, 1905, 3.

41. "National League: The Championship Record- Games Played Thursday, May 4," *Sporting Life*, May 13, 1905, 4.

42. "National League: The Championship Record–Games Played Monday, May 8," *Sporting Life*, May 20, 1905, 4.

43. Frederic P. O'Connell, "A Model Magnate: Taylor Always Roots and Never Weakens," *Sporting News*, May 20, 1905, 3.

44. J.C. Morse, "Boston Briefs: Manager Tenney Doing Well under Difficulties," *Sporting Life*, May 20, 1905, 10.

45. O'Connell, "A Model Magnate: Taylor Always Roots and Never Weakens," 3.

46. Frederic P. O'Connell, "Slow in Starting: Champions Have Many Setbacks on the Road," *Sporting News*, May 27, 1905, 4.

47. "National League: The Championship Record–Games Played Friday, May 12," *Sporting Life*, May 20, 1905, 5.

48. "National League: The Championship Record–Games Played Thursday, May 18," *Sporting Life*, May 27, 1905, 4.

49. "National League: The Championship Record–Games Played Monday, May 22," *Sporting Life*, June 3, 1905, 4.

50. "National League: The Championship Record–Games Played Friday, June 9," *Sporting Life*, June 17, 1905, 5.

51. "National League: The Championship Record–Games Played Tuesday, June 13," *Sporting Life*, June 24, 1905, 4.

52. Frederic P. O'Connell, "Fourth Straight: Collins' Champions Please Their Patrons," *Sporting News*, June 17, 1905, 4.

53. "National League: The Championship Record–Games Played Wednesday, June 14," *Sporting Life*, June 24, 1905, 4.

54. "National League: The Championship Record–Games Played Saturday, June 17," *Sporting Life*, July 1, 1905, 4.

55. "National League: The Championship Record–Games Played Wednesday, July 5," *Sporting Life*, July 15, 1905, 4-5.

56. "National League: The Championship Record–Games Played Saturday, July 8," *Sporting Life*, July 22, 1905, 4.

57. "National League: The Championship Record–Games Played Wednesday, July 12," *Sporting Life*, July 22, 1905, 4.

58. "National League: The Championship Record–Games Played Saturday, July 15," *Sporting Life*, July 22, 1905, 5.

59. "National League: The Championship Record–Games Played Wednesday, July 19," *Sporting Life*, July 29, 1905, 4.

60. Frederic P. O'Connell, "Rank Partisans: People Who Count on a Major League's Collapse," *Sporting News*, July 22, 1905, 5.

Notes

61. "National League: The Championship Record–Games Played Wednesday, July 26," *Sporting Life*, August 5, 1905, 4.

62. Frederic P. O'Connell, "True Sportsman: Taylor Agrees to Fall Series with Rival," *Sporting News*, August 5, 1905, 3.

63. "National League: The Championship Record–Games Played Sunday, July 30," *Sporting Life*, August 5, 1905, 5.

64. "National League: The Championship Record–Games Played Friday, August 4," *Sporting Life*, August 12, 1905, 4.

65. "National League: The Championship Record–Games Played Monday, August 7," *Sporting Life*, August 19, 1905, 4.

66. "National League: The Championship Record–Games Played Sunday, August 13," *Sporting Life*, August 19, 1905, 5.

67. Frederic P. O'Connell, "Prefers Rivalry: Taylor Opposed to Merger of Major Leagues," *Sporting News*, August 19, 1905, 3.

68. "National League: The Championship Record–Games Played Friday, August 18," *Sporting Life*, August 26, 1905, 4.

69. "National League: The Championship Record- Games Played Tuesday, August 22," *Sporting Life*, September 2, 1905, 4.

70. "National League: The Championship Record–Games Played Thursday, August 24," *Sporting Life*, September 2, 1905, 5.

71. "National League: The Championship Record–Games Played Tuesday, August 29," *Sporting Life*, September 9, 1905, 4.

72. "Willis Beats McIntire in Pitchers' Battle: Bostons Scored the Only Run, Although Brooklyn Twirler Batted Well," *Brooklyn Daily Eagle*, September 3, 1905, 5.

73. "National League: The Championship Record–Games Played Thursday, Sept. 7," *Sporting Life*, September 16, 1905, 4.

74. Frederic P. O'Connell, "Interest Waning: Only Fair Crowds Now Attend Boston Games," *Sporting News*, September 16, 1905, 1.

75. "National League: The Championship Record–Games Played Saturday, Sept. 16," *Sporting Life*, September 23, 1905, 4.

76. Frederic P. O'Connell, "Must Be Admired: Sportsmanship and Gameness of John I. Taylor," *Sporting News*, September 23, 1905, 5.

77. "National League: The Championship Record–Games Played Monday, Sept. 18," *Sporting Life*, September 30, 1905, 4.

78. "National League: The Complete 1905 Record–Games Played Tuesday, October 3," *Sporting Life*, October 14, 1905, 10.

79. "Brooklyns Scheming to Leave Last Place: Beat Bostons Again and Would Like to Have Sunday Game with Phillies," *Brooklyn Daily Eagle*, October 7, 1905, 9.

80. Frederic P. O'Connell, "Evenly Matched: Athletics and Giants Are Both Strong Teams," *Sporting News*, October 7, 1905, 4.

81. "New England News: Boston's Battle–For the Base Ball Supremacy of the Hub," *Sporting Life*, October 21, 1905, 12.

82. "Caught on the Fly," *Sporting News*, October 7, 1905, 6.

83. Frederic P. O'Connell, "May Land Nealon: Taylor Hopes to Sign Young First Baseman," *Sporting News*, October 28, 1905, 4.
84. Frederic P. O'Connell, "Taylor Hustling: Will Liven Up His Team with Fast Youngsters," *Sporting News*, November 4, 1905, 5.
85. Frederic P. O'Connell, "Title in Dispute: Parties to Boston Deal Can Not Agree," *Sporting News*, November 11, 1905, 5.
86. Frederic P. O'Connell, "Fallen Through: Dunn's Deal for Purchase of Boston Club," *Sporting News*, November 18, 1905, 2.
87. Frederic P. O'Connell, "Fear Litigation: Moneyed Men Will Not Buy Boston Stock," *Sporting News*, December 9, 1905, 1.
88. A.R. Cratty, "Pittsburg Points: Old League's Loss in the Retirement of Noted Magnate–That Deal for Willis," *Sporting Life*, December 23, 1905, 8.
89. "Tips by the Managers," *Sporting News*, December 23, 1905, 4.
90. Ralph S. Davis, "Will Do His Best: Willis Glad to Get Away from Boston," *Sporting News*, March 17, 1906, 7.

CHAPTER 6

1. Ed F. Ballinger, "Buccaneers- - - Thumb-Nail Sketches of Club Officials and the Players," *Pittsburgh Post*, April 19, 1917, 8.
2. "National League Notes," *Sporting Life*, September 16, 1911, 3.
3. John J. Evers and Hugh S. Fullerton, "Touching Second: The Science of Baseball," *Perry Daily Chief*, June 11, 1910, 3.
4. "Schulte May Break Record: Cub's Right Fielder Has a Mania for Home Runs and Fast Trotters," *Great Falls Daily Tribune*, September 24, 1911, 8.
5. Randy Roberts and Carson Cunningham, ed., *Before the Curse: The Chicago Cubs' Glory Years, 1870-1945*, (Urbana, Ill.: University Of Illinois Press, 2012), 106.
6. Evers and Fullerton, "Touching Second: The Science of Baseball," 3.
7. "In the Wake of the News: 'Wildfire' Schulte," *Chicago Daily Tribune*, April 25, 1929, 17.
8. Irving Vaughan, "Frank Schulte, Original 'Babe' Ruth, Victim of 'Heinie' Batch," *Democrat and Chronicle*, March 25, 1928, 16.
9. John W. Fox, "Name One Poem That Logan Wrote," *Binghamton Press*, December 7, 1956, 33.
10. "John Schulte a Suicide: Brother of Chicago National Outfielder Found Dead in Bed at Lestershire, N Y.," *Boston Daily Globe*, August 30, 1910, 6.
11. I.E. Sanborn, "Cubs Cheered Off: Thousands Watch Train Depart for Scene of Battle," *Sporting News*, October 20, 1910, 2.
12. "Tips by the Managers," *Sporting News*, October 27, 1910, 4.
13. Frank B. Hutchinson, Jr., "Chicago Chat: Murphy Taking Rule-Change Talk Seriously," *Sporting Life*, January 28, 1911, 2.
14. Ralph S. Davis, "Clarke Chimes In: Pirate Leader Now in War on Chicago Clubhouse," *Sporting News*, January 26, 1911, 2.

15. "Attack on Chicken Coop Produces Real Results: Adequate Quarters to Be Provided for Visiting Ball Players at the Cubs' Chicago Park," *Pittsburg Press*, January 24, 1911, 16.

16. I.E. Sanborn, "'Kick' No New One: Perfect Clubhouse for Guests Yet to Be Found," *Sporting News*, January 26, 1911, 1.

17. "National League Notes," *Sporting Life*, February 18, 1911, 3.

18. "Tips by the Managers," *Sporting News*, February 16, 1911, 4.

19. I.E. Sanborn, "Antics of Artie: Hofman Had Cub Pot at Boiling Point for Awhile," *Sporting News*, March 2, 1911, 1.

20. Frank B. Hutchinson, Jr., "Chicago Chat: Another Veteran 'Cub' Slated for Release," *Sporting Life*, March 18, 1911, 2.

21. Fox, "Name One Poem That Logan Wrote," 33.

22. I.E. Sanborn, "Means Rush Start: Major League Clubs Generally in Good Condition," *Sporting News*, April 6, 1911, 1.

23. "Baseball Notes," *Brooklyn Daily Eagle*, April 12, 1911, 1.

24. Richard G. Tobin, "Chicago Gleanings: Both Cubs and White Sox Make Poor Beginning," *Sporting Life*, April 22, 1911, 6.

25. "National League: The 1911 Championship Record–Successful Opening," *Sporting Life*, April 22, 1911, 8.

26. "National League Notes," *Sporting Life*, April 22, 1911, 9.

27. "National League: The 1911 Championship Record–Games Played Thursday, April 20," *Sporting Life*, April 29, 1911, 8.

28. R.G. Tobin, "Chicago Gleanings: The Cubs Starting Out with Every Indication of Making Their Usual Strong Fight for Honors," *Sporting Life*, April 29, 1911, 3.

29. "National League: The 1911 Championship Record–Games Played Wednesday, April 26," *Sporting Life*, May 6, 1911, 8.

30. I.E. Sanborn, "Windy City Woes: Both Teams Have Been Hit Hard by Accidents," *Sporting News*, May 4, 1911, 1.

31. "Schulte Fined for Slow Work: Manager Chance Puts $50 Plaster on Outfielder for Lack of Speed on Bases," *St. Louis Post-Dispatch*, April 23, 1911, 8.

32. I.E. Sanborn, "Hard Row for Cubs: They Go East in Anything But Good Condition," *Sporting News*, May 11, 1911, 1.

33. I.E. Sanborn, "Greed of Gotham: It Compelled Cubs to Play in the Rain and Lose," *Sporting News*, May 18, 1911, 1.

34. "National League: Standing on Tuesday Morning," *Sporting News*, May 18, 1911, 2.

35. "Ill-Fated Cub Player: Johnny Evers," *Sporting News*, May 25, 1911, 3.

36. "National League: Standing on Tuesday Morning," *Sporting News*, May 11, 1911, 5.

37. "National League: The 1911 Championship Record–Games Played Thursday, May 11," *Sporting Life*, May 20, 1911, 8.

38. "National League: The 1911 Championship Record–Games Played Wednesday, May 17," *Sporting Life*, May 27, 1911, 8.

39. "National League: The 1911 Championship Record–Games Played Thursday, May 18," *Sporting Life*, May 27, 1911, 8.

40. I.E. Sanborn, "Salaam to Chicago: Quaker City Eats from Hands of Cubs and Sox," *Sporting News*, May 25, 1911, 1.

41. "National League: The 1911 Championship Record–Games Played Wednesday, May 24," *Sporting Life*, June 3, 1911, 8.

42. "National League: The 1911 Championship Record–Games Played Saturday, June 3," *Sporting Life*, June 10, 1911, 9.

43. William Peet, "Nationals Will Face Old Hoodoo, Doc White, This Afternoon: Other Gossip and Comment," *Washington Herald*, June 12, 1911, 7.

44. Richard G. Tobin, "Chicago Gleanings: Manager Frank Chance, of the Cubs, Nearing the End of His Base Ball Days," *Sporting Life*, June 10, 1911, 3.

45. Chan. Richter, "Some Peculiarities: As Manifested Between Individuals in the National League," *Sporting Life*, June 17, 1911, 24.

46. "National League: The 1911 Championship Record–Games Played Sunday, June 11," *Sporting Life*, June 24, 1911, 8.

47. "Johnny Kling Refuses to Join Boston Club," *Bakersfield Californian*, June 12, 1911, 1.

48. "Frank Chance 'Beaned' 38 Times; Head Aches," *Bakersfield Californian*, June 12, 1911, 1.

49. "Chance Out of Game for Good: Chicago Manager, However, Refuses to Admit His Playing Days Are Over," *Buffalo Evening Times*, June 14, 1911, 6.

50. "National League: The 1911 Championship Record–Games Played Sunday, June 18," *Sporting Life*, July 1, 1911, 8.

51. "Schulte's Steal Gives Cubs Game: Poet Purloins Home in the Eighth, Beating Dooin's Daisies, 4 To 3," *Lake County Times*, June 19, 1911, 3.

52. "Schulte of Cubs Takes Pretty Bride," *Bridgeport Evening Farmer*, June 27, 1911, 7.

53. "Schulte Leaves Bachelor Ranks: Star Right Fielder of Cubs Finds Time to Marry Miss Mabel Kirby," *Lake County Times*, June 27, 1911, 3.

54. Handy Andy, "Schulte Leaves Bachelor Ranks: Star Right Fielder of Cubs Finds Time to Marry Miss Mabel M. Kirby," *Chicago Daily Tribune*, June 27, 1911, 12.

55. "Cupid Signs Life Contract with Frank Schulte, the Hard-Hitting Cub Ballist," *Ottumwa Tri-Weekly Courier*, July 11, 1911, 8.

56. I.E. Sanborn, "No Team Has Class: Nothing in National like Old Cub Machine," *Sporting News*, July 13, 1911, 1.

57. "National League: The 1911 Championship Record–Games Played Tuesday, July 4 (A.M.)," *Sporting Life*, July 15, 1911, 8.

58. "National League: The 1911 Championship Record–Games Played Tuesday, July 4 (P.M.)," *Sporting Life*, July 15, 1911, 8.

59. "National League: The 1911 Championship Record–Games Played Tuesday, July 18," *Sporting Life*, July 29, 1911, 8.

60. "National League: The 1911 Championship Record–Games Played Wednesday, July 19," *Sporting Life*, July 29, 1911, 8.

61. "National League: The 1911 Championship Record–Games Played Thursday, July 20," *Sporting Life*, July 29, 1911, 8.

62. "Schulte of Cubs and Luderus Out for Circuit Raps: Chicago and Philadelphia Sluggers Out for Home Run Honors," *Bridgeport Evening Farmer*, August 3, 1911, 7.

63. "National League: The 1911 Championship Record–Games Played Saturday, August 5," *Sporting Life*, August 12, 1911, 9.

64. "Tinker Benched by Frank Chance: Cubs Shortstop Suspended for Season and Fined for Indifferent Playing," *Times Dispatch*, August 6, 1911, 1.

65. I.E. Sanborn, "Tinker Out and In: Chicago Fans Given Something to Gossip About," *Sporting News*, August 10, 1911, 1.

66. "National League: The 1911 Championship Record–Games Played Sunday, August 6," *Sporting Life*, August 19, 1911, 8.

67. "National League: The 1911 Championship Record–Games Played Monday, August 7," *Sporting Life*, August 19, 1911, 8.

68. "National League: The 1911 Championship Record–Games Played Saturday, August 12, 1911," *Sporting Life*, August 19, 1911, 9.

69. "National League: The 1911 Championship Record–Games Played Wednesday, August 16," *Sporting Life*, August 26, 1911, 8.

70. "National League: The 1911 Championship Record–Games Played Thursday, August 17," *Sporting Life*, August 26, 1911, 8.

71. "National League: The 1911 Championship Record–Games Played Saturday, August 19," *Sporting Life*, August 26, 1911, 9.

72. Richard G. Tobin, "Chicago Gleanings: Frank Schulte after a New Major League Record," *Sporting Life*, August 26, 1911, 7.

73. "National League: The 1911 Championship Record–Games Played Thursday, September 7," *Sporting Life*, September 16, 1911, 9.

74. "Cubs Beat Reds; Gain on Giants: Twin Victory, 3 to 0 and 4 To 2, Puts Chance's Men One Game Behind Leaders," *Lake County Times*, September 8, 1911, 12.

75. "Fans Keeping Tab on Schulte's Work for Record of Runs," *Omaha Sunday Bee*, October 1, 1911, 2.

76. "Cubs Shut Out New York: Marquard and Crandall Hit Hard with Richie Steady," *Topeka State Journal*, September 28, 1911, 2.

77. "National League: The 1911 Championship Record–Games Played Thursday, September 28," *Sporting Life*, October 7, 1911, 8.

78. "New York Beats Chicago, 3 to 1: Giants Triumph over Cubs in Third Game of Series, Regaining Part of Previous Loss," *Omaha Sunday Bee*, October 1, 1911, 1.

79. "National League: The 1911 Championship Record–Games Played Saturday, September 30," *Sporting Life*, October 7, 1911, 9.

80. "The Final Week's Games: Games Played Monday, October 9," *Sporting Life*, October 21, 1911, 11.

81. "Short Lengths: Schulte's Auto," *Baseball Magazine*, May 1913, 68.

82. "Cobb and Schulte Win Automobiles," *Pensacola Journal*, October 12, 1911, 1.

83. "Get Buzz Wagons: Ty Cobb and Frank Schulte Winners in Auto Contest," *Evening Star*, October 12, 1911, 18.

84. "Cobb and Schulte Given Automobiles," *Richmond Palladium And Sun-Telegram*, October 13, 1911, 6.

85. "Ed Walsh Will Get an Automobile Too," *Brooklyn Daily Eagle*, October 13, 1911, 2.

86. I.E. Sanborn, "Cubs Game to End: Could Not Realize All Was but a Vain Hope," *Sporting News*, October 5, 1911, 1.

87. "A Crushing Defeat," *Lake County Times*, October 19, 1911, 3.

88. "Chicago City Series: Result of the Series," *Sporting News*, October 26, 1911, 8.

89. "Ed Walsh to Get an Automobile," *Lake County Times*, October 19, 1911, 3.

90. "White Sox Win!: The Local Championship of the Windy City," *Sporting Life*, October 28, 1911, 14.

91. "National League Notes," *Sporting Life*, November 25, 1911, 10.

92. "National League: Standing on Tuesday Morning," *Sporting News*, October 12, 1911, 7.

93. "Schulte a Great Ball Player," *Evening Times* (Grand Forks, North Dakota), October 31, 1911, 3.

94. E.J. Lanigan, "Schulte's Plaint: The Star Chicago Player and Leading Home-Run Hitter of the National League, Claims That Secretary Heydler Is Short Two Homers," *Sporting Life*, December 9, 1911, 7.

95. I.E. Sanborn, "Death Drafts Cub: Doyle Had Been Counted Sure for Third Base," *Sporting News*, February 8, 1912, 1.

96. Hugh S. Fullerton, "Murphy's Anti-Drink Rule May Not Have Good Effect: Frank Chance's Honor System Proved to Be the Right Thing in Past When Peerless Leader Could Watch Men, but Recruits Mistake Liberty for License," *Pittsburgh Sunday Post*, September 29, 1912, 4.

97. I.E. Sanborn, "It's All Over Now: Might as Well Put Tickets for Big Series on Sale," *Sporting News*, September 12, 1912, 1.

98. "Sports: Chance Suspends Frank Schulte," Lake County Times, September 9, 1912, 3.

99. "Sabbath Sport: Standing of the Clubs," *Day Book*, September 9, 1912, 14.

100. "Wildfire Schulte Back in the Game," *San Francisco Call*, September 18, 1912, 12.

101. "Football and Baseball: Anecdotes of Diamond and Gridiron," *Baseball Magazine*, November 1912, 80.

102. "Schulte Breaks 50 Bats Every Season," *Honolulu Star-Bulletin*, September 28, 1912, 9.

103. John Mooney, "Sports Mirror," *Salt Lake Tribune*, October 2, 1949, 2S.

CHAPTER 7

1. Ward Mason, "'Chief' Wilson of the Cardinals: The Man Who Holds the Record for the Greatest Number of Three-Base Hits Ever Made–A Heavy Hitter and Sterling Fielder," *Baseball Magazine*, October 1915, 75-76.

2. "Baseball By-Plays," *Sporting News*, October 24, 1912, 4.

3. "J. Owen Wilson: Outfielder of the Pittsburg National League Club," *Sporting Life*, September 19, 1908, 1.

4. A.R. Cratty, "In Pittsburg: Pitcher Leever Is Regarded as a Humorist," *Sporting Life*, February 29, 1908, 10.

5. James Jerpe, "On and Off the Field," *Gazette-Times*, April 19, 1913, 14.

6. A.R. Cratty, "In Pittsburg: A Problem Which Must Be Settled," *Sporting Life*, May 23, 1908, 5.

7. "J. Owen Wilson: Outfielder of the Pittsburg National League Club," 1.

8. Cratty, "In Pittsburg: A Problem Which Must Be Settled," 5.

9. A.R. Cratty, "In Pittsburg: Veteran Twirlers Fail to Keep Up Pace," *Sporting Life*, June 6, 1908, 6.

10. "J. Owen Wilson: Outfielder of the Pittsburg National League Club," 1.

11. Ralph S. Davis, "Slip Away Unsung: Pittsburgh Draws Curtain on 1911 Base Ball Season," *Sporting News*, October 12, 1911, 5.

12. Ralph S. Davis, "Easier for Clarke: Pirate Problems Not so Serious as a Year Ago," *Sporting News*, November 30, 1911, 1.

13. Ralph S. Davis, "Clarke Is Unsigned: Pirate Chief's Term of Service Has Expired," *Sporting News*, December 7, 1911, 5.

14. Ralph S. Davis, "Joy Not Unalloyed: Pirate Fans' Christmas Lacking in Good Cheer," *Sporting News*, December 21, 1911, 1.

15. "National League," *Sporting News*, January 4, 1911, 6.

16. Ralph S. Davis, "Pirates Cruise On: First Squad under Clarke Goes to West Baden," *Sporting News*, March 7, 1912, 5.

17. A.R. Cratty, "Pirate Points: Flag Day to Be a Holiday Fixture," *Sporting Life*, January 20, 1912, 11.

18. Ralph S. Davis, "Moore Blows Up and Pirates Win: Pirates Hand Their Notorious 'Jinx' a Beating after Sensational Pitchers' Battle–Quakers Get Only Four Hits Off Camnitz–Byrne and Wilson Contribute Home Runs," *Pittsburgh Press*, June 4, 1911, 1.

19. Cratty, "Pirate Points: Flag Day to Be a Holiday Fixture," 11.

20. "Enlarged Park to Be Dedicated Friday, May 26," *Pittsburg Press*, May 19, 1911, 26.

21. A.R. Cratty, "Pirate Points: Col. Dreyfuss Not Pleased With Results to Date–The Veterans of the Pittsburg Team Not Playing Up to Form and Expectation–Hope of a Glorious Finish Still Strong," *Sporting Life*, June 10, 1911, 2.

22. Ralph S. Davis, "Pirate Crew Grows: Clarke Has Reason for Bigger Training Squad," Sporting News, February 8, 1912, 2.

23. Ralph S. Davis, "Only Two Bad Ones: Leifield and Campbell Pair of Pirate Holdouts," *Sporting News*, February 15, 1912, 2.

24. Ralph S. Davis, "Donlin Man Needed: He's Expected to Put More Spirit in Pirate Team," *Sporting News*, February 22, 1912, 2.

25. Ralph S. Davis, "Donlin's Bon Mot: Salary No Object to Man on a Real Ball Team," *Sporting News*, February 29, 1912, 5.

26. Davis, "Pirate Cruise On: First Squad under Clarke Goes to West Baden," 5.

27. "Ralph S. Davis, "Pirate Crew Full: Leifield Yields to Game's Call after Many Days," *Sporting News*, March 21, 1912, 3.

28. W.B. McVicker, "Donlin Joins Owen Wilson on Sick List: Both Star Outfielders Are Victims of Colds, But Expect to Be Able to Oppose Cardinals Tomorrow," *Pittsburg Press*, April 10, 1912, 23.

29. Ralph S. Davis, "Dreyfuss in Doubt: Does Not Seem Enthusiastic over Miller on First," *The Sporting News*, April 11, 1912, 2.

30. "National League," *Sporting News*, April 11, 1912, 7.

31. W.B. McVicker, "Pirates Arrived Late in St. Louis: Train Connections from West Were Delayed and Railroad Officials Refused to Furnish Special Train," *Pittsburg Press*, April 11, 1912, 20.

32. "The National League: The 1912 Championship Record–The 1912 Opening," *Sporting Life*, April 20, 1912, 10.

33. "National League: Standing Tuesday Morning," *Sporting News*, April 18, 1912, 6.

34. James Jerpe, "Follow the Ball," *Gazette-Times*, April 14, 1912, 2.

35. James Jerpe, "Pirates Lose to Reds in 11-Inning Struggle: Pittsburgh Ties Score in Ninth, But in the Fatal Session Byrne Throws over Uncovered First and Deciding Run Goes Over–Adams and Fromme Pitch," *Gazette-Times*, April 16, 1912, 10.

36. "The National League: The 1912 Championship Record–Games Played Tuesday, April 16," *Sporting Life*, April 27, 1912, 10.

37. "The National League: The 1912 Championship Record–Games Played Thursday, April 18," *Sporting Life*, April 27, 1912, 10.

38. James Jerpe, "Follow the Ball," *Gazette-Times*, April 22, 1912, 11.

39. James Jerpe, "Follow the Ball," *Gazette-Times*, April 24, 1912, 10.

40. Jerpe, "Follow the Ball," April 22, 1912, 11.

41. James Jerpe, "Chief Wilson Is Hero for the Pirate Crew: Drives in Runs and Then Saves Day in Ninth by Catching Drive with Men on Bases–Carey Shines Also–Pittsburgh Takes Game, 5-3," *Gazette-Times*, April 24, 1912, 10.

42. Ralph S. Davis, "Reasonable as Yet: Pittsburg Fans Accept Alibi for Failure to Win," *Sporting News*, May 2, 1912, 2.

43. "The National League: The 1912 Championship Record–Games Played Saturday, April 27," *Sporting Life*, May 4, 1912, 10.

44. James Jerpe, "On and Off the Field," *Gazette-Times*, April 28, 1912, 2.

45. James Jerpe, "Follow the Ball," *Gazette-Times*, April 26, 1912, 12.

46. Davis, "Reasonable as Yet: Pittsburg Fans Accept Alibi for Failure to Win," 2.

47. "The National League: The 1912 Championship Record–Games Played Saturday, May 4," *Sporting Life*, May 11, 1912, 10.

48. Ralph S. Davis, "Jotted Down While Pirates Lost Again," *Pittsburg Press*, May 4, 1912, 8.

49. James Jerpe, "On and Off the Field," *Gazette-Times*, May 5, 1912, 3.

50. James Jerpe, "On and Off the Field," *Gazette-Times*, May 10, 1912, 12.

51. Ralph S. Davis, "Alibi of Pirates: Team Misses Services of Both Donlin and Wagner," *Sporting News*, May 9, 1912, 3.

52. Ralph S. Davis, "Jotted Down While Ames Beats Pirates," *Pittsburg Press*, May 16, 1912, 22.

53. "The National League: The 1912 Championship Record–Games Played Thursday, May 16," *Sporting Life*, May 25, 1912, 10.

54. James Jerpe, "On and Off the Field," *Gazette-Times*, May 24, 1912, 13.

55. Ralph S. Davis, "Corsairs Captured Exciting Struggle: Timely Hitting Beats the Cubs, Camnitz Is Wild, But Settles Down in the Pinches, and Is Given Wonderful Support," *Pittsburg Press*, May 26, 1912, 1.

56. "Not Wilson's Smashes," *Gazette-Times*, May 27, 1912, 8.

57. Ralph S. Davis, "Pirates Get Shade: Figure a Little Best of It on Chicago Trade," *Sporting News*, June 6, 1912, 2.

58. "Pirate Heaver Trains Hard as Real Sprinter: Claude's Speed and Fine Physical Condition Help Him Make Use of His Ability as a Batsman," *Pittsburg Press*, June 8, 1912, 8.

59. "National League: Standing on Tuesday Morning," *Sporting News*, June 13, 1912, 5.

60. Ralph S. Davis, "Clarke Will Play: He Might Be in Now but for a Broken Finger," *Sporting News*, June 13, 1912, 2.

61. "Caught on the Fly," *Sporting News*, June 13, 1912, 4.

62. James Jerpe, "On and Off the Field," *Gazette-Times*, June 18, 1912, 13.

63. James Jerpe, "On and Off the Field," *Gazette-Times*, June 21, 1912, 13.

64. James Jerpe, "On and Off the Field," *Gazette-Times*, June 24, 1912, 8.

65. James Jerpe, "On and Off the Field," *Gazette-Times*, July 7, 1912, 3.

66. James Jerpe, "On and Off the Field," *Gazette-Times*, June 27, 1912, 13.

67. James Jerpe, "On and Off the Field," *Gazette-Times*, June 25, 1912, 12.

68. Ralph S. Davis, "Hush Their Knocks: Hammers Laid Away as Pirates Win Some Games," *Sporting News*, June 27, 1912, 1.

69. Ralph S. Davis, "Pirates Have Hope: Think Western Clubs May Pull Giants Down," *Sporting News*, July 4, 1912, 1.

70. James Jerpe, "On and Off the Field," *Gazette-Times*, July 9, 1912, 10.

71. Ralph S. Davis, "Pittsburg in Print: Piratetown Figures Largely in News of the Day," *Sporting News*, July 18, 1912, 2.

72. "National League: Standing on Tuesday Morning," *Sporting News*, August 1, 1912, 5.

73. James Jerpe, "On and Off the Field," *Gazette-Times*, July 20, 1912, 9.

74. James Jerpe, "On and Off the Field," *Gazette-Times*, July 19, 1912, 10.

75. James Jerpe, "On and Off the Field," *Gazette-Times*, July 26, 1912, 10.

76. James Jerpe, "On and Off the Field," *Gazette-Times*, August 4, 1912, 3.

77. Ralph S. Davis, "New Pirate Shines: Mensor Seems to Have Won His Job with Pittsburg," *Sporting News*, August 8, 1912, 2.

78. A.R. Cratty, "Pittsburgh Pencillings: Young Mensor Upholds Predictions Made by His Employer," *Sporting Life*, August 10, 1912, 3.

79. James Jerpe, "On and Off the Field," *Gazette-Times*, August 11, 1912, 2.

80. James Jerpe, "On and Off the Field," *Gazette-Times*, August 17, 1912, 9.

81. James Jerpe, "On and Off the Field," *Gazette-Times*, August 21, 1912, 11.
82. "Hail to the Chief!" *Gazette-Times*, August 27, 1912, 8.
83. "League Record in Triples Made by the Pirates: Buccaneers Likely to Establish New World's Mark This Year–Wilson's Great Work Has Helped," *Pittsburg Press*, September 1, 1912, 2.
84. James Jerpe, "On and Off the Field," *Gazette-Times*, September 2, 1912, 8.
85. James Jerpe, "On and Off the Field," *Gazette-Times*, September 4, 1912, 10.
86. James Jerpe, "On and Off the Field," *Gazette-Times*, September 7, 1912, 10.
87. W.J. O'Connor, "Notes of Saturday's Battle at St. Louis," *Pittsburg Press*, September 8, 1912, 2.
88. James Jerpe, "On and Off the Field," *Gazette-Times*, September 14, 1912, 10.
89. James Jerpe, "On and Off the Field," *Gazette-Times*, September 12, 1912, 11.
90. Ralph S. Davis, "Pittsburgh's Kick: Pirate Fans Have Again Proved Rank Quitters," *Sporting News*, October 5, 1911, 2.
91. Ralph S. Davis, "One Lie Is Nailed: Fred Clarke Will Continue as Pirate Leader," *Sporting News*, October 10, 1912, 2.
92. James Jerpe, "On and Off the Field," *Gazette-Times*, October 7, 1912, 8.
93. "National League News," *Sporting Life*, October 19, 1912, 10.
94. Ralph S. Davis, "Record Is Spoiled: Dreyfuss Hoped He Would Not Have a Holdout," *Sporting News*, February 20, 1913, 3.
95. A.R. Cratty, "Pittsburg Points: Solons Endeavor to Place Blame for Corsairs' Bad Season–Jiggers," *Sporting Life*, September 7, 1912, 7.
96. James Jerpe, "Corrected Figures Crown Wilson 'Three Base' King: Lajoie Falsely Credited with 43 Triples in 1903, Though He Made Only 13–Pirate with 36 Last Last Season Broke All Records," *Gazette-Times*, March 14, 1913, 12.
97. D. Wiley Whitten, Jr., *Champions of Naught Six: The Story of the 1906 Cleburne Railroaders*, (Fort Worth, Tex.: Minor League Press, 2010), 136.

CHAPTER 8

1. Larry D. Mansch, *Rube Marquard: The Life and Times of a Baseball Hall of Famer*, (Jefferson, N.C.: McFarland & Company, Inc., 1998), 8-9.
2. Ibid., 10.
3. Ibid., 12.
4. Ronald A. Mayer, *Christy Mathewson: A Game-By-Game Profile of a Legendary Pitcher*, (Jefferson, N.C.: McFarland & Company, Inc., 1993), 3.
5. Mansch, *Rube Marquard: The Life and Times of a Baseball Hall of Famer*, 13-15.
6. Ibid., 19.
7. Rob Neyer and Eddie Epstein, *Baseball Dynasties: The Greatest Teams of All Time*, (New York: W.W. Norton & Company, 2000), 75.
8. Christy Mathewson, "Pitching in a Pinch: Or Baseball from the Inside," *Sporting News*, December 12, 1912, 6.
9. "Champion Giants' Roster: Pitcher R.W. Marquard," *Sporting Life*, October 12, 1912, 10.
10. "Baseball By-Plays," *Sporting News*, October 19, 1911, 4.

11. "Caught on the Fly," Sporting News, February 16, 1911, 6.

12. Christy Mathewson, "Christy Mathewson's Stories of the Big Leaguers: Some Sides to Training Camp Routine," *Gazette-Times*, March 10, 1912, 5.

13. Mathewson, "Pitching in a Pinch: Or Baseball from the Inside," 6.

14. "Caught on the Fly," Sporting News, October 12, 1911, 4.

15. Mathewson, "Pitching in a Pinch: Or Baseball from the Inside," 6.

16. "Baseball By-Plays," *Sporting News*, September 28, 1911, 4.

17. T.H. Murnane, "Things That Hurt: Wrangling and Rowdyism of the World's Series," *Sporting News*, October 26, 1911, 1.

18. "Baseball By-Plays," *Sporting News*, November 16, 1911, 4.

19. "Caught on the Fly," *Sporting News*, October 26, 1911, 4.

20. W.J. M'Beth, "Think Chase Done: Gotham Fans Discount Denials by Farrell," *Sporting News*, November 23, 1911, 1.

21. W.J. McBeth, "At Least a Truce: Major League War Seems in a Simmering Mood," *Sporting News*, December 28, 1911, 1.

22. "McGraw's Opinion of Cubans," *Sporting News*, December 28, 1911, 2.

23. "National League," *Sporting News*, December 14, 1911, 6.

24. "National League," *Sporting News*, November 30, 1911, 7.

25. Harry Dix Cole, "New York News: The Death of Ex-Secretary Knowles Deplored," *Sporting Life*, February 10, 1912, 6.

26. W.J. McBeth, "Death of Knowles: It Came as a Shock to Friends in New York," *Sporting News*, February 8, 1912, 1.

27. "Fred Knowles Dead: Former Secretary of the New York Giants Passes Away at Denver," *Brooklyn Daily Eagle*, February 1, 1912, 3.

28. W.J. M'Beth, "Still a Fluttering: U.S. League Fails to Locate Its New York Park," *Sporting News*, February 15, 1912, 1.

29. W.J. M'Beth, "M'Graw Is Worried: Epidemic in Texas May Spoil Training Plans," *Sporting News*, February 1, 1912, 1.

30. W.J. M'Beth, "All off in Gotham: United States League Is Ready for the Mourners," *Sporting News*, February 22, 1912, 1.

31. W.J. M'Beth, "Interest Faraway: New York Fans Scan News from the Provinces," *Sporting News*, March 7, 1912, 1.

32. McBeth, "Giants Are Better: More Evenly Balanced Than the 1911 Champions," *Sporting News*, April 18, 1912, 1.

33. "National League," *Sporting News*, March 14, 1912, 7.

34. "National League," *Sporting News*, April 4, 1912, 7.

35. "The National League: The 1912 Championship Record–The 1912 Opening," *Sporting Life*, April 20, 1912, 10.

36. "The National League: The 1912 Championship Record–Games Played Tuesday, April 16," *Sporting Life*, April 27, 1912, 10.

37. "The National League: The 1912 Championship Record–Games Played Friday, April 19, 1912," *Sporting Life*, April 27, 1912, 10.

38. "The National League: The 1912 Championship Record–Games Played Saturday, April 20," *Sporting Life*, April 27, 1912, 10.

39. "The National League: The 1912 Championship Record—Games Played Wednesday, April 24," *Sporting Life*, May 4, 1912, 10.

40. W.J. McBeth, "Mr. Fogel's Stall: It Shows Where Fault Lies in Rules of the Game," *Sporting News*, May 2, 1912, 1.

41. "The National League: The 1912 Championship Record—Games Played Wednesday, May 1," *Sporting Life*, May 11, 1912, 10.

42. "The National League: The 1912 Championship Record—Games Played Tuesday, May 7," *Sporting Life*, May 18, 1912, 10.

43. "The National League: The 1912 Championship Record—Games Played Saturday, May 11," *Sporting Life*, May 18, 1912, 11.

44. "Caught on the Fly," *Sporting News*, May 9, 1912, 4.

45. "Caught on the Fly," *Sporting News*, May 16, 1912, 4.

46. Ralph S. Davis, "Pirate Fans Waver: Begin to Lose Heart at Showing of Their Team," *Sporting News*, May 23, 1912, 2.

47. "The National League: The 1912 Championship Record—Games Played Thursday, May 16," *Sporting Life*, May 25, 1912, 10.

48. Davis, "Pirate Fans Waver: Begin to Lose Heart at Showing of Their Team," 2.

49. "The National League: The 1912 Championship Record—Games Played Monday, May 20," *Sporting Life*, June 1, 1912, 10.

50. "The National League: The 1912 Championship Record—Games Played Friday, May 24," *Sporting Life*, June 1, 1912, 10.

51. "The National League: The 1912 Championship Record—Games Played Thursday, May 30 (A.M.)," *Sporting Life*, June 8, 1912, 10.

52. "The National League: The 1912 Championship Record—Games Played Monday, June 3," *Sporting Life*, June 15, 1912, 10.

53. "Giants' Star Heaver Has Won 11 Straight Games," *Pittsburg Press*, June 4, 1912, 18.

54. "The National League: The 1912 Championship Record—Games Played Saturday, June 8," *Sporting Life*, June 15, 1912, 10-11.

55. "The National League: The 1912 Championship Record—Games Played Wednesday, June 12," *Sporting Life*, June 22, 1912, 10.

56. Ralph Davis, "Ralph Davis' Column," *Pittsburg Press*, June 14, 1912, 26.

57. "The National League: The 1912 Championship Record—Games Played Monday, June 17," *Sporting Life*, June 29, 1912, 10.

58. Ren Mulford, Jr., "Redbugs Wail: Feeling Fan Pulse among Rhinelanders," *Sporting Life*, June 22, 1912, 9.

59. "National League News," *Sporting Life*, June 15, 1912, 11.

60. "The National League: The 1912 Championship Record—Games Played Wednesday, June 19," *Sporting Life*, June 29, 1912, 10.

61. "Rube Marquard Aims to Beat Some Great Records: Giant Star Only Four Games Away from Record Made by Luby, of Chicago, in 1890," *Pittsburg Press*, June 23, 1912, 4.

62. "The Rube and the Records," *Sporting News*, June 27, 1912, 3.

63. W.J. McBeth, "No Mercy for Star: M'Graw Gives Marquard Tough Assignments," *Sporting News*, June 27, 1912, 2.
64. "The National League: The 1912 Championship Record–Games Played Friday, June 21," *Sporting Life*, June 29, 1912, 11.
65. Ralph S. Davis, "Hush Their Knocks: Hammers Laid Away as Pirates Win Some Games," *Sporting News*, June 27, 1912, 1.
66. "National League News in Short Metre," *Sporting Life*, July 6, 1912, 4.
67. "The National League: The 1912 Championship Record–Games Played Tuesday, June 25," *Sporting Life*, July 6, 1912, 10.
68. "The National League: The 1912 Championship Record–Games Played Saturday, June 29," *Sporting Life*, July 6, 1912, 11.
69. "The National League: The 1912 Championship Record–Games Played Wednesday, July 3," *Sporting Life*, July 13, 1912, 9.
70. Ed F. Bang, "Rube Marquard's Pa, Ma and Grandma Are His Most Ardent Rooters," *Pittsburg Press*, July 7, 1912, 2.
71. "Sports: Marquard Lost Till He Learned to 'Cut Loose and Let'er Go,'" *Pittsburg Press*, July 11, 1912, 15.
72. Rube Marquard, "Tips to Kids," *Pittsburg Press*, July 11, 1912, 15.
73. I.E. Sanborn, "Don't Forget Cubs: They're the Team That Greased Slide for Giants," *Sporting News*, July 18, 1912, 1.
74. "Caught on the Fly," *Sporting News*, July 18, 1912, 4.
75. "National League: Standing on Tuesday Morning," *Sporting News*, July 18, 1912, 5.
76. Sam Crane, "Modest Pitcher Hero: The Sensational Marquard, Who Was Stopped by the Cubs After 19 Consecutive Victories, and Thereby Deprived of the Opportunity to Establish a New Record, Has No Censure for Poor Support," *Sporting Life*, July 20, 1912, 1.
77. "National League: Standing on Tuesday Morning," July 18, 1912, 5.
78. "A Regrettable Incident," *Sporting Life*, July 20, 1912, 1.
79. Crane, "Modest Pitching Hero: The Sensational Marquard, Who Was Stopped by the Cubs After 19 Consecutive Victories, and Thereby Deprived of the Opportunity to Establish a New Record, Has No Censure for Poor Support," 1.
80. "Marquard Feat: Cost Him Dear in Strain Upon His Nerves," *Sporting Life*, July 27, 1912, 4.
81. Mansch, *Rube Marquard: The Life and Times of a Baseball Hall of Famer*, 108-110.
82. "National League News in Short Metre," *Sporting Life*, September 21, 1912, 8.
83. "Shirley Kellogg and Rube Marquard Wed," *Pittsburg Press*, September 17, 1912, 19.
84. "World's Series Notes," *Sporting Life*, October 19, 1912, 7.
85. "No Honors for Giants," *Sporting Life*, October 26, 1912, 8.
86. Jeffrey M. Katz, *Plie Ball: Baseball Meets Dance on Stage and Screen*, (Jefferson, N.C.: McFarland & Company, Inc., 2016), 33.

87. "Where Bills Change Weekly: Rube Marquard at the Victoria–John J. McGraw at the Colonial," *The Sun*, October 27, 1912, 4.

88. W.J. M'Beth, "Still on the Map: Much Base Ball News to Come Out of New York," *Sporting News*, November 7, 1912, 1.

89. Bozeman Bulger, "McGraw and Marquard Reach Parting of the Ways: Only Theatrically, However," *The World*, October 28, 1912, 12.

90. "Rube Marquard Guards Blossom from Irate Hubby: Giants' Pitcher Goes to Police Court with Her to Get Summons for Kane," *The World*, October 29, 1912, 1.

91. "Domestic Discord: Pitcher Marquard Still 'Mixing Them Up,' Though the World's Series Is Over–Alleged to Be the Cause of Friction in the Kane Household," *Sporting Life*, November 9, 1912, 4.

92. "Giant Pitcher Pays $2,254 for a Wife," *Rock Island Argus*, October 17, 1913, 3.

93. "'Rube' Eludes Detectives: Famous Pitcher Now a Fugitive from New Jersey Justice," *New-York Tribune*, November 9, 1912, 5.

94. "Rube Marquard Flees in an Auto from Irate Hubby: Surprised with His Leading Lady in an Atlantic City Hotel," *The World*, November 8, 1912, 1.

95. "Marquard Flees to Escape Arrest: Giant Pitcher Found in Hotel Room by Husband of Actress," *Bridgeport Evening Farmer*, November 9, 1912, 7.

96. "Marquard Sued for $25,000: Joe Kane Says Rube Stole Blossom Seeley's Affections," *The Sun*, November 14, 1912, 1.

97. "'Rube' Denies Fascination," *New-York Tribune*, November 20, 1912, 9.

98. "Caught on the Fly," *Sporting News*, November 28, 1912, 6.

99. "National League News in Short Metre," *Sporting Life*, November 30, 1912, 11.

100. "Sport Doings," *Day Book*, December 13, 1912, 10.

101. "The High Spots from the Sporting World," *Day Book*, December 16, 1912, 13.

102. W.J. O'Connor, "Marquard Says McGraw Is Jealous: Pitcher for Giants Says Manager Is Peeved Because Marquard Has Better Vaudeville Act–Will Become Farmer If He Doesn't Get $10,000 Salary," *El Paso Herald*, December 16, 1912, 7.

103. "Caught on the Fly," *Sporting News*, December 19, 1912, 6.

104. "Caught on the Fly," *Sporting News*, December 5, 1912, 6.

105. "Seeley's Spouse Gets Decree in 20 Minutes: Court Quickly Decides Suit in Which 'Rube' Marquard, of 'Giants,' Figured," *New-York Tribune*, January 16, 1913, 7.

106. "Tiresome Talk Says McGraw," *Sporting Life*, December 21, 1912, 9.

107. "Brush Dead: End Came While on Train," *Sporting News*, November 28, 1912, 1.

108. "Rube Marquard and Blossom Seeley to Be Married Today," *Los Angeles Evening Herald*, March 12, 1913, 11.

109. "When Marquard Signed to Pitch for N.Y.," *Day Book*, March 25, 1913, 19-20.

110. "Giant Pitcher Pays $2,254 for a Wife," 3.

CHAPTER 9

1. "Tris Speaker Has No System; He Is Just a Natural Hitter," *El Paso Herald*, August 21, 1912, 10.
2. "Tris Speaker Writes a History of His Life," *Baseball Magazine*, January, 1913, 92.
3. "American League Notes," *Sporting Life*, August 24, 1912, 13.
4. Glenn Stout, *Fenway 1912: The Birth of a Ballpark, a Championship Season, and Fenway's Remarkable First Year*, (Boston: Houghton Mifflin Harcourt, 2011), 7.
5. "Tris Speaker Writes a History of His Life," 92.
6. "Tris Speaker Has No System: He Is Just a Natural Hitter," 10.
7. Stout, *Fenway 1912: The Birth of a Ballpark, a Championship Season, and Fenway's Remarkable First Year*, 7.
8. Monty, "Speaker May Be New World Star," *Evening Standard*, August 23, 1912, 2.
9. Stout, *Fenway 1912: The Birth of a Ballpark, a Championship Season, and Fenway's Remarkable First Year*, 7.
10. Monty, "Speaker May Be New World Star," 2.
11. T.H. Murnane "Speaker's Case: Remarkable Experience of the Boston Club with This Player," *Sporting Life*, September 26, 1908, 9.
12. Stout, *Fenway 1912: The Birth of a Ballpark, a Championship Season, and Fenway's Remarkable First Year*, 7-8.
13. Murnane, "Speaker's Case: Remarkable Experience of the Boston Club with This Player," 9.
14. "Honorable Action: Of the Little Rock Club in the Matter of Outfielder Speaker," *Sporting Life*, September 5, 1908, 23.
15. Murnane, "Speaker's Case: Remarkable Experience of the Boston Club with This Player," 9.
16. "Honorable Action: Of the Little Rock Club in the Matter of Outfielder Speaker," 23.
17. Murnane, "Speaker's Case: Remarkable Experience of the Boston Club with This Player," 9.
18. "American League Notes," *Sporting Life*, August 29, 1908, 11.
19. Stout, *Fenway 1912: The Birth of a Ballpark, a Championship Season, and Fenway's Remarkable First Year*, 8.
20. "Wise Sayings of Great Men," *Sporting Life*, December 5, 1908, 4.
21. Paul J. Zingg, *Harry Hooper: An American Baseball Life*, (Urbana, Ill.: University Of Illinois Press, 2004), 82.
22. "American League," *Sporting News*, November 9, 1911, 6.
23. T.H. Murnane, "Russell Will Sell: Health Makes Boston Magnate Give Up His Club," *Sporting News*, November 16, 1911, 2.
24. "Caught on the Fly," *Sporting News*, November 2, 1911, 4.
25. "American League," *Sporting News*, November 16, 1911, 7.

26. T.H. Murnane, "Scattering Beans: Boston Players and Fans Quit Game for Winter," *Sporting News*, November 9, 1911, 5.

27. T.H. Murnane, "Boston under Way: Red Sox Organize and Braves Get a Manager," *Sporting News*, January 11, 1912, 2.

28. "American League News in Nut-Shells," *Sporting Life*, January 20, 1912, 7.

29. T.H. Murnane, "One Brave Is Out: Bill Sweeney Refuses to Sign Boston Contract," *Sporting News*, February 29, 1912, 1.

30. A.H.C. Marshall, "Boston Brief's: The Braves Virtually Marooned at Augusta, Ga.," *Sporting Life*, March 23, 1912, 8.

31. T.H. Murnane, "Tim Shifts Dates: Murnane Drops in to See How Red Sox Fare," *Sporting News*, March 21, 1912, 5.

32. "American League News in Nut-Shells," *Sporting Life*, March 30, 1912, 13.

33. T.H. Murnane, "Murnane Musings: He Has Become Firm Convert to Hot Springs," *Sporting News*, March 28, 1912, 2.

34. "American League," *Sporting News*, April 4, 1912, 7.

35. Murnane, "Murnane Musings: He Has Become Firm Convert to Hot Springs," 2.

36. "American League," April 4, 1912, 7.

37. T.H. Murnane, "Murnane Is Amazed: Takes Off His Hat to New Park at Cincinnati," *Sporting News*, April 11, 1912, 2.

38. "The American League: The 1912 Championship Record–Start of the 1912 Race," *Sporting Life*, April 20, 1912, 12.

39. "The American League: The 1912 Championship Record–Games Played Friday, April 12," *Sporting Life*, April 20, 1912, 12.

40. "The American League: The 1912 Championship Record–Games Played Tuesday, April 16, 1912," *Sporting Life*, April 27, 1912, 12.

41. T.H. Murnane, "Red Sox Hit Hard: Bad Weather Cost M'Aleer Three Good Days," *Sporting News*, April 25, 1912, 2.

42. "The American League: The 1912 Championship Record–Games Played Saturday, April 20," *Sporting Life*, April 27, 1912, 12.

43. "The American League: The 1912 Championship Record–Games Played Friday, April 26," *Sporting Life*, May 4, 1912, 12.

44. "The American League: The 1912 Championship Record–Games Played Saturday, April 27," *Sporting Life*, May 4, 1912, 12.

45. "The American League: The 1912 Championship Record–Games Played Tuesday, April 30," *Sporting Life*, May 11, 1912, 12.

46. T.H. Murnane, "Ward Flingers Off: Hub Perdue Only One to Show Real Class to Date," *Sporting News*, May 2, 1912, 2.

47. T.H. Murnane, "Boston's Odd Ways: Reasons for Poor Patronage at New Fenway Park," *Sporting News*, May 16, 1912, 1.

48. "Knockers and Their Vicious Criticism Hurt Ball Players: Tris Speaker Was Turned Down by Comiskey," *Evening Times* (Grand Forks, North Dakota), May 3, 1912, 3.

49. "The American League: The 1912 Championship Record–Games Played Wednesday, May 1," *Sporting Life*, May 11, 1912, 12.

50. "The American League: The 1912 Championship Record–Games Played Thursday, May 2," *Sporting Life*, May 11, 1912, 12.

51. "The American League: The 1912 Championship Record–Games Played Saturday, May 4," *Sporting Life*, May 11, 1912, 13.

52. "Will Hal Chase Figure in Trade?: Report That New York First Sacker Will Be Swapped for Speaker or Johnson," *Bridgeport Evening Farmer*, May 9, 1912, 8.

53. "The American League: The 1912 Championship Record–Games Played Friday, May 17," *Sporting Life*, May 25, 1912, 12.

54. "The American League: The 1912 Championship Record–Games Played Thursday, May 23," *Sporting Life*, June 1, 1912, 12.

55. "The American League: The 1912 Championship Record–Games Played Monday, May 27," *Sporting Life*, June 8, 1912, 12.

56. "Speaker after Record," *Republican News Item*, May 31, 1912, 5.

57. "The American League: The 1912 Championship Record–Games Played Tuesday, June 4," *Sporting Life*, June 15, 1912, 12.

58. "The American League: The 1912 Championship Record–Games Played Thursday, June 6," *Sporting Life*, June 15, 1912, 12.

59. "The American League: The 1912 Championship Record–Games Played Sunday, June 9," *Sporting Life*, June 15, 1912, 13.

60. "The American League: The 1912 Championship Record–Games Played Thursday, June 13," *Sporting Life*, June 22, 1912, 12.

61. T.H. Murnane, "Red Sox Go to Top: But Gifts and Feasting Are Big Item with Murnane," *Sporting News*, June 20, 1912, 2.

62. "The American League: The 1912 Championship Record–Games Played Wednesday, June 26," *Sporting Life*, July 6, 1912, 12.

63. "The American League: The 1912 Championship Record–Games Played Thursday June 27," *Sporting Life*, July 6, 1912, 12.

64. "The American League: The 1912 Championship Record–Games Played Saturday, June 29," *Sporting Life*, July 6, 1912, 13.

65. "Sporting Notes: Can Throw Straight–Tris Speaker Is Popular with Players and Fans," *Bemidji Daily Pioneer*, June 26, 1912, 4.

66. "The American League: The 1912 Championship Record–Games Played Wednesday, July 3," *Sporting Life*, July 13, 1912, 12.

67. "Is Tris New King?: If Boston Wins Pennant He Will Be So Declared," *Topeka State Journal*, July 9, 1912, 3.

68. T.H. Murnane, "Boston Back Again: Red Sox Have Put Old Town on Base Ball Map," *Sporting News*, July 11, 1912, 2.

69. "American League: The 1912 Championship Record–Games Played Friday, July 12," *Sporting Life*, July 20, 1912, 12.

70. "M'Aleer's Mind: Is Now Relieved on an Important Question," *Sporting Life*, July 20, 1912, 2.

71. "Speaker Clouts Homer in Tenth: Great Outfielder Wins for Boston by Driving Ball into Bleachers," *Sunday Star*, July 28, 1912, 1.

72. "'When Wood Slumps Red Sox Will Blow': Boss of the Climbers Says Boston Hurler Is Sure to Get His Bumps," *Washington Herald*, July 30, 1912, 8.

73. "Baseball Briefs," *Bismarck Daily Tribune*, August 14, 1912, 3.

74. "Mother Wants Tris," *Santa Fe New Mexican*, August 15, 1912, 4.

75. Norman M. Walker, "Borderland Auto Road Race Might Wind Up in El Paso with Good Profit: Tris Speaker Dragged into a Sob Story," *El Paso Herald*, August 20, 1912, 7.

76. T.H. Murnane, "A Century His Aim: Stahl Thinks 100 Games Will Win Flag for Red Sox," *Sporting News*, August 22, 1912, 2.

77. T.H. Murnane, "Murnane Says Tris Speaker Is World's Best Ball Player," *Salt Lake Tribune*, August 25, 1912, 1.

78. "The American League: The 1912 Championship Record–Games Played Tuesday, August 27," *Sporting Life*, September 7, 1912, 11.

79. "Taylor Is Largely Responsible for Boston's Success: Gathered Much of the Material Which Stahl Has Developed," *Washington Times*, September 5, 1912, 12.

80. "In the World of Sport: Three Stars in Great Race," *Arizona Republican*, September 8, 1912, 11.

81. T.H. Murnane, "Honors Go to Wood: Red Sox Star Beats Johnson in Challenge Battle," *Sporting News*, September 12, 1912, 1.

82. "The American League: The 1912 Championship Record–Games Played Friday, September 6," *Sporting Life*, September 14, 1912, 12.

83. "The American League: The 1912 Championship Record–Games Played Sunday, September 15," *Sporting Life*, September 21, 1912, 13.

84. "American League News in Nut-Shells," *Sporting Life*, September 21, 1912, 9.

85. "Speaker Bats Strong: Johnson Says He Has No Weakness at the Bat," *Evening Times* (Grand Forks, North Dakota), September 23, 1912, 3.

86. "American League: Standing on Tuesday Morning," *Sporting News*, September 26, 1912, 6.

87. "The American League: The 1912 Championship Record–Games Played Thursday, September 19," *Sporting Life*, September 28, 1912, 10.

88. "The American League: The 1912 Championship Record–Games Played Friday, September 20," *Sporting Life*, September 28, 1912, 10.

89. "Give Carrigan and Wagner Credit for Flag," *Bridgeport Evening Farmer*, September 17, 1912, 7.

90. "McAleer Rates Tris Speaker More Valuable Than Ty Cobb," *El Paso Herald*, September 18, 1912, 9.

91. "The American League: The 1912 Championship Record–Games Played Saturday, September 21," *Sporting Life*, September 28, 1912, 11.

92. "Chance Is Now in Line to Manage the Yankees: Batting Crown Again for Cobb," *Brooklyn Daily Eagle*, November 11, 1912, 2.

93. "Doyle and Speaker Voted Most Valuable Men," *Day Book*, October 4, 1912, 9.

94. "Tris Speaker and Larry Doyle Most Valuable to Teams," *Cairo Bulletin*, October 4, 1912, 3.

95. "Doyle and Speaker Voted Most Valuable Men," 9.

96. T.H. Murnane, "Through Tim's Eyes: World's Series Incidents Seen by Veteran Writer," *Sporting News*, October 17, 1912, 1.

97. "Sizzling Rally Fails to Hold off New York: Doubting Thomases 'Shown' by '$11,000 Lemon' That He Has the Goods," *San Francisco Call*, October 11, 1912, 11.

98. Gerald C. Wood, *Smoky Joe Wood: The Biography of a Baseball Legend*, (Lincoln, Neb.: University Of Nebraska Press, 2013), 147-148.

99. "Interesting Side-Lights on Big Battles; Also Incidents Noticed After the Games," *Sporting News*, October 24, 1912, 2.

100. "Tris Speaker Writes a History of His Life," 92.

CHAPTER 10

1. Charles F. Faber and Richard B. Faber, *Spitballers: The Last Legal Hurlers of the Wet One*, (Jefferson, N.C.: McFarland & Company, Inc., 2006), 120.

2. F.C. Lane, "'Dutch' Leonard's Three Ambitions: The Remarkable Achievements of a Twenty-Four-Year-Old Star," *Baseball Magazine*, November 1916, 48.

3. Faber and Faber, *Spitballers: The Last Legal Hurlers of the Wet One*, 120.

4. Lane, "'Dutch' Leonard's Three Ambitions: The Remarkable Achievements of a Twenty-Four-Year-Old Star," 48.

5. Faber and Faber, *Spitballers: The Last Legal Hurlers of the Wet One*, 120.

6. Lane, "'Dutch' Leonard's Three Ambitions: The Remarkable Achievements of a Twenty-Four-Year-Old Star," 48.

7. "American League News in Nut-Shells," *Sporting Life*, April 6, 1912, 13.

8. "Baseball By-Plays," *Sporting News*, April 15, 1915, 4.

9. Grant T. Reeves, "Echoes from Field and Club House: Calling Down the Manager—Handing One to Jesse," *Baseball Magazine*, September 1915, 67.

10. A.H.C. Mitchell, "Boston's Budget: Manager Stahl Settles an Important Matter," *Sporting Life*, January 25, 1913, 7.

11. "News Gathered from All Quarters," *Sporting Life*, November 16, 1912, 3.

12. Lane, "'Dutch' Leonard's Three Ambitions: The Remarkable Achievements of a Twenty-Four-Year-Old Star," 48-49.

13. Francis Eaton, "Deal for Red Sox Still Hangs Fire: Taylors Would Retire from an Active Part," *Sporting News*, November 6, 1913, 3.

14. Eaton, "Boston Says Farewell to M'Aleer as Boss of Red Sox: No Regrets Cabled to Jimmy," *Sporting News*, December 4, 1913, 1.

15. "New Red Sox Boss Started as Bell Boy," *Sporting News*, December 11, 1913, 5.

16. Eaton, "Boston Says Farewell to M'Aleer as Boss of Red Sox: No Regrets Cabled to Jimmy," 1.

17. "Late News Items: President Johnson Denies Sale," *Sporting News*, December 4, 1913, 1.

18. Eaton, "Boston Says Farewell to M'Aleer as Boss of Red Sox: No Regrets Cabled to Jimmy," 1.

19. Francis Eaton, "Lannin Is Elected President of Sox: Purchaser of M'Aleer's Stock Takes His Place," *Sporting News*, December 25, 1913, 1.

20. "Late News Items: Lannin Will Be President of Sox," *Sporting News*, December 4, 1913, 1.

21. Francis Eaton, "Boston Stirred Up Considerably: Much Happens in Base Ball Way in the Hub," *Sporting News*, January 15, 1914, 1.

22. Francis Eaton, "Red Sox Show No Jealousy of Tris: Team Mates Glad to See Him Land Big Money," *Sporting News*, March 12, 1914, 1.

23. Francis Eaton, "Red Sox Better but for Pitchers: Even in That Department They May Get By," *Sporting News*, March 19, 1914, 1.

24. Francis Eaton, "Boston Teams on Ways Homeward: Red Sox, Barring Wagner and Wood, Are Ready," *Sporting News*, April 2, 1914, 1.

25. "Caught on the Fly," *Sporting News*, April 9, 1914, 6.

26. Francis Eaton, "Boston Hopeful but Not Boastful in Its Claims: Third Place Would Satisfy," *Sporting News*, April 9, 1914, 1.

27. Francis Eaton, "Think They Can Stage a World's Series in Boston: Both Hub Teams in Dreamland," *Sporting News*, April 16, 1914, 1.

28. "The American League: The Junior League's Start," *Sporting Life*, April 18, 1914, 8.

29. "The American League: 1914 Championship Record–Games Played Friday, April 17," *Sporting Life*, April 25, 1914, 8.

30. Thomas Kirby, "Boehling Shows He Has Developed Into Star of Big Show: Boehling Shows Poise in Work on Slab That Was Missing in 1913," *Washington Times*, April 18, 1914, 12.

31. "The American League: 1914 Championship Record–Games Played Tuesday, April 21," *Sporting Life*, May 2, 1914, 8.

32. "Pitchers' Battle Ends When Darkness Comes," *Washington Times*, April 22, 1914, 14.

33. Francis Eaton, "Making Allowances: But Truth to Tell Boston Fans Are a Bit Disappointed at Showing by Their Ball Teams," *Sporting News*, April 30, 1914, 1.

34. "The American League: 1914 Championship Record–Games Played Wednesday, April 29," *Sporting Life*, May 9, 1914, 8.

35. "The American League: 1914 Championship Record–Games Played Monday, May 4," *Sporting Life*, May 9, 1914, 9.

36. "The American League: 1914 Championship Record–Games Played Friday, May 8," *Sporting Life*, May 16, 1914, 8.

37. "New Yorks Shut out by Red Sox in Drizzle- - -Federal League Now Preparing to Change Circuit: Keating Falters at End; Not so Leonard," *The Sun*, May 9, 1914, 10.

38. Francis Eaton, "Red Sox in Stride as West Appears: Outlook Clears for Carrigan's Uncertain Crew," *Sporting News*, May 14, 1914, 1.

39. "The American League: 1914 Championship Record–Games Played Thursday, May 14," *Sporting Life*, May 23, 1914, 8.

40. J. Ed Grillo, "Pertinent Comment on Happenings in Sportdom," *Evening Star*, May 15, 1914, 19.

41. Francis Eaton, "Lannin to Play to Game's Real Fans: More Quarter Seats and a Roof over Them," *Sporting News*, May 21, 1914, 1.

42. "The American League: 1914 Championship Record–Games Played Saturday, May 23," *Sporting Life*, May 30, 1914, 9.

43. "American League: Standing on Tuesday Morning," *Sporting News*, June 4, 1914, 5.

44. Francis Eaton, "Boston Again Finds Glory in Its Diamond Athletes: Braves Start on the Warpath," *Sporting News*, June 18, 1914, 1.

45. "The American League: 1914 Championship Record–Games Played Sunday, June 14," *Sporting Life*, June 20, 1914, 9.

46. "The American League: 1914 Championship Record–Games Played Thursday, June 18," *Sporting Life*, June 27, 1914, 8.

47. Francis Eaton, "Braves Make First Division Motions: Climbing Fast out of Cold Cellar Berth," *Sporting News*, June 25, 1914, 1.

48. Francis Eaton, "Feds Disturb Even Tenor of Red Sox: Outlaw Offers Take Players' Minds off Work," *Sporting News*, July 2, 1914, 1.

49. Francis Eaton, "Red Sox Make Jam of American Race: Mackmen Forced into Bunch by Carrigan Comers," *Sporting News*, July 9, 1914, 1.

50. "The American League: 1914 Championship Record–Games Played Wednesday, June 24," *Sporting Life*, July 4, 1914, 8.

51. "The American League: 1914 Championship Record–Games Played Friday, June 26," *Sporting Life*, July 4, 1914, 9.

52. "The American League: 1914 Championship Record–Games Played Monday, June 29," *Sporting Life*, July 11, 1914, 8.

53. "The American League: 1914 Championship Record–Games Played Thursday, July 2," *Sporting Life*, July 11, 1914, 8.

54. "The American League: 1914 Championship Record–Games Played Wednesday, July 8," *Sporting Life*, July 18, 1914, 8.

55. Francis Eaton, "Red Sox Lack Red Neck Stuff in Work: Entirely Too Gentle to Cope with Opponents," *Sporting News*, July 16, 1914, 1.

56. "The American League: 1914 Championship Record–Games Played Saturday, July 11," *Sporting Life*, July 18, 1914, 9.

57. "The American League: 1914 Championship Record–Games Played Wednesday, July 15," *Sporting Life*, July 25, 1914, 8.

58. "The American League: 1914 Championship Record–Games Played Monday, July 20," *Sporting Life*, August 1, 1914, 8.

59. "The American League: 1914 Championship Record–Games Played Monday, July 27," *Sporting Life*, August 8, 1914, 8.

60. "The American League: 1914 Championship Record–Games Played Wednesday July 29," *Sporting Life*, August 8, 1914, 8.

61. "The American League: 1914 Championship Record–Games Played Friday, July 31," *Sporting Life*, August 8, 1914, 9.

62. Tim Murnane, "Murnane Admits a Bee in His Bonnet: Can't See Where Any Team Has It on the Braves," *Sporting News*, August 6, 1914, 3.

63. "American League: Standing on Tuesday Morning," *Sporting News*, August 27, 1914, 5.

64. "The American League: 1914 Championship Record–Games Played Wednesday, August 5," *Sporting Life*, August 15, 1914, 8.

65. "The American League: 1914 Championship Record–Games Played Sunday, August 9," *Sporting Life*, August 15, 1914, 9.

66. "Carrigan Has Great Praise for Leonard," *Bridgeport Evening Farmer*, August 19, 1914, 7.

67. "American League Notes," *Sporting Life*, August 15, 1914, 10.

68. "'Dutch' Leonard Keeps Red Sox in Flag Race: Manager Carrigan Gives Much Credit to Southpaw for Boston's Present Showing," *Washington Times*, August 10, 1914, 10.

69. "Lone Run Gives Yankees Victory: Fisher Has a Shade Over 'Dutchy' Leonard in Pitching Duel," *New York Tribune*, August 14, 1914, 8.

70. "American League: Standing on Tuesday Morning," August 27, 1914, 5.

71. The American League: 1914 Championship Record–Games Played Wednesday, August 19," *Sporting Life*, August 29, 1914, 8.

72. "The American League: 1914 Championship Record–Games Played Friday, August 28," *Sporting Life*, September 5, 1914, 9.

73. T.H. Murnane, "Lannin's Ax Sharp for All Dead Wood: Loafers and Holdup Men Not Wanted on Team," *Sporting News*, September 3, 1914, 1.

74. "'Dutch' Leonard May Be out Rest of Year," *Washington Times*, September 3, 1914, 10.

75. "'Dutch' Leonard Is on Hospital List with Broken Hand," *Detroit Free Press*, September 5, 1914, 10.

76. "To-Day's Chat," *Franklin Evening News*, September 9, 1914, 3.

77. "'Dutch' Leonard Is Hurt: Capable Boston Pitcher Disabled in Rough House," *Daily Northwestern*, September 5, 1914, 12.

78. "Dutch Leonard Is on the Shelf: Friendly Wrestling Match Incapacitates Big Heaver," *Los Angeles Times*, September 25, 1914, 3.

79. "Is Baseball All Luck? Is It?: Read This Story of Dutch Leonard, Then Ponder a Moment," *Tulsa Daily World*, July 11, 1915, 7.

80. T.H. Murnane, "Tim Proclaims a New Allegiance: King M'Graw Is Dead, Long Live King Stallings," *Sporting News*, October 1, 1914, 1.

81. J.C. O'Leary, "No Baseball in Carrigan's Visit: But He Isn't Averse to Talking of Red Sox as Likely 1915 Champions," *Boston Evening Globe*, December 11, 1914, 7.

82. "American League Notes," *Sporting Life*, July 4, 1914, 10.

83. A.H.C. Mitchell, "The Red Sox: Only in Fair Shape, Thanks to Minor Injuries to Players–The Pitching Department the Problem of Greatest Concern to Manager Carrigan," *Sporting Life*, May 1, 1915, 8.

84. A.H.C. Mitchell, "Boston Red Sox: The Sensational Outburst of Pitcher Hubert Leonard Elicits a Prompt, Complete and Crushing Answer from President Lannin," *Sporting Life*, June 5, 1915, 9.

85. "Say Red Sox Owner Tries to Boss Team," *Bridgeport Evening Farmer*, May 29, 1915, 8.

86. "Mix-Up among Red Sox: Pitcher Leonard Claims President Lannin Is Running Club," *Evening Star*, May 27, 1915, 21.

87. "Say Red Sox Owner Tries to Boss Team," 8.

88. Mitchell, "Boston Red Sox: The Sensational Outburst of Pitcher Hubert Leonard Elicits a Prompt, Complete and Crushing Answer from President Lannin," 9.

89. T.H. Murnane, "Leonard's Attack Puts Lannin Wise: Gets a New Idea of Qualities of Some Players," *Sporting News*, June 3, 1915, 1.

90. "The Leonard Sequel: The Suspended Red Sox Pitcher Declares That Being in Presidential Disfavor, He Wants to Be Traded to Another Club," *Sporting Life*, June 12, 1915, 9.

91. T.H. Murnane, "Rowland in Good with Boston Fans: Incident Shows Sportsmanship of Chicago Leader," *Sporting News*, June 10, 1915, 1.

92. "Dutch Leonard, Old A. L. Hurler, Dies," *Brooklyn Eagle*, July 12, 1952, 7.

93. Alan Schwarz, *The Numbers Game: Baseball's Lifelong Fascination with Statistics*, (New York: Thomas Dunne Books–St. Martin's Press, 2004), 166-167.

CHAPTER 11

1. Dan Holmes, *Ty Cobb: A Biography–Baseball's All-Time Greatest Hitters*, (Westport, Conn.: Greenwood Press, 2004), 1-3.

2. "A Chapter from Cobb's Career: The Beginning of a Marvelous Record on the Diamond," *Baseball Magazine*, March 1912, 79-80.

3. Holmes, *Ty Cobb: A Biography–Baseball's All-Time Greatest Hitters*, 6-7.

4. Jonathan Weeks, *Baseball's Most Notorious Personalities: A Gallery of Rogues*, (Lanham, Md.: The Scarecrow Press, Inc.–Rowman & Littlefield, 2013), 176.

5. Holmes, *Ty Cobb: A Biography–Baseball's All-Time Greatest Hitters*, 9.

6. "By His Wife: Who Mistook Him for a Burglar, the Somnambulist Georgia Senator Was Shot Dead," *Cairo Bulletin*, August 11, 1905, 1.

7. "Charged with Murder: Mrs. Cobb Mistook Her Husband for a Burglar, Is Arrested," *Waterbury Evening Democrat*, August 11, 1905, 5.

8. "Woman Arrested at Grave: She Is Suspected of Murdering Her Husband," *Evening Star*, August 11, 1905, 16.

9. Joe S. Jackson, "Cold Shoulder For Tiger Brigade: Weather Man Refused Our Boys Farewell Augusta Game–Detroiters Bid Good-Bye to Training Camp Today–Visit Has Been Fairly Satisfactory–Players All in Pretty Fair Condition–Cobb's Mother Acquitted of Murder," *Detroit Free Press*, April 1, 1906, 13.

10. "American League: The Championship Record–Games Played Wednesday, August 30," *Sporting Life*, September 9, 1905, 6.

11. Ralph S. Davis, "Pittsburg Packed: Fans Eager to See Games in Smoky City," *Sporting News*, October 14, 1909, 1.

12. "Gossip of the Players," *Sporting News*, November 4, 1909, 4.

13. "Caught on the Fly," *Sporting News*, October 26, 1911, 4.

14. Mark S. Halfon, *Tales from the Deadball Era: Ty Cobb, Home Run Baker, Shoeless Joe Jackson, and the Wildest Times in Baseball History*, (Lincoln, Neb.: Potomac Books–University of Nebraska Press, 2014), 12-13.

15. Hugh Jennings–Manager of the Detroit American Club, "My Opinion of Ty Cobb: How the Greatest Player in the History of the Game Looks to His Own Manager," *Baseball Magazine*, March 1912, 15-16.

16. "Baseball By-Plays," *Sporting News*, February 15, 1912, 4.

17. Charles Leerhsen, *Ty Cobb: A Terrible Beauty*, (New York: Simon & Schuster, 2015), 280.

18. "Cobb Runs Amuck in Butcher Shop: Pulls Pistol on Proprietor in Row over Fish, Then Beats Youth," *Detroit Times*, June 22, 1914, 7.

19. "Cobb in Trouble: The High-Salaried Detroit Star Not Only Arrested for a Fight with a 'Butcher Boy' but Disabled for Play with a Broken Thumb," *Sporting Life*, June 27, 1914, 10.

20. "American League: Standing on Tuesday Morning," Sporting News, July 2, 1914, 5.

21. H.G. Salsinger, "Tigers Start Late to Gulfport Camp: Their Stay, However, Will Be as Long as Usual," Sporting News, December 3, 1914, 3.

22. H.G. Salsinger, "Detroit Snug as Blizzards Blow: Base Ball Storms Do Not Touch Tigertown," *Sporting News*, December 10, 1914, 3.

23. H.G. Salsinger, "Detroit Figures in the Story of Kauff: Might Be a Tiger If He Had Not Jumped to the Feds," *Sporting News*, December 17, 1914, 5.

24. H.G. Salsinger, "What Does Ruppert Want in This Life: Half Million Dollars' Worth of Advertising Already," *Sporting News*, December 24, 1914, 6.

25. "Jennings Not So Popular with Detroit Owners," *Bridgeport Evening Farmer*, April 7, 1915, 14.

26. "Press Pointers: A Word to Ty Cobb," *Sporting Life*, January 2, 1915, 14.

27. H.G. Salsinger, "Early Tigers Go South This Week: Favored Few Get Running Start at Hot Springs," *Sporting News*, February 18, 1915, 6.

28. "Major League Notes," *Sporting News*, March 4, 1915, 6.

29. "Tigers Start Training in Gulfport: Rain Elsewhere, but Sun Shines upon Camp," *Detroit Times*, March 1, 1915, 6.

30. H.G. Salsinger, "Jennings Decides on a Small Squad: Just the Pick of Players Will Go to Gulfport," *Sporting News*, February 11, 1915, 3.

31. "American League Notes," *Sporting Life*, March 6, 1915, 8.

32. H.G. Salsinger "Burns Back on His Job by May First: Kavanaugh Will Sub for Detroit's Invalid Player," *Sporting News*, March 25, 1911, 5.

33. Holmes, *Ty Cobb: A Biography–Baseball's All-Time Greatest Hitters*, 65.

34. "Major League Notes," *Sporting News*, March 11, 1915, 8.

35. "Major League Notes," *Sporting News*, April 8, 1915, 6.

36. H.G. Salsinger, "Salsinger Joins in the New Chorus: Long Training Trips in Disfavor with Detroit," *Sporting News*, April 8, 1915, 5.

37. Harold V. Wilcox, "Ty Cobb's Ambition: Is to Equal or Surpass Wagner's Wonderful Batting Record as Set Forth in 'Richter's History and Records of Base Ball," *Sporting Life*, April 10, 1915. 2.

38. H.G. Salsinger, "Detroit Pitchers Not Delivering: It Is Just as Has Been Feared Regarding Tigers," *Sporting News*, April 22, 1915, 3.

39. "The American League: The 1915 Campaign of President Johnson's League–The Opening Games," *Sporting Life*, April 24, 1915, 5.

40. Salsinger, "Detroit Pitchers Not Delivering: It Is Just as Has Been Feared Regarding Tigers," 3.

41. "The American League: The 1915 Campaign of President Johnson's League–Games Played Friday, April 16," *Sporting Life*, April 24, 1915, 5.

42. "The American League: The 1915 Campaign of President Johnson's League–Games Played Sunday, April 18," *Sporting Life*, April 24, 1915, 6.

43. "The American League: The 1915 Campaign of President Johnson's League–Games Played Monday, April 19," *Sporting Life*, May 1, 1915, 5.

44. "The American League: The 1915 Campaign of President Johnson's League–Games Played Tuesday, April 20," *Sporting Life*, May 1, 1915, 5.

45. "The American League: The 1915 Campaign of President Johnson's League–Games Played Wednesday, April 21," *Sporting Life*, May 1, 1915, 6.

46. "The American League: The 1915 Campaign of President Johnson's League–Games Played Sunday, April 25," *Sporting Life*, May 8, 1915, 6.

47. Chandler D. Richter, "Side-Lights on Base Ball: Tyrus Cobb's Batting Ambition," *Sporting Life*, May 1, 1915, 13.

48. Hugh Fullerton, "How the Champion Batters Grip the Old War Club," *The West Virginian*, May 7, 1915, 8.

49. "American League Notes," *Sporting Life*, May 8, 1915, 9.

50. "The American League: The 1915 Campaign of President Johnson's League–Games Played Wednesday, May 19," *Sporting Life*, May 29, 1915, 7.

51. H.G. Salsinger, "Being Human It Has Its off Days: These Remarks Concern Detroit's Wrecking Machine," *Sporting News*, May 27, 1915, 3.

52. "The American League: The 1915 Campaign of President Johnson's League–Games Played Sunday, May 16," *Sporting Life*, May 29, 1915, 7.

53. "American League Notes," *Sporting Life*, May 29, 1915, 10.

54. "The American League: The 1915 Campaign of President Johnson's League–Games Played Wednesday, June 2," *Sporting Life*, June 12, 1915, 7.

55. "Base Running and Hitting of Cobb Defeat Yankees," *Bridgeport Evening Farmer*, June 5, 1915, 8.

56. "Great and Only Ty Cobb Plays Game Each and Every Minute," *Bridgeport Evening Farmer*, June 9, 1915, 8.

57. "Base Running and Hitting of Cobb Defeat Yankees," 8.

58. "Great and Only Ty Cobb Plays Game Each and Every Minute," 8.

59. "Base Running and Hitting of Cobb Defeat Yankees," 8.

60. "The American League: The 1915 Campaign of President Johnson's League–Games Played Wednesday, June 9," *Sporting Life*, June 19, 1915, 6.

61. "The American League: The 1915 Campaign of President Johnson's League–Games Played Saturday, June 12," *Sporting Life*, June 19, 1915, 7.

62. "Local Shriners Will Honor Ty Cobb: Georgian Will Be Given Testimonial When He Comes Here with Detroit Tigers," *Evening Ledger*, June 10, 1915, 12.

63. "Caught on the Fly," *Sporting News*, June 10, 1915, 4.

64. Grantland Rice, "Fanning with Grantland Rice," *Evening Ledger*, June 10, 1915, 12.

65. Barry Faris, "Sports News: Cobb Still Sensational," *Bemidji Daily Pioneer*, June 16, 1915, 4.

66. Ty Cobb–Champion All-Around Player, "Ty Cobb Says- - -Almost Every Tiger Will Swear That Certain Club Is Stealing Signs on Home Grounds- - -Elated at Success," *Washington Times*, June 12, 1915, 13.

67. "Cobb Threatened by Ban Johnson: Will Drive Star out of Baseball If He Wrote Signal Stealing Article," *The West Virginian*, June 17, 1915, 8.

68. "Ty Cobb Not Worried by Johnson's Threats," *Harrisburg Telegraph*, June 15, 1915, 8.

69. Bozeman Bulger, "Ban Johnson's Threat to Banish Cobb from Game Is Not Taken Seriously: American League Leader's Latest Move the Crowning Diplomatic 'Bone' of Baseball–Yanks Make Room for Collegians To-Day," *Evening World*, June 16, 1915, 12.

70. "Cobb Threatened by Ban Johnson: Will Drive Star out of Baseball If He Wrote Signal Stealing Article," 8.

71. "Johnson Threatens to Stop Authoring: Intimates That Baseball Writers' Association May Investigate Detroiter's Writings," *Washington Times*, June 25, 1915, 15.

72. "Ban Johnson on Cobb's Case: The President of the American League Has Not Taken Official Cognizance of Cobb's Alleged Newspaper Charges of 'Signal-Tipping;' and Did Not Threaten to 'Drive Cobb out of Base Ball,'" *Sporting Life*, June 26, 1915, 2.

73. Peter Carney, "Cobb's Running: The Detroit Star Apparently out to Surpass the American League Base Stealing Records, at Least," *Sporting Life*, June 26, 1915, 6.

74. "Tyrus Cobb Greatest Player in the Game at Present," *Honolulu Star-Bulletin*, July 9, 1915, 8.

75. Damon Runyan, "Greatness of 'Ty' and 'Tris': The Difference Between the American League's Two Chief Star Players, Cobb and Speaker, Lies in Temperament and Mentality, Which Manifests Itself in Their Distinctive Work on the Diamond," *Sporting Life*, July 10, 1915, 2.

76. "Sons of Stars: Almost Sure to Follow in the Footsteps of Famous Fathers," *Sporting Life*, July 10, 1915, 11.

77. J. Ed Grillo, "Ban Johnson Issues Two Edicts: Ty Cobb Deserts the Company of Authors Voluntarily," *Sporting Life*, July 17, 1915, 7.

78. "Cobb Jealous of His Laurels," Brattleboro Daily Reformer, July 27, 1915, 4.

79. "Careful of Throwing Arm," *Tucumcari News* and *Tucumcari Times*, July 29, 1915, 6.

80. H.G. Salsinger, "Tigers Must Have Lot of Confidence: Defy All Traditions of Game as They Go East!" *Sporting News*, August 5, 1915, 3.

81. "The Race of the American League: Games Played Saturday, August 7," *Sporting Life*, August 14, 1915, 15.

82. Bill Evans, "Ty Cobb, Base Runner," *Brooklyn Daily Eagle*, August 16, 1915, 8.

83. Monty, "Ty Cobb Loses Batting Arm: Most Sensational Ball Player World Ever Knew Worried over Failing Muscles," *Ogden Standard*, August 21, 1915, 2.

84. "Cobb Rounds a10-Year Record in Big League: Celebrated Event with No Special Ceremony Except to Play Winning Ball," *Pensacola Journal*, August 27, 1915, 1.

85. H.G. Salsinger, "If Bill's Right It's All off with Tigers: Can't Gain Enough on Road to Head Red Sox," *Sporting News*, September 9, 1915, 3.

86. "Ty Cobb Never Loses Confidence Even in Worst Batting Slump," *Bridgeport Evening Farmer*, September 13, 1915, 12.

87. H.G. Salsinger, "Tigers Can't Lay It on to Pitching: Twirlers Did Their Full Part in Boston Series," *Sporting News*, September 2, 1915, 3.

88. "Crowd Mobs Ty Cobb; Call Cops," *Tacoma Times*, September 17, 1915, 2.

89. "Jennings' Tigers Land First Game from Sox: Detroit Returned Winner by 6 to 1 in Roughest Game Ever Seen in Boston," *Washington Herald*, September 17, 1915, 14.

90. "Crowd Mobs Ty Cobb; Call Cops," 2.

91. "Base Stealing Record Is Shattered by Cobb," *Washington Times*, September 24, 1915, 12.

92. "Another Steal for Cobb to Equal Milan's Mark: Georgia Peach to Date Has Purloined Eighty-Seven Sacks," *Washington Herald*, September 25, 1915, 8.

93. "Cobb Ties Up Record," *Detroit Times*, September 25, 1915, 6.

94. "Base Stealing Record Is Shattered By Cobb," 14.

95. "The Race of the American League: Games Played Monday, September 27," *Sporting Life*, October 9, 1915, 12.

96. "Tyrus Cobb Is Greatest Player: So Says Writer in September Issue of Baseball Magazine Who Has Studied Career of The Georgia Peach," *Daily Gate City*, September 13, 1915, 6.

CHAPTER 12

1. Bill Plott, "Jack Nabors–Part I," Anniston Star, September 8, 1968, 2-C.

2. "Baseball By-Plays," *Sporting News*, November 5, 1914, 4.

3. "Mack Says He Asked Waivers on His Veterans: Plank, Bender and Coombs Will Not Be Retained for 1915–Federals Made One a Big Offer," *Evening Ledger*, October 31, 1914, 1.

4. "Plank Secured at Last," *Sporting Life*, December 12, 1914, 8.

5. "Bender Also Becomes a Federal," *Sporting Life*, December 12, 1914, 8.

6. "Caught on the Fly," *Sporting News*, December 10, 1914, 6.

7. "Eddie Collins Sold to Chicago White Sox," *Sporting Life*, December 12, 1914, 1.

8. "Eddie Collins Sold by Mack to White Sox: Famous Athletic Second Baseman Will Play for 'Charlie' Comiskey, Who Takes over Ironclad Contract," *Evening Ledger*, December 8, 1914, 1 and 3.

9. I.E. Sanborn, "Collins' Capture: The Theme of the Day in the Windy City Where White Sox Followers Are Already Indulging in Pleasant Pennant Dreams," *Sporting Life*, December 19, 1914, 6.

10. "Eddie Collins Sold by Mack to White Sox: Famous Athletic Second Baseman Will Play for 'Charlie' Comiskey, Who Takes over Ironclad Contract," 3.

11. Chandler D. Richter, "Athletic Affairs: Why Manager Mack Was Amply Justified in Disposing of a Star Player Who Would, for Various Reasons, Have Been of Little Team Value in the Future," *Sporting Life*, December 19, 1914, 7.

12."Eddie Collins Sold by Mack to White Sox: Famous Athletic Second Baseman Will Play for 'Charlie' Comiskey, Who Takes over Ironclad Contract," 3.

13. "Player-Authors Barred from Earning Pin-Money: At Least, That Is Edict Issued by Ban Johnson- Baseball Czar Says He Will Not Permit Collins to Write News Articles," *Evening Ledger*, December 18, 1914, 12.

14. "Caught on the Fly," *Sporting News*, December 24, 1914, 7.

15. William G. Weart, "Loss of Collins Wakes Up Laggard Quaker City Fans: Realize Fault Is All Their Own," *Sporting News*, December 17, 1914, 1.

16. "The Philadelphia Writers–Once More Meet Friends at the Festive Board: The Eleventh Annual Dinner of the Local Sporting Writers' Association a Success–Announcement of Frank Baker's Retirement," *Sporting Life*, February 27, 1915, 9.

17. "Baker Has Been Ill: May Be Reason He Will Not Play This Year," *Evening Ledger*, February 17, 1915, 12.

18. "Connie Mack Declares Frank Baker Will Never Play with Athletics' Team Again: 'I'm Done with Baker; Shall Never Play on My Team,' Says Mack," *Evening Ledger*, April 26, 1915, 13.

19. "A New Pitching Record," *Sporting Life*, June 26, 1915, 10.

20. Bill Plott, "Jack Nabors–Part II," *Anniston Star*, September 12, 1968, 4-B.

21. "Mack Lands a Great Twirler: Has Purchased Youngster Who Broke World's Record in Pitching 13-Inning Hitless Game," *Ogden Standard*, July 24, 1915, 2.

22. "Connie Mack Lands Pitching Sensation: Nabors, of Georgia, Who Broke World's Hitless Inning Record, to Play Here," *Evening Ledger*, July 13, 1915, 11.

23. "Short Sports of Interest," *New York Times*, July 25, 1915, 5.

24. "Behold the Phillies! Precedent A-Smash; They Have Come Back: Athletics' New Pitcher a Young Giant," *Evening Ledger*, July 14, 1915, 10.

25. "Brooklyn Must Improve on Road or Lose Chance for the Pennant: Strong Array of Recruits Now with Athletics," *Evening Ledger*, July 27, 1915, 11.

26. H.C. Mitchell, "A Red Sox Deal for Strength: The Boston American Club Purchases Outright Jack Barry, Valued Member of the Disrupted $100,000 Athletics' Infield–A Deal That Puts the Red Sox in the Pennant Race Stronger Than Ever," *Sporting Life*, July 10, 1915, 1.

27. "'Eddie Murphy Day' at Shibe Park; Macks Clash with White Sox: Former Athletics Player, Now of Enemy Clan, to Receive Present–Bressler or Nabors and Faber to Pitch," *Evening Ledger*, August 9, 1915, 11.

28. "Nabors' Wildness Costly," *Washington Herald*, August 10, 1915, 8.

29. "Athletics Routed by Terrific Blows of Boston Red Sox: Foster Holds Mackmen to Three Hits–Nabors Relieves Wyckoff–Locals Amass Four Errors," *Evening Ledger*, September 1, 1915, 1.

30. William G. Wert, "Red Sox Impress Quaker City Fans: Wonderful Work by Barry Adds Much to Chances," *Sporting News*, September 9, 1915, 1.

Notes

31. "All Over but the Shouting! Phils Just About Clinch Pennant: Ty Cobb Tries a New Stunt, but Burns Was Taking a Nap," *Evening Ledger*, September 22, 1915, 10.

32. William G. Weart, "Connie Moves His Date up a Notch: Look out for New Athletics in Fall of 1916," *Sporting News*, September 23, 1915, 1.

33. "Baseball By-Plays," *Sporting News*, October 21, 1915, 4.

34. William G. Weart, "Public Weary of Baker Trade Talk: Mack Declares There Is Nothing in Any of the Rumors," *Sporting News*, December 2, 1915, 1.

35. "Developments of Day in Frank Baker Case," *Evening Ledger*, December 10, 1915, 19.

36. "'Home Run' Baker to Play with Yankees Next Year: Athletics' Slugger Says He Is Considering New Proposition Made by New York Club," *Evening Ledger*, December 10, 1915, 19.

37. "Sale of Baker Great Relief, Declares Mack: Connie Thinks End of Tiresome Affair Will Prove Great Benefit to Game," *Evening Ledger*, February 16, 1916, 15.

38. William G. Weart, "Bender Rare Sight in Philly Uniform: Big Surprise for Fans When Pat Moran Signs Chief," *Sporting News*, February 17, 1916, 1.

39. William G. Weart, "Phils Pull Stuff to Upset Tradition: Five of Moran's Men Bring Brides into Camp," *Sporting News*, March 16, 1916, 1.

40. William G. Weart, "More Pitchers Is Purpose of Moran: Mound Burden of Phillies Will Be Better Distributed," *Sporting News*, March 9, 1916, 2.

41. Weart, "Bender Rare Sight in Philly Uniform: Big Surprise for Fans When Pat Moran Signs Chief," 1.

42. Chandler D. Richter, "King Lameness Holds Forth in Camp of Athletic Team: Youngsters Are Stiff Today after Strenuous Drill by Mack and Thomas–Jack Nabors Looks Good for This Season," *Evening Ledger*, March 14, 1916, 15.

43. William G. Weart, "Phils in Condition to Show Best Paces: Florida Camp Continues Ideal for Getting in Shape," *Sporting News*, March 23, 1916, 1.

44. William G. Weart, "Rankest Gloom in Camp of Mackmen: Failure of Pitchers Depresses All Members of Team," *Sporting News*, April 6, 1916, 1.

45. Chandler D. Richter, "Mack's Pitchers to Be a Surprise," *Sporting Life*, March 25, 1916, 5.

46. "The Race of the American League: The Opening Games," *Sporting Life*, April 22, 1916, 18.

47. William G. Weart, "Phillies Beginning to Realize They Have a Fight on Hands: M'Graw Pulling Big Comeback," *Sporting News*, April 20, 1916, 1.

48. "The Race of the American League: Games Played Tuesday, April 18," *Sporting Life*, April 29, 1916, 13.

49. "The Race of the American League: Games Played Saturday, April 22," *Sporting Life*, April 29, 1916, 23.

50. "Beat Boston Again: Mackmen Bat Well and Win Second Time by 6 to 2," *Sunday Star*, April 23, 1916, 1.

51. Chandler D. Richter, "Mack to Have Strong Pitching Staff for 1917: Crowell, Myers and Nabors Have Proved Worth as Good Hurlers," *Evening Ledger*, April 24, 1916, 14.

52. "The Race of the American League: Games Played Friday, April 28," *Sporting Life*, May 6, 1916, 13.

53. "American League," *Ogden Standard*, May 4, 1916, 2.

54. "The Race of the American League: Games Played Wednesday, May 3," *Sporting Life*, May 13, 1916, 10.

55. "Jennings' Action in Pulling Cunningham from Mound Opened Eyes of Local Fans: Jennings Responsible for Failure of Detroit Staff to Show Expected Form," *Evening Ledger*, May 10, 1916, 16.

56. "The Race of the American League: Games Played Tuesday, May 9," *Sporting Life*, May 20, 1916, 12.

57. "The Race of the American League: Games Played Wednesday, May 10," *Sporting Life*, May 20, 1916, 12.

58. William G. Weart, "If Tigers and Browns Were All Mack Might Win Flag: Time to Stop Talk about Jokes," *Sporting News*, May 18, 1916, 1.

59. "American League: Standing on Tuesday Morning," *Sporting News*, May 25, 1916, 5.

60. "The Race of the American League: Games Played Saturday, May 27," *Sporting Life*, June 3, 1916, 13.

61. William Peet, "Nationals Again Lead American League- - -Athletics Humbled: Griffmen Win, Both Games of a Double-Header and Jump into First Place Again," *Washington Herald*, May 28, 1916, 13.

62. "The Race of the American League: Games Played Monday, May 29," *Sporting Life*, June 10, 1916, 10.

63. William G. Weart, "A Ruction Now and Then Tonic to Fans: But Fines from Tener Quickly Put Lid on Phillies," *Sporting News*, June 8, 1916, 1.

64. "Five Errors Offset Nabors's Efforts," *Ogden Standard*, June 17, 1916, 8.

65. "Moran Refused to Sacrifice Alexander to Clinch Game, but Robinson Ruined Staff: Larry and His Achievements," *Evening Ledger*, June 23, 1916, 12.

66. William G. Weart, "Phillies Take to Road without Fears as to What's in Store: A Steady Pace, Home or Abroad," *Sporting News*, June 29, 1916, 1.

67. "The Race of the American League: Saturday, June 24," *Sporting Life*, July 1, 1916, 10.

68. "Boston Beats Athletics," *Evening Star*, July 4, 1916, 11.

69. William G. Weart, "Mack School Gets Results with Rush: Pupil Lawry Already Classed as a Sure Comer," *Sporting News*, July 6, 1916, 1.

70. "American League: Standing on Tuesday Morning," *Sporting News*, July 20, 1916, 5.

71. "The Race of the American League: Tuesday, July 18," *Sporting Life*, July 29, 1916, 8.

72. "Other American League Game: Indians Scalp Athletics," *Evening Star*, July 22, 1916, 8.

73. William G. Weart, "Quakers Ought to Give Thanks for It: One Day of Rest after Session with Athletics," *Sporting News*, July 27, 1916, 1.

74. "The Race of the American League: Thursday, July 27," *Sporting Life*, August 5, 1916, 7.

75. William G. Weart, "Phillies Try Hard but Can't Advance: National Race a Mere Treadmill for Moran's Men," *Sporting News*, August 10, 1916, 1.

76. William G. Weart, "Philly Bleachers in Limelight Again: Sun God Blocks the Ball, Rigler Says Interference," *Sporting News*, August 17, 1916, 1.

77. Frederick G. Lieb, "Yanks Enjoy One Big Inning, Then Quit for the Day: Score Four Runs in Opener, Just Enough to Nose out Athletics, 4 to 3," *The Sun*, August 15, 1916, 12.

78. "Mackmen Drop Daily Game By 4 to 3 Score," *Ogden Standard*, August 15, 1916, 2.

79. Grantland Rice, "Cullop's Science Big Drawback to Mackmen: Two Yankees' Pitchers Conspire to Stop Ambitious Athletics," *New York Tribune*, August 15, 1916, 14.

80. "Baseball By-Plays," Sporting News, August 31, 1916, 4.

81. William G. Weart, "Macks Lose On, but They Play 'Em Hard: Browns Were Lucky to Escape with Two Games," *Sporting News*, August 24, 1916, 1.

82. Robert W. Maxwell, "Indians Find Nabors and Williams in Wild Form and Score Easily: Many Passes Enable Cleveland to Pile up Big Lead–Bagby Holds Macks," *Evening Ledger*, August 25, 1916, 1.

83. "Caught on the Fly," *Sporting News*, August 31, 1914, 4.

84. "Yankees Entertain Twenty-Five Fans: Smallest Crowd Ever Sees Locals Take an 8 to 2 Licking from Athletics," *The Sun*, September 9, 1916, 12.

85. "Has Confidence in Nabors: Connie Mack Expects to Make Great Pitcher out of Youngster–Lacking in Experience," *The Williams News*, September 14, 1916, 2.

86. "White Sox Win in Ninth," *Omaha Daily Bee*, September 20, 1916, 7.

87. Norman L. Macht, *Connie Mack: The Turbulent and Triumphant Years, 1915-1931*, (Lincoln, Neb.: University Of Nebraska Press, 2012), 72.

88. "Griffs Wide Awake," *Evening Star*, September 29, 1916, 18.

89. "Is 'Worst' Twirler in Major Baseball: Nabors, of Athletics, Wins One of 22 Games, Losing 20 in a Row," *Buffalo Sunday Times*, February 4, 1917, 61.

90. "Affairs of the Athletic Club: Has Confidence in Nabors," *Sporting Life*, February 17, 1917, 6.

91. Jonathan Fraser Light, *The Cultural Encyclopedia of Baseball*, Second Edition, (Jefferson, N.C.: McFarland & Company, Inc., 2005), 547.

92. "Big League Scouts Are All Looking over Bunch of Players on Connie Mack's Team: Connie Mack Was One of First Managers to Accept Military Responsibilities of Players," *Evening Ledger*, May 2, 1917, 14.

93. Plott, "Jack Nabors–Part II," 4-B.

CHAPTER 13

1. James C. Isaminger, "In the National Spot Light," *Sporting Life*, August 7, 1915, 8.

2. "Washington Gossip: 'Ty' Cobb Stirs Fans in Department Of Commerce," *Grenada Sentinel*, July 23, 1915, 6.

3. "Rube Marquard Is Superstitious," *Pittsburg Press*, July 11, 1913, 23.

4. Lyall Smith, "As of Today: Now Take 1916 A's—Go Ahead, I Dare You," *Detroit Free Press*, August 27, 1958, 21.

5. "Two Games for Red Sox: Defeat Athletics in Both Ends of Double-Header, 3 to 2 And 7 To 3," *Sunday Star*, June 25, 1916, 1.

6. Smith, "As of Today: Now Take 1916 A's—Go Ahead, I Dare You," 21.

Bibliography

BOOKS

Abrams, Roger I. *Legal Bases: Baseball and the Law*. Philadelphia: Temple University Press, 1998.
Anthony, Dave and Reynolds, Gareth. *The United States of Absurdity: Untold Stories from American History*. Danvers, Mass.: Ten Speed Press–The Crown Publishing Group, 2017.
Bogen, Gil. *Tinker, Evers, and Chance: A Triple Biography*. Jefferson, N.C.: McFarland & Company, Inc., 2003.
Bondy, Filip. *Who's on Worst: The Lousiest Players, Biggest Cheaters, Saddest Goats and Other Antiheroes in Baseball History*. New York: Anchor Sports–Anchor Books – Random House LLC, 2013.
Buckley, Edmund, ed. *Current Encyclopedia, Volume 2*. Chicago: Current Encyclopedia Company, 1902.
Cicotello, David and Louisa, Angelo J., eds. *Forbes Field: Essays and Memories of the Pirates' Historic Ballpark, 1909-1971*. Jefferson, N.C.: McFarland & Company, Inc., 2007.
DeValeria, Dennis and Jeanne Burke DeValeria. *Honus Wagner: A Biography*. New York: Henry Holt, 1995.
Faber, Charles F. and Faber, Richard B. *Spitballers: The Last Legal Hurlers oOf the Wet One*. Jefferson, N.C.: McFarland & Company, Inc., 2006.
Fleitz, David L. *Ghosts in the Gallery at Cooperstown: Sixteen Little-Known Members of the Hall of Fame*. Jefferson, N.C.: McFarland & Company, Inc., 2004.
_____. *Napoleon Lajoie: King of Ballplayers*. Jefferson, N.C.: McFarland & Company, Inc., 2013.
Freedman, Lew. *Connie Mack's First Dynasty: The Philadelphia Athletics, 1910-1914*. Jefferson, N.C.: McFarland & Company, Inc., 2017.
Gaines, Bob. *Christy Mathewson, the Christian Gentleman: How One Man's Faith and Fastball Forever Changed Baseball*. Lanham, Md.: Rowman & Littlefield, 2015.
Gay, Timothy M. *Tris Speaker: The-Rough-and-Tumble Life of a Baseball Legend*. Lincoln, Neb.: University of Nebraska Press, 2005.
Ginsburg, Daniel E. *The Fix Is In: A History of Baseball Gambling and Game Fixing Scandals*. Jefferson, N.C.: McFarland & Company, Inc., 1995.
Halfon, Mark S. *Tales from the Deadball Era: Ty Cobb, Home Run Baker, Shoeless Joe Jackson, and the Wildest Times in Baseball History*. Lincoln, Neb.: Potomac Books–University of Nebraska Press, 2014.

Hall, Alvin L. and Rutkoff, Peter M., eds. *The Cooperstown Symposium on Baseball and American Culture, 1999*. Jefferson, N.C.: McFarland & Company, Inc., 2000.

Hamersly, Lewis R. ed. *Who's Who in Pennsylvania*. New York: L.R. Hamersly Company, 1904.

Hawkins, Jim, Ewald, Dan and Van Dusen, George. *The Detroit Tigers Encyclopedia*. Champaign, Ill.: Sports Publishing LLC, 2003.

Holmes, Dan. *Ty Cobb: A Biography–Baseball's All-Time Greatest Hitters*. Westport, Conn.: Greenwood Press, 2004.

Hubbard, Donald. *The Red Sox Before the Babe: Boston's Early Days in the American League, 1901-1914*. Jefferson, N.C.: McFarland & Company, Inc., 2009.

Hubbard, Donald J. *The Heavenly Twins of Boston Baseball: A Dual Biography of Hugh Duffy and Tommy McCarthy*. Jefferson, N.C.: McFarland & Company, Inc., 2008.

Istorico, Ray. *Greatness in Waiting: An Illustrated History of the Early New York Yankees, 1903-1919*. Jefferson, N.C.: McFarland & Company, Inc., 2008.

Johnson, Steve. *Chicago Cubs Yesterday & Today*. Minneapolis, Minn.: Voyageur Press, 2008.

Jordan, David M. *The Athletics of Philadelphia: Connie Mack's White Elephants, 1901-1954*. Jefferson, N.C.: McFarland & Company, Inc., 1999.

Kaese, Harold. *The Boston Braves, 1871-1953*. 1948; reprint, Boston: Northeastern University Press, 2004.

Katz, Jeffrey M. *Plie Ball: Baseball Meets Dance on Stage and Screen*. Jefferson, N.C.: McFarland & Company, Inc., 2016.

Kelly, Robert E. *Baseball's Offensive Greats of the Deadball Era: Best Producers Rated by Position, 1901-1919*. Jefferson, N.C.: McFarland & Company, Inc., 2009.

Kimberly, Chuck. *The Days of Wee Willie, Old Cy and Baseball War: Scenes from the Dawn of the Deadball Era, 1900-1903*. Jefferson, N.C.: McFarland & Company, Inc., 2014.

Kiser, Brett. *Ghosts of Baseball's Past*. Lincoln, Neb.: iUniverse, Inc., 2006.

Leavengood, Ted. *Clark Griffith: The Old Fox of Washington Baseball*. Jefferson, N.C.: McFarland & Company, Inc., 2011.

Leerhsen, Charles. *Ty Cobb: A Terrible Beauty*. New York: Simon & Schuster, 2015.

Levy, Alan H. *Rube Waddell: The Zany, Brilliant Life of a Strikeout Artist*. Jefferson, N.C.: McFarland & Company, Inc., 2000.

Lieb, Fred. *Baseball As I Have Known It*. 1977; reprint, Lincoln, Neb.: First Bison Books–University of Nebraska Press, 1996.

Lieb, Frederick G. *The Pittsburgh Pirates*. 1948; reprint, Carbondale, Ill.: Southern Illinois University Press, 2003.

Light, Jonathan Fraser. *The Cultural Encyclopedia of Baseball, Second Edition*. Jefferson, N.C.: McFarland & Company, Inc., 2005.

Macht, Norman L. *Connie Mack and the Early Years of Baseball*. Lincoln, Neb.: University of Nebraska Press, 2007.

———. *Connie Mack: The Turbulent and Triumphant Years, 1915-1931*. Lincoln: Neb.: University of Nebraska Press, 2012.

Mack, Connie. *My 66 Years in the Big Leagues*. 1950; reprint, Mineola, N.Y.: Dover Publications, Inc., 2009.

Mansch, Larry D. *Rube Marquard: The Life and Times of a Baseball Hall of Famer*. Jefferson, N.C.: McFarland & Company, Inc., 1998.

Mayer, Ronald A. *Christy Mathewson: A Game-by-Game Profile of a Legendary Pitcher*. Jefferson, N.C.: McFarland & Company, Inc., 1993.

Mitchell, Eddie. *Baseball Rowdies of the 19th Century: Brawlers, Drinkers, Pranksters and Cheats in the Early Days of the Major Leagues*. Jefferson, N.C.: McFarland & Company, Inc., 2018.

Neyer, Rob and Epstein, Eddie. *Baseball Dynasties: The Greatest Teams of All Time*. New York: W.W. Norton & Company, 2000.

Nicholson, Lois P. *From Maryland to Cooperstown: Seven Maryland Natives in Baseball's Hall of Fame*. Centreville, Md.: Tidewater Publishers, 1998.

Nowlin, Bill. *The Great Red Sox Spring Training Tour of 1911: Sixty-Three Games, Coast to Coast*. Jefferson, N.C.: McFarland & Company, Inc., 2010.

Redmond, Patrick R. *The Irish and the Making of American Sport, 1835-1920*. Jefferson, N.C.: McFarland & Company, Inc., 2014.

Reisler, Jim. *Before They Were the Bombers: The New York Yankees' Early Years, 1903-1915*. Jefferson, N.C.: McFarland & Company, Inc., 2002.

Roberts, Randy and Cunningham, Carson, ed. *Before the Curse: The Chicago Cubs' Glory Years, 1870-1945*. Urbana, Ill.: University of Illinois Press, 2012.

Robertson, John G. and Saunders, Andy. *A's Bad as It Gets: Connie Mack's Pathetic Athletics of 1916*. Jefferson, N.C.: McFarland & Company, Inc., 2014.

Schwarz, Alan. *The Numbers Game: Baseball's Lifelong Fascination with Statistics*. New York: Thomas Dunne Books–St. Martin's Press, 2004.

Slusser, Susan. *100 Things A's Fans Should Know & Do Before They Die*. Chicago: Triumph Books, 2015.

Smiles, Jack. *"Ee-Yah": The Life and Times of Hughie Jennings, Baseball Hall of Famer*. Jefferson, N.C.: McFarland & Company, Inc., 2005.

Stout, Glenn. *Fenway 1912: The Birth of a Ballpark, a Championship Season, and Fenway's Remarkable First Year*. Boston: Houghton Mifflin Harcourt, 2011.

Thorn, John, ed. *Base Ball: A Journal of the Early Game, Volume 8*. Jefferson, N.C.: McFarland & Company, Inc., 2014.

Waldo, Ronald T. *Characters from the Diamond: Wild Events, Crazy Antics, and Unique Tales from Early Baseball*. Lanham, Md.: Rowman & Littlefield, 2016.

_____. *Honus Wagner and His Pittsburgh Pirates: Scenes from a Golden Era*. Jefferson, N.C.: McFarland & Company, Inc., 2015.

_____. *The 1902 Pittsburgh Pirates: Treachery and Triumph*. Jefferson, N.C.: McFarland & Company, Inc., 2015.

Weeks, Jonathan. *Baseball's Most Notorious Personalities: A Gallery of Rogues*. Lanham, Md.: The Scarecrow Press, Inc., Rowman & Littlefield, 2013.

_____. *Cellar Dwellers: The Worst Teams in Baseball History*. Lanham, Md.: The Scarecrow Press, Inc.–Rowman & Littlefield, 2012.

Westcott, Rich. *Great Stuff: Baseball's Most Amazing Pitching Feats*. New York: Sports Publishing–Skyhorse Publishing, 2014.

Whalen, Thomas J. *When the Red Sox Ruled: Baseball's First Dynasty, 1912-1918*. Chicago: Ivan R. Dee–Rowman & Littlefield, 2011.

Whitten, Jr., D. Wiley. *Champions of Naught Six: The Story of the 1906 Cleburne Railroaders*. Fort Worth, Tex.: Minor League Press, 2010.

Wiggins, Robert Peyton. *The Federal League of Base Ball Clubs: The History of an Outlaw Major League, 1914-1915*. Jefferson, N.C.: McFarland & Company, Inc., 2009.

Wood, Gerald C. *Smoky Joe Wood: The Biography of a Baseball Legend*. Lincoln, Neb.: University Of Nebraska Press, 2013.

Zingg, Paul J. *Harry Hooper: An American Baseball Life*. Urbana, Ill.: University of Illinois Press, 2004.

NEWSPAPER AND MAGAZINES

Alexandria Gazette (Alexandria, Virginia), May 17, 1901–September 20, 1912
Altoona Mirror (Altoona, Pennsylvania), September 27, 1929
Altoona Tribune and *Morning Tribune* (Altoona, Pennsylvania), February 16, 1904–September 28, 1929
Anniston Star (Anniston, Alabama), September 8, 1968–September 12, 1968
Arizona Republican (Phoenix, Arizona), March 26, 1912–September 19, 1915
Atlanta Constitution, August 10, 1905–August 15, 1905
Augusta Chronicle (Augusta, Georgia), August 11, 1905
Bakersfield Californian (Bakersfield, California), June 12, 1911
Baseball Magazine, November 1908–November 1916
Bemidji Daily Pioneer (Bemidji, Minnesota), June 26, 1912–June 16, 1915
Binghamton Press (Binghamton, New York), December 7, 1956
Bismarck Daily Tribune, August 14, 1912
Boston Daily Globe and *Boston Evening Globe*, August 30, 1910–December 11, 1914
Bourbon News (Paris, Kentucky), July 19, 1901
Brattleboro Daily Reformer (Brattleboro, Vermont), July 27, 1915
Bridgeport Evening Farmer (Bridgeport, Connecticut), June 27, 1911–October 26, 1915
Brooklyn Daily Eagle and *Brooklyn Eagle*, October 28, 1901–July 12, 1952
Buffalo Evening Times and *Buffalo Sunday Times*, December 12, 1910–February 4, 1917
Butler Citizen, (Butler, Pennsylvania), November 22, 1900
Butte Inter Mountain (Butte, Montana), June 10, 1902–October 20, 1903
Cairo Bulletin (Cairo, Illinois), August 15, 1904–October 4, 1912
Celina Democrat (Celina, Ohio), July 30, 1915
Chicago Daily Tribune, June 27, 1911–April 25, 1929
Chicago Eagle, August 19, 1916
Cincinnati Enquirer, August 30, 1910
Clovis News (Clovis, Curry County, New Mexico), August 13, 1915

Condon Globe (Condon, Gilliam County, Oregon), June 9, 1904
Courier Democrat (Langdon, North Dakota), October 28, 1915
Cut Bank Pioneer Press (Cut Bank, Teton County, Montana), July 23, 1915
Daily Gate City (Keokuk, Iowa), September 13, 1915
Daily Missoulian (Missoula, Montana), October 21, 1911
Daily Northwestern (Oshkosh, Wisconsin), September 5, 1914
Daily Pioneer (Bemidji, Minnesota), October 13, 1903
Day Book (Chicago, Illinois), September 9, 1912–October 16, 1913
Dayton Evening Herald, April 29, 1901–July 27, 1901
Democrat and Chronicle (Rochester, New York), March 25, 1928
Detroit Free Press, September 3, 1903–August 27, 1958
Detroit Times, May 20, 1914–September 25, 1915
Edmonton Journal (Edmonton, Alberta, Canada), September 9, 1912
El Paso Herald (El Paso, Texas), May 29, 1911–December 16, 1912
Evening Capital News (Boise, Idaho), June 4, 1914
Evening Ledger (Philadelphia, Pennsylvania), October 31, 1914–May 2, 1917
Evening News (Wilkes Barre, Pennsylvania), September 9, 1912
Evening Standard (Ogden City, Utah), August 15, 1912–October 2, 1912
Evening Star and *Sunday Star* (Washington, D.C.), January 5, 1901–September 29, 1916
Evening Times (Grand Forks, North Dakota), October 31, 1911–September 23, 1912
Evening Times-Republican (Marshalltown, Iowa), June 16, 1904
Fergus County Democrat (Lewistown, Fergus County, Montana), July 23, 1912
Fort Wayne News (Fort Wayne, Indiana), September 18, 1912
Franklin Evening News (Franklin, Pennsylvania), September 9, 1914
Gazette-Times (Pittsburgh, Pennsylvania), March 10, 1912–April 19, 1913
Grand Forks Daily Herald (Grand Forks, North Dakota), July 16, 1915
Great Falls Daily Tribune (Great Falls, Montana), September 24, 1911
Grenada Sentinel (Grenada, Mississippi), July 23, 1913
Guthrie Daily Leader (Guthrie, Oklahoma), September 10, 1915
Harrisburg Star-Independent and *Star-Independent* (Harrisburg, Pennsylvania), May 27, 1904–May 27, 1915
Harrisburg Telegraph (Harrisburg, Pennsylvania), June 15, 1915
Honolulu Star-Bulletin, July 25, 1912–July 9, 1915
Houston Daily Post, November 10, 1901
Indianapolis Journal and *Sunday Journal* (Indianapolis, Indiana), May 22, 1903–April 17, 1904
Indianapolis Sunday Star, May 6, 1917
Jamestown Weekly Alert (Jamestown, North Dakota), October 15, 1903
Kansas City Sun (Kansas City, Missouri), July 24, 1915
Lake County Times (Hammond, Indiana), June 19, 1911–September 21, 1912
Lewiston Evening Teller (Lewiston, Idaho), April 15, 1904
Lincoln County Record (Pioche, Nevada), June 14, 1901
Los Angeles Herald and *Los Angeles Evening Herald*, July 12, 1906–March 12, 1913

Los Angeles Times, September 25, 1914
Minneapolis Journal, March 29, 1901–May 17, 1901
Muncie Evening Press (Muncie, Indiana), September 18, 1912
New York Times, December 30, 1901–December 11, 1915
New-York Tribune and *New York Tribune*, March 21, 1901–January 4, 1920
North Platte Semi-Weekly (North Platte, Nebraska), July 27, 1915
Ogden Standard (Ogden City, Utah), July 24, 1915–August 15, 1916
Omaha Daily Bee and *Omaha Sunday Bee*, October 1, 1911–September 20, 1916
Ottumwa Tri-Weekly Courier (Ottumwa, Wapello County, Iowa), July 11, 1911
Pensacola Journal (Pensacola, Florida), October 12, 1911–August 27, 1915
Perry Daily Chief (Perry, Iowa), June 11, 1910
Perrysburg Journal (Perrysburg, Wood County, Ohio), July 21, 1911
Perth Amboy Evening News (Perth Amboy, New Jersey), July 8, 1912
Philadelphia Inquirer, April 29, 1916–August 26, 1916
Philipsburg Mail (Philipsburg, Granite County, Montana), May 17, 1901–June 28, 1901
Pittsburgh Post and *Pittsburgh Sunday Post*, September 29, 1912–April 19, 1917
Pittsburg Press, October 11, 1902–July 11, 1913
Port Gibson Reveille, (Port Gibson, Clairborne County, Mississippi), July 22, 1915–August 24, 1916
The Progress (Ocean Springs, Mississippi), July 23, 1904
Public Daily Ledger Maysville Republican, (Maysville, Kentucky), September 25, 1903–October 5, 1903
Register and Leader (Des Moines, Iowa), July 14, 1907
Republican News Item (Laporte, Sullivan County, Pennsylvania), May 31, 1912
Richmond Daily Palladium and *Richmond Palladium and Sun-Telegram* (Richmond, Indiana), January 20, 1904–October 15, 1911
Rock Island Argus (Rock Island, Illinois), April 24, 1902–September 22, 1915
St. Louis Post-Dispatch, April 23, 1911
St. Louis Republic, April 1, 1901–September 30, 1904
St. Paul Globe, February 19, 1901–October 10, 1904
Salt Lake Herald, December 6, 1903–February 7, 1904
Salt Lake Tribune, May 29, 1904–October 2, 1949
San Francisco Call and *The Call* (San Francisco, California), March 24, 1904–January 16, 1913
Santa Fe New Mexican, August 15, 1912–August 26, 1912
Scranton Tribune (Scranton, Pennsylvania), April 20, 1901–April 29, 1902
Scranton Truth (Scranton, Pennsylvania), September 18, 1912
Seattle Star, July 9, 1915
Semi-Weekly Messenger (Wilmington, North Carolina), June 6, 1902
Silver Messenger (Challis, Custer County, Idaho), October 15, 1901–October 29, 1901
Spirit of the Age (Woodstock, Vermont), July 20, 1912
Spokane Press, December 18, 1903–May 13, 1904

Sporting Life, February 15, 1896–February 17, 1917
Sporting News, October 15, 1898–October 9, 1946
The Sun (New York, New York), October 11, 1904–September 9, 1916
Sunday State Journal (Lincoln, Nebraska), September 1, 1907
Tacoma Times, September 17, 1915
Times Dispatch (Richmond, Virginia), August 6, 1911–September 23, 1912
Topeka State Journal and *Topeka Daily State Journal*, March 25, 1901–September 8, 1914
Tucumcari News and Tucumcari Times (Tucumcari, Quay County, New Mexico), July 29, 1915
Tulsa Daily World, July 11, 1915–June 20, 1915
Washington Herald, June 12, 1911–May 28, 1916
Washington Times, *The Times*, and *Evening Times* (Washington D.C.), March 27, 1901–September 24, 1915
Waterbury Democrat and Waterbury Evening Democrat (Waterbury, Connecticut), March 27, 1901–August 11, 1905
The West Virginian (Fairmont, West Virginia), May 7, 1915–March 3, 1916
The Williams News (Williams, Coconino County, Arizona), September 14, 1916
The World and *Evening World* (New York, New York), November 18, 1903–June 16, 1915
Youngstown Indicator (Youngstown, Ohio), August 21, 1902

WEBSITES

Ballparks of Baseball, http://www.ballparksofbaseball.com
Baseball Almanac, http://www.baseball-almanac.com
Baseball-Reference, http://www.baseball-reference.com
Biographical Directory of the United States Congress, http://bioguide.congress.gov
Brooklyn Public Library, http://bklyn.newspapers.com
Case Western Reserve University, http://case.edu
CDNC–California Digital Newspaper Collection, http://cdnc.ucr.edu
Chicago Public Library, http://www.chipublib.org
City of Philadelphia, http://www.phila.gov
The Encyclopedia of Arkansas History & Culture, http://www.encyclopediaofarkansas.net
Find a Grave, http://www.findagrave.com
Google Books, http://books.google.com
Google Newspaper Archives, http://news.google.com
Grove City College Athletics, http://athletics.gcc.edu
Historical Newspapers, http://www.newspapers.com
IBDB–Internet Broadway Database, http://www.ibdb.com
Iowa National Guard, http://www.iowanationalguard.com
The Lansingburgh Historical Society, http://lansingburghhistoricalsociety.org
LA84 Foundation Digital Library, http://digital.la84.org

Library of Congress, http://www.loc.gov
Major League Baseball, http://www.mlb.com
Nassau County–Long Island, New York, http://www.nassaucountyny.gov
National Baseball Hall of Fame, http://www.baseballhall.org
New-York Historical Society Museum & Library, http://sports.nyhistory.org
Paper of Record, http://paperofrecord.hypernet.ca
Philadelphia Bar Association, http://www.philadelphiabar.org
Project Ballpark, http://www.projectballpark.org
Retrosheet, http://www.retrosheet.org
Seamheads, http://seamheads.com
Society for American Baseball Research, http://sabr.org
TSHA–Texas State Historical Association, http://tshaonline.org
Ty Cobb Baseball Atheneum Repository Digital Holding Library, http://www.tycobb.org

Index

Numbers in **bold** indicate pages with photographs.

Abbaticchio, Edward "Ed," 85–86, 88
Acton, Rachel, 62
Adams, Charles "Babe," 115, 120, **130**
Adams, Franklin Pierce, 99
Adams Express Co., 58
Adams House, 174
Agnew, Peter, 64
Agnew, Samuel "Sam," 178
Akron, Ohio, 125
Albany Senators, 39
Alexander, Grover Cleveland, 140, 143, 187
All-American, 15, 200
Allentown, Pennsylvania, 69
Altoona, Pennsylvania, 21, 25, 35
Altoona Mountain City, 21
Altoona Mountaineers, 35, 83
America, viii, 131
American Association (major league), 4, 36, 44, 72, 129, 209
American Association (minor league), 32, 99, 117, 132, 134, 227
American Boy, 209
American League, ix, 4–8, 10, 12, 14–18, 22, 25, 29, 33–34, 38, 40–42, 44, 46, 49–50, 52–54, 58, 60–61, 65, 71–73, 81–82, 87, 89–90, 99, 108, 132, 134, 138, 155–56, 161, 164, 166–68, 171, 173, 178, 180–81, 183–84, 187, 190, 194–95, 199, 203–206, 211–13, 218, 227, 231
American League Park (New York), 28, 42–46, 48, 52
American League Park (Washington), 13, 42, 65
American League's Service Bureau, 72
American Magazine, 200
Ames, Leon "Red," 143
Anderson, John, 46, 50, 52

Anniston, Alabama, 193
Anniston Moulders, 216
Anniston Star, 212
Anson, Adrian "Cap," 200
Arborway Court, 174
Arkansas, 175
Armour, William "Bill," 21–23, 25–27, 29, 31, 34–35, 194
Athletics, 39
Atlanta, Georgia, 44, 194
Atlanta Crackers, 44
Atlantic City, New Jersey, 148
Atlantic League, 21, 39
Atlantic Ocean, 219
Augusta Tourists, 193–194
Austin, Texas, 113, 128
Austin Senators, 113
Ayers, Yancey "Doc," 176
Bailey, J.N., 105
Baker, John Franklin "Frank, Home Run or Bake," 136, 167, 176–77, 195, 212, 215, 217–18, 220
Baker, Wesley, 57
Ball, Cornelius "Neal," 36
Baltimore, Maryland, 15, 63
Baltimore Orioles, 5, 9, 17, 36, 40, 44, 61, 72, 76–77, 129, 134, 136, 182
Baltimore Terrapins, 213
Bandle, C.H., 156
Bankston, Wilborn Everett "Bill," 216
Barrow, Edward "Ed," 183
Barry, John "Jack," 214, 216–17
Bartenders' Union, 61
Baseball Hall of Fame, 92, 231
Baseball Magazine, 195
Baseball-Reference, x, 18, 187, 231
Baseball's Sad Lexicon, 99
Baseball Writers' Association, 205
Batch, Emil "Heinie," 96
Bates, John, 120
Bay, Harry, 28, 31, 64
Beck, Frederick "Fred," 94

Becker, David "Beals," 103
Bedient, Hugh, 159, 176–77, 179, 183
Bell, George, 97
Bellevue-Stratford Hotel, 213
Bemis, Harry, 23, 28, 33, 36
Bender, Charles "Chief," 137, 213, 217
Bennett Park, 12, 26, 46, 51
Benton, John "Rube," 142
Benz, Joseph "Joe," 202
Bergen, Florence, 81
Bergen, Harriet (Gaines), 81
Bergen, Joe, 81
Bergen, Martin "Marty," 77–81
Bergen, Martin, Jr., 80
Bergen, Michael, 81
Bernhard, William "Bill," 6–10, 16–17, 24–25, 28–29, 33
Bescher, Robert "Bob," 133
Bethune Avenue, 197
Billings, James B., 82
Birmingham, Ohio, 171
Birmingham Barons, 26
Bliss, John "Jack," 120
Blossburg, Pennsylvania, 95
Boehler, George, 222
Boehling, John Joseph "Joe," 176
Boland, Bernard "Bernie," 201
Bonds, Barry, 110
Bonner, Frank, 23
Boone, Lute "Luke," 184, 202
Boston, Massachusetts, 11, 16, 29, 40, 51–52, 54, 72, 77–78, 80, 83–84, 86–88, 90, 124, 156, 159–60, 164, 174–76, 178, 186, 223
Boston Americans, 8–9, 11–12, 14, 17, 27–34, 42–53, 61, 65–71, 87, 89–90, 154, 172
Boston Beaneaters, 6, 17, 75–91, 231
Boston Braves, ix, 118, 121–23, 126–27, 139, 143, 185, 212–13, 219

Boston Doves, 95, 227
Boston Red Sox, x, 110, 147, 150, 154–69, 171–72, 175–87, 198, 203, 205, 207–209, 216–17, 220–21, 223–27, 233
Boston Rustlers, 103–105, 107, 137
Bowerman, Frank, 23–24, 44
Bowman, Frank, 148
Bradford, Pennsylvania, 56
Bradley, Hugh, 159
Bradley, William "Bill," 26–28, 30, 33–34, 45, 49
Brain, David "Dave," 91
Bransfield, William "Kitty," 119
Braves Field, 187
Bremer, Eugene, 187
Bresnahan, Roger, 143
Bressler, Raymond "Rube," 227
Bright's disease, 198
Broadway, 147
Brock, Louis "Lou," 209
Brockton Shoemakers, 21
Brooklyn, New York, 21, 78, 96
Brooklyn Daily Eagle, 24
Brooklyn Superbas, 13, 16, 21–23, 40, 50–51, 81, 84, 86, 88–89, 92, 96, 102, 106, 114, 117, 122, 126–27, 139–41, 144–46, 154–55
Brookside Park, 132
Brookville, Pennsylvania, 59
Brouthers, Dennis "Dan," 200
Brown, Charles "Buster," 87
Brown, Mordecai "Three Finger," 103, 108, 171
Brown, Stewart, 193
Brush, John T., 48, 54, 132–33, 149
Buccaneers, 101, 126
Buckenberger, Albert "Al," 76–77, 82
Bucknell University, 9
Buckwheats, 59
Buelow, Frederick "Fritz," 32
Buffalo, New York, 14, 23
Buffalo Sunday Times, 227
Bulger, Bozeman, 191–92
Bunker Hill Day, 158
Burkett, Jesse, 11, 172–73, 188
Burlington Railroad, 119
Burnet House, 80
Burns, George, 169, 217, 221–22
Burns, James D., 11
Bush, Leslie Ambrose "Bullet Joe," 219–22, 225–27

Bush, Owen "Donie," 198, 201, 208
Butler, Pennsylvania, 59–60
Butler County, Pennsylvania, 57, 64
Byrne, Robert "Bobby," 120–21, 124
Caldwell, Ray, 202–203, 221
California, 15–16, 35, 60, 99, 175
California Angels, 72
California League, 60
Callahan, James "Nixey," 18, 161
Cambridge, Massachusetts, 43–44
Camden, New Jersey, 64
Camnitz, Samuel Howard "Howie," 120
Camp Dodge, Iowa, 228
Campbell, Arthur Vincent "Vin," 118, 121
Cannell, Wirt "Rip," 90
Cantillon, Joseph "Joe," 60
Canton, Ohio, 14
Canton Chinamen, 132
Carey, Max, 128
Carnegie, Pennsylvania, 64, 116
Carnegie, Andrew, 41
Carpenter, Charles F., 21, 35–36
Carpenter, William L., 197
Carr, Charles "Charlie," 33
Carrigan, William "Bill," 156, 167, 174–86
Carter, W.K., 148
Caruthers, Robert "Bob," 30
Cavet, Tillar "Pug," 184
Central League, 132
Chadwick, Henry "Father of Baseball," 68
Chalmers Motor Company, 108, 168
Champaign, Illinois, 100
Chance, Frank "the Peerless Leader," 95–106, 110, 122
Chapman, Raymond "Ray," 226
Charles River, 156
Charleston, South Carolina, 83
Charleston, Oscar, 18
Chase, Harold "Hal," 160
Chatham, Ontario, Canada, 57
Cecil County, Maryland, 76
Chesbro, Chad, 39
Chesbro (Chesebrough), John Dwight "Jack, Happy Jack or Chad," 31, 38–54, **55**, 70, 75, 143, 231

Chesbro, Mabel (Shuttleworth), 43
Chesbro, Martha, 51
Chicago, Illinois, 14–15, 42, 58, 60–62, 64, 67, 89, 97, 99, 102, 104, 109–110, 114, 120, 122, 125, 128, 149, 156, 160, 162, 216
Chicago Chronicle, 6
Chicago City Series, 109
Chicago Colts, 143
Chicago Cubs, x, 82–85, 87–88, 94–110, 115, 120–23, 125, 127–28, 133, 135, 140, 142, 144–47, 194, 232
Chicago Daily Tribune, 98, 105, 214
Chicago Orphans, 21, 60
Chicago River, 146
Chicago White Sox, 12, 27–28, 31–33, 46–47, 49–51, 54, 62, 66–69, 96–97, 108–109, 157–62, 164–65, 167, 175, 179–84, 186, 200–202, 204–205, 207, 213–14, 216–19, 224–27
Chicago White Stockings, 58, 110, 143
Christmas, 116
Cicotte, Edgar "Eddie," 165
Cincinnati, Ohio, 26, 42, 63, 80, 89–90, 105, 110, 120, 128, 142
Cincinnati Reds, 26, 34, 63, 83–87, 89, 92, 95, 98, 101–102, 105, 107–108, 117, 120–21, 124–25, 127–28, 133, 140–42, 154, 157–58
Cincinnati Red Stockings, 209
Cincinnati Tigers, 187
Clancy, Robert, 232
Clarke, Fred, 40, 47, 57–58, 60–61, 75, 91, 98, 112–16, 118–19, 121–22, 124–25, 128, 231
Clarkson, Walter, 44, 49
Class C level baseball, 46, 153
Class D level baseball, 212, 216
Cleburne, Texas, 153
Cleburne Railroaders, 153
Cleveland, Ohio, 20, 23–25, 35–36, 67, 131–32, 144, 167, 180, 206
Cleveland Blues, 21, 25
Cleveland Broncos, 17, 22–25

Index

Cleveland Indians, 71, 169, 200–201, 206, 222–26
Cleveland Leader, 17
Cleveland Naps, 17, 25–36, 43, 45–51, 64, 66–69, 102, 127, 129, 132, 155, 157, 161, 164, 166–67, 179–80, 182, 184, 195
Cleveland Spiders, 40, 225
Clingman, William "Billy," 29, 35
Cobb, Amanda (Chitwood), 191, 193–94
Cobb, Charlotte "Charlie" (Lombard), 195, 197
Cobb, Ty, Jr., 205
Cobb, Tyrus Raymond "Ty or the Georgia Peach," x, 1, 17, 108, 115, 136, 161, 163–68, 181, 184, 186, 190–209, **210**, 217, 230–32
Cobb, Georgia State Senator William Herschel, 191–94
Cochecton, New York, 94
Cole, Leonard "King," 101, 103, 108, 122–23, 140
Coleman, John, 91
Collins, Edward "Eddie," x, 165–66, 195, 213–14, 217–18, 227
Collins, James "Jimmy," 11, 77
Collins, John "Shano," 200–201
Collins, Ray, 175, 180
Colonial Theatre, 148
Colonials, 132
Columbia Park, 8–9, 11–12, 29–30, 45–46, 61, 65–68, 70
Columbus, Ohio, 27–28, 44
Columbus Buckeyes/Senators, 57
Columbus Senators, 21, 32
Comanche steamship, 219
Comiskey, Charles, 158, 160, 204, 209, 213–14
Comiskey Park, 180, 186, 227
Commerce, Georgia, 192
Conant, William H., 82, 86, 90–91
Congregational, 43
Connolly, Thomas "Tommy," 13, 28, 30, 32–33, 65, 167, 177, 182, 224
Conroy, William "Wid," 42, 46, 48, 50, 53
Conway, Massachusetts, 43
Cooley, Duff, 2

Coombs John "Jack," 137, 213, 217
Cooperstown, New York, 39, 72
Corbett, James "Jim," 61
Corriden, John "Red," 195
Corridon, Frank, 44
Corsicana, Texas, 160
Coumbe, Frederick "Fritz," 182
Coveleski, Harry, 201
Craig, Roger, 227
Crandall, James "Doc," 142
Cratty, A.R., 117, 129
Cravath, Clifford "Gavvy," x, 110
Crawford, Samuel "Sam," 27, 33, 107, 129, 184, 199–202
Crickets, 21
Criger, Louis "Lou," 53
Cross, Montford "Monte," 5, 46, 65, 69
Crowell, Minot "Cap," 221
Cuba, 137
Cuban, 137
Cumberland Valley League, 21
Cunningham, George, 222
Curley, Mayor James M., 176
Curtis, Clifton "Cliff," 227
Cuyler, Hazen "Kiki," 129
Czolgosz, Leon, 14
Dahlen, William "Bill," 13, 139
Dale, Richard C., 7, 10
Daly, Thomas "Tom," 179
Dane, Oscar, 62
Daniels, Charles W., 62
Danville, Illinois, 100
Daubert, Jacob "Jake," 102, 106
Dauss, George "Hooks," 198
Davis, Alfonzo "Lefty," 42
Davis, Harry, 65, 70, 136, 219, 224
Davis, Ralph S., 44, 123
Davis, Dr. T.A., 104
Dayton Old Soldiers, 21–23
Dayton Veterans, 21
Deadball Era, vii, viii, ix, xi, 1, 20, 38, 56, 94, 103, 112, 131, 152, 171, 190, 208–209, 211, 230–31, 233
Decatur, Alabama, 212
Decoration Day, 123
DeGrom, Jacob, 188
Delahanty, Edward "Ed," x, 4, 30, 169
Delahanty, James "Jim," 86, 164
Delaney, Bob, 148
Delaware College, 76

Delaware County League of Pennsylvania, 215
Delaware River, 64
Denver, Colorado, 137
Denver Bears, 228
Denver Grizzlies, 173
Department of Commerce, 232
Derringer, Samuel Paul, 92
Des Moines, Iowa, 113, 231
Des Moines Champs, 113–14
Detroit, Michigan, 27, 43, 166, 180–81, 202, 205–206
Detroit Free Press, 33
Detroit Journal, 25
Detroit Tigers, x, 9, 11–12, 17, 22, 26–27, 31–33, 45–46, 49–51, 54, 57, 66–70, 82, 91, 96, 108, 115, 129, 136, 157, 161–62, 164–65, 167–68, 177, 179, 181–84, 193–95, 197–203, 205–209, 213, 217, 219, 221–25, 232
Detroit Times, 208
Detroit Tygers, 203
Devore, Joshua "Josh," 138, 141, 144
Dinneen, William "Bill," 51–53, 186
Dobbs, John, 88
Dobson, Mrs. D., 105
Dogwood, Alabama, 212
Doheny, Edward "Ed," 75
Dolan, Albert "Cozy," 158
Dolan, Patrick "Cozy," 89
Donahue, Francis "Red," 5, 31
Donahue, John "Jiggs," 69
Donlin, Michael "Mike," 88, 118, 120–22, 125, 137
Donovan, Patrick "Patsy," 40, 71
Donovan, William "Bill," 202
Dooin, Charles "Red," 104, 125
Doolin, Michael "Mickey," 102, 125
Dope Book, 72
Dorchester, Massachusetts, 72
Dougherty, Patrick "Patsy," 48, 52–53, 66
Doyle, James "Jimmy," 99, 104–105, 109
Doyle, John "Jack," 102
Doyle, Lawrence "Larry," 108, 127, 129, 140, 145, 168
Dreyfuss, Barney, 40–42, 47, 57–59, 84, 114, 116–19, 126, 155

Drucke, Louis, 140
Dubuc, Jean, 200, 223
Duffy, Hugh, 17, 77, 87
Dunn, Frank V., 83–84, 86, 88–90
Dunn, John "Jack," 182
Dunn Field, 225
Dutchman, 25, 135, 172
Dwyer, Frank, 45
Eason, Malcolm "Mal," 103
East, 15, 39, 101, 117, 146
Eastern League, 23, 39, 76–77, 82
Eaton, Francis, 175
Ebbets, Charles, 22, 84, 139, 140, 154–55
Eddie Murphy Day, 216
Edmonson, W.C., 215
Edwards, Henry P., 25, 28, 32
Egan, Arthur "Ben," 182
Egan, John "Jack," 178
Egan, Richard "Dick," 133
1899 Boston Beaneaters, **93**
Elberfeld, Norman "Kid," 45, 48, 53, 66
Elberton, Georgia, 191–92
Elkton, Maryland, 81
Ellis, George "Rube," 101
Elmira, New York, 148
El Paso, Texas, 165
Emerson, Parson John, 43
Emslie, Robert "Bob," 142
England, 179
Engle, Arthur Clyde, 156, 168–69, 178, 184
Erb, Dr. Theodore, 70
Evans, William "Billy," 206
Evansville, Indiana, 100
Evening World, 45
Evers, John "Johnny," 85, 96, 102–104, 107
Exposition Park, 41, 59, 85, 89, 114
Face, Elroy "Roy," 150
Falkenberg, Frederick "Cy," 227
Fall River Indians, 2
Farrell, Frank, 154–155
Federal League, 180, 187, 198, 201–202, 205, 207, 213–14, 217
Feller, Robert "Bob," 71–72
Fenway Park, 147, 156–59, 164–66, 168–69, 174, 176, 178–79, 181–82, 184–85, 208, 220, 223, 233

Fenway Realty Company, 179
Ferris, Albert "Hobe," 53
Fifth Avenue Hotel, 16
Fillingim, Dana, 216
Finn, Michael, "Mickey," 113–14, 154
Finneran, William "Bill," 139
Finnigan (Finnegan), Joe, 64
First Regiment Band, 65
Fisher, Isaac Newton "Newt," 192
Fisher, Ray, 177, 181, 184
Fitzgerald, Mayor John "Honey Fitz," 174
Fletcher, Arthur "Art," 168
Flick, Elmer, 3, 5, 11, 15, 28–29, 49
Florida, 218–20
Fogel, Horace, 16, 140
Fohl, Leo "Lee," 224
Forbes Field, 116–17, 120–28, 141, 146, 231
Fordham Court, 174
Forest Hills, Massachusetts, 174
Fort Worth Panthers, 113
Fort Worth Polytechnic Institute, 153
Foster, Edward "Eddie," 222
Foster, George "Rube," 176, 179, 182–183, 217, 220
Foster, John B., 22, 149
Fourth of July, 143
Franklin, Pennsylvania, 57
Fraser, Charles "Chick," 6–11, 16–17
Freeman, John "Buck," x, 14, 45, 94, 106–107, 110
French, 1
Frenchman, 11
Fresno, California, 172–173
Friel, William "Bill," 31
Fullerton, Hugh, 110
Fultz, David "Dave," 11, 48
Ganzel, John, 46, 50, 53
Garden City Hotel, 173–74
Gardner, William Lawrence "Larry," 156–57, 169, 177–78, 181
Garvin, Virgil "Ned," 50–51
Gaspar, Harry, 107
Gaynor, Mayor William Jay, 139
Geier, Philip "Phil," 2, 9
Georgia, 190–92, 198
Georgia Alabama–League, 212, 216
Germany, 131

Gettleson, Leonard, 72
Gibson, Josh, 18, 230
Gibson, Norwood, 48
Gibson, Robert "Bob," 187
Gleason, Harry, 68
Glen Aubrey, New York, 95
Glendon. Martin, 33
Gobblers' Knob, 122
Gochnaur, John Peter "Dutch, Goch or Johnny," 20–36, **37**
Golden, Roy, 101
Goldman, Harry, 213
Gordon, Joseph, 45
Gowdy, Henry "Hank," 213
Grady, Michael "Mike," 87
Grand Rapids, Michigan, 57
Grand Rapids Furniture Makers, 57
Graney, John "Jack," 200
Greater Forbes Field, 117
Gregg, Sylveanus "Vean," 182
Griffin, Tobias "Sandy," 95
Griffith, Clark, 18, 28, 42–43, 45–46, 48, 50, 52, 75, 98, 164, 166, 185, 197
Grillo, J. Ed, 178
Groh, Henry "Heinie," 145
Grove City College, 59–60
Gruber, Abe, 45
Gulfport, Mississippi, 198–99
Gwynn, Anthony "Tony," 230
Hagerstown Lions, 21
Hall, Charles "Charley," 158–59
Hall, Marcus "Marc," 198
Hamilton, Earl, 178
Hamilton, William "Billy," 77–78, 209
Hamilton Boulevard, 197
Hammerstein's Victoria Theatre, 148
Handy Andy, 105
Hanlon, Edward "Ned," 16, 50–51
Harding, Howard, 197
Harmon, Robert "Bob," 119
Harrisburg, Pennsylvania, 69
Harrisburg Senators, 64, 78
Harrison, Mayor–Elect Carter Henry, IV, 100
Hart, William "Bill," 44
Harvard University, 43–44
Haskell, John "Jack," 9
Hauser, Arnold, 100, 120
Heidrick, Emmet, 27
Heilmann, Harry, 221–22

Index

Heinemann, Joe A., 59
Hemphill, Charles "Charlie," 23–24, 27
Henderson, Ricky, 209
Hendricks, John "Jack," 173
Hendrix, Claude, 125
Henriksen, Olaf, 184
Henry, John, 221
Herrmann, Garry, 63, 84, 154, 156
Herzog, Charles "Buck," 141, 168
Hesselbacher, George, 224
Heydler, John, 109
Hickman, Charles "Charlie, Charley or Hick," 28–30, 34, 36, 49
Hickory Grove, 95
Hilligan, Earl J., 72
Hilltop Park, 54, 102, 157–58, 162
Hite, Mabel, 120, 125
Hoblitzell, Richard "Dick," 120
Hodgson, George, 59
Hoffman, Daniel "Danny," 70
Hofman, Arthur "Solly," 99, 101, 122–23, 125
Hohnhorst, Edward "Eddie," 161
Homestead, Pennsylvania, 31, 64
Homestead Grays, 18
Hooper, Harry, 156–57, 162, 168, 172, 175, 177–78, 182, 233
Hornsby, Rogers, 18
Hot Springs, Arkansas, 114, 118–19, 156–57, 172, 175–76
Hotel Dunlop, 148
Hotel Hermitage, 148
Hotel Somerset, 160
Hough, Frank L., 7
Houston, Texas, 149
Houston Buffaloes, 153–54
Houston Chronicle, 159
Howard, George "Del," 91
Howard, Ivan, 184
the Hub, 91
Hubbard, Texas, 152–53
Hudson River, 54, 95
Huff, George, 95, 154, 160
Hughes, Charles A., 198
Hughes, Thomas "Tom," 42, 44, 49
Hulen, William "Billy," 2
Hulswitt, Rudolph "Rudy," 36
Humane Society, 63

Huntington Avenue Baseball Grounds, 9, 30, 45, 47, 51, 66, 70, 88–89, 159
Huston, T.L., 198
Hutt, Councilman Louis, 217
Hyatt, Ham, 119
Indiana, 100, 176
Indiana Avenue (Chicago), 104
Indiana Hoosiers, 198
Indianapolis, Indiana, 27, 62
Indianapolis Indians, 132, 227
International League, 182–83, 225
Interstate League, 21
Irish, 211
Isaminger, James A., 231
Jackson, Mississippi, 199
Jackson, George, 143
Jackson, Joseph "Shoeless Joe," 129, 161, 163–64, 168, 206, 224
Jacksonville, Florida, 137, 218–19
Jagmetty, Magistrate Joshua, 148
Jamaica Plain, Massachusetts, 174
Jamieson, Charles "Charlie," 222
Janvrin, Harold "Hal," 181, 233
Jeckyll-and-Hyde, 101
Jefferson Market Police Court (New York), 148
Jennings, Hugh "Hughie or Hughey," 136, 168, 194–96, 198–99, 206–207, 213
Jennings club, 21
Johnson, Adam Rankin, 179, 182
Johnson, Byron Bancroft "Ban," 4–5, 12, 14, 17, 24, 40–41, 44, 48, 61, 87, 156, 158, 174, 178–79, 183, 198, 204–205, 213–14, 224
Johnson, John G., 6–7
Johnson, Walter "King of the Pitchers," 71, 150, 161–62, 166, 171, 176, 184, 197, 202, 222, 226
Johnstone, James "Jim," 102
Johnstown Buckskins, 39
Jones, Fielder, 224
Jordan, Timothy "Tim," 94, 124
Joss, Adrian "Addie," 23, 29–30, 33, 49, 102, 171
Judge, Joseph "Joe," 222
Kachline, Cliff, 227
Kahoe, Mike, 31
Kane, Joe (Joseph Cahen), 147–49

Kane, John, 133
Kansas City, Missouri, 59, 61
Kansas City Blues, 80
Kansas City Cowboys, 36
Kansas City Monarchs, 187
Kauff, Benjamin "Benny," 202
Kavanagh, Martin "Marty," 202–203
Kearny, New Jersey, 115
Keating, Raymond "Ray," 178, 221
Keefe, Robert "Bobby," 105
Keefe, Timothy "Tim," 143–44, 187
Keeler, William "Willie," 11, 43, 45–46, 48, 50–51, 53
Keister, William "Bill," 36
Kelley, Joseph "Joe," 7, 63
Kellogg, Shirley, 147
Kendrick, W. Freeland, 203
Kentucky, 42
Kenzie, George, 148
Kerr, William, 76–77
Kilfoyle, John, 22, 31, 34
Killefer, William "Bill," 143
Killen, Frank, 80
Kilroy, Matthew Aloysius, 72
King George V, 179
Kleinow, John "Red," 52–53
Klem, William "Bill," 86, 123
Kling, John "Johnny," 102, 104
Klobedanz, Frederick "Fred," 78
Knabe, Franz Otto, 102
Knowles, Frederick "Fred," 137
Konetchy, Edward "Ed," 140
Koufax, Sanford "Sandy," 72
Krause, Harry, 171
Kuntzsch, George, 76
Kyle, Andrew "Andy," 128
Labor Day, 50, 69, 226
LaChance, George "Candy," 53
Lajoie, Celina (Guertin), 1
Lajoie, Jean–Baptiste, 1
Lajoie, Napoleon "Larry or Nap," 1–18, **19**, 24–25, 27–34, 45, 49, 69, 127–29, 162, 167, 190, 195, 199–200, 221, 225, 231
Lajoie Day, 162
Lake, Frederick "Fred," 77
Lancaster Links, 132
Lanigan, Ernest J., 7, 72, 129
Lannin, Joseph, 173–76, 178–87
Lannin Realty Company, 174
Lardner, Ring, 200

Latham, Walter "Arlie," 209
Laureate Boat Club Grounds, 95
Lauterborn, William "Bill," 86
Lavender, James "Jimmy," 122, 144
Law, John "Jack," 23
Leach, Thomas "Tommy," 40, 94, 114, 120–21, 123
League Park (Cleveland, Ohio), 17, 27–29, 31–32, 46, 51, 161, 201
Leechburg, Pennsylvania, 60
Leever, Samuel "Sam," 39, 75, 231
Leidy, George, 193
Leifield, Albert "Lefty," 89, 118, 123
Lemoore, California, 173
Leonard, David, 171–72
Leonard, Ella, 171
Leonard, Hubert Benjamin "Dutch," 171–73, 175–88, **189**
Lestershire, New York, 95, 97
Lewis, Allen, 72
Lewis, George "Duffy," 156, 161, 164, 166, 169, 172, 175, 178, 181
Library of Congress, 72
Lindaman, Vivan "Vive," 91
Little Red Book, 71
Little Rock, Arkansas, 154
Little Rock Travelers, 113–14, 154
Lizotte, Abel, 76
Lloyd Street Grounds, 11
Lobert, John "Hans," 133, 135
Lochhead, Robert "Harry," 9
Locke, William H., 119
Lockette, Mattie, 62
Loftus, Thomas "Tom," 57, 60
Long, Herman, 33, 36, 77
Long Branch, New Jersey, 72
Long Island, New York, 173
Loos, Ivan "Pete," 8
Lord, Harry, 157
Los Angeles, California, 60–61
Los Angeles Angels, 25
Los Angeles Dodgers, 72, 209
Louisville, Kentucky, 27, 62
Louisville Colonels (major league team), 40, 57–58
Louisville Colonels (minor league team), 26, 132
Love, Edward "Slim," 226
Lowe, Robert "Bobby," 77

Lowrey, George, 59–60
Lubricated Hog Chase, 59
Luby, John "Pat," 143
Luderus, Frederick "Fred," 106
Lumley, Harry, 96, 125
Lush, William "Billy," 49
Lynch, Thomas, 140
Lynchburg Hill Climbers, 76
Mace, Harry, 30
Mack, Connie (Conny), 4–9, 11–13, 15–17, 47, 57–65, 67–68, 70, **74**, 81–82, 97–98, 157, 195, 212–20, 222–27, 233
Mack, Katherine, 219
Magee (Magie), Jake, 95
Magee, Sherwood "Sherry," 102
Mahan, Henry W. 156
Maisel, Frederick "Fritz," 178, 184, 199, 205–206, 218
Majestic Park, 175
Major League Baseball, 231
Major Negro Leagues, 18, 187
Maloney, William "Bill," 85
Maris, Roger, 110
Marlin, Texas, 138
Marlin Springs, Texas, 134, 138
Marquard, Fred, 131–32
Marquard, Lena, 131
Marquard (Marquardt), Richard William "Rube, $11,000 Beauty, $11,000 Lemon or Watch," 103, 122, 131–50, **151**, 232–33
Marsans, Armando, 127
Marston, Charley, 2
Martin, Judge Jonathan Willis, 7
Maryland, 215
Mason, 191
Massachusetts, 39, 43, 51
Mathews, Robert "Bobby," 44
Mathews, Walter, 63
Mathewson, Christopher "Christy," 9, 88, 106, 108, 126, 133–37, 139, 141–42, 147, 168–69, 171, 205
Mathewson, Christy, Jr., 205
Mattern, Alonzo "Al," 107
Matthews, Harry, 216
Mays, Carl, 208
McAleer, James "Jimmy," 156–57, 162–64, 167, 173–74, 179
McAllister, Lewis "Sport," 33
McBeth, William J., 138
McCarthy, Alexander "Alex," 116, 119–21, 123

McCarthy, John "Jack," 29, 95
McCormick, James "Jim," 143
McCormick, William "Barry," 33, 65
McCreary, Robert, 191
McElwee, Leland "Lee." 227
McFarland, Edward "Ed," 5
McGinnity, Joseph "Joe," 18, 47, 143
McGraw, John, 5, 15, 132–40, 142, 144–45, 147–49, 154, 166, 168, 228
McGuire, James "Deacon," 53, 155
McGwire, Mark, 110
McHale, Martin "Marty," 181
McInnis, John "Stuffy," 214, 217, 220–21
McIntire, John "Harry," 88
McKechnie, William "Bill," 116
McKinley, President William, 14
McLain, Dennis "Denny," 54
McPherson, Reverend Walter H., 104
McRoy, Robert, 156, 162, 173–74
McTigue, William "Bill," 105
Melrose Park, 183
Melville, George D., 62
Memorial Day, 67, 141, 180
Memphis, Tennessee, 15
Memphis Egyptians, 113
Mercer, George "Win," 13
Mercer, Sid, 138
Meyer, William "Billy," 220
Meyers, John "Chief," 103, 108, 122, 142
Miami, Florida, 219
Middletown, New York, 39
Milan, Jesse Clyde, x, 195, 199, 205, 208, 222
Miller, Elmer, 140
Miller, John "Jack or Dots," 115–17, 119–23
Miller, Ward, 127
Milwaukee, Wisconsin, ix, 58–59
Milwaukee Brewers (major league team), 14
Milwaukee Brewers (minor league team), 4, 11, 57–59
Missouri Baptist Sanitarium, 68
Mitchell, Michael "Mike," 95
Mitchell, William "Willie," 200
Mobile Sea Gulls, 199
Monroe Monarchs, 187

Index

Montevallo, Alabama, 212, 228
Moore, Alonzo "Earl," 18, 26, 28, 32–33, 36, 47, 67, 103, 117
Moraga, California 172
Moran, John Herbert "Herbie," 127
Moreland, George, 71, 208
Morgan, Harry "Cy," 137
Morgan, Raymond "Ray," 176, 221
Morse, Jacob C. "Jake," 29–30, 40, 44, 84
Morton, Guy, 201
Mulford, Ren, Jr., 108, 142
Mullin, George, 22–23, 46, 51
Murnane, Timothy "Tim," 11, 83, 159, 165, 187
Murphy, Charles Webb, 98–99, 106, 109, 120–21
Murphy, Daniel "Danny," 66
Murphy, John (groundskeeper), 138
Murphy, John Edward "Eddie" (baseball player), 216–17
Murphy, Michael "Mike," 233
Murray, John "Red," 148
Murray, William "Billy," 76, 163
Mutt and Jeff, 121
Myers, Elmer, 220–23, 227
Nabors, Dr. Arthur H., 212, 216, 228
Nabors, Bill, 212
Nabors, Herman John "John Jack or Jack," 211–12, 215, 216–17, 219–28, 233
Nabors, James, 212
Nabors, Sarah Matilda (Foster), 212
Napoleon, Ohio, 33
Narrows, Georgia, 191
Nashville, Tennessee, 157
Nashville Volunteers, 26, 192
National anthem, 65
National Association of Professional Baseball Leagues, 23
National Baseball Museum, 72
National Commission, 154, 204
National League, ix, 2–7, 15–16, 21–22, 24–25, 40–42, 47, 57, 60, 77, 81–84, 87, 89–90, 94, 96–98, 102–103, 106, 109, 114–15, 121, 123, 125, 127–28, 133, 141–42, 147, 171, 174, 190, 199, 212

National League Park (Philadelphia), 102, 123, 128, 135
National Park (Washington), 162, 221, 226
National Union Day, 49
Navin, Frank J., 181, 198–99
Navin Field, 164, 183, 197, 200–202, 207, 223, 225
Negro American League, 187
Negro National League, 18
Negro National League II, 18
Negro Southern League, 187
Neil Park, 28
Newark, Delaware, 76, 81–82
Newark Indians, 225
Newburger, New York City Supreme Court Justice Joseph E., 149
New England League, 2, 21, 172
Newnan Cowetas, 212, 215–16
New Orleans, Louisiana, 15, 23, 25, 27, 99
New Orleans Pelicans, 26
New Orleans Picayune, 15
New Year's, 5
New York, 125
New York, New York, 30, 41, 43–44, 51, 84, 137, 139, 141–42, 144, 147–49, 160, 175, 219
New York City Supreme Court, 148–49
New York Cubans, 18
New York Giants, 9, 16, 23–24, 39, 41, 47–48, 54, 83–86, 88–89, 92, 97, 102–103, 106–109, 115, 121–28, 132–45, 147–49, 154, 166, 168–69, 173, 175, 187, 205, 216, 228, 232
New York Globe, 138
New York Herald, 143
New York Highlanders, 28–29, 31–32, 36, 38, 42–54, 62, 65–66, 68–70, 75, 134, 154, 157–58, 160–62, 167, 194, 231
New York Metropolitans, 129
New York Mets, 188, 227
New York State League, 21, 39, 95
New York Tribune, 225
New York Yankees, x, 54, 110, 177–78, 181, 184, 198,

201–205, 207, 216, 218, 220–21, 223, 225–26
Niagara Falls, 30
Nichol, Hugh, 209
Nicholl, Sam, 63
Nichols, Charles "Kid," 77
The Nineteenth Straight, 148
Norfolk, Virginia, 82
North Adams, Massachusetts, 38–39, 52
North Brookfield, Massachusetts, 81
Nunamaker, Les, 203, 221
Oakes, Ennis "Rebel," 140
Oakland, California, 172
Oakland Athletics, 209
O'Brien, Joseph "Joe," 137
O'Brien, Thomas "Buck," 157–58, 163, 169
O'Connell, Frederic P., 54, 86
O'Connor, John "Jack," 42, 195
O'Connor, Magistrate Keyran J., 148
Ohio, 17, 171, 176
Ohio–Pennsylvania League, 132
Olcott, Judge William, 45
Old West, 114
Oldring, Reuben "Rube," 220–21
O'Loughlin, Francis "Silk," 27–28, 33, 43, 51, 159, 168, 200, 203
$100,000 Infield, 217
Organized Baseball, 76, 202
Oriole Park, 17, 61
Orr, David "Dave," 129
Orth, Albert "Al," 42, 49
O'Toole, Martin "Marty," 112, 116, 118–23, 125–27, 141–42
Owens, Clarence "Brick," 224
Pacific Coast, 42–43, 149, 175
Pacific Coast League, 35
Paige, Leroy "Satchel," 187
Palace of the Fans, 101
Palm Beach, Florida, 219
Parent, Alfred "Freddy," 45, 53
Parnell, Roy, 187
The Passing Show of 1912, 147
Paterson Giants, 21
Patten, Case "Casey," 12, 18
Patterson, Roy, 18
Pawtucket Colts, 21
Pearson, Alexander "Alex," 31
Peckinpaugh, Roger, 221
Peitz, Henry "Heinie," 89
Pennsylvania, 17, 24, 29, 59

Pennsylvania Common Pleas Court No. 5, 6–7, 10, 16
Pennsylvania State, 116
Pennsylvania State League, 76
Pennsylvania Supreme Court, 16
Perdue, Herbert "Hub," 106–107, 143
Perkins, Ralph "Cy," 219
Pewaukee Lake, 59
Philadelphia, Pennsylvania, 6, 10, 13, 15–17, 48, 61, 64–65, 69, 91, 128, 135, 160, 196, 203, 213–14, 216–18, 220, 231
Philadelphia Athletics, x, 5–9, 11–17, 24, 28–30, 32, 34, 39, 45–50, 60–71, 81–82, 89, 97–98, 107, 136–37, 150, 154, 157–59, 161, 163, 165–67, 172–73, 176–77, 180–81, 183–86, 195, 203, 206–208, 211–27, 233
Philadelphia Inquirer, 72
Philadelphia North American, 9
Philadelphia Phillies, x, 2–10, 15–17, 24, 30, 36, 39, 82, 84–86, 101–106, 110, 117, 119, 123, 125–28, 135, 140–41, 143, 169, 187, 216
Philadelphia Quakers, 36, 91
Philadelphia Record, 10
Philadelphia Sporting Writers' Association, 215
Philadelphia Telegraph, 11
Philadelphia Times, 103
Philadelphians, 102
Phillippe, Charles "Deacon," 40, 75, 231
Piatt, Wiley, 5
Pick, Charles "Charlie," 220
Pickering, Oliver "Ollie," 28
Piedmont, Alabama, 212
Pinkerton Detective Agency, 61
Pipp, Walter "Wally," 221
Pittsburgh, Pennsylvania, 39, 44, 47, 58, 64, 112, 118–19, 121, 123, 145, 195
Pittsburgh Pirates, 2–3, 26, 39–42, 44, 47, 57–60, 75–77, 84–89, 91, 94, 97–98, 101, 108, 112–29, 133, 141–44, 146–47, 150, 154–55, 163, 165, 190, 195, 231
Pittsburgh Press, 50
Plank, Edward "Eddie," 11, 46–47, 65, 67–68, 213, 217

Plano, Butler County, Pennsylvania, 57
Planters Hotel, 119
Players' League, 36
Players' Protective Association, 5
Plott, Bill, 212
Polk Street (Chicago), 145
Polo Grounds, 84, 88, 124, 133, 136, 139–40, 142, 144, 147, 177, 204, 220, 225, 232
Porter, Mary, 145
Portsmouth Browns, 21
Poseytuck, 95
Poseyville, 95
Powell, John "Jack," 27, 52
Powers, Michael "Doc," 70
Prospect, Pennsylvania, 57
Providence Clamdiggers/Grays, 76
Providence Grays (major league team), 54, 143
Providence Grays (minor league team), 183
Pulliam, Harry, 83–84
Punxsutawney, Pennsylvania, 58
Quaker City, 9, 72, 218
Quebec, Canada, 1, 174
Queen of the Valley flyer, 69
Radbourn, Charles "Old Hoss," 44, 54, 143
Ralston, Judge Robert, 7, 10
Rankin, William M., 44, 46
Ray, Carl, 222
Raymer, Frederick "Fred," 87
Raymond, Arthur "Bugs," 103
Reach, Alfred "Al," 3, 6
Reading, Pennsylvania, 69
Reading Railroad's Main Line, 69
Record Book of 1913, 129
Redland, 90
Redland Field, 124, 127, 157
Reese, John "Bonesetter," 121–22, 207
Referee Collingwood, 60
Regulars, 118
Rehg, Walter "Wally,"180
Reitz, Henry "Heinie," 129
Retrosheet, vii
Reulbach, Edward "Ed," 101–102, 143
Rice, Grantland, 203, 207, 225
Richie, Elwood "Lew," 110
Richmond, Virginia, 39
Richmond Bluebirds, 39
Richmond Giants, 39

Richter, Chandler D., 103, 201, 220
Richter, Francis C., 2–3, 54
Richter's History of Baseball, 199
Rickey, Wesley Branch, 178
Rigler, Charles "Cy," 124, 139–40, 142–43, 168
Riley, Edwin L. "Eddie," 174–75
Risher, Howard, 64
Ritchey, Claude, 40, 89
Roanoke Magicians, 21, 39
Roaring Twenties, ix
Roberts, J. Doak, 153, 159–60
Robinson, Wilbert "Robbie," 134–35, 138, 144
Robison Field, 101, 118, 124–25, 128, 140
Rochester Bronchos, 82
Rogers, Colonel John I., 3, 5–10, 16
Rogers, William H. "Billy," 83–84
Rome Romans, 21
Roth, Andy, 193
Rowland, Clarence "Pants," 204
Royal Rooters Club, 174
Royston, Georgia, 191–94, 209
Royston Record, 191
Rucker, George "Nap," 144
Rudolph, Richard "Dick," 212
Ruppert, Jacob, 198
Russell, Allen, 226
Russell, Lillian, 97
Ruth, George Herman "Babe," x, 54, 182–83, 220
Ryan, John "Jack," 77
Ryan, Lynn Nolan, 72
St. Joseph, Missouri, 119
St. Joseph Drummers, 118
St. Joseph's Hospital (Syracuse), 109
St. Louis, Missouri, 24, 47–48, 50, 61, 64, 68, 78, 104, 119–20, 138, 160, 166
St. Louis Browns, 23–24, 27, 31–33, 44, 46–47, 49–52, 61, 66, 68–70, 79, 160–64, 166, 178, 180, 183, 185, 195, 201, 209, 224, 225–26
St. Louis Cardinals, 18, 31, 47, 85–87, 89, 92, 100–101, 106, 118–20, 123–24, 128, 140–41, 143, 146, 187, 209, 231
St. Louis Giants, 18

St. Louis Republic, 9, 14
St. Louis Terriers, 213
St. Mary's College, 172
St. Marys, Pennsylvania, 64
St. Marys' Volunteer Fire Department, 64
St. Patrick's Day, 211
St. Paul Saints, 99, 117
San Francisco, California 61, 149
San Francisco Seals, 35
San Joaquin Valley League, 172–73
Sanborn, Irving E., 99
Sawyer, Ford, 72
Schalk, Ray, 181, 186, 207
Schang, Walter "Wally," 221, 224, 226, 233
Schmidt, Charles "Boss," 199
Schrecongost, Freeman Osee, 46, 64, 67
Schulte, Frank M. "Wildfire," x, 94–110, **111**, 115
Schulte, John, 95
Schulte, John, Jr., 97
Schulte, Mabel (Kirby), 104–105
Schupp, Ferdinand "Ferdie," 187
Scott, James "Jim," 180
Scott, Lewis Everett, 176–77, 182, 184, 203
Scranton, Pennsylvania, 69
Scranton Miners, 21
Seattle Siwashes, 35–36
Section 10, 122
Seeley, Blossom, 147–49
Selbach, Albert "Kip," 48, 53
Selee, Frank, 76–82, 84, 95, 99
Selma River Rats, 212
Senior Circuit, 6, 87, 190
Seybold, Ralph "Socks," 12, 94, 107
Shafer, Arthur "Tillie," 142, **151**
Shanks, Howard "Howie" 176, 221
Shawkey, James Robert "Bob," 176, 216
Shean, David "Dave," 104, 106
Sheckard, Jimmy, 103, 108
Sheehan, Thomas "Tom," 222, 224, 227
Shelby County, Alabama, 212
Sheridan, John "Jack," 162
Shettsline, William "Bill," 4, 7–8
Shibe, Benjamin "Ben," 6–7, 16
Shibe, Thomas, 219
Shibe Park, 136, 163, 177, 181, 203, 206, 208, 212, 214, 216–17, 220–21, 223–24, 226–27, **229**
Shindle, William "Billy," 36
Shore, Ernest "Ernie," 182–83, 220
Shriners, 203
Siever, Edward "Ed," 18
Sioux City Indians, 228
1622 to 1628 L Street Northwest, 71
69th Regiment Band, 45
Slagle, James "Jimmy," 5
Smith, George "Germany," 21
Smith, Judson "Jud," 76
Smoky City, 40, 57
Snodgrass, Frederick "Fred," 136, 139, 168
Snowball Farm, 81
Soden, Arthur H., 82–83, 86, 90
Somers, Charles, 31, 34, 40–41
Sosa, Sammy, 110
South, 15, 25
South Atlantic League, 192
South End, 90
South End Grounds, 84, 86–88, 105, 107, 123, 139, 143
South Side Park, 27, 47, 49, 51
Southern, 26, 67
Southern Association, 26, 44, 113, 154, 192, 199
Southern Hotel, 24, 47, 78
Spanish influenza, 228
Sparks, Thomas "Tully," 39
Spartanburg, South Carolina, 65
Speaker, Archery, 153
Speaker, Nancy Jane, 153, 160, 165
Speaker, Tristram E. "Tris or Spoke," 152–69, **170**, 175–78, 181–82
Sporting Life, vii, 2–3, 22, 45, 54, 72, 117, 129, 201, 227
Sporting News, vii, 7, 14, 44, 46, 72, 86, 129
Sportsman's Park, 32, 47, 51, 68, 166, 180, 224
Springfield Maroons, 39
Stack, William Edward "Eddie," 103
Stahl, Charles "Chick," 77–78
Stahl, Garland "Jake," 65, 156–58, 162–63, 165–67, 172–74
Stahl, Jennie, 156
The Stain of Guilt, 62–63

Stallings, George, 3
Stanage, Oscar, 222
Starkloff, Dr. Max C., 68
Stars and Stripes, 71
Steele, William "Bill," 106
Steinfeldt, Harry, 99–100
Stevenson, Judge Maxwell, 7
Stovall, George, 51, 166
Stricklett, Elmer, 44
Strunk, Amos, 220
Suggs, George, 105
Sweeney, William "Bill," 127, 143
Sweet, Assistant Secretary Edwin F., 232
Syracuse, New York, 83, 107, 109
Syracuse Stars, 76–77, 95
Talladega Tigers, 212, 215–16
Tannehill, Jesse, 28, 39–44, 54, 70, 75
Taylor, General Charles H., 173, 179
Taylor, John "Jack," 85, 87
Taylor, John I., 87–88, 154, 156–57, 166, 172–75, 178
Taylor, Luther "Dummy," 23–24, 92
Tennessee-Alabama League, 193
Tenney, Frederick "Fred," 77–78, 82–85, 88–90
Terre Haute, Indiana, 100, 141
Tesreau, Charles "Jeff," 140, 147
Texas, 15, 113–14, 134, 138, 165–66, 168, 175
Texas League, 113, 153, 160, 202
Texas leaguer, 116
Thanksgiving Day, 116
Thomas, Ira, 214, 219
Thompson, James "Shag," 220
Thompson, Samuel "Sam," 3
Thoney, John "Jack," 27, 46
Three Base King, 129
Tinker, Joseph "Joe," 96, 106–107, 135
Tinker to Evers to Chance 99, 110
Titus, John, 86, 127
Toronto Royals, 23
Tri–State League, 35–36, 64, 83
Triumvirate, 82
Troy, New York, 95, 102
Troy Trojans, 95, 187
Turkish bath, 61
Turkish rugs, 98
Turner, Terrance "Terry," 32, 34, 49

Tuthill, Harry, 199, 207
Twitmeyer, Bill, 122
Unglaub, Robert "Bob," 48
Union Association, 21
The Union Scout, 59
Union Station (Chicago), 97
United States, ix, 1, 5, 228
University of Georgia, 192
University of Illinois, 95
University of Pittsburgh, 116
Upland, Pennsylvania, 215
Vargas, Juan "Tetelo," 18
Vaseline, 125
Veach, Robert "Bobby," 200–202
Virginia League, 21, 39
Virginia State League, 39, 76
Vitt, Oscar, 202, 221
Votes for Women, 199
Waddell, Florence (Dunning), 60
Waddell, George Edward "Rube," 29–30, 40, 50, 56–73, 132, 171
Waddell, May Wynne (Skinner), 63
Wagner, Charles "Heinie," 156, 167, 176
Wagner, John "Honus," 1, 11, 40, 57, 64, 112, 114–16, 118, 120–23, 127, 165, 190, 195, 200
Walker, Clarence "Tillie," 180
Walker, Norman W., 165
Walker County, Alabama, 212
Wallace, Roderick "Bobby," 27, 209
Walsh, Edward "Ed," 54, 108–109, 164
Walsh, James "Jimmy," 177, 224
Washington, D.C., 15, 30, 71–72, 204, 206, 232
Washington, Indiana, 62
Washington Herald, 208
Washington Nationals, 40
Washington Park, 84, 89, 96, 126, 139, 160
Washington Senators, x, 8, 10–13, 24, 28–30, 32–36, 42, 45, 47–49, 51, 65–68, 70–71, 106, 150, 156, 159–62, 164, 166–67, 175–77, 179–80,
184–85, 195, 197, 199, 207–208, 221–23, 226–27, 232
Washington Star, 198
Washington Times, 28, 62, 208
Watson, George, 50–51
Waverly, New York, 95
Weaver, Mayor John, 65
Weaver, Orville, "Orlie," 103
Webb, Earl, 169
West, 60, 175
West Baden, Indiana, 99, 118
West Coast, 15, 60
West Forty–Sixth Street (Cleveland), 144
West Penn Railroad, 60
West Side Grounds, 85, 98, 100, 103–105, 107–108, 115, 121, 128, 140, 144
Western Association, 12, 21, 63
Western League, 57, 113, 118, 173, 227
Western Pennsylvania, 57
Westervelt, Frederick, 161
Wheat, Zachariah "Zack," 127
Wheeling, West Virginia, 63
White, Guy "Doc," 33, 50
White Sox Park, 164
Wild Will Day, 202
Wild West Show, 114
Wildfire (trotting horse), 97
Wilhelm, Irvin "Kaiser," 85, 90
William F. & B.F. Downey's livery stable, 71
Williams, James "Jimmy," 40, 52–53
Williams, Ted, 230
Williamson, Edward "Ned," 110
Willis, James, 76
Willis, Mary (Minniss or Minnis), 81
Willis, Victor Gazaway "Vic, Granddaddy Longlegs, Uncle Victor or the Wolf," 6, 75–92, 126, 231
Wills, Maurice "Maury," 209
Wilmington, Delaware, 76
Wilmington YMCA, 76
Wilson, Arthur "Art," 139–40, 168
Wilson, Bernice (Mosely), 128
Wilson, John Owen "Chief," 112–15, 117, 119–29, 130, 231, 234
Wiltse, George "Hooks," 84, 141, 216
Windy City, 120
Winfield, Kansas, 114
Winnipeg, Manitoba, Canada, 84
Wisconsin, 59
Witt, Lawton "Whitey," 222
Wolfe, Wilbert "Barney," 31, 49
Wolverton, Harry, 86
Wood, Howard Ellsworth "Joe, Smoky Joe or Boy Wonder," 150, 156–58, 160–62, 164, 166–67, 169, 172, 175–76, 179–80, 182–83, 185–86
Wood, Laura (O'Shea), 176
Wood Street (Chicago), 145
Woodcock, Fred, 2
Woodrow Wilson Club, 232
Woonsocket, Rhode Island, 1
Worcester, Massachusetts, 173
Worcester Busters, 172–73, 188
World Series, 44, 89, 91, 96–97, 115, 126, 136–37, 147, 149–50, 163, 166, 168–69, 173–74, 181, 185, 187, 194–95, 211–13, 215
World's Fair (St. Louis), 50
World War II, ix
Wright, Clarence Eugene "Gene," 22–23, 31
Yanigans, 118–19
Yawkey, William H., 198
Yerkes, Stephen "Steve," 157–58, 168, 176, 184
York Penn Parks, 83
Young, Denton "Cy," 18, 45, 48, 65–66
Young, Irving, "Irv," 90
Young, Ralph, 202, 222
Youngstown, Ohio, 121–22, 156, 207
Zanesville, Ohio, 62
Zielke, George, 72
Zimmerman, Henry "Heinie," 99–104, 107, 121, 124

About the Author

RONALD T. WALDO is a historian and author who has written eight books on the subject of baseball history, with many devoted to examining the Deadball Era and the 1920s. A resident of Pittsburgh, Pennsylvania his entire life, he graduated from Point Park University in the spring of 1983 with a Bachelor's Degree in journalism and communications. Following his love and passion for baseball history, Mr. Waldo's first book, titled *Fred Clarke: A Biography of the Baseball Hall of Fame Player-Manager*, was released in December 2010.

Some of his other books include a biography about Hazen "Kiki" Cuyler, a compilation of stories connected to the life and career of Honus Wagner, and team related works on the 1902 Pittsburgh Pirates, 1925 Pittsburgh Pirates, and 1938 Pittsburgh Pirates. Mr. Waldo's most recent book, published in April 2017, is titled *Baseball's Roaring Twenties: A Decade of Legends, Characters, and Diamond Adventures*.

He also participated as a contributing author on the 2018 release, *Unlucky 21: The Saddest Stories and Games in Pittsburgh Sports History*, writing the chapter about the 1974-75 Pittsburgh Penguins hockey team titled "History Gone Bad: Chico and His Men Ruin the Pittsburgh Penguins' 1975 Playoff Party."

A longtime member of the Society for American Baseball Research, each of his four books covering baseball's Deadball Era received nominations for the Larry Ritter Book Award by that organization's Deadball Era Committee. Besides being an avid baseball historian, Mr. Waldo also loves following current baseball, football, hockey, and soccer.

www.ingramcontent.com/pod-product-compliance
Lightning Source LLC
Chambersburg PA
CBHW031429160426
43195CB00010BB/661